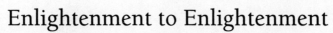

# Enlightenment to Enlightenment

# Enlightenment to Enlightenment

*Intercritique of Science and Myth*

## Henri Atlan

*Translated from the French by*
Lenn J. Schramm

STATE UNIVERSITY OF NEW YORK PRESS

© Editions du Seuil, 1986

Cover illustration, "La Promenade" by Roland Cat,
Courtesy Galerie Isy Brachot, Bruxelles-Paris.

Published by
State University of New York Press, Albany

© 1993   State University of New York

For information, address State University of New York
Press, State University Plaza, Albany, NY 12246

Production by Marilyn P. Semerad
Marketing by Lynne Lekakis

**Library of Congress Cataloging-in-Publication Data**

Atlan, Henri
    [A tort et à raison. English]
    Enlightenment to enlightenment : intercritique of science
and myth / Henri Atlan ; translated from the French by
Lenn J. Schramm.
        p.   cm.
    Includes index.
    ISBN 0–7914–1451–5. — ISBN 0–7914–1452–3 (pbk.)
    1. Science—Philosophy.  2. Reasoning.  3. Ethics.  I. Title.
Q175.A8613   1993
121—dc20
                                                            92–19023
                                                            CIP

10 9 8 7 6 5 4 3 2 1

*To Bela Rachel*

Sempiterna Temptatio, fit Zénon. Je me dis souvent que rien au monde, sauf un ordre éternel ou une bizarre velléité de la matière à faire mieux qu'elle-même, n'explique pourquoi je m'efforce chaque jour de penser un peu plus clairement que la veille.

(Marguérite Yourcenar, *L'Oeuvre au noir*)

I [Wisdom] was with [the Creator before the Creation] like a child to be raised [or, according to alternative readings proposed by Genesis Rabba (1,1), like a teacher, a craftsman, or an instrument providing the plans for building the world], a source of delight every day, rejoicing [or playing] before Him at all times, rejoicing [or playing] in His inhabited world, finding delight with mankind.

(Proverbs 8:30–31)

# Contents

## Introduction

# Right or Wrong?

The whole modern conception of the world is founded on the illusion that the so-called laws of nature are the explanation of natural phenomena.

Thus people today stop at the laws of nature, treating them as something inviolable, just as God and Fate were treated in past ages.

And in fact both are right and both wrong: though the view of the ancients is clearer insofar as they have a clear and acknowledged terminus, while the modern system tries to make it look as if *everything* were explained.

Wittgenstein,
*Tractatus Logico-Philosophicus,* 6.37ff.

In French this book was titled *A Tort et à raison,* which implies an untranslatable pun: "Right and Wrong." Not right *or* wrong, as mutually exclusive choices, as if right were synonymous with reason (French *raison*) and wrong necessarily equivalent to mixed up and confused (as in the French idiom *à tort et à travers*). Hence not only "Right *and* Wrong," but also "Wrong *and* Reasonable." Both oxymorons are only apparent, as we shall see in the course of this work.

Right *or* wrong? No, right *and* wrong—just as in the joke that is frequently (but probably *wrongly*) attributed to the Talmud. A rabbi was hearing a case involving two litigants. When the first had finished recounting his story, the rabbi, after long reflection, announced that he had decided that he was in the right. The other party quite naturally protested, and the rabbi agreed to hear his version. After the respondent had presented his case, the rabbi, again following long reflection, pronounced that he was in the right as well. When the rabbi's astonished students asked him how he could say that each of two contradictory versions of the same events was right, he responded, after a third long period of contemplation: "You're right too!"

The goal of the present volume is to show that there are several rationalities, different modes of being "right/reasonable/rational," all of them, despite their contradictions, legitimate ways of accounting for the data of our senses. Although the problem is hardly new, fresh life has been breathed into it by contemporary science, thanks to the quiet strength and modest triumph that have characterized science during the second half of the twentieth century. Science is everywhere, and nothing that pretends to make a true statement about reality can ignore it; while, on the other side, myth, religion, and metaphysics are all branded with the taint of illusion, if not indeed of hocus-pocus. As Bertrand Russell said, the only truth is scientific. At the same time, however, the quest for this truth, proceeding from the particular to the general, humbly restricts itself, by virtue of the conditions of application of its self-imposed rigorous methods, to objects that, because amenable to the latter, are carefully circumscribed and defined.

The result has been a disappointment with the nineteenth-century hope that science would explain everything and, what is more, provide a foundation for ethics; that science would help mankind live better, not only by virtue of its technological by-products, but also by shedding light on both the true and the good; that science would tell us how to live, in accordance with precepts we could believe in because, being "scientific," they would have once and for all dissipated the shadows of obscurantism and tradition. Behind this disappointment lurks the yearning to replace religious dogma with scientific dogma and thereby create a grand synthesis between the lights of reason and the illuminations of mysticism. The outcome has been a mysticism of science for which, once again, the only truth is scientific, but which cannot resign itself to staying within the narrow limits in which consistent reflexive critical thinking would contain it. Whence the oscillation between a naive materialist scientism and the no less naive spiritualist syntheses dressed in the oddments of mystic traditions vulgarized by pseudo-scientific jargon.

Here I want to defend the proposition that we are *right* to distinguish among the objects and methods of the physical sciences, the biological sciences, and the *sciences humaines*, with their different interests and stakes; as well as to distinguish all of these from the mystical and mythological traditions in which we have come to recognize a possible rationality that has quite different interests and stakes. By the same token, those who have attempted to unify all of these in a grand synthesis, embodied in some arcane lore that claims to reveal eternal and ubiquitous Ultimate Reality, are *wrong*.

Right and wrong according to whose lights? According to the lights of reason, of course: but those of an acrobatic reason, performing without a net, one that can no longer make use of metadiscourse and metatheory (meta-physics, meta-biology, meta-psychology, etc.). Are we right—is it reasonable—to trust in reason? If so, in what conditions? If not, how can we know this? The quest for illumination by the new mystics of this century, disappointed by "Cartesian rationalism," is a curious sequel to the *philosophes* of the Enlightenment.

*Light* and *illumination* are synonyms—but not always. The neo-alchemist confounding of Enlightenment and Illumination[1] is probably to be explained by an irrepressible need to ground ethics (and politics) in objective Truth, to the detriment of both scientific research and mystical traditions. One possible remedy is the serious humor of the multiplicity (and relativity) of games of knowledge, reason, the unconscious, language, possibilities, real-unreal, whose ceaseless transformations can advantageously replace the alchemical quest for Ultimate Reality.

The first chapter poses a number of questions based on the author's experiences (both first- and secondhand) during the 1960s and 1970s. These experiences orient the reflections in the subsequent chapters, because, although the questions that concern us have been widely debated and closely analyzed by centuries of philosophical activity, today they are asked in different contexts. The story of these experiences, as much or more so than long theoretical analyses, can help us conceive of the terms of some problems of civilization that are posed by the explosive development, in quantity and quantity, of science and technology.

The discoveries of the twentieth century have significantly modified how we conceive not only of nature, but also of the theoretical, moral, and political implications of our research activities. Quantum physics and relativity, followed later by molecular biology and most recently by computer science, have clearly had a fundamental effect on our thought about things, and even more on our thought about how we think about things. It cannot be denied that we are discovering, in us and around us, a new type of reason, one that is different from what the past centuries of science and philosophy had accustomed us to. But what is this new reason? Or, more precisely, wherein lies the novelty of this new reason—it being understood that it remains reason, in *direct continuity with classical reason*? Too often novelty, with its aura of the unprecedented, the marvelous, and the fantastic, dazzles us so far as to make us forget where it comes from. Thus a mysticism that lives comfortably with an irrationality that the new science is supposed to "confirm" has sometimes been able to overwhelm first-class scientists. On the other side (and also too often), some among their peers, seeking to remain "level headed," find no other resource than to turn away their eyes from the implications of this new reason, as if it were merely a question of perfect continuity with the combat and victory of classical reason over whatever is not itself; merely a triumphant sequel to the successes of the Enlightenment over the shadows of religious obscurantism and the irrational—Nietzsche's "black men" and Freud's "black mud." This combat did indeed take place and continues in our own time. But we are not dealing with an uninterrupted process, monotonic and unambiguous: the light is always mingled with darkness—and in direct proportion to how blinding it is. The thesis of this book is that we must first endeavor to circumscribe within the new science what is truly new, from the perspective of thought about things: not so much theoretical content, whose refutation is always pending and in which we must not "believe," despite the technological successes that accompany it; but, above all, the new relations between our rationality and things, it being understood that the things of nature remain what they always were, as does our discursive reason, which still operates in accordance with the principles of identity and noncontradiction. What has altered is the relationship between them; or, more precisely, the relationship between the abstract and the concrete, as it appears in modern scientific thought. What is new in the "new reason" is not so much reason itself as the manner in which we employ it to "explain" reality.

In parallel, because this novelty is recognized as such only in a limited sociocultural context—namely, that of the science and philosophy that have developed in the West during the past few centuries—the comparison naturally ensues with what has occurred in other sociocultural milieus, in the Near East and Far East and among the American Indians. There too we must detour past the alternative paths (basically identical with the two errors mentioned previously) of being dazzled by the richness and novelty (for us Westerners) of the harvests gathered by these non-Western traditions of knowledge, versus their outright dismissal from our mental world, lest we surrender to this fascination. The wise path is to keep a firm grasp on this comparison and to systematically adumbrate the differences rather than the similarities. The conscious or unconscious quest for a unified and closed lore, for knowledge of Ultimate Reality, is a source of confusion as well as an obstacle to authentic dialogue between cultures. The different experiences of thought, the different modes of using reason that people have developed on different continents over the ages, have nothing to gain from leveling comparisons and syncretisms that deprive them of their substance and of the legitimacy that grounds their portion of truth. This does not mean, however, that they should be ignored. Since the publication of Russell's *Mysticism and Logic* in 1918, many elements have appeared that belong both to the order of scientific logic and to that of mystical experiences.

Today we have reached the point where scientific explanations cannot be complete, because they are based on methods of observation and experimentation that carve up reality into separate domains and subdivide each domain into various levels of integration.

The passage from one level to another, in reality and in our knowledge thereof, is conditioned by the theoretical and technical tools at our disposal for performing such dissection. The inevitability of this problem has become clear thanks precisely to the success of molecular biology. In Chapter 2 we shall see how the problems raised by the observation of organized beings in nature have been totally rephrased by the biological and cybernetic context of the science of the last four decades. This will lead us to situate the frontiers of objective knowledge at the seams between levels of organization; that is, between the domains circumscribed by different scientific disciplines. The questions of physicochemical reductionism and of the mind-body problem are posed (again) in this context, giving us our first glimpse of the relativist consequences that flow from recognition of these frontiers.

Distinguishing between the reductionism of method, which is indispensable for the practice of science, and a reductionism of theories, we shall see that the latter, always motivated by extrascientific preoccupations—metaphysical if not indeed ideological—is often a source of confusion that sometimes leads to the opposite of the goals pursued. In classical reductionist mechanicism, for example, the image of the man-machine, which seems to be the zenith of materialism, is stood on its head, as it were, when we realize that machines are characterized by their purposefulness, which is actually that of their builder, the plan of the one who designed them in order to accomplish a particular task. In other words, the image of man-as-machine is not materialist *enough* and should be rejected by a consistent physicochemical reductionism. It still contains too many elements of teleology. Even the metaphor of the genetic program, which should expunge this defect from materialism, frequently reinforces it instead, especially when taken too seriously, too literally. The machine is not a good image, even if natural selection is invoked as the programmer. The play of molecular interactions, with no superadded purposefulness, not even teleonomic, is the only coherent physicochemical description of living systems. Purposefulness, whether in the form of a biological function and its meaning, or of intentionality—even unconscious intentionality—implies a projection by the observer, which can (also) be justified by the concern for convenience and relevance in a suitable description of what is observed at certain levels. We shall see how it is possible to artificially simulate situations in which "naive" observers, attempting to describe and understand the functionality they observe, would also be quite justified in making such projections. The purposefulness of a game, unlike that of the machine, is nothing more than its mechanism, that is, the rules that govern how it is played. These rules are not "adapted" to a task to be accomplished. This is why it is possible to change the rules; they will always be "adapted"—even if, as in loser takes all, they are reversed!—with no need for continual planning and optimizing by experts in operational research. We have learned that the specific property of a machine is not to obey the laws of mechanics, like a clock (the stars do that, too), nor, like a turbine or steam engine, to transform energy (nature does that, too), but rather to be programmable. As a consequence, the man-machine acquires a new meaning. Mechanics and thermodynamics banished the soul from the physical world, but the image of nature-as-programmer seems to invite it back—unless the programmer is another human being, wielder of power? Are we able to abandon the man-machine to the bygone centuries that could not escape its image, without rediscovering the man-as-pure-spirit it replaced, and instead welcome the *man-as-game*?

The post-positivist philosophers have helped expose the delusions of an omnipotent science, the same delusions whose offshoots are at the origin of the resurgence of mysticism and the irrational. On the other hand, the experience of the sacred, which dominated the origin of civilizations— but which in our own culture is allowed to be evidence at best for a deviant perception of reality, reserved to a handful of mystics, poets, and artists, and always suspected of unchecked subjectivity, if not indeed of pathology—has become, thanks to psychedelic experiences, a mass phenomenon, in some measure objectifiable, within the reach of (almost) everyone. The discovery in the West of the reality of the world of dreams and of the "social imaginary" (Castoriadis), first through chemistry and later through techniques of meditation and contemplation imported from the East, the groundwork for which had in large measure been laid by psychoanalysis and surrealism, merely reinforced and vulgarized the idea of an Ultimate Reality—precisely that which they unveil, as the original and undifferentiated Unity from which the diversity and multiplicity of symbols and individuals proceed; our Self, in particular, appears there as the singular locus of differentiation. This is why, not wishing to abandon this territory to delirium and the arbitrary, we shall reflect, in Chapter 3, on the rationality (or asserted irrationality) of mysticism and, in general, of traditions whose practice and teaching accord a central role to mystical experiences and to the transmission of narratives that we receive as myths. The goal is clearly not encyclopedic, but rather to distill out the features that make it possible to recognize the rationality of this discourse, while underscoring how this rationality is different, opposed to, or, better yet, "incommensurate" with that of the scientific method we practice in the laboratory.

The sciences developed out of a rupture with this type of experience, out of the radical distinction that English (unlike French) denotes by "experiment" vs. "experience." The effects of this rupture were not all bad, contrary to what certain nostalgic souls believe; for the numinous is always ambushed by confusion, which is the source of crime and, what is "worse," of error. The natural sciences developed methods for tracking down and running to earth the misidentification of their objects, the confusion of genres and the hidden contradiction. They cannot renounce these skills, even if their own domains of application are restricted by the conditions in which the methods can be applied. The main thrust of *science* is to pose *questions*. The main thrust of *mystical traditions* is to provide *answers*. It goes without saying that answers given by the latter cannot satisfy the questions raised by the former. Scientific questions call for certain types of answers that scientific theories attempt, generally imperfectly, to provide; but grand syntheses complete these partial answers by means of extrapolations in which the only vestige of science is the vocabulary employed, in a more or less rigorous fashion. On the other hand, mystical traditions offer answers to questions that have no scientific relevance, questions that are metaphysical in all senses of the term; but they seem to contend with the aforementioned syntheses or, on the contrary to reinforce them. If the two sorts of questions and answers can intermingle, without our being aware of this, it is because both employ reason; the uses are different, certainly, but the rationality is the same. If scientific reason can sometimes function as a myth, this is probably because, conversely, myths can operate with their own proper rationality. In fact, rational explanations of the universe are mythological in proportion as they assert themselves to be comprehensive, given that the scientific practice of our century, concentrating on efficacy and control, has increasingly renounced completeness.

The intellectual subtleties of mystical traditions consist of wondering about the questions to which these traditions offer, a priori, answers. Quite schematically, Jewish tradition, both talmudic and kabbalistic—to which I shall refer frequently because I know it, better than the others, from the inside—developed the art of questioning ad infinitum, by means of a particular sort of dialectic and critical reasoning, its own a priori answers; whereas the Buddhist tradition of *koans*, which I know only from the outside, developed the art of confounding—in the dual sense of confounding one's opponent and sowing confusion—the rational aspect of its own theoretical answers. These activities aim at satisfying two legitimate but mutually contradictory needs: to explain, that is, to give a sense to things, to eliminate their surprising and disquieting character and associate them with the already seen and already explained; and, at the same time, to clarify and elucidate, by distinguishing and separating, what must not be confused, while preserving the unique character of every experience—including that of the theoretician who has managed to explain by unifying, without confounding, a multitude of disparate objects.

Chapter 4 is an opportunity for both author and reader to step back and acquire a new perspective on the preceding observations, by reflecting on the rationality of natural phenomena and reconsidering the principle of noncontradiction and the reality of possible worlds. We shall demonstrate the undecidability of the rational or irrational character of reality, and the undecidability of this undecidability....

In Chapter 5 we shall analyze the inevitable role of interpretation in the practice of the various methods of knowledge available to us. Scientific theory discloses no more of the essence of things than do mythological systems and mystical revelation. Things are given us to interpret. Different rules and techniques of interpretation typify the various methods. And theory is inevitably interpretation—unless it is the possibility of interpretation; that is, the fact that we are capable of interpreting things and that sometimes this interpretation can be effective. In other words, in these interpretive games there is no Ultimate Reality to be discovered, except perhaps the very possibility of their existence and effectiveness; but this is not "real" (because it is only a possibility!) and can be spoken of only allusively, by means of a ruse, by demolishing language. This analysis leads to a relativism of knowledge that is nevertheless not to be confused with some nihilism or "confusionism" in which "everything is the same." Quite the contrary, the rigor of the rules of interpretation imposes itself all the more so—and becomes all the more attainable—in proportion as they are recognized as such, thereby permitting us to circumscribe their legitimate domains of application.

This attitude lies in direct continuity with certain currents of analytic philosophy that inherited the logical and linguistic tools of logical positivism but criticized the latter for the overly narrow, almost ideological, use it made of these tools and which characterized it through the 1950s. Popper, Quine, and their disciples occupy center stage in this movement. But already Wittgenstein, formulating questions that can no longer not be asked, had insights on which our own reflections are based, as do some of his commentators, such as Saul Kripke, or, among others, the "Friday afternoon" group of philosophers,[2] a faithful representative of this evolution, in which products of the American school attempted to integrate the achievements of Europe over the last decades. In their meeting, at Oxford, they assigned themselves the task of undertaking a new critique of scientific reason, rendered possible, today, by the increasingly operational character of the natural sciences, including the cognitive sciences; and, to this end, of setting scientific research in a broader context, while exposing the "underlying beliefs" and "ultimate presuppositions" that establish the framework within which each science is practiced in each age. Here we may hear an echo of the Nietzschean idea that the scientific ideal of explanation may itself at times be a myth (the "rational myth of the West"), perhaps in the service of the private interests of the new "priesthood" of a technocratic society. But here too we must guard against the meta-theoretical and all-encompassing temptation to seal ourselves up within a sociology of science or closed criticism, blind to itself, that might rely on the form of criticism instituted by this work.

Moreover, the attitude expressed by Popper in the Postscript to his *Logic of Scientific Discovery*,[3] namely, that science can be neither superficial nor authoritarian, in the final analysis reduces to an aesthetic and moral judgment on the value of human reason in general and of scientific activity in particular, despite the self-defeating digressions that have perverted its liberating vocation ever since, following the First World War, it became excessively guided, to his taste, by the quest for utility and mastery. Of course, Popper makes this aesthetic and moral judgment from within his own civilization and culture: Greco-Roman, Christian, humanist, Western. In other cultures, it is other activities, other asceses, whether intellectual, rational, or willingly irrational, those of mystical, artistic, and mythological traditions, that are the object of analogous value judgments; just as legitimately, we may add, and despite the recognition, there too, of deviations to which each of these traditions of knowledge and of interpretive ordering of things has given rise, deviations in which they too have immured and crushed those whom they were supposed to help set free. Because we know today that this is the case, skepticism—or the so-called epistemological nihilism that lies at its origin—can go beyond itself and lead to something other than plain nihilism. We need merely recognize the value, or rather the different and specific values, of each of these enterprises of knowledge—somewhat in the manner of the rabbinic judge with whom we began.

Thus this skepticism is not nihilist to the extent that is based on *belief* in *several* modes of trying to know and understand, even if their paths never intersect. Certainly this relativizes each tradition of knowledge, from the perspective of belief in its absolute and exclusive character; but at the same time it permits us to allow each of them, a priori, the possibility of having something to teach us, of containing something that speaks to our reason. We must not believe in any constituted knowledge, a posteriori and exclusively, so as to slam the door a priori to any possibility of believing in other forms of knowledge. We are not preaching here a return to obscurantism and confusion, for the coexistence of different and sometimes contradictory traditions envisioned here can be effected only in a praxis that does not suppress—quite the contrary—their differences and theoretical contradictions. What is more, it does not suppress our experience of Western civilization as central, because our own; nor the irreplaceable character, for each of us, of our linguistic tradition, that in which we have learned, with greater or lesser success, to name things so as to endow them with meaning. But neither does the reality of this experience prevent our reason and our imagination from showing us the no less central and irreplaceable character of other traditions, for those who have been nurtured by them. Tradition has it that in ancient times the sages of the Sanhedrin had to be conversant in each of the seventy languages of mankind. On this condition, their deliberations concerning natural and moral law—extending the activity of Adam, who named all things and beings—could avoid being frozen in a nominalism reducible to that of a single language.

The interest that the depositories of a tradition may have in accepting and becoming familiar with the values of others must allow them to not reject or dominate these others by force, even while they resolutely continue to advance along their own path. In this sense, and only in this sense, some traditions may perhaps pretend to greater "universality" than others—but not in the name of theoretical Universals, of revelation, or of reason, the discourses of which in any case speak only particular languages.

This attitude contrasts with that adopted by a public avid for grand unifying syntheses and for "scientific astrology" and other fads and fallacies, with the more or less implicit support of certain men of science, some of them quite eminent, who believe they have rediscovered in modern science the teachings of ancient traditions, especially those of the East. This current of thought, provocatively expressed at the famous Cordoba Colloquium of 1979, derives its origin and direct inspiration from the encounter between the two great upheavals in Western thought in the first half of the twentieth century: quantum physics and psychoanalysis. The role of Carl Gustav Jung in the establishment—and the dissemination by some of his disciples—of scientific-mystical neoalchemy is clear to any reader, not only of the proceedings of the Cordoba colloquium, but also of a 1952 volume he produced conjointly with one of the fathers of quantum physics, Wolfgang Pauli. An analysis of the misunderstandings between the two co-authors of that book, as well as of the Freud-Jung controversy concerning the criteria of scientificity of psychoanalysis, occupies a large part of Chapter 5. We shall see the difficulties encountered by the authors of these upheavals themselves when they endeavored to establish, despite everything, a continuity between the content of what they had discovered and the form of ratiocination to which nineteenth-century science had accustomed them. Quantum physics forced them to give over the naive realism that classical physics had previously nourished. Psychoanalysis, as a technique profoundly implying the subjective lived experience of human beings but that nevertheless did not renounce its claim to scientific rationality, forced its adherents to steer a course that was certainly fertile and original, but was often unable to avoid the two stumbling blocks that still threaten it today: an irrelevant scientific content, which is moreover always lagging behind the latest changes in physical and biological theory; and discoveries about the unconscious. The sui generis practice of therapy makes it possible to have a quasi-initiatory experience of the latter, but the theory has difficulty avoiding (though it sometimes succeeds) a language that more closely resembles that of art and illumination than that of scientific discourse. Moreover, it is with Freud and certain of those who attempt to maintain a Freudian (in form, albeit not necessarily in content) orthodoxy, that we find an intuition of what *today* appears to be the criteria of scientificity of a research *practice*: reproducibility whenever possible, leaving the door open to future refutation, and, above all, renunciation of complete explanation that would ground a monist metaphysics—in other words, the famous incompleteness of theory, by which science can keep itself open and always in motion and thereby distinguish itself from the static perfection of magic and myth.

In Chapter 6 we shall return to the snares laid by the quest for *the* Ultimate Reality behind the theories of physics, which compares and unifies the content of their discourses with that of mystical traditions. I have found it interesting, because unexpected, to offer a few examples drawn from the talmudic tradition; these demonstrate how the relativism of knowledge recommended here, far from being a sterile skepticism, actually permits a critique that is even more fruitful because it is not based on a metatheory that could produce a theory of critical thought. Recognizing the unbridgeable distance and the incommensurability of two modes of knowledge allows us, by jumping from one to the other, to have a radical exteriority toward each of them. The result is a critique that is not simultaneous, but rather alternating and reciprocal, and thereby always able to refresh its praxis, because it avoids setting itself up as an autonomous and overarching domain that would be the locus of a necessarily noncritical theory of critical thought.

But the best companion on these winding paths remains humor, whose smiles and laughter open up what was thought to be sealed. Approaching the paths of knowledge as games that must not be taken too seriously is the best guarantee of the serious nature of knowledge. This is why Chapter 7 conducts a dialogue among three philosophers who, each in his own fashion, have found in play the richest experience of the serious, if not indeed the tragic, side of the stakes of knowledge. The game as constitutive of the infant's Self and subsequently of the adult's culture (Winnicott), language games as constitutive of the social reality of knowledge (Wittgenstein), and various aspects of the game as symbol—that is, as an opening to the unreal-real being—of the world (Eugen Fink), teach us how to play the games of knowledge better.

We could not conclude this journey without encountering several times, along the turnings of our road, the question of ethics and its sources. For it is the anguished need for a true ethics, vouched for in some fashion by scientific truth, that pushes great minds to throw themselves into the arms of the grand unifying synthesis of scientific mysticism.

Because one absolutely cannot deduce value judgments from those of reality—what should be from what is—the desire to ground ethics in scientific knowledge was already debatable, even when it was still naively believed that science merely exposes what exists, uncovers reality. But these attempts appear to be even more in vain after we have recognized that every discipline is relative to the methods it employs and to the domains in which they are legitimately applied, without going so far as to consider those unfortunate experiences in which they were used to justify totalitarian regimes. In an attempt at "genealogical reflection," to use J. Beaufret's term, we shall suggest, in Chapter 8, a hypothesis that derives ethics from the internalization of rituals, themselves based, originally, on the integration in individual and social life of experiences of "another" reality, the reality of dreams and hallucinations, of shamans and prophets. We are thereby brought back to the separation between scientific and traditional disciplines, this time on the basis not only of their objects and methods, but also of their motivations. The true motive force of objective knowledge, which is based on measurement and calculation, is mastery of nature— despite all the proclamations about the value of disinterested scientific knowledge and of the search for truth in itself, whose role is simply to provide ideological justification for social mobilization around this project. Ultimately—and despite the efforts of the *philosophes* of the Enlightenment—the question of ethics remains in the purview of what survives of these mystical and religious traditions and continues to provide their chief impetus. Seen as aiming at self-liberation and self-*control*, one might think that this problem re-enters the domain of the scientific project to master nature by constructing artifacts that lead to "self-manufacturing" techniques,[4] because human beings are, after all, products of nature, and can also be turned into artifacts. But this would ignore the ambiguous status of the *sciences humaines*, in which human beings are simultaneously subject and object, whose discourse is more scientific in proportion as they are more objective and disinterested, and which, at the limit, are restricted to tailor-made domains of reality, cut to measure, lacking significant links to the lived experience of individuals. By contrast, traditional disciplines that proceed from the inside—from the irreducible intuition of the subjectivity of the "I"—toward the outside, thus projecting on the latter a "world soul," maintain a certain effectiveness, that of a humanization of nature, of animism in the positive sense, precisely by permitting one to postulate an ethics. In this object-subject of knowledge, the "hierarchies" are "tangled" to such an extent that imagination and even delirium can "take over" even more strongly than in nonhuman nature. Here the relationship to the world of possibles is different, because of the complexity provoked—or designated—by this entanglement of levels. (Almost) all possibilities—including those that are contradictory and hence logically impossible—can become real, that is, *truly* possible, if they are located at the source of the transformations of the possible into the real, that is, within the observer-actor, the subject-object himself.

To this effectiveness, which is limited in the real world, there corresponds another effectiveness, that of the sciences, which move from the outside toward the inside and succeed in mastering nature and, again in a limited fashion, in naturalizing human beings. But these respective efficacies are severely diminished when they pretend to unity and exclusive universality. Clearly they cannot renounce this pretension: for one thing, some form of reductionism that pretends to unify everything on a physical causalist basis is indispensable for scientific method; for another, the all-encompassing nature of Revelation or Illumination is the alpha and omega of rationalized mystical experience. Trying to resolve this contradiction through a syncretic discipline in which these two approaches come together is merely running away to an even greater pretension to monopoly and universality, in which their respective efficacies would certainly evaporate. It is far better, if we would keep them in motion and preserve their fruitfulness, to move between them and accept the monopolistic pretensions of each as a necessary rule of the game, without which it cannot be played; not only the games in progress, but also those of the future, whose stakes we do not yet know.

In some milieus, two questions are posed whenever one hears about the latest news or the latest theory: "Is that supposed to be serious?" and "Where are you talking from?" The latter question already casts doubt on the seriousness of the answer to the former! The first question is raised in Chapter 7. As to the second, this entire book tends to show that one can and must speak from several different places, about science from where it is practiced, about myth from the world of those who live it; but as a consequence it becomes possible to speak of one from the place of the other, and vice versa. This is still relativism, of course, but also the "nontriviality" of individuals who maintain their autonomy (von Foerster, Dupuy).

"And where is Truth in all of this?" you may ask. As a result of the overwhelming but exalting successes of the technology derived from the natural sciences, in our age there is the scientific—and everything else. We have come to believe that the only truth is scientific truth and that only science deals without illusions with the search for the Truth about nature and ourselves. Everything else (our subjectivity in our passions, art and myth, not to mention religion) can be no more than an ornament, if it is not in fact so much hocus-pocus. Following in the wake of the illusions of the Enlightenment, we have had to live through the disillusionment of the twentieth century to understand that scientific Truth, too, is only an embellishment on reality. Certainly it lights our way, but we fashion it to do precisely this, like an illumination in a manuscript or a fancy candelabrum, or like the streetlight of the old joke—the one under which we look at night for a key we lost somewhere else, because it's too dark to see in the place where we lost it. The real is not true. It is content with being. We construct one truth around it, and then another, like a decoration; not arbitrarily, to be sure, but with certain goals and ends. If we would attain an objectifiable mastery of nature, we must work within the constraints of the experimental method and of the logical truth functions. The successful attainment of our objectives allows us to continue; failure leads us to change the objective and to build a different candelabrum, if we can. Other goals—such as understanding, explaining, persuading, loving and being loved, unifying our inner life and our objective or intersubjective experiences, causing justice and love to reign among responsible human beings—all these impose different constraints on how we construct truth.

A certain modesty in the exposure of truth leads us to reclothe it with multiple but fitting veils. Evidently naked Truth can be "contemplated" only without words and in darkness.

Once again, the relativism defended here does not imply that anything goes and everything is the same. Quite the contrary: the distinctions on which it rests—between disciplines, between domains of legitimacy, between games with different rules, and so forth—lead to other distinctions, such as that between reason and unreason, or between wisdom and folly, as well as between different ethics of life and knowledge. These distinctions are the indispensable point of departure if one would have any hope of ultimately arriving at a certain de facto universality, one that is not an illusion, by virtue of the confrontation of and dialogue between cultures. Only a universality of practice can be attained, and not the illusory universality that ostensibly flows from a theoretical universality posed a priori. Because of the limitations of languages, universality cannot be one of concepts and discourse. The sole exception, to a certain extent, is scientific language, but at the cost of its amorality and leveling, which condition its transparency and the operationality of its techniques. To go beyond these limitations, the only possible universality of values is that which is built up, step by step, through struggle, coexistence, and dialogue. And its only guarantee is good will, without complacency, toward the other, the strange, and the stranger.

Verbal and written information and helpful comments have been provided on various occasions by my colleagues and friends M. Biezunski, M. Dufour, J.-P. Dupuy, F. Fogelman-Soulié, J.-C. Giabicani, D. Girard, B. Kohn-Atlan, S. Kottek, J.-M. Lévy-Leblond, M. Milgram, S. Mosès, M. Olender, B. Shanon, I. Stengers, G. Vichniac, and G. Weisbuch. I would like to thank all of them.

## Notes

1. In common usage the difference between these two synonyms seems to be one of connotation and primary meaning: *illumination* is associated with "illuminati" and the idea of revelation, whereas *enlightenment* calls to mind the Enlightenment, with its dependence on reason. In the 1960s certain circles coined the term *enlightment* for the inner light that leaves reason aside, but three decades later it cannot be said that the coinage is current.

2. S. Mitchell and M. Rosen, ed., *The Need for Interpretation* (London: Athlone Press, 1983).

3. Karl R. Popper, *Realism and the Aim of Science*, ed. W. W. Bartley (London: Hutchinson, 1983).

4. M. Foucault, "Usage des plaisirs et techniques de soi," *Le Débat* 27 (1983), pp. 46–72; and the remarks by T. Orel, "A propos des techniques d'auto-façonnage," *Sociétés* 1 (1984), pp. 32–33.

*Chapter 1*

# (Experimental) Proceedings

*A Radio Encounter between Assiduous Listeners of*
*"Cultural" Broadcasts, a Biologist, and a Philosopher*

The topic proposed by the radio program was how "science" can help people resolve their problems. More precisely, "since we can no longer believe in religion and ideologies have failed us, only science remains as a source of truth in which we can believe. Only from it can we (and therefore must) learn how to live. Given its brilliant successes, including sending men to the moon and discovering the secrets of life, it is abnormal that it does not help us more in knowing how to live and be happy. It is the duty of men of science like yourselves to tell us what we must do and how to do it."

The biologist and philosopher, *without prior consultation between them*, responded to this demand made by the show's audience and hosts with a refusal, which they justified by explaining that it was a case of mistaken identity and in particular an error about the goal of scientific research, which is not the enunciation of moral law. This encountered an indignant reaction on the part of the hosts, who felt that their two guests were not playing by the rules of the game. The latter took turns defending themselves vigorously, while the demand itself became ever more pressing and even aggressive, culminating in the assertion: "Your attitude is that of traitors who are dodging your obligations to society. Society has allowed you the great privilege of engaging in a profession you like, which gives you many benefits, intellectual satisfaction, the opportunity to travel, etc.

17

So you owe it something, and especially to those of us who do not enjoy such privileges. Your side of the bargain is to tell us what we must do."

This dialogue of the deaf became a traumatic experience when the hosts, to confound the two unfair players, played tapes made by other scientists who were willing to play by the rules. These proved to be self-confident speeches about how the thermodynamics of irreversible phenomena can teach us to organize our life in society and about the moral philosophy that can be "scientifically" deduced from the most recent theories of neurophysiology. The two allies, outflanked, found themselves obliged to condemn these colleagues whom they esteemed for their achievements in science and to demonstrate how the latter had exceeded their field of competence. But of course the battle was lost even before it was begun and merely reinforced the idea that "these two individuals were a bad choice. They are not representative of the community of good and responsible scientists upon whom we can and must count. Fortunately there are others. We'll repeat this program later, we hope with a better choice of guests."

## November 1978: The President and the Biologists

On November 28, 1978, the president of France appointed three renowned French biologists to "study the consequences that the discoveries of modern biology are apt to entail for the organization and functioning of society, to make note of those biotechnology applications that offer the greatest benefit for human progress and happiness, and to propose appropriate means for applying them."[1]

After a year of work these scientists, assisted by a team of specialists, produced a report entitled *The Life Sciences and Society*, which received fairly broad coverage in the print and broadcast media. This full and fair report highlighted the "hot spots" of contemporary biological research, the great advances made in recent years, and the enigmas still to be solved. The last section, "Interactions between Biology and Society," and the conclusions of the report expressed the consensus of the vast majority of prudent practicing biologists, who are aware of the limits on what may reasonably be expected of their discipline in domains such as politics, society, and ethics, which go considerably beyond it. The problem is not the report's content—not surprising, given the identity of its authors—but its very existence, or rather the solemnity surrounding its commissioning and submission. Of the three studies that President Giscard asked the biologists to undertake (see above), only the last two were really within their domain of competence: to make a list of the most useful applications of biotechnology and to propose appropriate means for applying them, with all the limits inherent in a prognostic study that attempts to peer into the future. Restricted to these two questions, the study would have served to direct research policy in biology and have been rather more in the province of a minister of research than of the president of France. Analogous studies could have been carried out with regard to the research orientation of other disciplines in the physical and social sciences. But the peculiar nature of this report involved the first item in its authors' commission: "study the consequences...for the organization and functioning of society." Evidently this is what interests not only those responsible for research policy, but also those responsible for the conduct of public affairs in general, and justifies the presidential commission and its attendant solemnity. At the same time, the commission constitutes an astonishing short-circuiting of all the intermediate echelons and, above all, of other important persons whose domains of competence are no less relevant for the study requested: sociologists, philosophers, moralists, artists. Once again, the report's contents make a felicitous attempt to make amends for this approach. We read that

> sooner or later, however, the development of the [life] sciences will have to attach itself more closely to the future of society, its hopes, its ethics.... What is needed above all is profound and protracted reflection by a group comprising not only scientists and politicians but also individuals with other fields of expertise. This is where social planning and ethical imperatives join forces.[2]

As its concluding lines point out: "Contrary to what one would sometimes have us believe, it is not on the basis of biology that a particular idea of man can be shaped. On the contrary, it is on the basis of a particular idea of man that biology can be used in the service of the latter."

But what concerns us here above all is the reason for the commission. Why should the president of France feel a need to ask biologists—and only biologists—to help prepare a forward-looking study of the organization and functioning of society? The answer was provided by one of the president's spokespersons, who told the press, several days after the publication of the report, that the president's future decisions would be the appropriate ones because they would be instructed by Science. This explains the underlying motivation for the commission and also why the science called upon was biology, which fascinates the general public more than any other because of its real or supposed relations with (scientific) Truth, on the one hand, and (individual and collective) Life, on the other. The president wanted the same thing as the public, who expect to find in scientific discourse a guarantee of the truth and correctness of social and political, and even ethical, behavior. The contents of the report, which to some extent warn against this expectation, do not counterbalance its very existence as a response to, and justification of, the commission.

Since then, France has a new president and new political constellation. The new and more democratic approach to the problems of scientific research culminated in a national colloquium on research and technology in 1982; efforts have been made to modernize scientific research and increase its budgets, despite corporate and trade-union obstacles. There is a contradiction between the desire for competitive and aggressive research that would succeed on the technological and industrial plane and "put an end to the crisis," on the one hand, and aspirations for a convivial and fraternal society that permits the flourishing of the greatest number. But the same implicit postulate is held by all: scientific progress is the only sure and indisputable value that satisfies the consensus of (almost) everyone when it is a question of choosing the right directions in the social and political arenas.

## Versailles, 1974

This was an international colloquium of molecular and cellular biologists, immunologists, and neurophysiologists, who met with physicists, biophysicists, and mathematicians to discuss some of the questions posed by the study of intercellular communications. There were passionate presentations about the experimental strategies that had led, at the end of long and patient labor, to the elucidation of molecular structures that serve as substrates for exchanges of information between cells or between the organism and some of its specialized cells, or for the collective behavior of a cluster of cells in the course of differentiation. There were equally passionate presentations of formal models, mathematical or otherwise, kinetic, thermodynamic, or simply logical, that provide a coherent representation of the cooperative mechanisms through which the collective behavior of cells is produced from molecular and membranal interactions. At that point a physicist mounted the podium to deliver his invited paper. This was Brian Josephson, a specialist in superconductivity who had discovered the celebrated effect that bears his name and won him the Nobel Prize.

First surprise: he wrote on the blackboard a list of reference works meant for anyone who wanted to delve more deeply into the subject of his talk, and it ran from the *Bhagavad Gita* to the teachings of Maharishi. After that he spoke of the results of experiments in transcendental meditation, which triggered various astonished reactions in the audience. The lecture continued with a description of the state of consciousness obtained through such meditation. Then he "explained" this state of consciousness by invoking the possibility that brain cells could attain the same state as that of matter at a temperature close to absolute zero, precisely in those conditions where superconductivity effects are observed. Conductivity without resistance, which characterizes these effects, would thus also be found in cerebral structures, under the effect of meditation! There he had gone too far: a molecular biologist, who had earlier described the detailed experiments that had led to the discovery of the structure of hemoglobin, literally exploded. "Nothing forces us," he said furiously to the physicist, "to listen to your wild speculations. You are not respecting the implicit conventions of a scientific conference. Each of us is reporting on the results of reproducible experiments that in principle anyone can repeat in the laboratory. This is not the place for you to talk about the states of your soul." To which the physicist retorted calmly: "What I am talking about is the result of reproducible experiments performed with the aid of a technique that anyone can apply in order to verify this reproducibility!" The session broke up in the uproar that ensued.

## California, 1967–1968

The hippy movement was born, developed, and grew on the wings of hallucinogenic trips, stimulated chiefly by LSD. In addition to its psychedelic effects on sense perception and other modified states of consciousness, LSD always produces neurovegetative effects that may be perceived as pleasant or not, depending on context, such as sweating, palpitations, vasodilatation and vasoconstriction, fatigue, and so forth. These phenomena are felt as waves of heat flowing through the body, which a physician has no trouble recognizing and attributing naturally to these neurovegetative effects. For the hippies, however, it was a flux of cosmic energy whose overflow quite naturally accompanies the expansion of perception that characterizes a trip, just as LSD makes one sensitive to the vibrations that everybody produces in his or her surroundings, good and bad "vibes," which can produce amorous ecstasies or rage reactions. They could have only a dialogue of the deaf, or almost so, with the physician-physicist who, armed with his physiological and physical interpretations, insisted that energy and vibrations have nothing to do with the "real" effects of LSD. No communication is possible because the (reproducible!) effect of LSD is precisely to transform the perception of reality so that the hallucination, *although perceived as different* from normal perception, is accompanied by a sense of reality that *nothing* distinguishes from the normal sense of reality associated with real objects outside a "trip." At the same time, though, it is most difficult for scientists looking on from the sidelines to admit that the hippies' is a correct usage of the notions of energy and vibration, even after themselves experiencing this transformed perception of reality. And should this experience persuade the scientists that these notions express it better than the more prosaic explanation that invokes neurovegetative and sympathetic-antipathetic effects, what remains of their science and their critical mind after they have completed these adventures? And how will they react to the scholarly dissertations of their psychoanalyst colleagues about psychic energy, its circulation, its investments and disinvestments, transposing all the properties of physical energy, including the law of its conservation, when no known form of physical energy (heat, mechanical, electrical, chemical) is involved? This would be a third "scientific"(?) use of the word *energy*, one that has little in common with the other two—and not counting our normal daily use of the word ("he got up full of energy today").

## Cordoba, 1979—Science and Consciousness: Two Views of the Universe[3]

Scientists, some of them well known, met with individuals nurtured by the great religious traditions of East and West, of Islam and Israel. There was also a large contingent of psychoanalysts (most of them Jungians), who, by virtue of the peculiar status of the discipline, found themselves in a third camp of knowledge and practice. The aim of the meeting was to resume the dialogue, which had been interrupted several centuries earlier, between the search for rational explanations of the world and its latest achievements in twentieth-century science, on the one hand, and the teachings of mystical traditions about the hidden aspects of reality, on the other.

Center stage was occupied by quantum mechanics (or, in more general terms, subatomic physics) and the cosmic consciousness. This time the same Nobel laureate physicist whose talk was interrupted at Versailles was able to develop at leisure his theories that interpret the experiences of transcendental meditation in terms of physics, and physics in terms of states of consciousness. This represented a new approach to physics; the guarantee of its scientific nature resided in the fact that the knowledge on which it is based and which derives from mystical and spiritual traditions "is based on experiences with well-defined, controlled states of consciousness."[4] Of course this approach is grounded in the abrogation of the subject-object distinction, a distinction that is only a harmful moment in the Western mode of thought and of which, happily, the Eastern traditions are free. Moreover, Western science is ready to go beyond this distinction and thereby to link up with the mystical traditions, thanks to the recognition of the role of the observer in quantum mechanics and of the role of the computation of probabilities in descriptions of reality! Finally, biology, especially that which focuses on the nervous system, must not lag behind physics in furthering this fusion and its discoveries, providing the keys to a unified articulation of matter-life-consciousness.

These themes recur again and again, in different garbs. throughout the 500 pages of the conference proceedings. After physics through the lens of the Vedic tradition of India and the teachings of the Maharishi Mahesh Yogi, it was the turn of the Tao of physics, which explains how a new vision of reality is imposed by the fact that "concepts like matter, object, space, time, cause and effect, etc., are totally different in atomic and subatomic physics from the corresponding classical ideas.... A new world view is now emerging which turns out to be closely related to the views of mystics, especially to those of the mystical traditions of the Far East (Hinduism, Buddhism, Taoism)."[5] The misleading vision of reality from which we emerge is of the world as an inert machine composed of isolated entities, separated from consciousness and the soul by a Cartesian dualism cast in the form of Newtonian mechanics, the model that dominated all scientific thought from the second half of the seventeenth century until the end of the last century. Opposed to this are both the Eastern vision of an "organic," "dynamic," "alive" nature and that suggested by modern physics, a "cosmic web" composed of patterns where "ultimate reality" is no longer that of the "isolated basic building blocks" but a "dynamic web of interrelated events."[6]

Statements by the physicist Werner Heisenberg, juxtaposed with others by a Tibetan Buddhist, Lama Govinda, and others, persuade us that quantum physics speaks an "Oriental" language.

Another interpretation of the role of probabilities, it too invoking the role of the observer in quantum mechanics, makes it possible to cross another barrier on the road toward the unification of cosmos, matter, and consciousness: that which has hitherto prevented us from considering the parapsychological phenomena of psychokinesis and precognition to be scientific![7] With the aid of information theory, we are to understand that *observer* refers not to the operation of observation and measurement[8] but rather to the direct influence of the observer's consciousness (or of the cosmos through the observer?): "The fundamental problem thus raised has not yet been fully penetrated; it certainly goes to the root of the relation between cosmos and consciousness."[9]

The author of this paper, O. Costa de Beauregard, also relies on certain equations in subatomic physics, in which elementary particles can "climb back up" the timeline, and on the quantum-mechanics problem of nonseparability. He concludes:

> The associated past-future and knowledge-organization symmetries mean (as can be shown in terms of formulae) that the observer is also an actor, and therefore that what parapsychologists call "psychokinesis" must logically be accepted. "Precognition" too must be logically accepted if the future exists in actuality, and if convergent waves are not to be discounted.
>
> The indirect transmission of messages to Elsewhere along Feynman lines implies "telepathy" and "telekinesis"—and *this* is what frightened Einstein, twice mentioning "telepathy" in this connection in 1949, Schrödinger, using the word "magic" in 1935, and de Broglie, seeing in 1956 an "incompatibility with our conventional ideas of space and time."
>
> In the Vedas, it is often stated that separability is an illusion, depending on our pragmatic approach; that higher states of consciousness involve a knowledge of the past, the future, and the Elsewhere, and also the possession of paranormal powers.[10]

This same thesis is then developed in greater detail by another physicist,[11] based on an analysis and interpretation of the problem of measurement in quantum mechanics, which goes under the name of the collapse of the wave function.

In general, at this Cordoba colloquium we encounter a series of convergent interpretations all of which lead, *grosso modo*, to the same conclusions: the unity of matter and spirit in a cosmic spiritualism that describes the universe in terms of consciousness, will, and interior life and that coincides on this point with the teachings of the mystical traditions (both major and minor).

## Initial Questions

Having had the opportunity to study and practice one of these traditions from the inside, I cannot avoid asking two types of questions. *How* is this second-order fusion effected—a fusion of scientific and mystical traditions that have long been separated (at least explicitly), of materialism and spiritualism, suddenly converging in a shared recognition of the cosmic fusion of matter and spirit? To what extent is this fusion confusion, both with and without the play on words? Second, *why*? Why is there this convergence, this unanimity in the quest for unity, to the point that the representatives of religious and spiritualist traditions sometimes seem to have been outbid by the physicists, when it is clear that physics by itself, if it raises problems like any developing science, in no way imposes such interpretations?

The shifts of meaning that accompany spiritualist interpretations of information theory, of the Einstein-Podolsky-Rosen inseparability paradox, of Heisenberg's uncertainty principle, of the effects of observation and measurement in quantum mechanics, have been frequently analyzed and condemned.[12] But basing a "model for psychokinesis" on the quantum-mechanics measurement problem known as the collapse of the wave function certainly represents a zenith in this genre, and one that we ought to analyze in detail.

## Cosmic Consciousness and the Collapse of the Wave Function

In the formalism of quantum mechanics, an elementary particle such as an electron and its behavior are described by a mathematical function (the wave function) that can be used to represent the probability of the presence of a given quantity of energy in a region of space. In interference fringe experiments, which can be conducted with these particles, just as with light waves, by making them pass through the experimental equivalent of two adjacent slits, the interference results from the fact that the wave function of each particle is spread out in space over a region that includes both slits. In certain conditions, the probabilities of its passing through one or the other slit are equal. A beam composed of a large number of electrons will be statistically distributed between the slits, reproducing conditions that are in every way similar to those produced by light waves and giving rise to the phenomenon of interference fringes. But the situation changes when each electron is considered individually as a particle localized in space: then it can pass only through one slit or the other, not through both of them at the same time. In fact, the passage of individual electrons can be detected; the measurement apparatus of the detector indicates only a single position (one slit or the other) for each electron. It is as if, prior to detection by the apparatus, each electron occupies a position spread out in space over both slits, just like a light wave, and in keeping with its wave function; but the mere fact of detecting its emergence from one of the slits reduces its wave function to the single region of space that covers only that slit. What is more, the usual idea that the detection and measurement apparatus introduces a perturbation of the electron *is not enough to account for this reduction.* The formula applied (Schrödinger's equation) can describe this perturbation in the form of a modified wave function that takes the quantum state of the measurement device into account. Because of the mathematical properties involved (the linear superposition of two or more different wave functions), the modified wave function still covers both slits. No matter what physical system of observation and measurement is employed, including the human eye and brain, if it obeys the physical laws described by quantum mechanics it will not modify the wave function of the observed electron so that it no longer covers both slits. Observation of the measurement device, however, indicates a single position of the needle on a dial, for example, indicating the electron's passage through only one slit. The usual conclusion is to say that the mere fact of observing the particle entails the collapse of the wave function; that is, its reduction to a single region of space. This reduction cannot be explained by the physical properties of the measurement device, because all agree that these are fully described by Schrödinger's equation.

This difficulty has led a number of leading physicists (including E. Wigner and John von Neumann) to conclude that in this case observation calls into play a system that does not obey the laws of quantum mechanics. Because these laws are supposed to apply to all material reality, they deduce that the effect of observation on the wave function is that of some nonmaterial reality, which can be only the mind of the observer. For a physicist this "explanation" raises at least as many problems as it solves, because in this context the mind of the observer is defined only operationally and negatively: whatever it is, in a human being, that registers the unique position of the needle on the dial of the measuring device does not obey the Schrödinger equation! From there to attributing to this "act of consciousness" the properties that introspection, certain psychological theories, and spiritualist traditions attribute to it is a considerable leap, which those who offer an idealist interpretation of quantum physics do not hesitate to make.

In fact, as we shall see,[13] this interpretation is by no means imposed by quantum mechanics itself. It is rather the result of a certain epistemological approach to physics, which is *often held even by physicists who think they are opposed to it,* including several who were present, in the minority, at the Cordoba conference. This approach involves confounding reality as it is *described* by physical science with what is called "physical reality," in the sense of the reality of matter itself.

As we shall see later, many of these physicists hold this attitude, which actually rests on a simple, if not simplistic, materialist metaphysics; the failure of this metaphysics leads some of them to its equally simplistic idealist antithesis. But to go from there to using this idealism as a "model of psychokinesis," a physical foundation for paranormal powers that modify matter by direct action of mind and will, remains quite a distance, and so lighthearted a crossing of that gulf leaves one flabbergasted. Yet it all seems to be perfectly logical. This is why it is important to try to take apart the mechanisms of these "deductions": because the mind of the observer acts on the wave function and reduces it during the observation, there "must" be continuity between human consciousness and matter, a continuity that can be formalized using information theory, with the shift of meaning we have already spoken of, namely, from the computation of probabilities used in an objective description of the sequence of events to the perception of information by a human mind with its psychological and even spiritual dimensions. The result is a "theorizing" about the possibility that human consciousness and will can deform and modify macroscopic samples of matter by direct action at a distance, thereby giving a "physical explanation" to the phenomena that are regularly reported—and no less regularly disputed—under the rubric of psychokinesis.

## Confusions of Levels and Disciplines

We are dealing here with one of the most common characteristics of these shifts of meaning in the use of scientific language, to which we shall return at greater length: a change in the level of organization (of observation, of relevance, etc.) with a jump over an entire series of intermediate levels. If the solution of the problem of the reduction of the wave function really implied the possibility of action at a distance by human consciousness on matter, it ought to be manifested first of all on the level of the wave functions of elementary particles. In other words, the simplest psychokinetic experiment to conduct, as well as the most persuasive, would be to force all the electrons in a beam to pass through a single slit and thereby suppress the interference phenomenon. Such experiments have never been reported. Those that are spoken of imply an effect at quite a different level of organization of matter, macroscopic samples whose form or structure is supposed to have been modified; and that is quite a different world than that of the wave functions of elementary particles reduced during observation of their passage one by one through a defined region of space.

The nonphysical (idealist but not necessarily spiritualist) interpretation of this reduction by the observer's mind is initially merely a negative interpretation that

1.  Takes note of the fact that the formalism of the Schrödinger equation is insufficient to describe what takes place during observation;

2.  Supposes that this formalism exhaustively describes physical reality; what is more, that its structure is the structure of physical reality and that everything outside it must be nonphysical. Note that this hypothesis is often shared by materialist physicists who, as a result, agree to consider the problem of measurement in quantum mechanics as one posed by physical reality and not only as a shortcoming of the theory.[14]

At first—with von Neumann, for example—all of this was merely the statement of a theoretical difficulty and was expressed only by posing a provocative question (along the lines of "if so, everything happens as if" the mind of the observer reduces the wave function) to underscore the difficulty. But this prepared the ground for the most extreme spiritualist interpretations, in which the mind of the observer that acts on the measurement is no longer a negation or a shortcoming of the formula, but is thoroughly confounded with the subjective experience[15] that we have of our own existence, thought, imagination, and memory—in short, of everything that constitutes our inner life. Nothing, except perhaps the misuse of the word *mind* or *consciousness,* justifies such a leap. Even if one allows the interpretation of the measurement as the reduction of the wave function by the observer's mind, this effect ought to be produced during any observation, by any observer, even a nonphysicist who has not the slightest knowledge of quantum mechanics and wave functions. To put it another way, it should be an effect of observers' minds even unknowingly—without their being conscious of it. It would thus be the unconsciousness of their mind or their unconscious mind at work. This is why, in such a case, paranormal powers would be—paranormal: they would be observed only in particular circumstances. But then who would prevent quantum physicists, who are themselves aware of it, from exercising their mind on the wave function so as to modify at will, by action at a distance on the measurement devices, the results of their experiments? The answer is that for such physicists, as we have seen, and unlike what the spiritualists would make of it, the mind in question has no operational content. No one knows how it works on matter at a distance. It is merely a word invoked when others, such as *God* or *Nature,* are unable to plug up a hole in the theory. In other words, we lack either a theory of consciousness formulated at the same level of organization as that of subatomic phenomena (but then it would no longer involve human consciousness, a mental phenomenon, but would be a theory of observation and measurement in subatomic physics), or a theory of mind at the level of human mental process and language, in interaction with other levels of reality and observation, and *with no discontinuity* down to the level of subatomic physics. But such a theory would be a theory of knowledge, which can be the result only of metascientific philosophical reflection on the conditions in which scientific knowledge is produced.

The preceding also suggests a third way; namely, invoking precepts that can play the role of this theory of consciousness but that are derived from different traditions of knowledge, foreign and even antithetical in their approach to the scientific knowledge that has evolved in the West. Without standing sentry over scientific knowledge, it is important to reflect on the implications of such an exercise and on the conditions in which these perilous transpositions can lead to fruitful intuitions or to delirious platitudes.

The incidents reported above include an element—exemplary and farcical when renowned scientists are involved, as in the second and fourth cases—of confusing levels and of brutal analogical transpositions lacking the perspective of distance. Languages and theories elaborated in a particular discipline and meaningful as explanations of the phenomena described at the level of observation characteristic of that discipline are transposed unchanged to other levels, corresponding to other disciplines, where these languages and theories no longer have the same meaning: the superconductivity of solid-state physics used to "explain" the nature of the modified states of consciousness produced by a technique of meditation; or, moving in the opposite direction, the mind of the observer, perhaps confounded with a cosmic consciousness, used to "explain" the paradoxes of quantum mechanics in subatomic physics. For most scientific researchers the outrageous nature of these transpositions is so evident and their improper character has been so frequently denounced that one is astonished that they crop up with such regularity under the pen and in the mouths of renowned scientists who have demonstrated their talent and originality in undeniably scientific labors. Most often the problem arises only because of the social standing of the researchers: the same theses would have no impact were they put forward by undergraduates or by nonscientists. They would be immediately labeled, in the worst case, as formidable errors to be rejected out of hand without even being examined and, in the best case, as surrealist diversions displaying more or less talent.

Yet the phenomenon, by virtue of its repetition, demands that we take a look. Why are these transpositions, so obviously delirious, continually rehashed by those whom one has the right to expect would be least susceptible to them? And why are they so often found in a mystical context, whether that of ancient traditions or of a mysticism of science lending out its vocabulary while surreptitiously or overtly denaturing it? What is the function of these curious and multiform dialogues between Western science and traditional beliefs whose participants, long before Cordoba, include Newton with alchemy and Oppenheimer with Hinduism—not to mention the long line of scientists-philosophers-mystics, Jews, Christians, and Moslems, from the talmudic sages through Teilhard de Chardin, by way of Maimonides, Avicenna, the kabbalists, and the Sufis? One cannot merely dismiss this phenomenon as a delirium without consequences. Not only are its social consequences far from negligible; the refusal to discuss it in the name of some rational purity that might be compromised cannot be justified even from the point of view of rational critical reflection on the practice of science.

It is consequently out of the question to fall back on the classical scientific position in which pure science, the result of triumphant rationalism, does not tolerate the proximity of any other mode of thought or apprehension of reality; in which *poetic* and *philosophical* (not to mention *mystical,* of course) are pejoratives that designate second-order, metaphorical discourse. This position found its supreme expression in the program of logical positivism, the full-fledged battle plan of an ideology in which the natural sciences, in association with formal logic, are supposed to provide the exclusive model of liberating thought and knowledge, sheltering humanity from the errors of irrationalism and their extensions in modern totalitarian mythologies. The intention was praiseworthy, but in practice it wound up as a sterile ideology that subjected the totality of mankind's lived experiences to a one-dimensional law, that of the formal, the technical (the techno-logical), and the operative, eventually denounced by Marcuse and Habermas, among others. In parallel, the pretension of logical positivism to account for the practice of scientific discovery in its social, psychological, and historical contexts had ever greater difficulty justifying itself in the face of the critiques of Kuhn, Lakatos, Quine, and Feyerabend; while the works of Wittgenstein and Popper appeared like worms in the apple of this scientific ideology, gnawing away at the very core of logical positivism, with which they shared the adventure while rejecting its axioms.[16]

On the other hand, modern epistemology, with its devastating critique of the rules that were supposed to guarantee access to truth and eliminate error, cannot justify this type of confusion, of which we have noted several examples; even if Feyerabend[17] hoped to counterbalance the new scientific dogmatisms by recommending that Darwinian theory and the biblical account of creation be taught in the schools in parallel! For all that the vanity of the quests for any criterion of demarcation between what is and is not scientifically permissible is quite evident in this critique, the result is not that everything is all one and the same. The fact that there is something of the irrational in real science, that it participates against scientists' will in their thought processes, which they would devote entirely to the realization of a program for the rational comprehension of the universe, and that in this regard the handbooks that recount a history of science in which reason always triumphs over darkness and error are telling tales, does not imply that nothing distinguishes the rational from the irrational, light from darkness (even if these distinctions are not identical). Finally, it does not imply that the distinct is not more distinct and thereby different from confusion.

Thus it is not a case of throwing back into the arms of obscurantism every attempt at dialogue between traditional lores and scientific knowledge (which also has a traditional aspect) and even less of banning a priori any attempt at analogical transposition from one scientific discipline to another. But neither is it possible to accept everything and confound everything. Even if we understand that the purity of the crystal of rationality is an optical illusion, that it is totally immersed in the irrational and in error, which even serves it as a point of departure, the converse is not true: not every error or hallucination bears within itself the germ of greater rationality. Hence it is important to try to know when one is still in those seas that are simultaneously fertile and dangerous, where fantasy and rationality can mate, and when one has been carried away by a current that confuses everything. On the other hand, the dialogue between scientific knowledge and traditional knowledge can take—and has done so effectively—quite different forms, as a function of the goal pursued and the social and ideological context in which it is conducted. Here too it is important to be able to distinguish a questioning and curious encounter from a welter of mutually reinforcing dogmas about "ultimate reality."

Our purpose here is not to seek new rules of demarcation but to understand what takes place—among both the general public and scientists—when these differences are abolished. More precisely, we want to analyze the mischief provoked by the sort of confusion we have seen several examples of, again, not in order to pontificate new rules aimed at eliminating this mischief but in order to try to pave a road that is no less necessary for all that it is naturally tortuous and muddy. There is a narrow path between outright rejection of everything that is not the light of reason, as the West has represented itself for the past few centuries, and acceptance on principle of all confusions, on the pretext that "anything goes."[18] There is a narrow path between—again—the crystal of ready-made academic knowledge, already established and petrified in "light having finally triumphed over the darkness of the past," and the smoke of free associations where the inadequacies of those petrifications are used to justify obscurantist regressions. But this path also connects the crystal, whose rigorous and luminous structure is a bedrock and guarantee of existence, and smoke, whose unpredictable swirls alone can lead to the still unknown.[19]

To reach that point, we must recognize that knowledge activities are games, in which the serious is not serious and only humor can be warranted as serious. Then the rule of rules, when we are dealing with the game of games and not with the search for some phantom "ultimate reality," consists of letting them play, letting them meet through differences and contrasts rather than through similarities.

## Notes

1. Letter from President Valéry Giscard d'Estaing to F. Gros, F. Jacob, and P. Royer, published with the report, *Sciences de la vie et Société* (Paris: Le Seuil, 1979).

2. Ibid., p. 280.

3. *Science and Consciousness: Two Views of the Universe, Edited Proceedings of the France-Culture and Radio-France Colloquium, Cordoba, Spain,* ed. Michel Cazenave, trans. A. Hall and E. Callander (Oxford: Pergamon Press, 1984). Unlike the previous cases, this is a case of indirect experience from press reports and published proceedings.

4. Brian D. Josephson, "Conscious Experience and Its Place in Physics," in ibid., p. 9.

5. Fritjof Capra, "The Tao of Physics," in ibid., p. 21.

6. Ibid., pp. 22–28.

7. Olivier Costa de Beauregard, "Cosmos and Consciousness" in ibid., p. 43.

8. Addressing this question of the relations between entropy and information in a 1972 work on information theory (Henri Atlan, *L'Organisation biologique et la théorie de l'information* [Paris: Hermann, 1972]), I indicated the reservations elicited by this abusive psychologizing and subjectivist interpretation of the probabilistic theory of information, even when it was expressed in a more moderate fashion and in the context of otherwise extremely interesting work. Nothing allows us to speak of information in the common meaning of the term, and even less of mental process or consciousness, when we are dealing with probabilistic measurements of information, where what is measured is only the a priori uncertainty regarding the interaction between a mensurable event and a measuring device, leaving aside any meaning and any other effect that this event might have on human mental processes. Here the thesis is even more radical.

9. Costa de Beauregard, "Cosmos and Consciousness," p. 35.

10. Ibid., pp. 43f.

11. Richard Mattuck, "A Quantum Mechanical Theory of the Interaction between Consciousness and Matter," in ibid., pp. 49–65.

12. See, for example, J.-M. Lévy-Leblond on the "uncertainty relations" he suggests calling "inequalities": *Bulletin of the Society of Physics* (Paris), supplement to no. 14 (April–May 1973), p. 15. See also J.-M. Lévy-Leblond and F. Balibar, *Quantique (rudiments)*, (Paris: Interéditions, 1984), Chapter 3; on the EPR paradox, M. Mugur Shächter, "Réflexion sur le problème de la localité," in *Actes du colloque du centenaire d'Einstein* (Paris: Centre national de la recherche scientifique, 1980), pp. 249–264; on information theory, Atlan, *L'Organisation biologique*, pp. 197–200.

13. See Chapter 6.

14. See Chapter 6 for a discussion of the attitude taken by F. Selleri, who in Cordoba represented the materialist physicist opposition.

15. Not only with subjective experience, moreover, but also as the object of diverse disciplines such as the branches of psychology (experimental, behavioral, analytic), linguistics, psycholinguistics, and psychosociology. This is why, quite naturally, those carrying on the dialogue with the spiritualist physicists at Cordoba included not only adherents of mystical traditions but also practitioners and theoreticians of psychology, here almost exclusively Jungian psychoanalysts. This role that psychoanalysis *can* play (but which it is not condemned to play, Jungian perhaps more so than Freudian, although the latter is not immune) as the cement in these fusions is clearly linked to the special position of this discipline, as thoroughly analyzed by Jacques Lacan, who located it between and alongside science, magic, and religion (J. Lacan, *Ecrits* [Paris: Le Seuil, 1966], Chapter 7). We shall return to this point in Chapter 5.

16. D. Lecourt, *L'Ordre et les jeux. Le positivisme logique en question* (Paris: Grasset, 1981).

17. Paul Feyerabend, *Against Method* (London: NLB, 1975).

18. Ibid.

19. See Henri Atlan, *Entre le cristal et la fumée* [Between crystal and smoke] (Paris: Le Seuil, 1979).

*Chapter 2*

# Scientific Knowledge and Levels of Organization

### *Biological Organization*

The observation of different levels of organization in nature has revealed new limits to scientific knowledge. In addition to those traditionally accepted in physics—the infinitely small and the infinitely large—we are now cognizant that at the seams between levels there are limits imposed by the partition into different levels by disciplines based on different techniques. Recently the existence of these levels has begun to be recognized as well as questioned, as the new biology provides the materials and tools for the physical chemistry of natural organizations. Formerly, physics imposed its paradigm on the natural sciences essentially in the form of an atomic theory and subsequently of a theory of elementary particles, in which the subdivision of matter into ever-tinier particles, down to "indivisible" elements, would ipso facto lead to knowledge of ultimate reality. In a materialist conception of the universe, reacting against theology, the ultimate reality that constitutes matter is confounded with the ultimate reality of the universe, a new avatar of the one God and capable in every respect of relacing the Spirit-God of theology. This materialist conception could develop fully only in the cultural context and age (from the eighteenth through the first half of the twentieth century in the West) when idealism and the phenomenology of mind were refined and promulgated as the uncrossable horizon of philosophy, culture, and civilization. In fact the very same,

35

though ostensibly rival, pretension characterized all the materialist philosophies of science, from Voltaire and the Encyclopédistes through Laplace, the Comtean positivists of the nineteenth century, and the logical positivists of the early twentieth century.

In this context, the organization of life was a poor relation twice over, as well as an object of rivalry: whether as a particular instance of Spirit at work in nature, so that its organized and teleological character was proof of its divine origin—or, at least, its spiritual origin, by analogy to the organizing faculties of the human spirit; or as a particular instance of the application of the laws of physics, so that the physicochemical nature of living matter was proof that the ultimate reality of living beings (molecules, atoms) is no different from that which the materialist view assigns to the entire universe.

At first sight, it seems that the new biology (since 1950) awarded the palms to the latter conception, after the long and futile defense waged by its rival, vitalism, which was nourished exclusively by the inadequacies of biology before the advent of molecular genetics. Molecular biology and neurochemistry have come to serve quite often as the foundation for materialist reductionism, or, more precisely, for the links that complete the chain, enabling the reduction of the life sciences one to another and ultimately to physics, and thereby the establishment of a single unity based on a full-fledged materialism: from psychology to neurophysiology, from neurophysiology to biochemistry, and from biochemistry to quantum mechanics. In fact these reductions pose many problems and constitute working hypotheses for research much more than complete and coherent theories. Such theories should permit an inverse causal chain from physics to psychology, so that the composition of a symphony or discovery of a scientific law could be described adequately in the language of neurophysiology, which could then be *fully* translated into the language of biochemistry, and finally, once again completely, into quantum equations.

The fact that this is not so, but that, nevertheless, there can be no science without such a postulate and that belief in this postulate carries with it a danger of dogmatism and illusion at least as large as that linked to theology and spiritualism—this is what I wish to discuss here.

Although it is true that the practical and theoretical successes of molecular biology have managed to sweep away spiritualism and vitalism to the point that they no longer have a place in the life sciences, this does not mean that the classical reductionist-materialist conception has triumphed. Molecular biology has imposed a new paradigm, different from that of physics, in which organization on different levels of integration has become the keystone of the new scientific knowledge and the point of departure for new questions.

It is certainly at the transition from inanimate to animate that its effect has been most evident and immediate. But molecular biology has also produced some non-negligible fallout with regard to the transition from life to the mind, a transition that is noted as always there, in the background, whenever one would make science go awry, at the junction of all the shifts of meaning, due to abusive extrapolations or incongruous confinement in petrified analogies. In effect, molecular biology, along with computer science (from which it has borrowed some of its vocabulary and key concepts[1]), has reinforced the tendency to displace the classic mind-body problem and base it on new, functionalist foundations. The latter are certainly not a reiteration of a strongly reductionist materialist credo or its negation in spiritualism, but rather a species of materialism refined by structuralism, or even a structuralism impregnated with materialism.

Its first traces can be found among the philosophers of language known as the logical positivists, who wanted to eliminate all metaphysics from their field of study and recognize only the analysis of the truth conditions of propositions. For Ayer,[2] for example, the mind-body problem was not a problem of the relations between two entities that coexist in each of us, which might or might not be reducible to one another, because the existence of the body and of the mind is not posed in terms of primary overarching entities. *Mind* and *body* (the same could be said of *matter* and *consciousness*) are only words that designate logical constructs we use to establish a relationship among various experiences. The problem in its classic form is created by improper use of language, a metaphysical usage that attributes existence and a hidden, indeed transcendent, reality—substance—to what is only the result of partial and unverified logical constructs based on improperly extrapolated experiences. The problem should arise only within scientific discourse, as a problem of relations between two disciplines: biology, which organizes observations and experiments on living systems, and psychology, which organizes observations and experiments on the production of desires, ideas, beliefs, feelings, relational behavior, and so forth. Among these behaviors, the objects of psychology, one also encounters, recursively, the production of speech, including scientific discourse, of which biology and psychology are particular cases.

More recently, however, the new biology has discovered and posited the organization of matter as its true object,[3] in two ways. First, it has had to borrow from the information sciences and study of artificial organizations (programmable machines, automata) the fundamental concepts that permitted its theoretical advances. Second, it has had to consider the existence within a *single* living organism of several levels of organization or integration, as they have been called. This has forced it to reconsider the interrelations of the various scientific disciplines as well as their relations with the reality that they endeavor to describe and explain. The same object—an organism—is now simultaneously a physical (atomic), chemical (molecular), biological (macromolecular, cellular), physiological, psychological, linguistic, and social object. The science of this object, to the extent that it is all of these at once, is that of its organization into levels of integration, carved up by the various disciplines. Thus the question of the transition from or reduction of one to another has become central and drives research forward.

The classification of the sciences is no longer based exclusively on philosophical concerns: it is imposed by the very objects studied, whose levels of organization are separated and studied, each by a particular discipline. This means that studying the object as a whole requires studying the seams between the levels, which itself reduces to the possible dialogues between or reductions of one discipline to another.[4]

Suddenly the question of reductionism is no longer posed as a corollary of a materialist metaphysics, but once again, and perhaps with greater precision—as for the logical positivists—with regard to scientific discourse and the possibility of unifying the languages of the different disciplines. This time the desire or need for unification does not have only metaphysical motives (at least on the surface), because it seems to be imposed by the very object of study, the living organism around which these disciplines meet. To deny this unity seems to be to negate the unity of the organism itself, when the simple observation that makes it possible to identify its existence and operation provides prima facie evidence thereof. But here the metaphysical demon slips in again and makes us shift from the supposed unity of the object to the coerced unity of the disciplines that deal with it. It is evidently here that the two rival metaphysics, materialist and idealist, make their reappearance. Instead of seeing the unity of the organism in its organization itself, despite all the practical and methodological difficulties this involves, it is easier to *want* to reduce this unity (even if it is impossible to satisfy the want) to that of Matter, or, symmetrically, to the unity of Spirit.


## From the Experience of Separation
## to the Joy of the Encounter

Recognizing that the organization of reality on different levels is the true object of the science of the natural organizations known as living beings leads to an uncomfortable situation if one is still nostalgic for ultimate reality. This (monotheistic?) nostalgia for unity of being, as it unfolds within science, produces two symmetrical temptations: the temptation of "strong" reductionism, which expresses materialist metaphysics (as opposed to "weak" reductionism, which is limited to a praxis without which the scientific process cannot exist); and the temptation of a spiritualism of the cosmic consciousness or of the qualitative mathematics of some neoalchemy. This multilevel organization is at least as much that of the organizing discourse by means of which we dissect, unify, label, classify, explain, predict, and master reality, as it is of reality itself. The levels of organization are levels of knowledge as well as levels of reality, because they correspond to our different ways of organizing reality (that is, to adorn it with and at the same time discover in it some order), thanks to the various scientific disciplines. We can subscribe to Heisenberg's dictum that there is no science of nature, but only a science of the knowledge that human beings have of nature. Certainly we must be careful to guard against understanding him in an idealistic sense, for this science is itself the product of nature, because it is the product of human beings who are themselves the product of nature.

This loop is none other than that of the recursion of language, which organizes reality (and thereby gives it sense and meaning) while being at the same time a product of that organization. But recognizing the existence of this loop by no means eliminates the duality of our experiences, those of our senses and those of our imagination, those of some "objective" external reality and those of our inner life[5]—in short, the concrete and the abstract—even if the line of demarcation between the two is a function of each person's experiences and education. Of the two, the experience of logical discourse is a source of discomfort or wonder, because it is difficult to classify: are we dealing with logic and rationality that belong to reality, or with some matrix created by our thought and projected onto reality? This question has never stopped haunting scientists and logicians, from Galileo's idea of the universe as a book whose language is mathematics, or Poincaré's idea that mathematics is the language human beings use when they study nature, through Einstein's opinion that nothing is more incomprehensible than the fact that the world is comprehensible[6] and Wittgenstein's statement that "belief in the causal nexus is *superstition*."[7] It is posed and posed again only on the basis of our double, divided experience of the concrete and of the abstract.

Today, when the God of Kepler, Tycho Brahe, and Newton is no longer guarantor of the unity of the world and of reason, scientific praxis supposes and at the same time creates this unity in an empirical, logical process in which "facts" are supposed to be observed in reproducible conditions that ground their objectivity and thus their concrete "external" reality; at the same time, logic binds these facts to one another, grounds the coherence of their fabric and thereby the degree of "interior"—or at least intersubjective—reality of the theoretical and practical knowledge that results from them. In this process, the rules that underlie the two types of results (experimental protocols and rules of logic) rely on each other to guarantee themselves against the dangers (of error, of misapprehension, of illusion, of delirium?) that would accompany experience of each of these realities in isolation. A certain guarantee of "truth" is provided by the facts, an external guarantee against the perils of the imagination, while the scope and coherence of logic is the interior guarantee of the possible generality and thus very existence of knowledge.

Of course the process of so-called objective knowledge, a rather paradoxical expression if you think about it, consequently eliminates the nonreproducible and the illogical, that is, a significant portion of the experiences of our individual subjectivity (and of intersubjectivity as well, to the extent that subjective experiences can be shared although they are nonreproducible and perfectly irrational). But even when the field has been limited in this way, it still causes problems by both its successes and its failures; by its successes, indeed, perhaps more than by its failures. Whatever theoretical response may have been imagined to justify this unity of the concrete and of the abstract—especially the loop created by the recursivity of language, organizer of the organization that produces it—it does not eliminate the immediacy of our experience of two different realities. The attempts by theoreticians to formalize these double rules and derive (objectively?) from them some criteria of demarcation that would make it possible to decide whether a proposition is or is not scientific have always failed. Extrapolated from particular examples, they have always been belied by observation of the history and practice of scientific discovery, which is richer than theory and supplies many counterexamples. What is more, at the end of this critique of the search for the criterion of scientificity (which always carries a connotation of a criterion of truth) we find ourselves back at Feyerabend's "anything goes"[8] or Quine's multiplicity of possible theories,[9] and are thus led to a radical relativism that, as we shall see later, does not necessarily lead to nihilist skepticism.

If the objective (and practice) of these sciences is to discover laws, the latter are not, despite their common designation, laws of nature. What we so designate are rather the rules—provisional and if necessary modifiable—of the game played by the community of scientists in their quest to know the laws of nature. This is why, of course, the successes of this process are so astonishing, whenever a theoretical prediction is really verified. That a machine runs, that bridges do not collapse, that the missile hits its target—these are even more astonishing when one knows how they work than when one does not: the feeling of wondering terror produced by ignorance is then replaced by astonishment that the abstractions of a large number of physical and mathematical theories, which make possible even more abstract computations, have nevertheless succeeded in producing something concrete that works. Nothing can eliminate the immediate and habitual character of our experience of the two different realities, the concrete and the abstract; but the observation that "it works" forces us to recognize that, at that time and place, they met. It is the habitual and irreducible nature of this experience of duality that explains the (almost sexual) joy of researchers when, during the experimental verification of a theoretical prediction, they have, exceptionally, the opposite experience.

It is true that physicochemical biology provides special occasions for this joy. On the one hand, predictions can be made through a large number of theoretical steps and way stations; on the other hand, experimental confirmations are expected of "objective" systems in which the natural part (living beings whose complex organization is not our doing) is larger than in the laboratory artifacts represented by ideal physical experiments. In the practice of the physical sciences the astonishment has been attenuated (relatively speaking) because, for them, the objective reality of facts becomes more remote from the hard facts of observation of nature and approximates a reality that, although certainly concrete, is artificially assembled in experimental devices that are imbued with the theory that directed and oriented their organization. The case is very different when predictions based on theories of the physical chemistry of solutions, for example, are to be verified in living cells. The experience of growing cells in laboratory culture, using everything known of their biology, while overcoming the technical obstacles (cell death, contamination, the great variability despite the standardization of procedures, etc.) that always exist, as if to remind us of the resistance of matter and of these organisms' independence of our desire for reproducibility, uniformity, and rationalization; and then, on those same cells, of making measurements (of membrane potential or ionic concentrations, for example) that will provide sufficiently precise and reproducible verification of computations based on equations (theory of chemical potential, the Nernst-Goldman equations, the Onsager relation) that are derived from the abstractions of chemical and statistical thermodynamics (both of them combining algebra, probability theory, and the idealized empiricism of gas theory) as applied to theories of electrolyte solutions, osmosis, and membrane permeability:[10] this experience generates a sense of preestablished harmony or mastery of events (depending on one's disposition and temperament!) that all the theoretical rationalizations of the philosophy of science have proven unable to diminish. This is fortunate, for only this experience of the amalgamation in a coherent unity produced "objectively" (that is, by stubborn nature that is independent of our desires for rationalization) of diverse elements derived from remote domains of theory engaged with such different empirical realities—only this experience is potent enough to carry the day, while maintaining the surprising and nontrivial character that makes it interesting.

In addition, it is this sense of harmony and unity that convinces not only someone who has ventured a prediction and observed its verification, but also anyone who is capable of following the details of the experimental protocols, theories, and hypotheses that led to the predictions. It is certainly the joy of this unification, which every researcher expects and provokes, that underlies the profound sense of the unity of science that is so quickly confused with the unity of the world. What more elegant proof could there be of this unity than the history of discoveries made by physicists during the 1950s, which spawned the great leap forward in molecular biology? Quantitative theoretical interpretation of x-ray diffraction experiments on crystalline DNA led to the double helix model (a theoretical construct that no one has ever "seen," of course, at least for the moment). Then this model, coupled with the biological role that DNA was perceived to play in the hereditary transformation of viruses and bacteria, led, as a test of the hypothesis "gene = DNA," to the prediction of the semiconservative nature of the replication of DNA during cell division. Finally, techniques of isotope tagging of cells led to measurements verifying this prediction. And, after the lapse of twenty years, all of this eventually culminated in the spectacular mastery represented by genetic recombination and cloning. This sequence must inspire one with awe at such unity in diversity, as well as with skepticism concerning any vision of the world that does not postulate the existence of this unity on the basis of the theories of physics, the "fundamental" discipline.

Other examples of this scientific joy, which produce even more spectacular beliefs and professions of unifying faith, are provided by the successes of the reductionist method as applied to the study of the brain. The systematic study of the nervous system of mollusks provides a view of the cellular and molecular mechanisms of the phenomena of learning with behavioral modification and long- and short-term memory.[11] The modification of a defensive reflex, acquired ("learned") under the effect of specific stimuli, is first of all related to the facilitative action of a particular neuron on a synapse of the reflex arc. This is in turn explained by a series of enzymatic activations leading to the phosphorylation of the membrane potassium channels, closing these channels and thereby reducing the flux of potassium ions in the presynaptic terminal. This prolongs the electric depolarization that accompanies the excitation of the afferent path of the reflex arc and thereby increases the flux of calcium ions penetrating this terminal. The result is an increase in the number of transmitter molecules released in the synapse and thus a more intense stimulation of the post-synaptic neuron in the reflex arc—whence the facilitative action in question. Finally, the same modification, depending on whether it is retained by short-term or long-term memory, does or does not entail the synthesis of new molecules of enzymatic proteins. All of this—this series of observations along with the experimental protocols that permitted it—establishes a fabric of extraordinary bridges between observation of macroscopic behavior and a sequence of precisely determined cellular and molecular events that obey the normal laws of enzyme biochemistry and molecular biology. This is an even more spectacular example of the success of the reductionist method than the previous ones, because of its possible implications for the mind-body problem. Of course, the complexity of the mammalian brain and, a fortiori, of the human brain, is incommensurable with that of the nervous system of an aplysia, whose several hundred neurons and their interconnections can be identified and studied almost one by one. But if one takes these experiments together with computer simulations of automata networks representing simplified neurons, the results make it possible to unify in a single theoretical framework—sometimes called "neoconnectionist"[12]—structural and functional observations on quite distinct levels of organization. The joy of reunion after separation is even greater when these results are confirmed on actual neuronal networks grown in culture!

## The Temptations of Reductionism

This experience of the unity of science, grounded in physics, is often used to justify a reductionist attitude whereby everything in nature must be explainable on the basis of causal sequences of physical phenomena. Taken to the extreme, this attitude leads to a materialist monism that excludes not only spirit, but also thought, as an autonomous phenomenon, and will, desire, and any intentionality in the expression of an autonomous self. It also leaves no room for affectivity, to say nothing of the world of art and esthetics that a sophisticated science should be able to explain by "reducing" it to physical phenomena, to molecular interactions in the brain, for example. But if reductionism is clearly a metascientific philosophy when expressed in this way, it also covers a practice that cannot be dissociated from scientific research as this has evolved until our own time. It is important to distinguish this reductionist practice from philosophies of the same name, which have recently been severely buffeted both by physics itself and by the science of organized artifacts.

The reductionist practice consists of separating a whole into its parts in the hope that the properties of the parts will explain those of the whole.

To the extent that analysis, which breaks down an aggregate into its constituent parts, is an indispensable element of all scientific research, all scientific activity entails the reductionist praxis. Only a reductionist postulate enables science, as practiced today, to exist. The opposing postulate of the irreducibility of the living to the inorganic, or of the mental to the living and the physicochemical, no longer serves as more than a brake on this method of knowledge (even if this was not the case until the nineteenth century, when, for example, Pasteur's discoveries about the absence of spontaneous generation were viewed, on the contrary, in a vitalist context, where it was important to establish that "life comes only from life"). But this postulate of unity can be applied either as the a priori ground, the content of which cannot and need not be made explicit, or as the knowledge that, on the contrary, is a conclusion to be derived—by extrapolation, which is why it remains a postulate—from science. In both cases we are dealing with a metascientific postulate; the difference is whether it is posited "prior to" science, as the precondition of its practice, or "after" science, in which case it serves as the point of departure for metaphysics.

The distinction between the two sorts of unity thus postulated, and the corresponding types of reductionism—"weak" and "strong," respectively—is important. The former is indispensable for and presupposed by scientific practice. The latter is the result of the belief in this axiom, in the form of a naive materialist metaphysics that can be just as mystifying as the theological or cosmic-spiritual beliefs it rejects.

Studying the "hierarchical" structure of living organisms, that is, their organization into different levels, the biochemist A. Peacocke[13] correctly distinguishes two hierarchies: a hierarchy of systems and processes from one of theories and concepts. It is only of the latter that one can speak with full knowledge of the case. It entails a nonreducibility of one level to another, in that the concepts of one level cannot be linked to and superimposed on those of another; nor can the laws of a higher, more comprehensive level be *derived* from those of a lower level.[14] Supplementary constraints that cannot be derived from these laws—for example, initial conditions and limit conditions or a process of irreversible evolution in which random factors have intervened—are also determining elements. But this does not prevent the processes from being the same at all levels; that is, biological processes are merely physicochemical processes. This allows a reductionist methodology that presupposes a unity of processes—examples are physicochemical biology and subsequently molecular biology—to be effective. In this way such a methodology can coexist with an epistemological antireductionism that recognizes that theories are not reducible to one another. This is already the case with chemical theories (of chemical affinities and reaction rates[15]) as they relate to physical theories. Similarly, biological theory is autonomous vis-à-vis physics and chemistry, in the sense that some biological concepts cannot be conceived of or translated into the terms of physics and chemistry (such as sexuality, function, adaptation, species, evolution), even if, once again, biological *processes* are envisioned as being physicochemical ones. For "questions of reduction, and so of emergence, are epistemological and linguistic, they are about logical relations holding between theories, descriptions, conceptual schemes, and so on, as applied to natural hierarchies."[16] The methodological concern for unity is not opposed to this epistemological antireductionism; moreover, the former may and even must hold sway—precisely as a methodology or as the rule of the game—even if the arguments supposed to *prove the existence* of this unity, starting from scientific theory, remain in dispute. Hence there is a distinction between the concern for methodology that is necessary for the pursuit of scientific activity and the concern for metaphysics that leads to a belief possessed of the same status as all idealisms, for, as Heidegger put it, "materialism has absolutely nothing to do with material. It is itself a form of spirit."[17]

This distinction in fact comes back to the positivist attitude, noted earlier, to the mind-body problem that always haunts these questions. So long as it is not being walled up by ideology in its own turn, this attitude is certainly the healthiest and most fruitful, because it allows the problem to be shifted from its normal metaphysical context, where it is insoluble, to the context of the relations between biology and psychology. These interdisciplinary relations raise different problems due to different techniques of observation and experimentation and different languages, each suited to its own goals and not overlapping. The difficulty is that in the real world we know, from other sources, that these objects of different disciplines coexist within a single organism and probably even coincide there: it is the same organism, with biology describing the anatomical, biochemical, and electrical properties of the brain, whereas psychology, or simply any individual person's speech, describes the properties of a mind, of a human being endowed with intentions, consciousness, and an unconscious, with desires and responsibilities. These two types of discourse, physicochemical and biological on the one hand, intentional and individualized on the other, do not overlap; in fact, they are often juxtaposed by the rules of their own games. Nevertheless, they deal with a reality, the human organism, which we want to believe is one, in a certain fashion, and about which we know, moreover, that the operation of the brain is a necessary if not sufficient condition of its mental activity. It is this, clearly the core of the difficulty, that creates the whole problem.

## The Mind-Body Problem

Under the influence of the so-called cognitive sciences, a new discipline that groups psychologists, linguists and psycholinguists, logicians and philosophers of language, neurobiologists, and computer scientists with a special interest in artificial intelligence, we can attempt to apply to the mind-body problem what has been learned about the logical structure of other organized systems, natural and artificial, in which there are also different levels of integration characterized by different properties and specific techniques and languages to deal with them. Resting the problem on a *functional* rather than a metaphysical basis,[18] the question becomes, initially, what causal relationship exists between the operation of a computer that performs a complicated task under the control of a program written in a high-level language, and the physical state of its millions of electronic components.

A direct answer to this question, transposed to the brain and its millions of neurons as the physical substrate of mental activities, requires us to distinguish between strong and weak reductionism. The former is untenable, because it is contradicted as soon as one passes a certain threshold of complexity, even staying within the context of the operation of artificial physicochemical systems. The second is correct, but, in the case of a machine, trivial, for it hardly goes beyond noticing that the machine's operation is limited by the constraints imposed by its components.[19] Strong reductionism holds that the analysis that breaks down the whole into its parts is *sufficient* for comprehending the properties of the whole, in a mental reconstitution wherein the latter are entailed, more or less automatically, by the properties of the parts.

But the reductionist postulate can be verified only in simple organizations, where the parts are associated among themselves in an additive and linear fashion, such that common sense can immediately grasp a property of the whole as the sum of the properties of the parts. Today, however, we are familiar with many organized material systems where this is not the case, so that reductionist philosophies are no longer acceptable—although this does not mean that we must regress to invoking spirits or mysterious vital principles. In particular, the strong reductionist postulate cannot be verified in the case of the operation of automata networks (of which computers are a particular case). To put this another way, it is just as difficult to predict the behavior of the whole of such networks from the properties of the parts as in the case of a cell reduced to its molecules or a brain reduced to its neurons.

True, in systems of moderate complexity these difficulties may some-times be surmounted; then, however, strong reductionism is even less capable, for these situations provide an occasion to catch on the fly, as it were, phenomena of emergence from one level to another, even though there is no mystery at the component level. In effect, the solutions found then do indeed permit us to deduce the properties of the whole from those of the parts, but *in a nontrivial fashion*, using nonlinear mathematical mod-els in which the operation of the whole is not merely the sum of the opera-tions of the parts. As a result, it is the model of organization that is impor-tant for the properties of the whole, whereas the properties of the parts usually play the role of constraints on the organization's performance rather than producing it directly. Even in the case of deterministic machines (or deterministic models of natural systems), once their opera-tion can be described only through complicated systems of equations, it is not enough to know the properties of the parts to understand those of the whole: knowledge and comprehension of the logic of the system of equa-tions is indispensable, for that logic produces certain counterintuitive effects opposed to what the common sense of simple linear addition would suggest.[20] This phenomenon, which can already be observed at the level of a single membrane (whether natural or artificial) that is supposed to be crossed by water and many solutes, to which the membrane is unequally permeable,[21] leads the author of a transport model used to predict the pas-sage of the different substances to conclude that reductionism has its lim-its, even though his is only an extremely simplified model of a cell mem-brane, which is itself an isolated element in the organization of a single cell. Knowledge of the transport fluxes of each molecular species in isolation *in no way* makes it possible to predict that of all species together, without a system of equations that describes their coupled behavior. Now this system of equations includes solutions that are *astonishing*, that is to say, *unpre-dictable* (because counterintuitive) *before the computation is performed*. The computation itself frequently can be performed only by a computer, and iteratively, so that the solution produced by the computer is scarcely differ-ent from experimental results. The results of a computer simulation of an experiment and of a real experiment are equally unforeseeable, although the former are in principle contained a priori in the equations that compose the model.[22]

We see, then, how reductionist philosophies are overwhelmed, not by the existence of mysteries and unresolved difficulties, but on the contrary by the success of mathematical tools, their scope extended by computers, when applied to the analysis and synthesis of complex artificial organiza-tions. It is how the difficulties of the synthesis are resolved that reveals the insufficiency of the reductionist postulate (and thus its falseness, because it is supposed to be sufficient). This becomes clear when determinist models prove effective. It is even more evident, of course, when the only effective model contains probabilistic elements and predicting the behavior of the whole, even through the complication of the model, itself involves a measure of indeterminacy.

This obtains all the more in our present case, where we are dealing with complex natural organizations such as developing cellular systems or the brain, of which we do not even have a complete model. Affirming that the behavior of the brain in its mental activities is the consequence of the activity state of its neurons, and that every thought or sensation can be described in the form of one of these states, is an obvious assertion but *quite empty as long as we do not know this description.* Equally evident and equally empty is the analogous assertion that the performance of a computer running a complicated task is the consequence of the activity state of all of its electronic components. In the latter case, too, it is practically impossible to describe the computer's physical state and the logical relationship between this state and the function performed, because of the series of different levels of organization, from machine language up to application software.

If we are ever able to describe the state of neuronal activity corresponding to every thought or sensation (the ideal of a research program based on the hypothesis of the existence of mental images), the philosophical consequences will certainly be quite different from those drawn today, relying on reductionist philosophies, as if we already possessed this knowledge. The *manner* in which the neuronal state "determines" the integrated operation of the brain is probably neither more simple nor more trivial than that by which the electronic state of a computer determines its logical operation. This already excludes a strong reductionist paradigm, even though the structure of the computer is known in full.

As we have seen, such a paradigm would imply the possibility of translating into the language of physics all the phenomena described and explained in the languages of other disciplines. By contrast, weak reductionism—like Fodor's "token physicalism"[23]—derives its conclusions from the fact that, to accomplish the same function at a global level of organization, a machine or a program can employ quite different physical substrates obeying different physical laws (valves, springs and clockwork, dials, semiconductors, enzymes, nerve cells). Conversely, the same electronic machine (a programmable computer), obeying the same physical laws at the level of its components, can be programmed to perform extremely diverse tasks described in terms of logical instructions that have only the remotest link with the physical state of its components. Here too the reason is that several levels of organization exist, ranging from that of the components and their interconnections to that of the high-level programming language, going by way of the binary machine language and assembly language. What is relevant at each level is the organization of that level as described in its own language. This is why, *even when there are translation languages* (e.g., compilers) that make it possible to go from one level to another, down to that of machine language, each level is *to a certain extent irreducible* (de facto if not de jure) to the previous levels.[24] The translation of a program into machine language is merely a series of zeroes and ones, where no one can discover any meaning whatsoever, and certainly not that of the task that the program is performing and of the logic of its organization adapted to this task. This irreducibility derives not only from the fact that the translation is performed level by level, *without any jumps*, but also from the fact that the translation is itself local, in that its only effect is to group and integrate the elements of one level in more general units on the higher level. The type of logical connections that can then be established *among* these more general units is not contained in the translation language. It is rather the property of the programming at that level, which has its own meaning. And this meaning, for all that it needs the lower levels and the translation languages, is not reducible to them, in the sense that it cannot be deduced from them.

This situation—once again new, in that it results from the organization in different levels of integration—is easily transposed to analysis of human (or animal) cognitive faculties as they relate to the hardware of neurophysiological organization. D. C. Dennett puts it this way:

> Since we are viewing AI [artificial intelligence] as a species of top-down cognitive psychology, it is tempting to suppose that the decomposition of function in a computer is intended by AI to be somehow isomorphic to the decomposition of function in a brain. One learns of vast programs made up of literally billions of basic computer events and somehow so organized as to produce a simulacrum of human intelligence, and it is altogether natural to suppose that since the brain is known to be composed of billions of tiny functioning parts, and since there is a *gap of ignorance* between our understanding of intelligent human behavior and our understanding of those tiny parts, the ultimate, millennial goal of AI must be to provide a hierarchical breakdown of parts in the computer that will mirror or be isomorphic to some hard-to-discover hierarchical breakdown of brain-event parts.[25]

However, unlike the unitary ideal of Oppenheim and Putnam,[26] the relationship to physics as the fundamental discipline cannot be that of strong reductionism; describing elementary events in the language of physics is insufficient for predicting observations and laws at levels of integration described by other disciplines, while at the same time preserving the types of problems that they tackle and maintaining the specificity warranted by their level of observation and description.[27] The only possible physicalism, which is really rather trivial though not devoid of meaning, observes that the organization at a higher level cannot be just anything, taking into account the constraints[28] imposed by the physical laws that reign locally, in "token" fashion, in the matter of which the machine is made. To put it another way, if these bits of matter, governed by the laws of physics, are indispensable to the integral functioning of the machine—and therefore impose constraints on its organization—they are not sufficient for this operation. What is more, the same operation can be performed by another machine in which there are different bits of matter and physical laws that apply locally (a rattrap or a corkscrew can be put together from different physical components, obeying the laws of mechanics in quite different manners or obeying entirely different physical laws).

## Reductionism, Self-Organization, and Levels of Observation

As we have seen, then, the very successes of robotics and artificial intelligence render reductionist theses quite untenable. Even in a machine there can be de facto emergence and nonreduction, despite the possibility of passing from one level to another, of translating from the language of one to that of the other. This also demonstrates that nonreductionism does not necessarily revert to spiritualism, for the properties of the integrated level emerge as a result of the machine's organization on different levels of integration and not because of a soul or spirit inserted into the machine.

It might be objected that we are dealing here with a man-made organization that is merely an extension of the mind of its builders. By way of reply, we should analyze the properties of self-organizing systems; that is, natural physicochemical organizations (or their computer simulations) where the emergence of new properties at an integrated level is not the result of any action planned by builders and programmers.

The idea of self-organization,[29] which developed during the 1960s on the substratum of information theory, thermodynamics, and chemical kinetics, is currently enjoying a new vogue, thanks to theories of automata and artificial intelligence. Without repeating details published elsewhere,[30] we can say here that self-organization necessarily implies interactions among different levels of integration that are at the same time different levels of observation. In the context of the principle of "complexity from noise," describing self-organization as the use of random disturbances to create functional complexity is tantamount to describing the creation of new—and hence as yet unknown—meanings in the messages transmitted from one level to another. Precisely because these meanings are unknown, however, this description has to be made indirectly, in a negative fashion, employing a model from which the meaning of the message is explicitly absent, whereas its existence is implicit in the operation of the system observed. To put it another way, what appears to be "organizational chance" to someone observing the system from the outside implies the creation of new meanings—still unknown to this observer—within the system itself. Technically, this is expressed by a change in the sign of the ambiguity function, which, negative when it expresses the effects of noise at one level, becomes positive at a higher level when it expresses an increase in diversity and complexity.[31]

This sign change is only a special (mathematicized) case of a more general (and perhaps more immediately comprehensible) logical property that characterizes any change in the level of organization and consists of a transformation from distinction and separation at an elementary level into unity and synthesis at a more integrated level.

The components at a certain level, viewed individually, are distinguished one from another by properties of exclusion, separation, and differentiation that make it possible not to confound them in a single amalgam. But these same elements, viewed as components of a whole, are necessarily united by the common properties that, at least from the perspective of these common properties, cancel out their differences. Put another way, one can pass from an elementary level to a more integrated level only by transforming the properties of separation into those of union.

Thus at the atomic level of physical structure we distinguish—at least conceptually—atoms one from another by their nuclear and electronic structure so as to individualize and identify them. When we pass to the molecular level, however, these atoms are joined by bonds that involve what is common in their structure. In a covalent bond, for example, a property of their outermost electronic shell, which distinguishes two atoms, serves to unite them. These properties of separation/combination of atoms in molecules are the source of the chemical affinities of molecules, which constitute—vis-à-vis the atomic properties—the emergence of new properties that can be observed only at the level of the whole, the molecule, even though they are clearly a consequence of the properties of the parts, the atoms.

Similarly, the transition from molecules to cellular organisms involves considering what the properties that distinguish and separate the different molecules have in common. This leads to the emergence of the properties of the whole, of the cell, expressed in terms of information theory and cybernetics. An analogous procedure accompanies the transition from single cells to multicellular organisms, where communication between cells involves a relationship of properties (often membranal) that at the same time distinguish the cells from one another.

This is quite general and even rather trivial, because the very manner of asking the question about the combination of disparate elements into a whole implies a change of perspective, such that what were properties of separation between elements must be transformed into, or at least make room for, properties of the cohesion of these same elements at a higher level.

Perhaps less trivial is the relationship between this change of sign, this passage from segregation to integration, and the emergence of new properties at the higher level: the new (chemical) properties of molecules vis-à-vis the (physical) properties of atoms; the new (biological) properties of living cells vis-à-vis the (chemical) properties of molecules; the new (physiological and specific) properties of organisms, vis-à-vis cellular properties; the new (psychological) properties of animal behavior and the human mind, vis-à-vis the neurophysiological properties of the nervous system; and the new (sociological) properties of human (or animal) groups vis-à-vis the properties of individuals.

As we see, the emergence of specific properties at a more comprehensive level of organization corresponds to the establishment of a distinct discipline with its own tools of observation and analysis and its own specialized language: physics, chemistry, cellular biology, physiology and embryology, psychology, sociology. This gives rise, moreover, to a question that may not have a definite answer: to what extent does the separation of an integrated system into different levels of integration exist "objectively"? Or does it depend instead on the techniques of observation, experimentation, and analysis by which we have access to these different levels?

It is quite clear that the image we make ourselves of the organization of a living organism is a mental reconstitution of images provided by quite different techniques, each adapted to a different level: chemistry and biochemistry for the molecular level, microscopy and physiology for the cellular level, anatomy and general physiology for the organic level, and so on. *It is impossible to simultaneously observe all levels with the same precision.* Biochemical techniques that allow one to observe certain molecular properties entail the destruction of the cells; whereas observing the properties of intact cells requires other techniques, in which molecular properties cannot be observed with the same precision.

This renders the problem insoluble, because it involves observing and describing how the articulation between two levels takes place for the system itself (and in some fashion independent of the means of observation with which we have access thereto), whereas by definition we do not have direct access to the locus of this articulation. This is the problem we try to resolve by means of the theoretical models we create, sometimes without wishing to, even if only to explain or at least to name the technical successes of the reductionist method, in which manipulations at an elementary level generate reproducible and controllable effects at the level of the organism. But the explanatory power of these models usually leaves us unsatisfied, because they involve either metaphors whose limits are quickly apparent (e.g., the genetic program) or formal models that are generally negative (e.g., the probabilistic models of statistical thermodynamics and information theory), and these latter in some way make us aware that we do not have direct experimental access to the locus of these articulations between levels.

All the same, sometimes *the situation is turned on its head as a consequence of the development of new techniques of observation or the discovery of new experimental and analytical tools*, which can give us direct access to what was previously perceived only negatively or metaphorically at the join between two different levels of organization. The two levels were relatively well known, each separately, but the seam between them had remained a mystery because there was absolutely no overlap between their techniques of observation and theoretical languages. Then the discovery of new techniques that provide access to what takes place between these levels quickly leads to the development of a new field of knowledge, a new discipline with its own tools and language. A spectacular example[32] of such a revolution was provided by molecular biology, on the seam between chemistry and biology. The hypothesis that I wish to propose here is that language, especially natural language as a process of creating meanings, can play a similar role in the transition from the physiological to the psychological.

## Language as the Locus of the Articulation between the Physiological and the Psychological

In the case of molecular biology we are dealing with the articulation between the molecular and cellular levels of the organization of living beings. The transition from one to the other could long be represented only with great difficulty, because the techniques of chemistry and biology were very different and hardly overlapped. The development of techniques of biochemistry and macromolecular biophysics, reinforced by cybernetic and genetic theories, made it possible for the languages of chemistry and biology to overlap to some extent.

But this is neither totally true nor quite so simple. In effect, this overlap was made possible only by the *establishment of a new discipline*, with its own techniques and language—those of molecular biology, which studies biological macromolecules. In other words, it is just as if a new level of organization, the macromolecular, was defined between chemistry and biology, once the discipline that studies it had managed to establish its methods and language.

We can apply the same scheme to our language, and perhaps with even greater profit, because, recursively, we cannot do without it to describe and try to explain reality. In effect, human language, too, is found at the seam between two levels of organization that coexist in the individual but constitute two almost completely separate domains from the point of view of the disciplines that deal with them: general physiology and neurophysiology, on one hand, and the various methods of studying the mind, on the other. In other words, this is a way in which the old problem of the relationship between mind and body, or between thought and brain, can be placed in a more general context and perhaps become more susceptible to analysis: the context of the problem of the links between different levels of organization in a self-organizing system, where language can be considered the locus of articulation between two levels.

What is more, just as with molecular biology between chemistry and biology, language quickly becomes its own level of organization, interpolated between the levels that it joins, because it is an object of observation, experimentation, and theory, the object of a discipline that deals with a particular field of knowledge. Therefore it seems that we should divide the transition from brain to thought into two that may be easier to conceive of, brain-language and language-thought.

One might be discouraged by the idea that we have taken a step backward: instead of a single transition between two levels, we now must deal with two transitions. Whenever the articulation between two levels begins to lose its mystery, once it can be identified, observed, and studied in itself, it imposes its own techniques and language and automatically becomes a relatively autonomous intermediate level. This merely recreates the question of articulations, which now must be asked about the seam between this intermediate level and the two preexisting ones, below it and above it. Molecular biology is a perfect example of this, but it also shows why we ought not be discouraged: despite everything, the distance between levels seems to diminish (although the number of levels increases), even if, perhaps, it is never completely eliminated except asymptotically, at infinity, and even if it is perhaps impossible to totally overcome the conceptual void between the different levels of organization, because we are always dealing with different conditions of observation. Thus the development of molecular biology as a field interpolated between chemistry and biology did not totally eliminate the initial gap. This is why biological research still has something to study. But instead of the enormous distance between physical chemistry and life, previously considered to be irreducible, we are now asking the apparently simpler questions of the transition from *chemical organization* to *the organization of information-bearing macromolecules*, on the one hand, and of the transition from the *level of these macromolecules* to that of the *physiological properties of organisms* (structure and function), on the other hand. That is, the gaps between *chemistry and molecular biology*, and between *molecular biology and physiology*, seem to be smaller than formerly.

The same applies to language, seen simultaneously as the locus of the articulation between the physiological and the psychological and as the level of organization and field of knowledge interpolated between the two. Here too the seemingly irreducible conceptual gulf between brain and thought is replaced by questions that are perhaps more easily analyzable, relating to the transition between brain and language, on the one hand, and between language and mind, on the other. The role of formal (computer) languages in functionalist theories and the conceptual revival that these have brought to analysis of the brain-thought problem are a good illustration of this, despite their inadequacies.

The first transition, that from physiology to language, can be conceived of easily enough, thanks to information and communication theory, which posits signs without meaning or, more precisely, signs whose meaning is not known to us—in other words, a language that our thought cannot understand. This is explicitly the case in communication theory, where signals are considered to be such on the basis of the observation of regularities and the probability of errors or perturbations of these regularities, and the meaning of the signals is irrelevant. This first transition can also be conceived of by analogy to the study of formal languages and generative grammars, where the question of meaning (the semantic aspects of language) can be treated only by means of simplifying approximations. On the other hand, the transition from language to thought seems to be precisely that of the emergence of meaning.

## Creation of Meaning and Neoconnectionist Models

If one accepts this hypothesis, the question of the body-thought relationship can perhaps be reduced, in large measure, to that of the creation of the meanings of a language. Some progress has already been made here, thanks to machine models that simulate the creation of functional meanings. Of course such meanings are simpler than those of natural language, but they are meaningful messages all the same.

These studies naturally continue prior studies on possible models of self-organization. In general, beyond the formalisms and mathematical techniques used in different theories, we have been able to characterize self-organization as an optimum between a rigid and immutable order that cannot be modified without being destroyed, such as that of the crystal, on the one hand, and ceaseless renewal that knows no stability, such as the swirling chaos of smoke, on the other. This intermediate state is not frozen and can react to unexpected disturbances by changes that are not simply the destruction of the preexisting organization but rather a reorganization that permits the appearance of new properties. These properties may take the form of a new structure or behavior. Nothing a priori makes it possible to predict these properties in specific detail—this is precisely their novelty. We have come to understand how, under the effect of perturbations that tend to produce a disorganizing effect, some systems can reorganize themselves and take on new structural and functional properties that are to a certain extent unpredictable a priori. These systems, which are characterized by disorganization followed by reorganization, can serve as a working model for the study of how living beings adapt to change and perhaps even of how they invent.

But we must not see these reorganizations simply as the rearrangement or permutation of interconnected elements. Each rearrangement must have a corresponding new functional organization that results from the creation of new meanings in the information transmitted from one part to another or from one level of organization to another. Without this creation, the recombination would not result in the appearance of new functions or new behaviors.

The operation of most of the machines with which we are familiar corresponds only to a single combination of its components; any other combination would lead to malfunction or breakdown. For disorganization to produce reorganization the meaning of the relations among the parts must be transformed. *This is why the creation of meaningful information is at the core of the phenomena of self-organization.* It is not enough to say this; it is still necessary to present mechanisms through which meanings can create themselves. This is without doubt a process quite as paradoxical as that for devising self-programming programs. It involves designing organizational models capable of modifying themselves and of creating unforeseen meanings that astonish even the designer. These paradoxes are resolved by the simultaneous use of two ingredients that are usually ignored in classic computer models: on the one hand, a certain degree of indeterminacy and randomness in the evolution of the model, which permits the appearance of something new, not determined by the program; on the other hand, cognizance of the observer's role and of the context in the definition of the meaning of the information, such that the new and unexpected can acquire meaning and not be merely chaos and random disturbances.

What a self-organizing process can be is summarized, ultimately, by the fact that it allows chance to acquire a functional meaning, a posteriori and in a given context. The study of automata networks with both structural and functional self-organizing properties allows us to tackle the mechanisms by which messages (or stimuli) can acquire nonprogrammed meanings for a machine.

In an automata network one can build a mechanism by which a set of a priori meaningless messages is subdivided into some that can be recognized by the network (which reacts to them with a particular response) and some that are not recognized (and therefore elicit no reaction). This behavior simulates, in an extremely elementary fashion, that of a cognitive system for which certain classes of sequences have meaning whereas others do not. The criterion of demarcation is a particular internal structure, a particular path between two elements of the network that is singularized and stabilized as a structure that can have this self-organized function, in partly random fashion. This structure, which thereby produces meaning, was itself produced in part by chance, through the history of its previous encounters with unexpected events. It has no other meaning per se than the production of this demarcation that creates meaning.[33]

Among the advantages it shares with all so-called neoconnectionist models (see note 12), this model offers an alternative to the usual metaphor of the computer as the exclusive reference for a functionalist approach to biological and psychological organization and to the mind-brain problem. Envisioning only the rules of computer programs as they exist today (deterministic and sequential), Fodor could imagine in his "language of thought" (see above) only mechanisms of deterministic and localized encoding; this led him to a relatively static vision of encoded representations as the sources of meaning in natural language and thought. The new directions in artificial intelligence research, based on probabilistic programs and parallel processing and on the heuristics of behavior, considerably modify the conclusions that can be drawn from the analogy with the computer sciences, while retaining the advances of functionalism over the classical—and rival—metaphysics of the mind-body problem. Hence today, just as in our automata networks, dynamic processes are privileged over states, and delocalized and partially stochastic procedures of the creation of meanings over representations. These are principles of modeling about which there is long-standing agreement that they more closely approximate what takes place in the brain,[34] principles that the neoconnectionist approach has readopted while applying new mathematical and computing tools. These tools result mainly from recent advances in the physics of disordered systems and phase transitions and from new studies in artificial intelligence, based on the massive use of parallel processing and probabilistic programming.[35]

Thus different modes of using the indeterminate and random are being explored and mastered. The possibility is developing of modeling the use of the approximative analogy, indispensable in processes of self-organization and learning new things,[36] of the "vagueness" that Wittgenstein recognized as an indispensable feature, characteristic of the "perfect logical order" of everyday language[37] and of the fluidity and "slippability" of concepts.[38] The first relatively precise description of such processes, concerning ecosystems with complex dynamics, has been put forward under the name *buffered stability.*[39] Similar descriptions are found in connectionist models, as a general property of most automata networks with multiple attractors.[40] The relatively new result produced by these studies, which makes it possible to use network dynamics to model learning machines and associative memories, is that the existence of multiple highly unstable attractors that change from one type to the other under the effect of disturbances or changes in the initial conditions does not prevent the existence, at a more general hierarchical level, of groups of more closely spaced attractors in larger basins. On the contrary, great stability can be observed at this level if one allows the definition of this "buffered" stability to admit differences of detail among attractors and focuses on an approximate and partial similarity represented by several macroscopic spatiotemporal properties, formalized precisely by such a group of relatively closely spaced attractors. When an "energy" function can be defined for such a network, such that each attractor corresponds to a minimum of this function, the groups of attractors are characterized by basins containing several local minima. The transition from one to another within such a basin can serve as a model of the type of cognition called "associative memory," where a form is recognized on the basis of another that is not totally identical to it.

Finally, the system of recognizing sequences described previously, where the criterion of recognition is resonance with a particular structure of the network, itself created by a self-organizing dynamic, is in some fashion related to Gibson's theory of "direct" or "instantaneous" perception.[41] In this theory, perception of a shape is not the result of a two-stage process: reception of signals and their subsequent processing by application of a rule for representation. Instead, an external shape, located in the environment, is perceived at the same time as signals are received, through a sort of resonance phenomenon between a structure in the environment—not necessarily evident to the eyes of the observer—and an internal structure of the cognitive system. The latter defines a possible functional meaning of the external structure for the system. The functional self-organization of a network of automata that recognizes sequences demonstrates that this type of behavior, where meanings are created at the same time as they are recognized, is less mysterious than it seems, for it can be simulated by a relatively simple combination of deterministic and probabilistic programming.

## Self-Reference in Language and White Space on the Page

Of course, these meanings are not the same as those of everyday human languages, but they do reproduce one of their properties. It is clearly not a matter of simulating natural language, even if only because of the absence of the specific trait of the latter that distinguishes it from animal languages, for example: self-reference, the possibility of designating the language itself in the language (and in particular by means of the word *language*). In these models, the meaning of a message or a sequence of signals is defined as the effect of this message on the receiver, which may be an animal or a machine rather than a human being. This definition is clearly more limited than what we experience—but still do not know how to define precisely—each time we understand the meaning of phrases in the natural language that we speak or write. But there is certainly some overlap, for it is indisputable that when I understand a message a change of state is produced in my brain at some stage in the process. This effect of the message on the brain, viewed as a receiver, is certainly one part of the phenomenon by which we understand—or create—the meaning of the message.

The reducibility of the mind-brain relationship to the creation of meaning in natural language can perhaps shed light on all transitions from one level to another. We use this very same mind when we try to think all these transitions, including that from body to mind. This phenomenon of recursion or invariance of scale is all the more astonishing when we realize that language itself, as a process of creating meaning, is also a multilevel system that organizes itself creatively. As in any self-organizing system, here too meaning is created by the interactions among different levels.

The transition from one level to another within language involves "white space" (caesuras, pauses) that simultaneously separates and combines words and sentences. It is there, in that white space, in the unsaid, that meaning is created. Meaning is created at the junction of two levels— the level of words and the level of sentences. Words are separated and defined by the white space that separates them and then combined into sentences by the same white spaces that join them. White space is a non-symbol, a nonsign that seems to be the source of meaning, whereas signs without white space would be meaningless.

Thus white space reproduces, in language, the locus of the transition from one level to another; it is where the internal meanings of language are created at the same time as the negativity of interruption and division between these signs is transformed into composition and reunion. Perhaps we are dealing here with what plays the role, in natural language, of the two necessary ingredients mentioned previously in our discussion of artificial models of functional self-organization: indeterminacy and the desire to explain the conditions of observation and of the context.

## Psychosomatic Organization and Unconsciousness of Self

Under the influence of psychoanalysis, which, despite its various avatars,[42] has not renounced its scientific pretensions, the approach to the mind-body problem from its human psychological aspect has benefited in recent years from the cybernetic vocabulary of biology and theories of biological organization. P. Marty,[43] one of the founders of the Paris psychosomatic school, found in the dynamics of organization the conceptual tool for describing psychological processes with biological references, both in general and sometimes in their details. For him, psychological organization appears to be an aggregate of emergent properties of biological organization. The dynamics of organization and disorganization provides Marty with an elaborate and detailed theory of psychosomatic pathology, in which psychological and somatic processes can be described as a single temporal continuum.[44] As was seen by Canguilhem[45] with regard to the theory of self-organization and complexity from noise, the cybernetic metaphor provides a content for Freud's intuitions about the death wish by displacing it from its initial economic framework, dominated by the obscure and deceptive notion of psychic energy.[46] Similarly, A. Bourguignon[47] employs the theory of self-organization to anchor in plausible biological processes both the normal and pathological psychological development of the child interacting with its mother and its environment.

Through all these attempts, we see that the frontiers of knowledge are located not only—as is frequently believed—in the infinite and the infinitesimal, but also at the articulations between levels of organization of reality, which correspond to different fields of knowledge whose techniques and language do not overlap. Because we cannot have direct access to them, we have only extremely limited technical and theoretical means for speaking of these articulations and how they appear *between* the fields of scientific knowledge. Nevertheless, they seem to be the place where whatever it is that constitutes the autonomy of a complex system resides.

This is why what we are bumping into in these shadow zones is perhaps, as was seen by Hofstadter,[48] the recursivity of the self. And it is precisely there that we must guard against falling into the spiritualist error that asserts we know what the self is, on the basis of our subjective experience of self-consciousness.

Just as we are attempting to obtain an objective grasp of the concept of meaning in nonhuman systems of communication, the self under discussion here is not necessarily the human self, and thus largely unconscious. The molecular and cellular self of the immune system can provide us with one example, and the self of self-modifying computer programs with another example.

The correct approach consists of attempting to grasp these notions through analysis of nonhuman situations and proceeding in such a way that the experience of our own subjectivity appears only secondarily, as a particular case.

It is always possible, after the fact because easier, to modify the application to this particular case of subjective experience, taking into account the particular position occupied by the observer. There is no circularity in this, because the observer of whom we are speaking is not our subjectivity, but rather the sum total of operations of measuring and of defining the logical relations between these operations.

Hence we are dealing here not with logical circularity, but with a recursive phenomenon in which language plays a fundamental role: spoken and written language occupies the seam between two levels of organization, but itself serves to describe and analyze all of these levels and at the same time is itself a self-organizing multilevel system.

In other words, every organization of life incorporates two aspects of language: not only the aspect of linear sequences of combinatory signs that convey information, but also that of an autonomous multilevel organization that creates meaning.

At this crossroads, where the shadow of what might be called "not necessarily human self-unconsciousness" appears, Douglas Hofstadter rightly saw the threefold overlap of chaos, creation of meaning, and autonomy of the self.

## Weak Reductionism

This overview of the problems posed by multilevel natural organizations indicates that we must accept both a unity of processes that we do not (yet?) know and the diversity of the disciplines that subdivide them and allow us to learn about them, progressively and partially. This leads to the perception of a unity of science that can be only the unity of its *practice*, motivated by its *successes*. The successes are technical, relating to mastery and control; the practice is that of weak reductionism, for which physics remains, to a certain extent, the fundamental discipline, even though the other sciences cannot be totally reduced to it.

We have just seen how even the question of the relationships between matter and mind can be approached—from the angle of the brain-thought problem—in a de facto reductionist process that characterizes scientific *practice*. In this procedure we have encountered the influence of the information sciences and paradigms of the computer and artificial intelligence, which allow us to explode the alternative between strong reductionism and spiritualist holism by demonstrating that properties of the whole can emerge *in machines*. As we have seen, however, this influence creates new theoretical difficulties that must always be borne in mind. For lurking in this process is the danger of going no further than the provisional syntheses that are always possible—if only for purposes of pedagogy or popularization—at the price of tentative extrapolations, generalizations, and global explanations. Weak reductionism consists, inter alia, of not giving into this temptation; at the same time, the unity of the processes continues to be postulated and physics—because of its successes—continues to be the paradigmatic discipline, the one whose method should be emulated. This reductionist praxis often leads the practitioners of each discipline, anxious to preserve the prudence and rigor without which their discipline would not exist, to fall back on themselves—at least in their practice as scientists—and renounce the need for total explanation.

But when it is a case of studying complex systems organized into different levels of integration, this excessively hermetic compartmentalization is no longer possible, because it destroys the very object of study. Then reductionist practice redons its unifying garb and discourse, still guarding itself against falling back into a strong, metaphysical reductionism. Just as for the latter, *the causal search for physical phenomena* remains indispensable, but its meaning differs from that spontaneously attributed to it by the strong reductionism of physicalist metaphysics in at least two points.

The first point concerns the transition from one level to another, such that the properties of the higher level are considered to be determined by those of the more elementary level. This transition cannot be seen as a simple causal determination of the same type as cause and effect relationships in a temporal sequence of events that determine one another on the same level of observation and organization. Neither can it be seen as a simple relationship of spatial inclusion of the parts in the whole; nor, as Oppenheim and Putnam would,[49] as an association of these two relationships, the causal and the inclusive, where parts *spatially contained* in the whole *causally* determine its properties. As we have seen, even in artificial machines the determination of the whole by its parts implies a qualitative leap, with the emergence of new properties that cannot be observed in the parts and cannot be described by a simple association of the properties of these parts. What is more, this determination takes place thanks to the relationships among the parts that are not merely spatial contiguity but also functional connections. The latter create more-relevant spaces (reaction spaces, more or less complex topological spaces[50]) than the usual Euclidian space.

The second point in which the meaning of reductionist practice applied to multilevel organizations differs from physicalist metaphysics concerns the nature of the physical phenomena that analysis makes it possible to place in causal relationship: these are physical in that they are described by physics, and not because they are immediately available through direct sensory apprehension of the physical reality—in the material sense—of which the universe is composed.[51] In other words, reductionist praxis derives from physics, when necessary, the concepts it finds useful for describing the properties of atoms and molecules, or measurable energy exchanges between well-defined systems composed of atoms and molecules, or mathematical formulas that have solved certain physical problems. But it does not infer, from the operational success of its concepts, a theoretical discourse on the unity of reality. (Even less can this unity be described on the apparently uncontestable basis of macroscopic material reality, that of objects directly perceived by our senses, as a truly materialist metaphysics would do if it could ignore the problems posed by mathematical abstraction in physics.)

The nonrenunciation of reductionism, although limiting it to a praxis that conditions science without deriving any unitary theoretical consequences from it, is evidently troubling if one can conceive reality only through a unified knowledge whose field would be coextensive with that of the natural sciences. For this pragmatic reductionism circumscribes the domain of legitimacy of science; it indicates the limits of the scientific process, which can progress only by *forcing itself* to be reductionist, only by "playing the reductionist game," whereas "believing in it"[52] would be evidence of great naivete—the naivete of believing in the objective truth, in some fashion or other, of the "fact" of the reducibility[53] of the real to some unique ("ultimate") reality, whether material or not, on the basis of scientific theories. This same naivete is found among spiritualist physicists who discover Spirit at work in the reduction of the wave function. In their defense we may cite, without condoning their approach, the oft-noted ambiguous role of mathematics in science.

## The Role of Mathematics

The privileged role of mathematics in scientific explanation and practice has certainly been partly responsible for this fascination with the unity of everything and its opposite. In effect, the mathematical representation of phenomena has properties that seem to be opposed point for point to those of the process of the natural sciences.

First, mathematical and scientific models work in opposite directions:[54] whereas for physicists a model is an abstract representation of a portion of reality, the mathematicians' model (like the painters') is that slice of reality from which they (sometimes) derive inspiration and which mathematics (or the work of art), while maintaining an independent existence, can if necessary represent. As the linguist Y. R. Chao put it, "in mathematics a model is more concrete than what it is a model of, while in the social sciences [and, I would add, in the natural sciences] a model is more of an abstraction."[55] Thus in the nineteenth century, logicians searched nature for geometric models—every geometry, both Euclidian and non-Euclidian, being basically a noninterpreted set of signs.

This variance in attitude is not only the fortuitous result of the different habits of different disciplines. It is also associated with a different appreciation of what an explanation is. What does it mean to explain or comprehend a phenomenon, if not to reduce it to something already known? If the object of knowledge is mathematics itself, that is, a system of formal relations, it is the possibility of interpreting these relations by reducing them to known phenomena—known because observed and reported by our senses—that permits us to understand it: this is the mathematicians' attitude. If, on the other hand, the object to be understood is a body of observations constituting what we consider to be a physical system, it is the antithetical operation—the possibility of abstracting and formalizing these observations—that constitutes an explanation.

In practice these two processes are superimposed, which entails some confusion in the attempts at modeling the nervous system, for example, found in the literature. Sometimes the model is used in the mathematicians' sense of the term, and the process goes from mathematical theory to the system; at other times it is a natural-science model, and the method proceeds from the system to its mathematical formalization. This difference is found in everyday language as well, where *model* sometimes means a simplified concrete representation (like a maquette or statue) and sometimes a set of ideal standards whose concrete realizations are imperfect approximations thereof. As Chao says, these differences can be traced back to the ancient opposition between things and ideas: "Things are imperfect examples of pure ideas; ideas are partial abstractions of real things. One is a model, in a sense, of the other; the other is a model, in the other sense, of the one."[56] To put it another way, in one sense an object is a model of an idea; in another sense, however, an idea is a model of a thing.

Second, the subject-object distinction *seems* to disappear in the mathematical representation of natural phenomena, because the effectiveness of the abstraction whose source is in the constructs of human thought suggests that it is nevertheless an objective reality. In fact the (spontaneous? universal?) agreement with regard to mathematical rationality grounds an intersubjectivity that creates a form of constraining abstract objectivity (mathematical logic) as the basis of the consensus of the scientific community.

Third, here too strict causal determinism is sometimes abandoned in favor not only of probabilistic methods but especially of the variational methods that are so important in mathematical modeling. The use of function optimization methods (potential or otherwise) in physics introduces a sort of end-seeking that is held in check, for the scientific consensus, only by the rationality and logical rigor of the formalism applied.[57]

For these reasons, the use of mathematics is imposed "naturally" and incorporated automatically in the practice of science; often it even has the look of an ideal, of which physics is the model (in the mathematical sense) to be imitated by the other sciences and of which logico-empiricist analytical philosophy seeks to be the theory (that is to say, to model, in the physicist's sense). On the other hand, it never stops posing problems for anyone who reflects on the fundamentals of science and will not accept without flinching a trivial and necessarily still theological faith in a preestablished harmony. Precise analyses thereof can be found, for example, in the work of M. Serres[58] on the origin of mathematics, or rather its origins, for he offers at least four (or five) scenarios; and of Richard Feynman[59] and J.-M. Lévy-Leblond[60] on its relations with physics. We will keep coming back to these questions, which have engaged the greatest minds, from different points of view—including that of logic (Chapter 4) and of the reality of physical interpretations (Chapter 5)—always hinging, ultimately, on the difficulties posed by a preestablished harmony[61] that can be spoken of only in one of the registers, whether that of the formal abstract or that of the immediately perceptible "natural."

This is also why scientific discourse is incessantly torn between the need to explain by assembling and unifying on the basis of abstraction and theory, on the one hand, and the need for rigor, which often compels it to renounce them. In the latter case one must be content with a predictive operational description, whether formalized, deterministic, probabilistic, or in natural language. Such a description is tantamount to saying: "Everything happens as if...in such and such experimental conditions; the result is that...in those conditions."[62]

Surrendering to the need to explain, for a practitioner of the natural sciences, is necessarily, at least at the outset, to yield to the reductionist movement. That is the form in which, historically, the universal need for explanation and rationalization has been prominent in the West as one[63] of the motivating factors of the development of the natural sciences. That is why, quite naturally, "scientific explanation," as opposed to other types of "explanation" (metaphysical, mystical, animist) can proceed only from "bottom to top" and in a reductionist fashion. But we have also seen that yielding to this need by posing straightaway, and almost as a necessity (even under the false modesty of a "plausible hypothesis"[64]), a unity of science that itself rests on the unity of the "ultimate reality of matter" corresponds to a metascientific position that all too easily ends up in mystical spiritualism.

By continuing the "Democritan process"[65] of classical reductionism in the quest for smaller common parts, one discovers "within" elementary particles not other "material" particles, in the sense of our macroscopic experience of matter, but Mind incarnated (if the term is appropriate here) in abstract formulas that cannot be reduced to this macroscopic experience. More precisely, one believes one has discovered Mind if one believes in the truth of the Democritan postulate about the unity of the real on the basis of a unique reality ("the ultimate reality of matter") of ultimate constituent parts: when the materiality of these constituents dissolves in the abstract formalism of quantum physics, the formalism itself—or rather its presumed source in Mind—becomes the mirror of this ultimate reality.

When an equation is the only way to describe or represent this "ultimate reality," physics, the fundamental discipline, seems to be supported exclusively by mathematics. As a result, the ground of materialism gives way and its metaphysics dissolves in the abstractions of a quantum metaphysics. The physical model of the natural sciences (and of the mathematician) leads back to the mathematical model of the physicist: the loop is closed. The lower level, the foundation, rests on something that seems to proceed from the highest level, that of the logico-mathematical structures of thought, itself the object of psychology, which is based on physiology, which is in turn based on quantum physics, which is in turn based on mathematical logic, and so on.

To avoid this endless loop, one must evidently suppose a preestablished harmony between abstract mathematical structures and concrete nature, or instead traverse the ladder in the opposite direction, from top to bottom, as mystical traditions do systematically. Alternatively, one can eliminate the problem by banishing the psychological and linguistic sciences from the ranks of scientific disciplines, as Oppenheim and Putnam[66] did in their reductionist period.

In all cases we are dealing with a sort of misapplied "monotheism" that makes the same error, whether in its materialist or its spiritualist version: wanting to identify some "ultimate reality" associated with "matter" or "mind." In fact these can cover only inappropriate extensions to the entire universe of our sensory experiences of macroscopic external reality, on the one hand, and of our proprioceptive and introspective experiences of our inner life, on the other.

Nevertheless, the errors of these two "monotheisms" are not symmetrical, from the perspective of scientific method, precisely because of the practical advantages of materialism and reductionism. We must "play the reductionist game," for without it the entire edifice of scientific discourse would crumble; or, more precisely, its progress would grind to a halt—not for metaphysical or theoretical reasons, but, once again, for pragmatic and historical ones. Hence scientific knowledge is constituted on three foundations:

1.  Causal, nonvoluntarist and nonintentional explanations, even if modes of causality more complex than linear and single-determination causality are employed;

2.  "Bottom-up" rather than "top-down" explanations,[67] that is, explanations proceeding from the most particular to the most integrated level of organization, even if the part-whole relationship is more general than that of spatial inclusion mentioned previously;

3.  The subject-object distinction, postulating an objective existence for things beyond individual subjectivity, even if the role of measurement and observation in the constitution of objects cannot be ignored.

It is difficult to satisfactorily cast this process into theory, as is amply demonstrated[68] by the criticism of those in the positivist line who were among the last to attempt it. Fundamentally, we can see quite clearly that we accept science a priori, not because of theoretical justifications that one can only attempt to detach, with great effort and *post factum*, from science as practiced, but simply because of its success at prediction and manipulation. Also, it matters little whether the three implicit principles or postulates[69] that guide this practice—presuppositions on the basis of which, by a scarcely or poorly formulated consensus, the publications and discourse of the scientific community are effectively produced—are the result of contingent historical reasons. What is important for our purposes is only whether the limits these presuppositions created, by precluding their antitheses (albeit in a relative and sometimes even contradictory fashion), are criteria of demarcation that a logical empiricist philosophy would eventually establish, or are rather the arbitrary result of a necessarily partial praxis that has merely banished, ad hoc in each individual case, whatever hampers its pursuit of operational success, in accordance with frequently divergent "interests."[70] In any case, the effectiveness of scientific knowledge—which makes us accept it as it is, a priori (or reject it!)—is found in that process and with those limitations, which, practically speaking, make it exist. To seek to suppress them and utter discourses that deny the subject-object distinction and proceed top down, and in which causality is replaced by the finality of a conscious or unconscious will, is to seek to replace scientific knowledge with another mode of knowledge,[71] mystical, for example.

As we shall see later, this may be perfectly legitimate, even from an ostensibly "rational" point of view, taking into account mainly the field and "interest" one would assign to this knowledge. On the other hand, to abolish these limitations *without leaving science behind* is not only illusory but also self-destructive: it is to assert a mode of knowledge that would be reduced to nothingness, because it lops off the branch it is sitting on; or, alternatively, that would be All, because, like God, it coincides with and merges into everything and its opposite. In the latter case, however, the limitations of language (formalized or not, theological or otherwise) distort excessively, and only complete silence is appropriate. It is within and thanks to these limitations that scientific knowledge is constructed: using the vocabulary, theoretical tools, and experimental method of science outside these limits merely creates ridiculous and sterile monsters such as scientology, mathematical theology, and various scientific astrologies—in short, what Freud dreaded in Jung (and in himself as well, of course, as in each of us) while designating it "the black...mud of occultism."[72]

Nevertheless, as we saw at the outset, the temptation to fuse into the unity of the All is great, not only outside but also within science. We have recounted episodes in which this temptation was particularly prominent, with the Cordoba conference as our paradigm or model. But we have also seen how reductionist scientism, too, does not escape this temptation, when science is not a praxis, but is used as explanation and ideology. This temptation probably corresponds to a profound need that we have difficulty renouncing in our daily life, that of explaining and rationalizing. I am myself succumbing to this need when I try to "understand" the phenomenon of Cordoba, to explain and rationalize it. In my defense, I do not pretend that my enterprise is a scientific study. For if the need to understand and explain is one of the motivating factors of science (the other being that to control and build), it goes well beyond the limits of scientific production. This impatient need pushes us to metascientific explanations in which bits and pieces of science are integrated, digested, metabolized, and combined in a grandiose or a ridiculous fresco,[73] depending on the talent of the visionary.

## Biological Functions and Intentionality:
### The Outflanking of the Scientific by
### the Quotidian and the Ethical

We have seen that self-consciousness and the creation of meaning probably constitute the core of the mind-body nexus. We have also seen how this problem can be tackled—if not resolved—through a weak reductionist, but still reductionist, process. This involves the reciprocal buttressing of cybernetics and biology, back-and-forth observations of biological structures and functions simulated by computer models such as learning machines and self-organizing automata networks. But we must discern why this process cannot lead to a metaphysics of mind and intentionality, in either sense: neither denying their reality nor affirming their ubiquity in nature. Strong reductionism, exalting its initial results into a science of truth, cheers itself with a unitary materialist metaphysic that allows only an illusory reality to our subjective experience of conscious intentions—with its corollary of freedom and responsibility—and to unconscious intentions of the sort described by psychoanalysts. But this attitude, so comfortable on the plane of theoretical coherence, is out of touch with our daily life, especially its social and judicial aspects, including the daily life of the very individuals, philosophers or scientists, who defend it; it is not lived, because it is quite *unlivable*. At the other extreme, weak reductionism leads to a pragmatic attitude, not so comfortable on the theoretical plane, but one *that we can live with*.

The difficulty arises from the fact that observation of meaningful behavior, meaningful in the sense that it represents the accomplishment of a function, tends to make us associate the origin of this meaning with a focused intention, which determines in advance the object to be obtained by this function, the task to be realized—the criterion by which a behavior is appropriate or inappropriate, meaningful or absurd. Modern biology has been devoted exclusively to separating intentionality from finality—teleology from teleonomy—using the metaphor of the computer program, theories of biological adaptation revived in the context of neo-Darwinian evolution, and models of self-organization. But this effort, although it leads on the operational plane to the production of fruitful hypotheses and models that permit predictive and effective manipulation, merely shunts aside the problem on the theoretical and philosophical plane.

When, in our daily life, particularly our social life, we observe a message or behavior that makes sense, we cannot avoid ascribing an intention to the transmitter of this message or to the one who behaves in this fashion. Evidently we are projecting from our own experience when we express ourselves and behave in an intentional fashion with the aim of saying or doing something. But the reality of our life in society—including the research laboratories and philosophy departments where reductionist theories are elaborated—would crumble without this projection, which each person makes without even thinking about it. Without it the very notion of personal responsibility and its derived judicial concept of an "individual and legal person" would have no effect. It is hard to see how neuronal interactions can be considered responsible for a crime or a good deed, appreciated and judged as such by other neuronal interactions. At the other extreme, an external observer who surveyed the behavior of a functionally self-organizing probabilistic automata network, without knowing its structure, would be tempted to attribute intentionality to it. And this seems to hold true for every creation of meaning when observed in the round, from the outside.

In fact, bringing these automata models as evidence is going too far, extrapolating to the absurd, and should permit us a better comprehension of what takes place when we observe natural systems that create meaning, such as animals or other human beings, and attribute intentions to them, by projection. When we see a dog trying to locate its master and to this end following a strategy that has it, for example, first look for a door and open it, if it is partially closed, then recognize a vehicle that can transport it, while seeming to comprehend the function of this vehicle, and then use it to arrive at its goal, we describe a behavior that is evidently purposeful,[74] as if this dog had an intention from the outset, namely, to find its master, and as if all its subsequent behavior was guided by this intention. We find it quite natural to describe this phenomenon in such terms and do not question the legitimacy of the description. In fact, we extend to the dog a behavior of which we have inner experience—our own intentional, purposeful actions that consciously aim at realizing an objective. But now let us observe behavior that is in every point similar to that of the dog, except that the agent is an isolated cell, for example, a white blood cell whose function is to swallow and digest foreign bodies, bacteria, or dead cells, of which the organism must be rid: here too we see the cell head for its prey, go around any obstacles, change its shape to thread through a narrow passage if necessary. Yet we do not attribute an intention to this end-seeking behavior; on the contrary, we look for and often find a physicochemical causal mechanism that explains the phenomenon: the hunted cell or bacteria secrete a substance that diffuses through the milieu and stimulates the membrane of the white blood cell. Under the effect of this signal, which can take the form of changes in the concentration of certain ions, contractile molecules whose shape depends on ionic concentrations—due to phenomena of electrostatic attraction and repulsion—change shape. This causes a deformation of the entire cell, producing amoeboidal motion in the direction of those regions where these stimulating substances are more highly concentrated, that is to say, in the proximity of the prey, and so forth.

Similarly, the attractive movements of spermatozoa by an ovum are explained by a chemiotactism of this same type, acting on the flagella that constitute the locomotor apparatus of the spermatozoa, and certainly not by some conscious intention—or even unconscious, in the psychoanalytic sense—and even less by a strategy of seduction!

Somewhere between the behavior of isolated cells and that of the dog we erect a barrier that keeps us from speaking of intention with regard to the cells, but not with regard to the dog. But where is this barrier located? On which side of it would we place algae? A clam? A frog?

Another example of the same barrier is even more subtle because it separates closely related species within a single genus: bats. The various species of bats constitute a unique subject for study because they constitute an evolutionary line with progressive encephalization, similar to another line that interests us even more, that which leads from the primates to man. In the latter case, too, we observe evolution producing new species with a larger brain in proportion to body weight and with different behaviors. Paul Pirlot[75] of Montreal spent many years studying the different species of bats and attempting to correlate species' alimentary behavior and brain size. In general terms, some species are insectivores and eat more or less automatically, thanks to a very well-developed ultrasonic sense that enables them to detect and unfailingly swallow up any insect passing sufficiently close within a given angle. Other species are fruit eaters or nectar eaters like bees, while the vampires feed on the blood of various mammals—sheep, human beings, and others—by biting their veins while they sleep.

Contrary to what specialists had thought, Pirlot was able to show that the most highly evolved species, those with the greatest brain development, are not those with the best sonar, who always function with precision, but rather the vampires, whose alimentary behavior is among the most insecure, requiring extremely varied strategies of approach, depending on the type of animal they are attacking, its shape, where it is sleeping, and so on. To put it another way, the species that developed earlier, the sonar-guided insectivores, possess what is certainly a precise alimentary behavior, but of an automatic and machinelike type, reflex in the mechanical sense; whereas the more recent species, with the more developed brain, behave in ways that seem to require purposeful intelligence, strategy, and planning, where the goal is posed in advance and the means of attaining it are improvised as a function of circumstances, like the dog we were discussing previously, or indeed like ourselves.

Here too, then, within the single genus of bats, we can distinguish species whose behavior is explained by a purely causal mechanism—the operation of sonar that triggers lingual motion with the direction and range required to trap without fail the insect flying by—from species whose diversified and adaptive behavior can be described in purposeful and intentional terms.

On the one hand, we explain observations by analogy with our subjective experience: "We do something in order to do this or that, with a view to this or that end"; hence, "The dog barks *in order to* attract attention, *with a view* to finding its master," and so forth. On the other hand, we disqualify these "in order to's" and "with a view to's" and accept only "because": because of a difference in ionic concentration, because of a change in molecular form, and so on. A consistent biologist would apply the same interpretation to the dog as to the white blood cell and the spermatozoön and reject explanations by "in order to" and "with a view to."

However, this is not very practical in everyday life, because purely causal and physicochemical descriptions of canine behavior, even if possible, would be extremely complicated: the slightest movement of a paw calls into play a considerable number of elementary events at the level of the cells of the nervous system, of different muscles involved in the movement, and so on. Most important, somehow this type of explanation always seems to miss the essential point; namely, the accomplishment of a particular function that gives meaning to the aggregate of elementary phenomena we observe in an integrated action, a behavior that to our eyes has a meaning.

In other words, the intention lies in the meaning we attach to things, and this meaning is produced by observation of the functional effects of things. The barrier we erect between causal explanations and intentional explanations certainly does not exist in things themselves; it derives from our interpretation of what we observe, either as behaviors or messages that have a meaning because they seem to accomplish a function, or as behaviors or messages whose functional meaning we cannot or do not wish to see—sometimes for reasons of convenience and fertility of research. We do not want to see it, in a correct research methodology, because this functional meaning is located on a totally different level of organization and complexity, for example, the function of the spermatozoön as the reproductive agent of the individual and the species. To include this functional meaning in our account of the behavior of the isolated spermatozoön would imply, today, a purely verbal and metaphysical explanation; for example, that by Nature or Natural Selection.

On the other hand, whenever we do see such a functional meaning and want to take it into consideration with regard to things we observe, we have a tendency to invert our attitude and to ascribe an intention to their origin. We are led to speak in this fashion of machines and computers, whose behavior seems to be intentional, when we observe them creating meaning, as in our example of networks that are nevertheless quite simple and devoid of mystery.

The next step, which we take quite naturally, is to ask whether an "intelligent" machine can suffer. A cell, an amoeba, a bacterium, or even a frog, or a dog—can they suffer? Once again, the question is where the barrier should be placed. But this time we are tempted to go in the other direction and to project the inner experience of our own subjectivity on anything that exists and functions with apparent meaning. The question of whether machines can "think," "suffer," predict, follow an autonomous strategy, and so on, is beginning to be the subject of serious logical and philosophical debate.[76]

In fact, the reasons we set the barrier of intention and meaning, without which creativity and responsibility do not exist, in a particular place cannot be objective reasons related to the nature of things, independent of the context in which we observe them.

We have seen that in practice, in our everyday life, it is sometimes simpler for us to set aside the coherent attitude of the biologist and rest content with "it happens as if," acting as if our dog, or our neighbor's, really has intentions and projects.

Taken to the extreme, moreover, there is no proof that I must accept this type of interpretation for any being other than myself: when I attribute an intention to another human being, there too I am projecting, by analogy, my own experience. The difference is that in the latter case one can perhaps refer to the articulate language in which we describe all of this and without which there could be neither science nor philosophy, a language that is common to that other human being and myself—but only more or less, and with many ambiguities.

Hence whatever causes us to place the barrier in one location rather than elsewhere, to attribute intention and projects, as well as suffering and the possibility of creating, to other human beings and maybe even to their dogs, but not to a blade of grass, a bacterium, or a machine or automaton—what makes us erect this barrier there rather than elsewhere—cannot be justified by objective and scientific considerations, but chiefly by the ethical motivations at play in our relations with other human beings and with nature. In our daily life we accept or reject these choices because of their psychological and social consequences. The criteria are psychological and social, related to our own conduct in daily life rather than to the objective knowledge of things we pursue by means of the scientific method.

This does not mean, of course, that we ought not to erect this barrier, only that we must understand it as a truly animist projection that goes beyond the limits of scientific method and that we cannot do without in our daily life. But we should be aware of this fact and erect the barrier in a place that, though it may be arbitrary from the perspective of objective knowledge of structures and of hidden functions, is determined by our immediate perception of things that we recognize without reflecting; that is, to erect the barrier of intention and projects *at the point where we can recognize a human form, characterized by body and language,* onto which we can project our own subjective experience. In other words, it is the immediate experience of skin, body, and words, a prescientific or postscientific experience motivated by a concern for ethical behavior rather than by objective knowledge, that makes us detect intention, projects, and creativity, as well as freedom and responsibility, inside a skin that encloses a body which, it turns out, more or less resembles mine.

Under the combined influence of behavioral biology and ethology, on the one hand, and of artificial intelligence, on the other, some authors evince a tendency to award scientific status to nonconscious, natural, and not necessarily human intentionality, from which human intentionality is derived.[77] They place the barrier at the level of animal or even plant behavior: intentionality is ascribed not only to the dog, who responds to its master's call in unusual conditions, adjusts its actions by anticipating certain of his habits after they have been modified, and invents a new strategy for maintaining the framework of communication that will allow it to recognize a later call, but also to a climbing plant, which spreads to the other side of a wall while "searching" a way out of the shade, "hoping" that the other side of the wall will be exposed to sunlight. Of course this is not to ignore the difficult problems of translation that the intentional character of the language used in these descriptions poses for physicalism. Even if we know that the movements of plants are governed by tropisms whose physicochemical mechanisms are well understood, and that those of the dog can be reduced, in principle, to more or less complex conditioned reflexes, the description of their overall behavior cannot avoid this intentional language. The use of quotation marks—which seems to be imperative for the plant, though rather less so for the dog—fixes nothing. It merely signals the difficulty, as if to say: "I know very well that it isn't 'really'[78] like that, but 'everything happens as if' and I don't know how to say it any other way." Hence this language must be used by all good weak reductionists, whether "functionalist" or "token physicalist," even if at the same time they endeavor to render it more scientific through the analysis and construction of formal computer languages in which indices of intentionality[79] could be used if required, defined by the success of a comprehensive task to be accomplished. Extending this thesis to the utmost, while looking for a way to translate into programming language the most specific properties that ordinary language ascribes to human beings (beliefs, desires, knowledge, consciousness), D. C. Dennett[80] was led, naturally and quite irresistibly, to envision conditions in which a computer could suffer. In such conditions, it would seem no stranger for a computer to be suffering than for a dog to be in pain, not to mention a mollusk with its rudimentary nervous system or an amoeba or a paramecium, concerning which, as for the plant, we no longer really know whether it suffers with or without quotation marks.

To put it another way, intentionality, like other mental phenomena and like all biological functions adapted to the efficient realization of purposeful tasks (respiration, digestion, reproduction, communication, and so forth), can be treated as an emergent property at the level of organization where such intentional behavior cannot be ignored without depriving the level of its specificity. The attempts in this direction are most interesting, but we must note their implicit postulate. Although it arises from a sort of unconscious anthropomorphism and animism of natural language, this type of description rests on a postulate of the intelligibility and rationality of reality that is even stronger than that which grounds a priori the process of rational explanation of nature by science. In effect, as Dennett remarks,[81] these intentions that we ascribe to natural systems are abstractions of a sort, in which a rationality resembling our own is ascribed to these systems with regard to the choice of means and their suitability to the ends pursued. Natural systems, in this case animal or plant, are supposed a priori to display rational behavior; it is this supposed rationality that enables us to understand them and to explain them using our own rationality. As was suggested by H. Simon,[82] this amounts to analyzing natural systems as if they were artifacts; that is, attributing to them the same type of rational adaptation of means to ends that we endeavor to introduce into the structure of our organized machines. To put this another way, it is an even stronger postulate than that of a rational intelligibility of nature; namely, that of an *intentional* rationality in nature. The postulate of habitual causal rationality is verified only if one circumscribes extremely limited domains where such a rationality can be observed, thanks to methods that eliminate from the field of research, by construction, any reality that might not be rational. Gregory Bateson,[83] among others, underscored the naivete of believing that nature complies with these exigencies of rationality outside the domain we demarcate with such precision so that we can impose them on it.

If we want to go further and deal now with a postulate of *intentional* rationality, the limitations that would be imposed by a method able to verify it scientifically are even stronger. Contrary to what the mystics of science often think, this postulate does not let us say whatever we will by projecting our subjective experience of intentionality onto nature, when the former is itself an object of research that we do not (yet?) know how to formalize. To remain within a scientific process, while respecting the rules of the game, entails that this intentionality be objectified, while of course maintaining the classic separation between subject and object. That is to say, it is indeed a stronger postulate, because even more restrictive.

Thus we see how, whatever end we grasp it by, scientific knowledge stretched into a unifying metaphysics produces symmetrical temptations to which the mystics of science succumb. They would recognize intentions and projects everywhere that functional meaning appears to us, even in a bacterium or an automaton, or, on the contrary, deny their existence anywhere, including in other human beings, and even within myself, when I play the game of seeing myself from the outside, objectively. These are the two pitfalls dug for us by the desire for unification and grand synthesis at any price: the spiritualist trap and the strong-reductionist trap.

The desire that science provide a comprehensive explanation plays the role, when one succumbs to it, of a temptation, lurking within scientific praxis, that is more appropriate to mysticism. It can be eluded through skeptical critique and the restoration of the requisite distance between even the most firmly established scientific theory (especially the most "established") and reality—by accepting the pluralist character of this approach, taking into account the plurality of scientific disciplines as they are practiced, always from bottom to top, but with white space, the "token" physicalism of the functionalists, or a weak reductionism, that is, without the support(?) of a unifying explanatory metaphysics; where the white spaces of language are accepted as being those that also divide the disciplines, while the dynamic of the process itself endeavors incessantly to overcome them—using language in which new white spaces appear.

Quite different are the mystical traditions in which the need to explain, as a profound motivation, proceeds explicitly from top to bottom in a process that is a priori unified, on the basis of illumination—no longer progressive elucidations as part of the search for dispersed islands of light, in the hope of increasing their size, but illumination by a primordial light to which one's perception of reality must be adapted.

# Notes

1. See Atlan, *Entre le cristal et la fumée*, Chapter 1.

2. A. J. Ayer, *Language, Truth and Logic*, 2d ed. (New York: Penguin Books, 1946).

3. In this connection, see François Jacob, *La Logique du vivant* (Paris: Gallimard, 1970); H. Atlan, *L'Organisation biologique* and *Entre le cristal et la fumée*; A. R. Peacocke, *The Physical Chemistry of Biological Organization* (Oxford: Clarendon Press, 1983). More and more authors are attempting to analyze the consequences of multilevel organization for biological theories, in particular those of ecological systems and evolutionary mechanisms. One of the difficulties stems from the fact that the different hierarchical levels can be defined in various ways, depending on which of their modes of interrelation are considered—inclusion, genealogy, or other—as well as on the fact that the individuals on which evolution acts extend to other levels (molecules, species, populations) than that of individual organisms. (For a review, see N. Eldredge and S. N. Salthe, "Hierarchy and Evolution," *Oxford Surveys in Evolutionary Biology* [1984], pp. 184–208.)

4. Particular mental states (desires, pleasures, pains, strategies that themselves imply rationality) are spontaneously ascribed to human beings, but also to a dog and, sometimes, to a fish; but what about an amoeba, or, better still, a white blood cell observed in motion under the microscope, joining with other phagocytes to surround and swallow their prey? Similarly, in certain conditions and with some reservations, one can pose the question with regard to automata. It is easier to deny all of this everywhere and invoke "molecular interactions," or to affirm its existence everywhere in the name of the "cosmic consciousness in cells." What I want to defend here is the right to draw limits that may seem to be arbitrary but that are often not far removed from those suggested by superficial observation and everyday nonscientific language.

5. The difference between experiment and experience.

6. See Chapter 6, n. 84.

7. Ludwig Wittgenstein, *Tractatus Logico-Philosophicus*, trans. D. F. Pears and B. F. McGuinness (London: Routledge and Kegan Paul, 1961), 5.1361.

8. Feyerabend, *Against Method*.

9. Willard van Orman Quine, *Word and Object* (Cambridge, Mass.: Technology Press of the Massachusetts Institute of Technology, 1960). Viewing scientific method from the perspective of its relations with truth, Quine criticized Peirce's idea that the application of the rules of the method should bring us ever closer to the truth, in the form of an ideal theory, like an asymptotic limit. For Quine, there is no reason to believe that there must exist a unique ideal result to this activity of elaborating a theory of our sense data: "We have no reason to suppose that man's

surface irritations even unto eternity admit of any one systematization that is scientifically better or simpler than all possible others. It seems likelier, if only on account of symmetries or dualities, that countless alternative theories would be tied for first place. Scientific method is the way to truth, but it affords even in principle no unique definition of truth. Any so-called pragmatic definition of truth is doomed to failure equally" (p. 23).

10. For an introduction to this chapter in physicochemical biology see, for example, E. Shechter, *Membranes biologiques. Structures, transports, bioénergétique* (Paris: Masson, 1984).

11. E. R. Kandel and J. H. Schwartz, "Molecular Biology of Learning: Modulation of Transmitter Release," *Science* 218 (1982), pp. 433–343.

12. See p. 57. For an introductory review, see *Cognitive Science* no. 9 (1985); J. L. McClelland and D. E. Rumelhart, "Distributed Memory and the Representation of General and Specific Information," *Journal of Experimental Psychology (General)* 114, no. 2 (1985), pp. 159–188; D. Broadbent, "A Question of Level: Comment on McClelland and Rumelhart," ibid., pp. 189–192; D. E. Rumelhart and J. L. McClelland, "Levels Indeed! A Response to Broadbent," ibid., pp. 193–197. See also F. Fogelman-Soulié, "Théorie des automates et modélisation des réseaux," *Jeux de réseaux* (Paris: Centre national de la recherche scientifique, 1986), pp. 13–24. In particular, the encounter between cell biology and models of artificial intelligence takes place in the study of threshold automata networks, in which learning is simulated by modifications of the strength of the connections that result from the dynamic evolution of the network. Continuing earlier work by F. Rosenblatt, M. L. Minsky, and S. Papert on perceptrons (see Atlan, *L'Organisation biologique*), by K. Nakano ("Associatron: A Model of Associative Memory," *IEEE Transactions on Systems, Man and Cybernetics*, SMC-2 [1972], pp. 380–388), by T. Kohonen ("Correlation Matrix Memories," *IEEE Transactions on Computers*, C-21 [1972], pp. 353–359), and by S. I. Amari ("Characteristics of Random Nets of Analog Neuronlike Elements," *IEEE Transactions on Systems, Man and Cybernetics*, SMC-2 [1972], pp. 643–657), simulations of self-organizing networks have made it possible to study learning mechanisms on such networks (S. I. Amari, "Learning Patterns and Pattern Sequences by Self-Organizing Nets of Threshold Elements," *IEEE Transactions on Computers*, C-21, no. 11 [1972], pp. 1197–1206). The principle is that different steady states of the network correspond to different patterns that it can learn (by modifying the connections and thresholds whose composition determines these steady states); pattern recognition then consists of the network's evolving in a spontaneous ("self-organizing") manner to the steady state that corresponds to it, in response to a stimulus that places the network in a state that is not very different but is not necessarily identical ("associative memory").

13. Peacocke, *Physical Chemistry of Biological Organization*.

14. This translation of concepts from one level to another, and the ability to derive laws (relations among concepts) observed at one level from those of another

level are the conditions posed by the philosopher E. Nagel and recently reiterated by the biologist F. J. Ayala for accepting that epistemological reduction is possible; i.e., that a discipline dealing with a particular level of organization (such as biology) can be reduced to another "basic" discipline (e.g., physics) that deals with another, more elementary level (E. Nagel, *The Structure of Science* [New York: Harcourt, Brace and World, 1961]; F. J. Ayala, "Biology and Physics: Reflections on Reductionism," *Old and New Questions in Physics, Cosmology, Philosophy and Theoretical Biology [Essays in Honour of W. Yourgrau]*, ed. A. Van der Nerve [New York: Plenum Press, 1983]).

15. Even though in the simplest cases—but only these—these quantities can be deduced from molecular structures calculated on the basis of Schrödinger's equation, not even their existence could have been deduced from it had not observation and classification by chemical methods permitted the prior definition of the notions with their normal chemical meaning, irreducible (in the sense stated) to that of the concepts of atomic physics. (See below how Feynman attacks this question in *The Feynman Lectures on Physics*; and see also M. Bunge, "Is Chemistry a Branch of Physics?" *Zeitschrift für allgemeine Wissenschaftstheorie* 13, no. 2 [1982], pp. 209–223.)

16. Peacocke, *Physical Chemistry of Biological Organization*, p. 269.

17. Martin Heidegger, *Der Satz vom Grund* (Tübingen: Pfullingen, 1958), p. 199.

18. Jerry A. Fodor (*The Language of Thought* [New York: Crowell, 1975], and "The Mind Body Problem," *Scientific American* [January 1981], pp. 124–132) is one of the authors most representative of this "functionalist" attitude. He too distinguishes "token physicalism," which corresponds fairly closely to our weak reductionism or to the unity of the processes in the reductionist method of Peacocke, continuing in the line of Nagel and Ayala, from a typological physicalism that corresponds to the epistemological reductionism of these authors, or to our strong reductionism, in which it is possible to translate into the language of physics, leaving nothing behind, all the phenomena that are today described and explained in the language of other disciplines. If this functionalist attitude makes it possible to escape the metaphysical dilemma of monism (materialist or mystical-spiritualist) and dualism (another form of spiritualism), preserving the advantages of the reductionist praxis but not yielding to the mirages of the unitary explanation, it nevertheless has the defect, at least in its initial form, of sticking too close to the metaphor of the programmable computer as the sole model for the cognitive and linguistic functions of the brain. In particular, it distorts the entire problem of representation in psychology (see Henri Atlan, "Noise, Complexity and Meaning in Cognitive Systems," *Revue internationale de systémique* 3, no. 3 (1989), pp. 237–249; and B. Shanon, "The Role of Representation in Cognition," in *Thinking*, ed. J. Bishop, J. Lockheed, and D. N. Perkins [Hillsdale, N.J.: L. Erlbaum, 1987], pp. 33–49; as well as the recent evolution in the work of Hilary Putnam [see n. 26]). The new developments in artificial intelligence, which repeat and renew the prob-

lem of self-organizing systems (see below), have enlarged the scope of this metaphor. Jerry Fodor's *The Modularity of Mind* (Cambridge, Mass.: MIT Press, 1983) seems moreover to take note of the limits of these approaches in which the only "computations" imaginable were those of finite determinist automata.

19. This may not be negligible, in that the machine's limits of performance can thus be posed in terms of computation time, complexity of the problems that can be solved, etc. Transposed to the analysis of natural systems, these measurements are even more important, in that they can be correlated with empirically observed limitations (see, n. 28).

20. A. Jacquard, "Le piège de l'addition," in *Au péril de la science* (Paris: Le Seuil, 1982), pp. 41–45.

21. D. C. Mikulecky, W. A. Wiegand, and J. S. Shiner, "Reductionism vs. Wholism: The Role of Network Coupled Models," "A Simple Network Thermodynamic Method for Series-Parallel Coupled Flows: 1. The Linear Case," *Journal of Theoretical Biology* 69 (1977), pp. 471–510; D. C. Mikulecky, "A Simple Network Thermodynamic Method for Series-Parallel Coupled Flows: 2. The Non-Linear Theory with Applications to Coupled Solute and Volume Flow in a Series Membrane," ibid., pp. 511–541.

22. On computer models and their difference from analytical mathematical models, see the discussion in H. Atlan, "Postulats métaphysiques et méthodes de recherche," *Le Débat*, no. 14 (July–August 1981), pp. 83–89; "L'émergence du sens et du nouveau," in *L'Auto-organisation, de la physique au politique*, ed. P. Dumouchel and J.-P. Dupuy (Paris: Le Seuil, 1983), pp. 115–138.

23. See n. 18.

24. This holds even more for natural systems in which there are no languages for translating from one level to another. With a very few exceptions (the description of simple chemical phenomena in the formalized language of quantum physics), it is natural language, not yet formalized, with all its ambiguities and "tangled hierarchies" (Douglas Hofstadter, *Gödel, Escher, Bach* [New York: Basic Books, 1979]), that serves as the language for translating among the various disciplines. We are closer here to the impossibilities of authentic translation from one natural language to another, as analyzed, for example, by Quine ("On the Reasons for Indeterminacy in Translation," *Journal of Philosophy* 67 [March 1970]), than to determinist and unambiguous translation algorithms, like the compilers of programming languages.

25. D. C. Dennett, "Artificial Intelligence as Philosophy and Psychology," in *Brainstorms* (Montgomery, Vt.: Bradford Books, 1978), Chapter 7, pp. 113–114.

26. In the wave of double-helix biology, Oppenheim and Putnam wrote an article on the unity of science (P. Oppenheim and H. Putnam, "The Unity of Science as a Working Hypothesis," in H. Feigl, G. Maxwell, and M. Scriven, ed. *Minnesota*

*Studies in the Philosophy of Science,* vol. 2 [Minneapolis: University of Minnesota Press, 1958], pp. 3–36) that is a veritable manifesto of triumphant strong reductionism. The language of physics, the basic discipline, will, according to them, come closer and closer to replacing those of the other disciplines. Significantly, even though they thought they had found in the infant fields of molecular biology and cybernetics the justification for the purest unitary materialism, they described the different levels of organization of reality as "levels of reduction." One of their presuppositions was that the relations between levels could be envisioned only in the form of spatial inclusion. This may be why the levels of mental process and of the disciplines that deal with it—psychology, linguistics, etc.—did not even appear among the six levels of reduction they proposed. These six levels were limited, "from bottom to top," to those of elementary particles, atoms, molecules, cells, multicellular organisms, and social groups; i.e., those among which a relationship of spatial inclusion can indeed be observed. By contrast, thought and language, not to mention feelings and beliefs, cannot be situated vis-à-vis living organisms either as the whole or as parts, from the perspective of the *spatial* relationship of parts to the whole (see p. 62). As a result, psychology and psycholinguistics cannot even have the status of scientific disciplines, even though they, quite as much as sociology, can be characterized by their objects of observation and their theories and are therefore no less scientific than the latter. For Oppenheim and Putnam, though, they seem to have the status of angelology or demonology, bent on studying the properties of things that do not exist.

Somewhat later this strong reductionism began to take hard blows from Popper's disciples and other practitioners of analytic philosophy, as is evidenced by an article on the same subject but with quite different inspiration and content: J. Agassi, "Unity and Diversity in Science," *Boston Studies in the Philosophy of Science* 4 (1969), pp. 463–519. Finally, some years later, Hilary Putnam himself ("Reductionism and the Nature of Psychology," *Cognition* 2, no. 1 [1973], pp. 131–146), making honorable amends, described his previous position, which he had shared with most philosophers of science of his generation, as "wrong." Revealingly enough, it was the analysis of the status of psychology that stood at the center of his argument. The reductionist thesis he had formerly defended implied that the human brain could be assimilated to a Turing machine and that "psychological states of a human being are Turing machine states or disjunctions of Turing machine states" (p. 136). This is the thesis he now rejects, because, inter alia, it ignored "societal beliefs and their effects on individual behavior" (p. 146). In general, his main criticism concerns the explanatory power of reductionist theories, even when they work, which decreases in proportion as they are situated on a level of organization that is more remote from (i.e., more elementary than) the more global level that is to be explained. For "from the fact that the behavior of a system can be *deduced* from its description as a system of elementary particles it does not follow that it can be *explained* from that description" (p. 131). This is because the explanation relies on the characteristics that are relevant to a situation to be explained; and these characteristics appear only on the level where the phenomena to be explained are perceived. See below for Feynman's objections to such a unitary metaphysics (n. 51).

In more recent work still, Putnam carries his break with reductionism farther and exposes the weakness of functionalism viewed as a computational theory of thought that takes the computer metaphor too seriously. This theory resurrects a reductionism of mental states, no longer to physicochemical states but rather to computational states (of some hypothetical software), which cannot themselves be reduced to the physical states of the hardware. In this vein, Putnam criticizes Chomsky and his idea of an innate organ of language and even more so Fodor and his theory of localized mental representations. He relies, inter alia, on the central role he ascribes to interpretation and the modes of formation of the convictions on which our appreciation of reality are based—as much through our scientific language as through our habitual way of using language. He abandons the last vestiges of a mentalist theory of linguistic meaning, which persisted in his 1975 papers, and, like many contemporary philosophers who have been disappointed by logical positivism, sees no more than a social construction in the meaning of words. For a review of his later position, see Hilary Putnam, "Meaning and our Mental Life," *The Kaleidoscope of Science* (Dordrecht: Reidel, 1986), pp. 17–32.

27. This is why the theory of mental objects (Jean-Pierre Changeux, *Neuronal Man: The Biology of Mind*, trans. Laurence Garey [New York: Pantheon Books, 1985]) is either self-evident, in its general form (a cerebral state corresponds to each concept, sensation, emotion, etc.), but not very helpful (so long as we do not know what constitutes cerebral states), or deceptive, if it suggests that these states can be described in terms of electrical and/or biochemical activities of groups of neurons, skipping over the levels of observation of experimental psychology, linguistics, and psycho- and sociolinguistics. Such a jump is as little justified as is that of Brian Josephson, mentioned in Chapter 1, associating mental states with the quantum states of cerebral tissue while skipping over all the intermediate levels, including that of the neuron.

28. For psychologists of this new school, the discovery of these constraints themselves, in the relevant aspect of their repercussions for mental function, could be the result of experimental studies; for example discoveries, using the techniques of experimental psychology, of invariance in the maximum number of events that our cognitive system can process simultaneously or in the relationship between short- and long-term memory and the time constants measured. Constraints and limits appearing at the integrated functional level would thereby steer research to the neurophysiological level to find their physicochemical basis there. See, for example, G. A. Miller, "The Magic Number Seven, Plus or Minus Two," in D. C. Hildum, *Language and Thought* (Princeton, N.J.: Van Nostrand, 1967), pp. 3–31.

29. See Atlan, *L'Organisation biologique*.

30. See Atlan, *Entre le cristal et la fumée*, and, for more recent studies, Dumouchel and Dupuy, *L'Auto-organisation*; H. Haken, ed. *Synergetics: An Introduction to Non-Equilibrium Phase Transitions and Self Organization in Physics, Chemistry and Biology* (Berlin: Springer-Verlag, 1978); S. German, "Notes on a Self-Organizing Machine," in G. E. Hinsdale and J. A. Anderson, ed., *Parallel Models of Associative*

*Memory* (Hillsdale, N.J.: L. Erlbaum, 1989), pp. 237–264; M. Milgram and H. Atlan, "Probabilistic Automata as a Model for Epigenesis of Cellular Networks," *Journal of Theoretical Biology* 103 (1983), pp. 523–547; T. Kohonen, *Self Organization and Associative Memories* (Berlin: Springer-Verlag, 1984); S. Wolfram, "Computation Theory of Cellular Automata," *Communications in Mathematical Physics* 96 (1984), pp. 15–57; H. Atlan, "Two Instances of Self Organization in Probabilistic Automata Networks: Epigenesis of Cellular Networks and Self-Generated Criteria for Pattern Discrimination," in J. Demongeot, E. Goles, and M. Tchuente, ed., *Dynamical Systems and Cellular Automata* (London: Academic Press, 1985), pp. 171–186; D. d'Humieres and B. A. Huberman, "Dynamics of Self Organization in Complex Adaptive Networks," in ibid., pp. 187–196.

31. See Atlan, *Entre le cristal et la fumée*, Chapter 4.

32. An older example is the overturning of scholarly classifications of the plant and animal worlds produced by the observation of intermediate forms as a result of the microscope and the biochemistry of photosynthesis.

33. Henri Atlan, "Information Theory and Self-Organization in Ecosystems," in R. E. Ulanowicz and T. Platt, ed., *Ecosystem Theory for Biological Oceanography, Canadian Bulletin of Fishing and Aquatic Science*, no. 213 (1985), pp. 187–199; "Two Instances of Self-Organization"; "Création de significations dans des réseaux d'automates," in *Jeux des réseaux*, pp. 65–79; "Self-Creation of Meaning," *Physica Scripta* 36 (1987), pp. 563–576; D. Pellegrin, "Capacités de reconnaissance des réseaux booléens aléatoires," *Cognitiva 85: De l'Intelligence artificiale aux biosciences*, pp. 419–424; H. Atlan, E. Ben Ezra, F. Fogelman-Soulié, D. Pellegrin, and G. Weisbuch, "Emergence of Classification Procedures in Automata Networks as a Model for Functional Self-Organization," *Journal of Theoretical Biology* 180, no. 3 (1986), pp. 371–380. These continue work undertaken over the course of a number of years on the dynamics of random Boolean automata networks with properties of structural self-organization (S. Kaufmann, "Behaviour of Randomly Constructed Genetic Nets: Binary Element Nets," in C. H. Waddington, ed., *Towards a Theoretical Biology*, vol. 3 [Edinburgh: Edinburgh University Press, 1970]; H. Atlan, F. Fogelman-Soulié, J. Salomon, G. Weisbuch, "Random Boolean Networks," *Cybernetics and Systems* 12 [1981], pp. 103–121; F. Fogelman-Soulié, E. Goles-Chacc, G. Weisbuch, "Specific Roles of the Different Boolean Mappings in Random Networks," *Bulletin of Mathematical Biology* 44, no. 5 [1982], pp. 715–730; F. Fogelman-Soulié, "Réseaux d'automates et morphogenèse," in Dumouchel and Dupuy, *L'Auto-organisation*, pp. 101–114; H. Atlan, "L'Emergence du nouveau et du sens," ibid., pp. 115–138; S. Kaufmann, "Boolean Systems, Adaptive Automata, Evolution," in E. Bienenstock, F. Fogelman-Soulié, and G. Weisbuch, ed., *Disordered Systems and Biological Organization* [Berlin: Springer-Verlag, 1986], pp. 339–360). These networks are composed of elements connected in such a way that each has a separate input from two neighbors and sends two output signals to two other neighbors. Each element can have only two states and always sends the same output signal to its two neighbors, equal to its current state. Thus each element

receives two binary signals from its neighbors. The network functions in parallel and discretely; i.e., after each unit time interval all elements change their state together, following the calculation rules characteristic of each of them. From the pair of binary signals they receive, each automaton calculates its next state by applying the Boolean algebraic function that characterizes it. The sixteen two-variable Boolean functions are the sixteen possible ways of establishing a correspondence between a binary number and a pair of two binary variables. This can be represented easily by listing the sixteen different ways in a matrix with two entries, each of which can be either 0 or 1, crossed against four elements that are each either 0 or 1. Except for the two constant functions (0 or 1, no matter what the input signals are), the other fourteen Boolean functions are assigned at random to the different network elements. Because the initial state of each automaton is selected at random, the initial state of the network is macroscopically homogeneous. At each time interval, each automaton calculates its next state, and the network thus evolves from one state to another until it stabilizes, usually quite rapidly, in a final state characterized by a nonhomogeneous macroscopic organization with spatial and temporal structure. The network divides into subnetworks whose elements are stable and oscillating subnetworks whose elements change their state cyclically, passing indefinitely through the same periodic sequence of states that is relatively short, taking into account the size of the network ($n$ elements) and the total number ($2^n$, large but finite) of possible states. Thus we have here a dynamic of structural self-organization in which, starting from a homogeneous initial state, we observe the emergence of spatiotemporal forms due to the evolution of the network toward one of its attractors. The number and stability properties of these attractors bring such networks close to the models of learning machines and associative memory already mentioned.

In addition, however, once installed in their final structured state in which some elements are stable and others periodic, these networks can also function as systems that are able to recognize external patterns presented to them. The patterns in question are binary sequences of 0 and 1 arranged in a particular way and imposed on an element of the network that serves as the input to the recognition system. These sequences have a perturbing role that destabilizes some stable elements. Curiously, though, the effect of some sequences is to stabilize previously oscillating elements. This phenomenon is explained by the resonance between a particular *partially* periodic structure in these sequences and a particular succession of states of different network elements connected in a particular path between the input element and that whose stabilization constitutes the "response" (at the "output") of the recognition system. The structure of the stabilizing (i.e. "recognized") sequences is only partially periodic; that is, it is made up of a series of binary signals, repeated *with variations*. Typically, such a series is represented by 0s, 1s, and asterisks (e.g., 00* 1* 01** 1*0); when this series is repeated so as to constitute a periodic binary sequence, the asterisks are replaced by random 0s and 1s. The resulting pseudo-periodic (or quasi-random) structure defines not a single sequence recognized by the stabilization of an oscillating element, as would be the case were the structure truly periodic, but rather a class of such sequences realized by all the possible permutations of replacing asterisks with a binary signal. Recognition consists of distinguishing a signal that belongs to this class from every other perturbing sequence. Hence the criterion of recognition is just a given pseudo-periodic structure whose stabilizing property is merely a consequence of the final state of organization of the network.

34. See the chapter on neurocybernetics in Atlan, *l'Organisation biologique*.

35. G. E. Hinton and J. A. Anderson, ed., *Parallel Models of Associative Memory* (Hillsdale, N.J.: L. Erlbaum, 1981); J. J. Hopfield, "Neural Networks and Physical Systems with Emergent Collective Computational Abilities," *Proceedings of the National Academy of Sciences USA* 79 (1982), pp. 2554–2558; B. A. Huberman and T. Hogg, "Adaptation and Self-Repair in Parallel Computing Structures," *Physics Review Letters* 52, no. 12 (1984), pp. 1048–1051; S. Kirkpatrick, C. D. Gelatt, M. P. Vecchi, "Optimization by Simulated Annealing," *Science* 220, no. 4598 (1983), pp. 671–680; D. H. Ackley, G. E. Hinton, T. J. Sejnowski, "A Learning Algorithm for Boltzmann Machines," *Cognitive Science* 9 (1985), pp. 147–169; D. L. Waltz and J. B. Pollack, "Massively Parallel Parsing: A Strongly Interactive Model of Natural Language Interpretation," ibid., pp. 51–74; D. Amit, H. Gutfrund, H. Sompolimsky, "Storing Infinite Number of Patterns in Spin Glass Models of Neural Networks," *Physics Review Letters* 55 (1985), pp. 1530–1533; G. Y. Vichniac, "Cellular Automata Models of Disorder and Organization," in Bienenstock, Fogelman-Soulié, and Weisbuch, *Disordered Systems and Biological Organization*, pp. 3–20; P. Peretto, "Mécanique statistique et réseaux de neurones formels," in *Jeux de réseaux*, pp. 97–106; R. Rammal, G. Toulouze, and M. A. Virasoro, "Ultrametricity for Physicists," *Review of Modern Physics* 58 (1986), p. 765; G. Toulouse, "Verres de spins et applications de la physique statistique aux problèmes complexes," in F. Fogelman-Soulié and M. Milgram, ed., *Les Théories de la complexité* (Paris: Le Seuil, 1991).

36. Atlan, *Entre le cristal et la fumée*, p. 144; "Noise, Complexity, and Meaning in Cognitive Systems."

37. Wittgenstein, *Tractatus* 5.5563; see also below, Chapter 7, p. 306.

38. D. R. Hofstadter, "Analogies, Roles, and Slippability: Fluid Transfer of Concepts between Frameworks," *Cognitiva 85: From Artificial Intelligence to the Biosciences* (Paris: Cesta-Afcet-Arc, 1985), vol. 1, p. 47.

39. M. P. Austin and B. G. Cook, "Ecosystem Stability: A Result from an Abstraction Simulation," *Journal of Theoretical Biology* 45 (1974), pp. 435–458.

40. On the notion of dynamic attractors, cf. R. Thom, *Structural Stability and Morphogenesis: An Outline of a General Theory of Models*, trans. D. H. Fowler (Reading, Mass.: W. A. Benjamin, 1975); and D. Ruelle, "Les attracteurs étranges," *La Recherche*, no. 108 (February 1980), pp. 132–144.

41. G. E. Michaels and C. Carello, *Direct Perception* (Englewood Cliffs, N.J.: Prentice-Hall, 1981).

42. See below, Chapter 5, pp. 209–225.

43. P. Marty, *L'Ordre psychosomatique* (Paris: Payot, 1980).

44. P. Marty, *Mouvements individuels de Vie et de Mort* (Paris: Payot, 1976).

45. G. Canguilhem, "Vie," *Encyclopedia Universalis*, vol. 16 (Paris, 1977), pp. 764–769.

46. See below, Chapter 5, p. 214.

47. A. Bourguignon, "Fondements neurobiologiques pour une théorie de la psychopathologie. Un nouveau modèle?" *Psychiatrie de l'enfant* 24, no. 2 (1981), pp. 445–540.

48. Hofstadter, *Gödel, Escher, Bach*.

49. See n. 26.

50. E. Bienenstock, "Dynamics of Central Nervous Systems," in J. P. Aubin, D. Saari, and K. Sigmund, ed., *Dynamics of Macrosystems* (Berlin: Springer-Verlag, 1985), pp. 3–20.

51. Richard Feynman, in Feynman, Robert B. Leighton, and Matthew Sands, *The Feynman Lectures on Physics* (Reading, Mass.: Addison-Wesley, 1963), cannot avoid the question of reductionism on the basis of physics, "the most fundamental and all-inclusive of the sciences...the present-day equivalent of what used to be called *natural philosophy*, from which most of our modern sciences arose." Significantly, those other sciences (described as "sisters" rather than as "daughters") are chemistry, biology, astronomy, geology, and *psychology*, whereas the "relation of physics to engineering, industry, society, and war, or even the most remarkable relationship between mathematics and physics" are merely mentioned, due to "lack of space" (vol. 1, chapter 3, p. 1); the last of these is discussed at length in Feynman's *The Character of Physical Law* (Cambridge, Mass.: MIT Press, 1967). For Feynman, the question of the theoretical grounding of these sciences by physics returns as an imperative or an explanatory ideal that comes on its own. But he adds himself to the list of authors already cited, philosophers and scientists, who defend a nontriumphalist position, composed of the pragmatic coexistence of a de facto reductionism as the moving force of scientific explanation in the process of generation, along with an acute awareness of the obstacles to elaborating a theory of this reductionism and having it accepted as the metaphysical foundation of a unitary theory of science. These obstacles are of two sorts. Some are connected with the aforementioned difficulty of translating the phenomena studied by the other disciplines and the laws they have established into the language of physics. Even the case of its nearest relative, inorganic chemistry (see Bunge, "Is Chemistry a Branch of Physics?"), shows how these difficulties are not totally overcome in practice, even if they are in principle. The other kind of obstacle is even more important: it is related to physics's property of not integrating history, in that physical laws (including those of evolution) are supposed to be themselves eternal and outside of time. For

Feynman, only a physics that takes account of a *possible history of physical laws*, by asking the question, "Here are the laws of physics; how did we get there?" could speak of the same problems as sciences that incorporate history, such as astronomy (the history of the universe), geology (the history of the earth), and biology (evolution). This is a very strong indication that, unlike strong reductionists as well as spiritual physicists, Feynman does not fall into the realist error of assimilating the description of reality given by physics to reality itself. This appears quite clearly in his conclusion, which, *taken out of context*, might be charged with being antiscientific or even mystical. In effect, for Feynman, if there is a unity of nature (and not of science), it is that of a glass of wine in which one can certainly describe various phenomena: physical (fluid mechanics, optics, atomic physics), astronomical and geological (of the glass), of course biological (fermentation), and even psychological (the pleasure of inebriation). But these sciences are only the effect of our minds, which, for the sake of convenience, divide their objects of investigation into segments—physics, biology, geology, astronomy, psychology, etc.—although nature knows none of that.

52. If science implies belief, let it be what Feynman suggested as its definition: "Science is the belief in the ignorance of experts.... Science doesn't teach anything: experience teaches it. If they say to you: 'Science has shown such and such,' you might ask, 'How does science show it? How did the scientists find out? How? What? Where?'...And you have as much right as anyone else, upon hearing about the experiments (but be patient and listen to *all* the evidence), to judge whether a sensible conclusion has been arrived at. In a field which is so complicated that true science is not yet able to get anywhere, we have to rely on a kind of old-fashioned wisdom, a kind of definite straightforwardness. I am trying to inspire the teacher at the bottom to have some hope, and some self-confidence in common sense and natural intelligence. The experts who are leading you may be wrong.... I think we live in an unscientific age in which almost all the buffeting of communications and television, words, books, and so on, are unscientific. As a result, there is a considerable amount of intellectual tyranny in the name of science" (Richard P. Feynman, "What is Science," *The Physics Teacher* [September 1969], p. 320).

53. H. Putnam, criticizing the theses he had once defended (see n. 26), rightly observed that the fact "that these two sides of psychology [that which is "extremely close to biology," and that produced mainly by "societal beliefs and their effects in individual behavior"] are not distinguished very clearly is itself an effect of reductionism" ("Reductionism and the Nature of Psychology," p. 146).

54. H. Atlan, "Modèles d'organisation cérébrale," *Revue d'EEG et de Neurophysiologie* 5, no. 2 (1975), pp. 182–193.

55. Y. R. Chao, "Models in Linguistics and Models in General," in *Logic, Methodology and Philosophy of Science*, ed. Ernest Nagel, Patrick Suppes, and Alfred Tarski (Stanford, Calif.: Stanford University Press, 1962), p. 558.

56. Ibid., p. 559.

57. See Chapter 5, p. 164.

58. Michel Serres, *Le Passage du Nord-Ouest* (Paris: Minuit, 1980).

59. Feynman, *Character of Physical Law.*

60. J.-M. Lévy-Leblond, "Physique," in *Encyclopaedia Universalis*, vol. 13 (Paris, 1977), pp. 4–8; "Physique et mathématiques," in *Penser les mathématiques* (Paris: Le Seuil, 1982). These relations consist simultaneously of a "mathematical polymorphism of physics" (a single physical law can be expressed in different mathematical formulas, equivalent from the mathematical point of view but different from the perspective of physics) and a "plurivalence of mathematics in physics" (the same equations govern quite different phenomena, belonging to physical domains that have no obvious connection).

61. For J. Ullmo ("The Agreement between Mathematics and Physical Phenomena," in M. Bunge, ed., *The Critical Approach to Science and Philosophy* [London: Collier-Macmillan, 1964], pp. 350–359), it is in the structure of the group, in the sense of set theory, that one must seek the common denominator of our ratiocination and our sense data, which permit us to perceive repetition and regularity. That is what grounds the accord between mathematics and the nature of things in physics. I do not know whether this resolves the problem or whether it is instead merely shifted, to the extent that the structure of the group is itself, like every logical structure, already an abstraction. It would in some fashion be the privileged locale in which the preestablished harmony unfolds.

62. "Science, by its successes, has engendered in our culture two attitudes that are hard to reconcile, and the dangers it poses...give rise to a third. Impressed by the correctness of the predictions of physics, we respect the verdict of experience. On the other hand (as were demonstrated by the celebrations of the centenary of Einstein's birth, in the spring of 1979), we render homage to the greatest physicist of the twentieth century as to a hero of pure thought, fantasy, and imagination" (P. Jacob, *De Vienne à Cambridge: l'héritage du positivisme logique de 1950 à nos jours* [Paris: Gallimard, 1980], p. 10).

63. The other motivating factor is the need for control and manufacture, which subsists in all cases, even when scientific and technical discourse renounces the need to explain.

64. Oppenheim and Putnam, "The Unity of Science as a Working Hypothesis."

65. Ibid.

66. Ibid.

67. The metaphors of top down and bottom up, so often used in this context, are ambiguous, and we must specify the sense in which we are using them. In organizations into different levels of integration, as well as in the question of the possible reduction of one discipline to another, all the way to physics, said to be the

"basic" discipline, the "lower" levels (the "foundations") designate those that are less integrated, down to the "lowest," that of the elementary constituents, which supports the entire edifice; whereas the "highest" level designates the most integrated one. It is in this sense that we are using the metaphor here. But *top* and *bottom* are often used to designate, respectively, the abstract and the concrete, or the general and the particular, so that a deductive method is viewed as moving downward, "top down," whereas induction is a "bottom up" process. This, for example, is what Gaston Bachelard does when he analyzes the role of mathematics in *The New Scientific Spirit*, trans. Arthur Goldhammer (Boston: Beacon Press, 1964) as that of an "applied rationality," or even, in *The Philosophy of No*, trans. G. C. Waterston (New York: Orion Press, 1968), of a "descending rationality." This usage can be assimilated to the previous, moreover, by considering abstraction to be a form of inclusive generalization and integration (even if the inclusion is not spatial). Furthermore, as a characteristic function of our thought, it can be viewed as one of the emergent properties produced by the organization of our cognitive apparatus. As we shall see (Chapter 5, n. 102), this ambiguity, in a reversal of perspective, explains why the mystic process can be seen as a progressive elevation toward illumination, whereas that of the scientist is seen as a downward motion—precisely that of descending, empirico-logical rationality, in which logical deduction finally overcomes, in some fashion, empiricism. We shall attempt to demonstrate how this inversion is false when it concerns not the mechanisms of discovery (in which anything can happen) but rather the logic respectively appropriate to mystical and scientific discourse.

68. See, for example, the works by Lecourt, *L'Ordre et les Jeux*, and by Jacob, *De Vienne à Cambridge*.

69. Above we called them the "foundations" or "bases" on which scientific knowledge rests. It is always risky to take such metaphors literally, as is attested by Heidegger's *Der Satz vom Grund*. There the implantation of a principle in the earth, its *grounding* in the *ground*, where it becomes a "basic principle," is not far from an ideology of the Fatherland as the "foundation" of civilization. The diversity of languages, with their untranslatable specificity, like that of the modes of knowledge, makes it possible to escape too rigorous a conditioning. For example, the Hebrew *av*, which means both principle and father, relates to a masculine generative connotation rather than to the rooting of plants in Mother Earth.

70. Using the terminology of Jürgen Habermas, *Knowledge and Human Interests*, trans. Jeremy J. Shapiro (London: Heinemann, 1978); see Chapter 5, p. 160.

71. Even Bachelard's "non-Cartesian epistemology" (*The New Scientific Spirit*) retains these modalities that condition the scientific method. It is the simplicity of the natural object that disappears, as well as substance, replaced by a reality that is constructed, progressively and by "rectifications," by an applied rationality in which theory and mathematics, brought face to face with experience, play a privileged role. Although Bachelard has been accused of idealism—a charge open to debate—the fact that he saw in quantum physics a "dematerialization of matter" led

him to oppose only a "naive materialism." On the contrary, he vigorously opposed the spiritualist confusion—even in the study of the scientific "spirit"—that claimed to find in nuclear physics the alchemical tradition of transmutation (Gaston Bachelard, L'Engagement rationaliste [Paris: Presses universitaires de France, 1972], p. 67). His "non-Cartesian epistemology" must be understood as the rejection of naive Cartesianism and not as a mysticism of science or a sort of scientific irrationalism such as we encounter today, in which the "East" is the attracting pole and the "Cartesian West" the repelling pole. For naivete spares no camp. In the same fashion, the subject-object relationship serves as the spearhead for this scientific irrationalism. We have already seen the confusion between the role of observation in physics and that of the subjectivity of the observers. In anthropology, too, the analysis of societies in which the subject-object distinction is not so clear-cut as in the West (M. Mauss, Louis Dumont) does not lead anthropological science, which remains a Western science, to renounce its own principle of objectivity.

72. See below, Chapter 5.

73. The phenomenon of Carl Sagan's Cosmos is an example of these frescoes. It can serve as a model for all attempts to vulgarize scientific theories of the origin of the universe and evolution, removed from the experimental context in which they were born. Within this context, they continue to play an operational role by virtue of the objections made to them and the attempts to refute them. Outside this context, by contrast, they typically play the role of mystifying and occluding unitary explanations against which A. Jacquard (Au péril de la science), distinguishing established science from science as process, correctly warns.

74. See the precise and documented critique of the use of different forms of teleological language in biology and philosophy, as related to the functional explanations and descriptions of life, in Réjane Bernier and Paul Pirlot, Organe et Fonction (Paris: Maloine, 1977).

75. P. Pirlot and J. Pottier, "Encephalization and Quantitative Brain Composition in Bats in Relation to their Life-Habits," Review of Canadian Biology 36 (4) (1977), pp. 321–336.

76. See, for example, Dennett, Brainstorms, and H. L. Dreyfus, What Computers Can't Do, 2nd ed. (New York: Harper and Row, 1979).

77. In addition to D. C. Dennett, already noted, we should mention a number of studies still at the stage of posing the problem, such as C. I. J. M. Stuart, "Physical Models of Biological Information and Adaptation," Journal of Theoretical Biology 113 (1985), pp. 441–454; and M. A. Boden, "Artificial Intelligence and Biological Reductionism," in M. W. Ho and P. T. Saunders, ed., Beyond Neo-Darwinism: An Introduction to the New Evolutionary Paradigm (New York and London: Academic Press, 1984), pp. 317–329.

78. But note that I am myself forced to put quotation marks around really, because the issue is precisely the status of reality vis-à-vis the language of description.

79. The use of feed-forward and feedback loops in cybernetic systems is a first step in this direction.

80. D. C. Dennett, *Brainstorms*. Note that his negative answer to the question of whether a computer can feel pain does not stem from any intrinsic limitation to the possibilities of a machine as compared with those of a living organism, but rather from the impossibility of establishing an unambiguous and operational link, translatable into an algorithm, between neurophysiological data on pain and our subjective experience of pain. We could perfectly well simulate on a machine the behavior of someone who suffers and says so, by incorporating into it a structure that reproduces our full neurophysiological knowledge of pain paths. But we still would not be certain that the machine was suffering, even when it said so (see also Wittgenstein on the meaning of "I am suffering," referred to in Chapter 9).

81. Dennett, *Brainstorms*, p. 28.

82. H. Simon, *The Science of the Artificial* (Cambridge, Mass.: MIT Press, 1969).

83. Gregory Bateson, *Men Are Grass: Metaphor and the World of Mental Process* (tape of the Lindisfarne Fellows, June 9, 1980), *The Lindisfarne Letter* 11 (West Stockbridge, Mass.: Lindinsfarne Press, 1980). See Chapter 4, n. 7; Chapter 7, p. 299.

# Chapter 3

# Mysticism and Rationality

Both the adjective *mystical* and noun *mystic* have two opposing connotations.[1] One of these, pejorative, designates the approximation, imprecision, and lack of rigor that take shelter behind the existence of some hidden reality or discourse. Only faith in this reality or discourse allows access to it, because it is incommunicable and its origin is mysterious. In this sense, the hidden and mysterious paper over the unintelligible, the arbitrary, and, carried to the extreme, just about anything. They provoke a strong suspicion of unmastered error, of falsehood, even of trickery: here mysticism goes hand in hand with mystification.

But there is another, positive, connotation, that which has always been attributed to those called, often without any clear reason, "authentic mystics," who are supposed to have access to uncommon experiences and for whom the hidden and mysterious, although unintelligible, indicate something real—or, at least, an interesting, original, and "true" psychic experience.

This positive connotation of mystic experience has been reinforced in recent years by two related phenomena. During the 1960s, the psychedelic revolution in the United States provided tens of thousands of persons, generally young and raised in the positivist and pragmatic canons of Western civilization, with direct and rapid access, by means of hallucinogenic substances, to experiences that (as was soon noticed) reproduced at least in part the content of those described by mystics of all religious traditions. Although these observations had their precursors, noted by writers and poets like Aldous Huxley and Henri Michaux, or by marginal experimentalists such as Watson and Heim, they had not strongly penetrated the daily life of our civilization. For at least two years in the 1960s, though, the systematic use of nonaddictive and non–habit-forming hallucinogens (LSD, mescaline, psilocybin, and so on) diffused through the most diverse social milieus, leading individuals who had were in no way prepared for it to the discovery of "other" realities. It is the mass and reproducible character of these experiences that gave them an "objective" reality; whereas formerly, in the best of cases, if their reality had not been denied pure and simple, they had been relegated to the practically impenetrable subjectivity of illuminati, poets, and artists.

This experience had an enormous cultural effect, including criticizing and relativizing the philosophical and scientific tradition that Western thinkers had previously considered to be the sole reference, the unique standard against which the traditions of other civilizations were to be evaluated, if they were not simply ignored. In particular, the Far Eastern traditions of India, China, and Japan—soon followed by the West's own mystical traditions, Christian, Jewish, and Muslim, rediscovered and reevaluated—penetrated mass culture in the United States and then in Europe. The traditional foundations of the critical method (law of noncontradiction, subject-object dualism, the postulate of objectivity, the reductionist materialism of the experimental method) were called into question and juxtaposed to the illumination of the mystics' cosmic consciousness, which almost anyone could henceforth discover thanks to hallucinogens and techniques of meditation.

Curiously enough, however, this new attitude toward existence, this new source of values, unifications, and exclusions (certainly new to the West) soon came to need to justify itself and itself became the object of rationalization: it is not easy to escape one's own socio-cultural conditioning.[2]

While India, China, and Japan avidly absorbed the cultural products of Europe and America that accompanied industrialization and technological development, Western societies absorbed foreign traditions, but without ceasing to be American or European society. Here the capacity to metabolize everything, which characterizes the culture of these societies, is expressed by ambiguous rationalizations, rationalizations of the irrational that penetrate not only the masses and the media, but also the more or less aristocratic circles of "enlightened" thinkers. Among the latter there seems to have developed a syncretism combining the rational elucidations of the "conscientious" scientist and the illumination of the mystic: F. Capra's *Tao of Physics*, R. Ruyer's *Princeton Gnosis*, and, more recently, the proceedings of the Cordoba colloquium are among its most familiar manifestations. In defense of these confusions—perhaps explaining if not justifying them—may be cited the fact that the traditional teachings of the East, unlike

Christianity, did not inherit a tradition of opposing and resisting empirical science and critical methods. What is more, access to these teachings is not embarrassed by a prior Faith in a personal God.[3] Instead, these discourses about Reality, the Infinite, Nonduality, designated by exotic names (Brahma, Tao, etc.) serve more as invitations to inquiry than as crystallizations of dogma. But this functions only at the infantile level of common catechisms. We need merely open the books and study them in their own language to recognize two facts:

1.  All mystical traditions that attempt to rationalize their discourse come up against the same problems (even if they resolve them differently): infinite-finite, impersonal-personal, divine-human. Works such as those by H. Corbin,[4] Gershom Scholem,[5] and contemporary Christian mystics who encountered Hindu spirituality[6] attest at the same time to the common foundations and individuality of these traditions. The differences in the solutions they propound are initially no more than different accents on one or another pole of a shared dialectic. But these different stresses lead, in the realm of practical behavior and legislation, to the enormous contrasts and distances that separate the sociocultural reality of the civilizations that are nourished by them (unless we consider their doctrines to be rationalizations of these sociocultural products as they relate to the discovery of this common ground of mystic experience).

2.  The Reality involved here (Brahma, the *Einsof* of the kabbala, the theologians' *Deus absconditus*) has nothing in common, save for the word itself, with the reality uncovered by scientific research, even though, in both cases, the object is to expose a hidden reality. For mystics, the former is the invocation of an infinite transcendence, one, absolute, compared to which the latter is multiplicity and relativity, division, fall, and illusion (*maya*) for those who believe implicitly in the truth of its appearances. The unifying endeavors of physics, aimed at finding a unified theory and single formula, must not deceive us: far from designating an Absolute whose immediate and ineffable attainment is the province of the Illumination of the saint (or prophet, or redeemed), they are the result, on the contrary, of an empirical-mathematical confrontation in which nothing is supposed to escape quantitative discourse, determined by the conditions of measurement and mensurability.

This does not rule out studying these traditions. They do not stop at the ecstatic experience of the ineffable, but call on the intellect and on discursive reason, probably ever since their origins. They did not wait for the development of Western science and philosophy to make use of the human rational faculties, which were nourished by them and which carried them forward and renewed them over the centuries. This is why dialogue is possible between the Eastern traditions and the scientific and philosophical tradition—if it is carried out on the basis of the differences between them rather than their similarities, sustained by the light of reason rather than by the dazzle of Illumination.

It is because the facile comparisons of the syncretism of modern science and Oriental traditions are prejudicial both to Western rationalism and to Eastern traditions that we ought to take them apart. We should make these dialogues possible because they can be fruitful and profitable, but we must also respect the rules of the game that each of the parties plays on its own field, so that the metafield on which they meet is not merely a fusion where both disappear. This enterprise is clearly risky and unavoidably tentative, in that it consists of laying down rules (metarules) for the game (metagame) in which games with different rules are set to playing each other! But the enterprise is also necessary, because, on the one hand, these games with their different rules (those of scientific research and those of mystical Illumination) can no longer ignore each other, while, on the other hand, their shameless interpenetration can only overturn the chessboard, shuffle the cards, making it impossible to continue any game or even to begin it.

This is why it is important to locate, even if only approximately, the type of coherence admitted by mystical traditions and that by which their rationality, when manifested, is different from scientific rationality. The question does not reduce to that of the rational and the irrational that are encountered, in varying degrees, everywhere, but rather to that of the relationship with reality, of concrete-abstract relations, of the rapport between reason and reality, between representations (theoretical, formal or analogical, artistic, revealed) and those things they represent and from which they flow: the belief in the reality of these representations and the question of the boundaries of delirium, illumination, and theoretical explanation.

## The Rights of Irrationalism: Unreason and Antireason

In this domain, simplifications are not acceptable: rationalization versus irrationalism; the nonduality that characterizes Oriental thought versus the Judeo-Christian dualism of Creator and creation, subject and object; polytheism or atheism versus monotheism; and so on. In fact, the nonduality of the Orient is perhaps not as contradictory to certain Western mysticisms as is believed.[7] The multiplicity of divine names and persons in the most Orthodox Jewish kabbalistic tradition sometimes seems to come close to polytheism if not indeed to atheism.[8] All of this must lead to extreme caution when considering vulgarizing summaries, even in the positive sense of the term. Rather than trying to mix all of this together, an impossible task in the limits of a single chapter or even a single book, I shall attempt to characterize to the extent possible, by successive steps, the type of relations that exist between mystical traditions and the use of reason, so as to differentiate them from the use of reason by Western scientific praxis.

Anthropologists and philosophers have made attempts at such differentiations.[9] We shall return to them. But our perspective here is different. For the moment we shall not consider the hidden rationality of magical or ritual practices that anthropology sets out to discover. Instead, we shall be looking for the type of conscious rationality (or irrationality) expressed in the texts and discourses of mystical traditions.

The relations between these traditions and reason are multiform and frequently ambiguous. Sometimes it is a matter of a more or less violent rejection of reason and a systematic search for the irrational as a means to break out of the confinement imposed by reason and, especially, rational discourse. Over the centuries, the obligations of rhetoric, the snares of discourse, and the increasingly abstract and disincarnate character of formal (mathematical, philosophical) languages that try to escape these snares have persuaded many sensible people, those who have come into contact with the concrete presence of experiences that are more or less overwhelming and ineffable, of the limited and deceptive character of rational argument. Of course the difficulty arises from the fact that these individuals nevertheless feel the need to speak and to communicate the content of these experiences, to recognize themselves among similarly "turned-on" individuals,[10] and, if possible, to group themselves into (religious) communities.

At the outset, though, it is the massive and overwhelming character of the experience that lights the fuse; no normal form of expression seems to be appropriate, except perhaps (militant) silence or paradoxical and contradictory discourses that are themselves soon (paradoxically, at a second level) systematized into an antireason in which a certain regularity in the use of logical contradiction can be recognized and theorized into a relatively coherent discourse. This, too, is quickly recognized as limiting and inadequate and must in its turn be denounced as a new trap of words and reason. Leaving aside rare exceptions, these games of hide-and-seek generally end up in platitudes and catechisms of no great interest or utility other than serving as stereotyped professions of faith for religious communities that no longer preserve more than a distant recollection of the initial experiences, from which their "presence" has almost completely dissipated.

This, it seems to me, is why this conscious and militant antireason lacks serious manifestation in the modern West outside of various forms of art and of the realization (or attempts to realize) the passions.

Only the modern West is so deficient, however; the mystical traditions of the Orient and the medieval West furnish us with texts and testimony in which there is still something living, in which something is said through the ruptures and fissures of discourse. When we receive these texts and testimonies in the here and now, though, it is difficult for us to separate their "mystical" value from their artistic value, as if esthetic experience were the only "presence" commonly accepted and recognized in the modern West. This experience, like that of the passions, certainly has a sexual component; this is why psychoanalysis is the most recent avatar of these games of reason-antireason, of language-antilanguage, in which the platitudinous catechisms follow profound illuminations. This is also why the question about the relationship between science and psychoanalysis, fertilizing the same ground, continues to be asked, leading to clearly different positions with conclusive stakes, such as those of Freud, Jung, and Lacan. It is probably not by chance that at Cordoba, among the spokesmen of non-Western mystical traditions and physicists of already-perverted new alliances, Jungian psychoanalysts provided the third force required for the "lay" and "scientific" religious discourse whose need is regularly expressed in the types of manifestations discussed in the introduction to this volume.

Just as the sexual requires a certain hygiene (that of Eros, where modesty plays a major role), so too is it necessary to distinguish, within these manifestations, the assumed and militant antireason, which does not lack grandeur and richness, from simple stultifying unreason.

In religious phenomena, the search for rationality and demand for the irrational often overlap whatever is the object of the cult or the origin of the phenomenon: a god, God, an ideology, Science and Reason itself. Only in its militant antirational mystical form, if one may say so, can the religious phenomenon be considered as a particular case of subordination to the passions or to a passion, perhaps to what Christians call the Passion. All passionate spiritualities share a common hermetic character that cannot be transmitted to anyone who is not inflamed by it. On the other hand, the religious phenomenon, as the locus of belief and dogma, is often expressed in a discourse that considers itself to be rational, at which point it evidently stops claiming to be irrationality or systematic antirationality. But the rationality that it asserts is only apparent, because it merely uses language and rhetorical forms to develop the dogmas and mysteries whose contents are posited a priori as so many mysterious acts of faith that are inaccessible to reason or experience.

It is precisely in this form, which asserts its rational grounding or justification, that the religious phenomenon comes closest to a form of unreason or even delirium. On the contrary, in its most valuable aspect the religious phenomenon must be considered to be surrender to a passion, usually grandiose, that can be transmitted and expressed only by its own existence, just as artists, to express themselves, can use only their own irreducible mode of expression. In other words, it is essentially a phenomenon of which one cannot speak, as is regularly witnessed by the subjects of the mystical experiences of all traditions; just as one cannot speak of music to someone who has never heard it, nor of painting to someone who cannot see. One can describe the exterior manifestations of this religious passion, evolve hypotheses concerning the processes that trigger it, interpret it in psychoanalytic, physiological, or sociological terms; but all who are possessed by it speak of its denaturation by language—what is said does not express the reality because the reality in question is ineffable.

"All my life I have spent among the Sages," said Rabbi Shimon (son of Rabban Gamaliel, the head of the Sanhedrin), "and I have found nothing better for the body than silence; not exegesis, but practice, is the main thing. Multiplying words leads to error."[11]

"The tao is silent," declared Raymond M. Smullyan, a mathematician and philosopher, in his book of that title,[12] which nevertheless extended to 225 pages, marked by a talent and humor that allowed him to present a Western discourse on this silence from the East![13] For his part, the Benedictine monk H. Le Saux, who became the Indian Swami Abhishiktananda, in contact, inter alia, with a sacred mountain where he lived the life of a hermit, and also with the two gurus Gnanananda and Ramana Maharshi, found that he was too "talkative,"[14] because he felt a need to teach and communicate.

The mystical experience, like that of Eros, is one of fusion-and-separation, or of separation-and-fusion, for which discursive language is poorly suited. The latter can certainly separate to better reunite or reunite to better separate in scholarly dialectic. But by no means can it separate and reunite at the same time; and even less because it wishes to be rigorous and approximate as closely as possible the logical ideal based on the principles of identity and noncontradiction. In this, such a language differs from poetic and sacred languages that can do so, playing incessantly on themselves between one level and another and presenting themselves straight off as antinomic and contradictory. As we shall see, it is understood that what they want to say is what they do not say, and vice versa. For Le Saux, his relationship with the gurus (and with the mountain) was the occasion of his experience of the "mystery of unity," of nonduality; of what the Zen master Suzuki called (in a manner scarcely audible in the West) "absolute subjectivity," in which interior and exterior are unified in the overtones of the self, beyond even the encounter with Eros, which is merely "a fusion where two become one." Between guru and disciple, Le Saux speaks not of "fusion or even of acquired unity," but of a return "to the plane of the original nonduality."

> Advaita (nonduality) always remains incomprehensible to someone who has not first lived it, existentially, in his encounter with the guru.
> ...What do the words used by the guru mean? Their entire power resides in their internal resonance. Seeing it, hearing it, one attains the epiphany of the self, this foundation of the self to which each of us aspires in essence, even if we do not know it. The true guru is inside one who, with neither sound nor words, renders audible the attentive soul, the "you are that," the tat-vam-asi of the vedic Rishis. And this true guru projects himself in an external form, whatever it may be, at the desired moment in order to help cross the ultimate step.[15]

Descriptions of this sort can be found in all mystical traditions; the differences among them turn on the ethical question of what should be done next.[16] We shall return to this. It is always a matter of the same impossibility of using words to speak of what words cannot describe, alongside the necessity of doing so if one wishes to leave silence behind. Asking about the possibility of understanding the word god as meaningful, Emmanuel Levinas encounters in a philosophical context the same impossible exigencies of "another thought that—neither assimilation nor integration—would not reduce the absolute with its novelty to the 'already known' and would not compromise the novelty of the new by deflowering it in the correlation between being thought and being what the thought imitates." For Levinas, these needs are satisfied by "the idea of the Infinite in us that 'contains more than it can contain, more than its capacity of cogito,'" that "thinks in some fashion beyond what it thinks."[17] Levinas's wager consists of trying to express this using the discourse of Western philosophy, following—and profoundly renewing—the tradition of a long line of Jewish and Christian philosophers.

In another context, Lacan's struggle with and against language derives from the fact that the acquisition of language is indispensable to the maturation of the infant and alone saves the child from psychosis; but at the same time it is achieved only by repression and denial, by the installation of the lure of the conscience, such that, carried to the extreme, only psychotics are still in touch with their truth.[18] One hopes to find the response to the challenge in the psychoanalytic technique of listening to what the words do not say but mean (or to what they say but do not mean, depending on where the subject of *meaning* is). This is why Lacan could not avoid the question of the relationship between psychoanalysis, on the one hand, and mysticism and magic, on the other.[19]

It is probably in the Orient that one encounters the most radical type of responses to this impossibility of simultaneous silence and speech that mystics confront, however. Words cannot contain the absolute, but words are indispensable to any expression of the absolute, because other modes of expression (gestures, images, even silence itself) also have their limitations. A kabbalist of the early twentieth century[20] explained this obligation of concealing "secret" wisdom (which nevertheless fills the libraries) by reference to the talmudic principle of "revealing one ell while hiding two," or "if a word has any value silence is worth twice as much."[21] He gave three reasons, in increasing order of importance, for this concern to disclose only by concealing and to speak only by remaining silent. The first involves opportunity: not speaking so as to say nothing and saying only what is necessary in a given context and toward a determined goal. The second concerns precisely the ineffable character of what is to be spoken, for "language can master nothing of the properties of these things, because of their extreme delicacy and spirituality." Only certain individuals receive the heaven-sent gift (and permission) to "wrap" these things in words and explain them in a fashion such that "only they will understand them who are suitable for understanding them." Rabbi Shimon bar Yohai (traditionally considered to be the author of the *Zohar*[22]), and Rabbi Isaac Luria, the founder of the sixteenth-century school of Safed, have been considered to be the most accomplished privileged vehicles of these wrappers and garments in a systematic form. This is why their works have become the indispensable intermediaries for all who would penetrate "the interiority and soul of the Torah," to climb the ladder for themselves, "with the aid of books and teachers."[23] The third reason for hiding this wisdom concerns its possible misuse by those "who do not fear the Name [the Tetragrammaton]" and, diverting it from its object of knowledge and illumination, would reduce it to manipulation for the sake of private interests; viz., the dangers of idolatrous and superstitious perversions such as have appeared, inter alia, in what is known as "practical Kabbala,"[24] a close relative of magic and sorcery.

Thus in Jewish mysticism, too, illumination is at the same time the final destination in the ascesis that aims at ethics and sainthood only and the point of departure in the systematic exposition focused on teaching (Torah) and rational knowledge. Unlike Far Eastern traditions, however, the Jewish exoteric tradition itself eclipses this preoccupation. Illumination is part of its esoteric aspect, while, from the outside, Jewish tradition can be known and lived principally through talmudic legalism, tempered by midrashic legends and scholastic rationalizations of the Maimonidean type. Nevertheless, this experience of illumination by the unity that fills all, which cannot be expressed in words but must nevertheless be handed on, has given rise to the most suggestive descriptions and exhortations by rabbis of the most Orthodox circles, who to this day continue to be nourished by the kabbalistic tradition.[25]

The systematic distortion of language by the use of contradiction and paradox, and even of nonsense, to continually undo what an affirmation could establish, without, however, making do with a simple negative—such is the method used in the attempt to grapple with this impossibility. Each tradition uses this method in its own fashion. The ancient Jewish texts, the Midrash and Kabbala, employ a complex exegetical tradition—it too non-Western—with four levels of meaning, where positive and negative, affirmation and negation, presence and absence are interwoven in a subtle tissue that I have elsewhere endeavored to analyze.[26]

But except for silence and for works of art in which the explicit appears only to manifest the unsaid, Zen *koans* are probably the best example of mystical antireason. We find in them the most provocative uses of paradox and contradiction. To offer one example among so many, quite typical:

> Once as Yaoshan was sitting, Shitou saw him and asked: "What are you doing here?" Yaoshan said, "I'm not doing anything." Shitou said: "Then you are just sitting idly." Yaoshan said: "If I were idly sitting, that would be doing something."
>
> Shitou said: "You said you are not doing; what aren't you doing?" Yaoshan said: "Even the saints don't know."[27]

Or again: "Toku-san, still another great one, used to wield his staff freely even before a monk had opened his mouth. In fact, Toku-San's famous declaration runs thus: 'Thirty blows of my stick when you have something to say; thirty blows just the same when you have nothing to say.'"[28]

One might think we were dealing with infantile games, or a sort of paralogism that makes us regress to the teachings of the sophists denounced by Aristotle as "what appear to be refutations but are really fallacies instead"[29] and that have long since disappeared from anything that has any pretensions of being considered serious thought in the West. But this is not so. What we have here is not unreason, in the sense of the improper use of reason, but rather antireason, firmly grounded on an acute awareness of the paradox introduced by the use of negation in the expression of what is. This is in fact one of the cruxes of impossibility associated with language in its relations with what is: language entails words that state as much, if not more, of what they do not designate as of what they do designate. When it comes to the experience of a single, undifferentiated reality, that of the "nonduality" of illumination, the words that dissect out reality from the perceived world rationalized by the intellect can only lead back to this duality whence we began. But because one cannot do without words, because the paths of illumination are taught in master-student relations that are also made of words, the *koans* play with them and mystify those who listen, in order to better demystify the use of words. "Use your spade which is in your empty hands." "Walk while riding on a donkey." "Talk without using your tongue"—these are examples cited by Suzuki to explain the relationship between Zen and the intellect that the *koans* want to exemplify.

> The intellect is needed to determine, however vaguely, where the reality is. And the reality is grasped only when the intellect quits its claim on it. Zen knows this and proposes as a *koan* [literally a public document!] a statement having some savor of intellection, something which in disguise looks as if it demanded a logical treatment, or rather looks as if there were room for such treatment.[30]

All of this appears rather clearly (if the term is not out of place here) in one of the most celebrated and analyzed of all koans: "The monk asked Joshu: 'Does a dog have a Buddha-nature, or not?' [Joshu answered:] 'Mu.'" Now *mu* means "no," but everyone agrees to see in it not an answer to the content of the question (does a dog have the nature of the Buddha?), but a negation of the question itself, what Douglas Hofstadter calls the "unmode," the "unasking" of the question;[31] better yet, a positing of negation itself, and even better, the positing of the sound or the effect "mu" that the disciple must penetrate to go beyond the aporias of questions-and-answers. In his book on Gödel's theorem, which combines in rare fashion humor and profundity, Hofstadter compares the Zen masters' acute awareness of the limitations of language, which one must nevertheless employ, with that of mathematicians vis-à-vis formal systems.

> Relying on words to lead you to the truth is like relying on an incomplete formal system to lead you to the truth. A formal system will give you some truths, but [as Hofstadter later shows

when he presents Gödel's Theorem] a formal system—no matter how powerful—cannot lead to all truths. The dilemma of the mathematician is: what else is there to rely on, but formal systems? And the dilemma of Zen people is: what else is there to rely on, but words? Mumon states the dilemma very clearly: "It cannot be expressed with words and it cannot be expressed without words."[32]

The plot thickens: *mumon,* which means "no-door," is the name of a twelfth- or thirteenth-century Chinese master who wrote obscure commentaries on *koans* entitled *Mumonkon* ("doorless door" or "doorless barrier"), for whom Joshu's "no"—or, more exactly, the sound *mu* of this "no"—is the "barrier of the patriarchs" on the road to Illumination.

> If you want to pass this barrier, you must work through every bone in your body, through every pore of your skin, filled with this question: "What is 'MU'?" and carry it day and night. Do not believe it is the common negative symbol meaning nothing. It is not nothingness, the opposite of existence. If you really want to pass this barrier, you should feel like drinking a hot iron ball that you can neither swallow nor spit out....
> I will tell you how to do this with this koan: Just concentrate your whole energy into this MU, and do not allow any discontinuation. When you enter this MU and there is no discontinuation, your attainment will be as a candle burning and illuminating the whole universe.[33]

As in the saying of Rabbi Shimon, son of Rabban Gamaliel, cited previously, here we have a militant attitude calling for the whole person to act on his or her body and affects, perfectly expressed by D. T. Suzuki who, while defending himself against being "an anti-intellectualist through and through," declares:

> Whatever statement one may make on any subject, it is ineluctably on the surface of consciousness as long as it is amenable in some way to a logical treatment. The intellect serves varied purposes in our daily living, even to the point of annihilating humanity, individually or en masse.[34]...
> The will in its primary sense...is more basic than the intellect.... The one great will from which all these wills, infinitely varied, flow is what I call the "Cosmic (or ontological) Uncon-

scious," which is the zero-reservoir of infinite possibilities. The "*Mu!*" thus is linked to the unconscious by working on the conative plane of consciousness. The koan that looks intellectual or dialectical, too, finally leads one psychologically to the conative center of consciousness and then to the Source itself.[35]

But this position of antireason, for which equivalents can be found in certain Western esthetic movements, is very difficult to maintain outside the extremely restricted circles where silence coherently overcomes the temptation of militant discourse, didactic exposition, or religious preaching. When this is not the case, these discourses cannot *not* employ at least some ostensible form of rationality to explain, justify, add, exhort—in short, in the final reckoning to say something about beliefs, using meaningful words. Illumination degenerates into faith and religious belief, the most common scene of mystification, because there reason talks nonsense, just like the sophists, but with other means. This is the reason of theologians, ideologues, and theoreticians of the mystery of meaning and the meaning of mystery, where all shots are permitted: when rational discourse stumbles up against contradictions or incoherencies, theology or mystery hastens to pick up the baton and stop up the holes.

## Order and Chaos in Symbolic Rationality

All the same, the relationship between mystical traditions and reason is not always one of militant antagonism or involuntary perversion. Alongside these voluntarist currents, all of the great mystical traditions have intellectualist currents that value reason. Each in its own fashion has found other means to use the language of words and reason without being imprisoned by it. To perceive the effective rationality of these currents and how it differs from scientific rationality, a detour through our understanding of myth and poetry as languages may prove useful. We have learned to decipher, in what we in the West call myths and receive in poetic or symbolic form, a certain use of reason that is not necessarily conscious but is not necessarily unconscious either.

Poetry has accustomed us to a usage of words in which what is actually said goes well beyond what is ostensibly said without its being, for all that, nonsense/unreason or antireason. We know that the game has different rules than prose discourse. The studies on this point by the poet Claude Vigée[36] are particularly illuminating. Whereas the language of prose aims at unicity of *meaning* and precision of content, culminating in philosophy, formal languages, and mathematics, poetic language seeks a purity of *form* that culminates in the unicity of the work, such that any modification of form would be a flaw or even destruction.

Nevertheless, these two types of expression remain closely related, since both cases involve the use of language. The relation between them is one of negative reciprocity: what is unicity for one is multiplicity for the other. The ideal of one, which at a certain level—whether of meaning or of form—is the anti-ideal of the other, reappears when the level changes. The unique form of the work of art speaks only thanks to the multiplicity (tending at the limit to infinity) of meanings and levels of meaning. What is more, this infinity of possible meanings can overtake pure form without meaning. Conversely, the univocal meaning of formal language no longer requires any restriction of form—for all that it is called formal. It is called formal because it reduces meaning to pure syntax devoid of semantics: the meaning of its signs is reduced to that of the relations among them, in which the role of their significata is merely conventional and interchangeable. At this price it obtains the univocality of meaning and absence of ambiguity that necessarily entail acceptance by every rational mind. This is what permits an algorithmic (i.e., mechanical and automatic) translation that is immediate and free of loss: unlike poetic language, the exchange of signs required by such a translation is a trivial matter. The form of the meaning, which constitutes the entire sense of a poem, going beyond its words taken individually and due to the polysemy of its words, has no importance in formal languages, because the words have only a single sense that is identical in all propositions and is independent of the form of these propositions. This is why, paradoxically, what is expressed in a proposition of formal language is independent of the particular form of that proposition: that form, by construction, is only a particular case of the unique general form that defines the syntax of the language—unlike the particular form of a poem, which is unique and cannot be reduced to that of a universal syntax.

These reciprocal inversions of unicity and multiplicity of form and meaning in poetry and prose may be at the origin of what Pirsig calls the "search for Quality," in a novel of rare profundity[37] in which Zen, the motorcycle, and rhetoric are the occasion for an astonishing excursion to the frontiers of logical reasoning. He proposes an inversion of the roles of quality and reality, which makes him appear to himself and others as mad or mystical, both at once and alternately, continuing the line of ancient intuitions[38] today renewed[39] on various sides. One may also think about the Intense, intensity as such, invoked by Yves Bonnefoy[40] when he wonders about an element that was not taken into account "in the calculations today which attempt to situate exactly the significance of poetry," or when, for him, the (young) reader "understands everything in the polysemies through comprehensive intuition, through the sympathy that one unconscious can have for another,... in the great burst of flame which delivers the mind—as formerly the negative theologies rid themselves of symbols." After the discoveries of the role of the unconscious in poetic creation and of the autonomy of the signifiers in the text, here too the "precision of study" comes to restrain and oppose the impatience of intuition by uncovering its illusion. For Bonnefoy, though, it is a question of a combat between "loyal adversaries."[41]

Thus poets tell us (even in prose!) about the type of positive relations that can be maintained between mysticism and discursive reason. Everything occurs as if it were a question of dividing the world into two kingdoms that are found, in somewhat different fashion, in the symbols of myth. As D. Sperber demonstrated so clearly,[42] symbolic language can be approximated by the use of quotation marks. These mean "your attention, please, we are speaking from another point of view, at another level of perception and description of reality, where meanings are no longer the same." Above all, these other meanings suggested by quotation marks are not necessarily found in another lexicon already lying to hand. The most interesting cases are those in which they are merely hinted at by the use of quotation marks and the interweaving of levels they imply and are thereby created at the moment they are uttered. The deciphering of symbols reveals their rationality in the form of these structures of relations, which have been illuminated by the studies of Lévi-Strauss and his disciples, in which the ideal of formal language reappeared.

It is always a matter of finding an order or of making it appear (creating it) by a change of level in a discourse that is otherwise, and from another perspective, chaos, confusion, and contradiction. Yet something in the form of this chaos indicates that another order could be projected onto it. This is what I have defined elsewhere as nature's property of complexity[43] and richness: an apparent disorder in which we have reason to believe we can find a hidden order. The partition into two kingdoms, of order and disorder, overlaps that between rational discourse about reality and the experience of a reality with no reason.

Every scientific system rests on the postulate or faith in the ability of reason to disclose an order beneath the complexity and apparent chaos of our experience of the world. From this point of view, symbolic and interpretive thought goes as far as possible down the path of faith in the possibilities of reason: nothing is accepted as devoid of meaning. Every phenomenon, even the most fortuitous and confused, every myth, even the strangest and most enigmatic, finds an explanation that renders it rational by means of a change of level—the symbolic explanation—in which reason appears not only in what is said overtly, but also symbolically, "between quotation marks."

Everything proceeds as if the fortuitous, the absurd, and the random were excluded from reality. A series of events or an a priori disparate aggregate of randomly associated facts is united by causal relations in one fashion or another. It seems as if our reason cannot bear the absence of order and reason in things. As Dan Sperber puts it: "Symbolic thought is capable, precisely, of transforming noise into information."[44] It is remarkable that poetic creation (and artistic creation in general) also ends up transforming noise into information, albeit at a different level, as we saw earlier. Claude Vigée has provided a gripping description of the different stages of the poetic experience:

> It is in the violent and lucid flame of the initial emotion that the disparate elements among which the poet "discovers unheard relations" are welded into accurate images.... No apparent order allows itself as of yet to be distinguished in this indescribable welter of sounds, images, undatable memories, which issue at the same time from the most secret regions of the soul and from its least intimate domain: that of learned signs. This experience rather resembles a throw of the dice: by means of everything that the past has accumulated in us, we would vanquish chance by means of chance, in order thereby to attain a superior reality of the spirit over which it no longer has any dominion.... A nascent coherence is suddenly established in the sounds and images of the primitive chaos. The "useful" (i.e., those that can fulfill their representative function for the affective consciousness) verbal and imaginative elements organize themselves according to the central rhythmic motion and the forces that emanate from it as from a magnet. Thereafter the unused materials become obstacles to creation. They are shunted off to the psychic frontiers and soon lapse into oblivion.... A perceptible structure is substituted for the void and chaos that existed previously.[45]

Like Caillois, for whom "it is a question of organizing poetry," for Valéry it is a matter not "of passing too simply from disorder to order, but of controlling self-variance...: awareness does not move toward unity, but on the contrary toward an organized multiplicity.... Distinguishing a 'psychesthetic chaos' from a 'form' that thwarts it while using it." And while searching for its marks in thermodynamic irreversibility, it is from the side of the "mystical element" of Wittgensteinian language, at the same time limitation and reunion, that his poetics derive.[46]

I would say rather "*although* searching for its marks in thermodynamic irreversibility." In fact, transforming disorder into order, thwarting chance while using it, making "complexity from noise"[47] and "order from fluctuations"[48] are recognized today as the principles of natural organizations based on the thermodynamics of open systems—of which living beings are particular cases. But is that really the same thing? Is the experience of the creation of information from noise, of order from disorder, in symbolic thought and artistic creation, the same as that produced by scientific observation of nature and of the living world?

It certainly is not if one takes these expressions as literal descriptions of what is, of "reality." For in one case we are dealing with experiences of the operation of language and thought, in the other with experiences of observations of nature interpreted in physical and mathematical theories (information theory, thermodynamics, and system dynamics). On the other hand, these expressions probably do designate experiences that are quite similar, if we realize that both are descriptions of descriptions; that is, descriptions that take into account the position of the observer and describer, an individual endowed with reason who confronts the complexity of the brute data of his or her experience of nature.

Nevertheless, a more profound difference remains, again linked to the status of contradiction and paradox, which are to be eliminated from scientific discourse, whereas they are not only permitted but even endowed with particular "monstrative" virtues, as we have already seen, in mystical discourse. Even though symbolic thought and poets do not resort to active antireason and a quasi-systematic search for contradiction, the experience of contradiction and paradox, *despite* the effort to introduce order (or rules) and rationalize, acquires a positive content, at least provisionally, because it leads back to an irreducible originality of these attempts to introduce order: that of symbolic thought and the change of logical level indicated by the "quotation marks"; or that of the poet and the poet's subjectivity.

For the scientific method, on the contrary, contradiction and paradox are intolerable scandals that threaten to undermine the entire structure. We are familiar with the role of the logical paradoxes that haunted the quest for the foundations of mathematics during the nineteenth and early twentieth centuries. They were not exploited to return to the ineffable or even to the irreducible, but rather to run them to earth, so as to make them surrender, if possible, and eliminate them or, in total despair of success, to evade them, as Russell tried to do. Similarly, the discovery of organizational randomness by the nascent sciences of complexity must not be understood, under pain of being profoundly denatured, as a manifestation and demonstration of an irreducible paradox that leads back to some "higher" or "deeper" elsewhere. Quite the contrary, it is a question of removing, by means of an appropriate formalism, the contradictions that appear in the usage of the notions of order, complexity, and organization, transposed without retouching from their usage in everyday language to scientific discourse on observations of nature. Natural language tolerates and even uses uncertain—because multiple and interlocking—significations, which in some cases rule out the use of univocal and adequate definitions. But what is no defect for everyday language[49] is assuredly one for scientific research (even if, along with Wittgenstein, we hold that the imitation of the natural sciences, including, inter alia, their "craving for generality," is the source of great confusion in *philosophy*[50]).

Scientific theories of complexity and organization cannot rest content with observing the contradictions and underlining the paradox. On the contrary, they must resolve these contradictions and eliminate the paradoxes. If, as in the example of complexity from noise, the apparent paradox is eliminated by taking the role of the observer into account, this must not itself induce error by suggesting that it involves a return to subjectivity. Whenever the role and status of the observer are taken into account in the natural sciences (an approach that began, at least explicitly, with quantum mechanics), we are dealing not with the subjectivity of an individual but of a theoretical being (the ideal physical observer) that is merely a shorthand reference for the totality of measurement and observation operations possible in the given conditions of the practice of a scientific discipline, and we are taking into account the corpus of knowledge characterizing that discipline at a given moment. The role shift by this ideal physical observer, to one of individual subjectivity and consciousness, is one of the main sources of misunderstanding and confusion in the spiritualist deviations of quantum mechanics and of course also in those of the new theories of order and complexity.

As we have seen, it is rather the individual, in his subjectivity and in the experience of his inner illumination (the "Self"), who is the point of departure of the mystical and poetic experience—even if it is subsequently a matter of extending this interiority to the All, in which no inside or outside is recognized; or of expanding the Self to the totality of being, or going even further, through the "I" and "Thou" (Buber, Rosenzweig) and the "face of the other" (Levinas), to one beyond Being, an infinity that opens and shatters everything.[51]

## Reason as Complement of Illumination

Of course, this is often merely a point of departure for these mystical traditions, which do not stop there. The possibility—indeed the necessity—of not staying put in the experience of illumination, of progressing[52] and of saying leads them, at least in certain cases, to use reason as a tool of progression and discourse. Reason no longer serves as a perverse foil, as in the *koans*, but is instead a valuable aid to be used correctly, with scrupulous observance of its rules.

Thus most great traditions dispose of a certain cohabitation or complementarity between mystical experience and rational discourse. A difference of accent may be observable between the traditions of India and those of the Mediterranean world: the role of rational discourse in the former, although undeniable (e.g., in some commentaries on the Upanishads and the Bhagavad Gita, or in a thinker like Sri Aurobindo[53]), is smaller than that of the experience and practice of the ineffable and of illumination. The contrary is true in traditions such as Judaism, Christianity, and Islam. The exoteric character of the mystical tradition of exercises and illumination in the Far East, where unity is lived outwardly in the mode of polytheism, while reflection and unifying consciousness are reserved to the esoterism of brahmans or monks, may correspond to this different accent—unlike Judaism, for example, where the monotheistic and legalistic exoterism corresponds to a mystical and multiform esoterism, bordering on an overt polytheism reserved for masters and initiates.

Whatever the case may be, in some of the great texts of these traditions and the commentaries on them one can find a certain rationality of mysticism, close to though different from symbolic thought, which it might be useful to analyze here. Even though we would then find ourselves confronting a certain rationality, in that the principles of identity and noncontradiction apply to it, the reality to which that rationality refers itself and that to which it applies constitute a domain peculiar to itself. Hence it is relatively easy to show—and this seems to me of great importance for the argument of this book—that scientific rationality is radically different from it.

In other words, the existence of mystical tendencies in science, avowed or not, must be supplemented by the existence of a rationality of mysticism, it too conscious or not, which can amply explain the confusions that we regularly witness—explain but not justify them. We shall see that there remain irreducible differences that must be kept in mind in the interest of the fruitful pursuit of both processes.

Plato recognized a necessary complementarity between reason and divination; the latter was needed to supplement the former as a means of gaining access to truth, whereas reason's task was to test the content of this truth. A passage in the *Timaeus* is particularly suggestive here:

> Herein is a proof that God has given the art of divination not to
> the wisdom, but to the foolishness of man. No man, when in

his wits, attains prophetic truth and inspiration, but when he receives the inspired word, either his intelligence is enthralled in sleep or he is demented by some distemper or possession. And he who would understand what he remembers to have been said, whether in a dream or when he was awake, by the prophetic and inspired nature, or would determine by reason the meaning of the apparitions which he has seen, and what indications they afford to this man of that, of past, present, or future good and evil, must first recover his wits. But, while he continues demented, he cannot judge of the visions which he sees or the words which he utters; the ancient saying is very true—that "only a man who has his wits can act or judge about himself and his own affairs." And for this reason it is customary to appoint interpreters to be judges of the true inspiration. Some persons call them prophets, being blind to the fact that they are only the expositors of dark sayings and visions, and are not to be called prophets at all, but only interpreters of prophecy.[54]

This complementarity resurfaces in diverse forms in the aforementioned monotheistic religions—Judaism, Christianity, and Islam—where the exercise of reason is one source of knowledge, alongside revelation and experience (personal or that transmitted by trustworthy witness).

Within these traditions, however, it is interesting to study the separation between two forms of using reason: one properly theological, influenced by medieval philosophy and scholasticism; the other, probably the heir of gnostic traditions, considered to be more particularly mystical and thus always somewhat suspect of irrationality. In fact, we can recognize, perhaps with greater ease today, that the more rationalist of these two streams is not the one you think. In the theological current, reason complements, in the sense of merely adding to, dogmas and acts of faith posited or received a priori. The so-called mystical currents of these traditions, however, use reason as a tool to sort, verify, and express discursively, starting from the raw data of revelation. These two aspects are already present, but united, in the Platonic text just quoted. They seem to have been gradually separated until they wound up opposed, split between the so-called rational philosophers of medieval theology and the mystical thinkers (kabbalists, sufis) of these same traditions.

Y. Jaigu opened the Cordoba colloquium by recalling that that city was the venue where this separation crystallized in Islam, between the rationalist Aristotelian philosopher Averroes and the mystic Ibn Arabi, as discussed by H. Corbin in "Creative Imagination in the Sufism of Ibn

Arabi."[55] Given the mutual influence of Jewish and Muslim thought in that era, it is hardly astonishing that, on the Jewish side, this same separation between ostensibly rationalist and mystical philosophers coalesced around Maimonides, the great Jewish thinker born in Cordoba. This separation between "philosophers" asserting the rational tradition and "kabbalists" asserting the esoteric and mystical tradition became prominent after his time.

Before that separation, however, one could observe in the works of one and the same author, as in those of Plato, the two forms in which mystics use rational discourse: one explicitly mystical and suspected of irrationalism by the other camp, the other theological and scholastic and claiming exclusive title to rationality. Two important, albeit very different, examples of this are the poet-philosophers Judah Halevi and Solomon Ibn Gabirol. For the former, mystical content supported by poetic form is found in a philosophical work (the *Kuzari*); for the latter, by contrast, the two are totally separated, by language (Hebrew for the mystical poems, Arabic for philosophical works), by style, and by readership.[56] The same cleavage appears subsequently in Maimonides' oeuvre, between the rationalist philosopher writing in Arabic and rejected by a large portion of the traditional Jewish public, on the one hand, and (rather than a Hebrew poet integrated into the mystical current of Judaism) the legal authority who occupies a central place in the post-talmudic juridical tradition. Contrary to appearances, there is no great distance between the foundations of this juridical tradition (which are certainly not Greek philosophy) and the mystical currents of Judaism, as later manifested by such rabbis as Joseph Caro, Schneour Zalman of Lyady, the Gaon of Vilna, or Joseph Hayyim of Baghdad, all of whom were simultaneously masters of Kabbala and of the legal tradition. This is why, up to and including Maimonides, there was no clear opposition in Jewish tradition between the "mystical" and "rational" currents; the line of demarcation between them more or less bisected the work of the authors themselves. Only afterward do we find Jewish theologians, claiming descent from Maimonides the philosopher, author of the *Guide for the Perplexed*, clashing with the kabbalists (who rejected that Maimonides, even while fully accepting his juridical corpus). It is the content of this clash, and what was it stake in it,[57] that interest us, by exemplifying two opposing conceptions of the rational and the nonrational. These same opposing conceptions are found today, when the question involves not the use, properly speaking, of reason, but a particular idea of the relations between reason and reality.

## Scholastic Theology and Kabbalistic Rationality

In our analysis of certain aspects of this confrontation between Jewish theologians who proclaim themselves rationalists and kabbalists considered to be mystics by their opponents (and sometimes even by themselves), we shall see that the true rationalists are not the ostensible ones.

The former group soon took up with a caricature of rationalism in the form of an ostensibly rational theology. Repeating, in a different historical and philosophical context, the progress of the author of the *Guide for the Perplexed*, they used reason only on the basis of a priori notions such as the existence of God, revelation, the chosenness of Israel, redemption—all of which are articles of faith. Without denying the authenticity of Maimonides' role as a recognized master in Jewish tradition, we must note that alongside his traditional Hebrew law codes, accepted by all, he found it necessary to write this controversial work in Arabic, a work of scholasticism inspired by Judaism and destined precisely for the perplexed, whose intellectual roots lay in scholasticism. The rabbis who claimed his mantle, perhaps more than Maimonides himself, were the spearheads of so-called rationalist Judaism.[58]

The articles of faith are posited by definition as so many postulates that, in the final analysis, can be accepted only by means of the obscure and mysterious mechanisms of faith. The sole object of subsequent rational ramifications is to draw coherent results from the acceptance of these dogmas. There is an unmistakable resemblance here to medieval Christian and Islamic scholasticism, which proceeded in the same path, as well as to all later attempts to reconcile the exigencies of reason and faith. Today we must recognize that these attempts at reconciliation are perfectly unreasonable, in that the demands of reason cannot be reconciled with articles of faith, posited a priori and by definition as irrational.

But whereas in the Christian world, *grosso modo*, this incompatibility was, after Pascal, soon recognized, the Jewish world was more restrained: energetic sequels of this mode of thought can still be found in the nineteenth and twentieth centuries. It seems as if Jews, unlike Christians, found it repugnant to affirm the irrational and thus incomprehensible and mysterious character of the foundations of their religion, ethics, and even history. Of course, some rabbis have always affirmed this; but they are treated—and rightly so—as mystics, and their teachings received with a measure of caution. In the Christian world, on the contrary, the zealots of gratuitous, unjustified, even absurd faith are considered to be in the mainstream of religious tradition. The other sect is tolerated on the periphery, as useful for converting a few poor souls who could not be directly touched by grace.

This Jewish discomfort with accepting the irrational as a foundation of Judaism can be readily comprehended if we consider the exceptional importance that all the ancient Jewish traditional texts have given to studying the Torah. This study, for its own sake, as a mental exercise, is presented by the Talmud as the foundation of Judaism, rather than some phenomenon of faith, even if the latter plays a role in traditional practice. Most of the rabbis were thus loathe to abandon the attempt to present Jewish teaching in an ostensibly rational form. Their only mistake was to seek this end by applying the method of medieval theologians and endeavoring to reconcile irreconcilables.

In parallel to this current there developed kabbalist thought. For the rabbis who were the masters of the Kabbala there were no articles of faith or a priori dogmas. The usual ideas covered by the term *religious faith* are not ignored in the texts of these authors, but they do not serve them as fundamental principles. On the contrary (and it is in this sense that Kabbala has been accused of atheism or heresy[59]), sometimes they are approached asymptotically, with the discovery in them of meanings quite different from those found in the theological catechism. If the theological process seems to be deductive, from top to bottom, starting from articles of faith, the other seems to be inductive, bottom to top, working by successive abstractions that begin with the experiences of the human body and its development, language, and biblical myth.[60] A formula that frequently reappears in these texts[61] to represent this process is drawn from the Book of Job (19:26): "Through my flesh I will see the divine."[62] This "divine" is described in Kabbala in concrete words that designate formal structures, presented in a lore so abstract that its object is not immediately apparent; although, subsequently, it can receive content and be applied to various fields of lived experience, psychological, ethical, mythical, historical, mystical, liturgical, and so forth. The divine worlds that these books describe in minute detail appear as the aggregates of related elements, so that one does not know at first whether one is speaking of God, of man, of the world, of Israel, and so on. Or rather, it seems to be a case of all of this at the same time, in a muddled and contradictory fashion. In fact, it is initially none of these, but merely a formalism in which concepts cannot be exhaustively defined by reference to a concrete or even representable reality, but only by reference to one another. In this formalism, to take one example, what is called "worlds" or "sephirot" or even "persons," as well as the different ways of writing the "names"—this has neither more nor less concrete existence than vector spaces or the parameters of mathematicians. This formalism is rational, in that the relationships among its concepts are accessible to reason. But it is clear that the content of these concepts is at first abstract and uncommon.

As we shall see shortly,[63] there is a confusion between *rational* and *common* that prevents us from recognizing abstract forms of rational discourse, because they are too abstract and refer to uncommon experiences; or, on the contrary, that makes the jump which leads to considering all forms of rational discourse as equivalent, including those that are no whit different from delirious rationalizations. The former attitude makes it impossible to see rationality in any symbolic or poetic thought and views it as only more or less militant irrationality. The latter attitude causes us to accept and even to fuse in a single amalgam all formal uses of reason, without considering their context and the direction in which proceed.

In a universe of thought where "uncommon," because too abstract, is confused with "irrational," kabbalistic thought is perceived as irrational, much as the mode of thought of modern physicists initially seemed irrational to certain of the older generation, who could never get used to it. The classic rationalists were led astray by this mode of thought and qualified it as mystical without searching any further. We can also understand how, from that starting point, a host of even well-disposed exegetes saw in Kabbala only the mystical tendency of a religion, "Jewish mysticism," and persisted in trying to give a theological content, a sort of theodicy, to kabbalistic concepts, even if it tortures them somewhat. In fact this was possible only thanks to a property of these formalisms (which can also be found in the physics of several centuries later): if one wishes to give concepts a content that is not abstract—that is, representable—one winds up with a description of the phenomena that is not only partial but also contradictory. However, this contradictory nature arises strictly from the representation, with its images and references to immediate sensory perceptions, and disappears if one holds fast to the formal relations that are alone adequate to the object of this discourse.

To do this, of course, we must accept that knowledge of what is not directly accessible to the senses can pass only through an abstract formalism and that concrete representation must be dispensed with. As Rabbi S. Heikel-Eliashof says in one of the last great kabbalistic works,[64] written at the beginning of this century, the initial notions of this wisdom are "only comprehensible" (by intellectual knowledge and through language) but "not attainable" (by the senses). This is an astonishing declaration when one considers that the kabbalists continue the prophetic tradition of seers or visionaries, so that it is justified to view them as the extension of a mystical tradition. But the meaning is clear when we remember that the goal of kabbalistic *writings*, especially the later (Lurianic) ones, and of these authors' attempts at systemization is to make an abstraction of the means whereby inspiration, "vision," and "unveiling" are produced, in order to derive from them formal patterns that obey the requirements of maximum generality and of the most perfect rational coherence possible. Thus one of the subjects of the sometimes tragic eighteenth-century dispute that pitted the strict and elitist mitnaggedic kabbalists[65] who gathered around the Gaon of Vilna against the generally more popular hasidic kabbalists had to do with the credence to be placed in revelation through dreams, visions, *maggidim*,[66] and other *benot qol*,[67] of which both groups had experience. The former[68] maintained that no credence should be accorded them a priori; the sole guarantee was to be found in the possibility of integrating them into a rational discourse that would be accessible and comprehensible independent of these experiences. In this they were merely repeating the old talmudic adage: "The sage takes precedence of the prophet."[69] The written texts are intended to "purify" the image and representation by means of formal reason. Thus it is evident that if we can conceive of the use of reason only through images and representations, these latter can only drop us back into the fuzziness and "impurity" of visions, the contradictions remain insoluble, and this kabbalistic thought cannot be viewed as other than an irrational mystery. A similar process leads to the idea that science rediscovers the fantastic and irrational. This "scientific" irrational may be voluntary and asserted to be such. But it may also be hidden behind an all-around confusion between, on the one hand, the new form of using reason and the new abstract-concrete relations established by mathematical physics and, on the other hand, the authentic mystical traditions that engaged in a quest for and cultivated the irrational, as we have seen. Unlike these traditions, kabbalistic texts, far from hunting for the irrational, asserted that they were passing the form of their discourse through the filter of stringent reason—more stringent, certainly, than that of the theologian-philosophers, even though the latter's reference to Aristotelian philosophy, via Maimonides, served them as a rationalist flag. In fact, studying their texts, one can recognize that they did not do so badly, if one is sensitive to this form of abstract reason in which the relationship with reality does not necessarily pass by way of sensory experience. A true rationality of mysticism can then appear, very different from the false rationality of the theologians, closer to symbolic thought and, what is more, not unrelated to the rationality of a mathematics, on the one hand, and psychoanalysis, on the other.

In the abstraction of its formal structure, which we can characterize here as invariance of paraphrase,[70] it resembles a mathematics abstracted not from geometrical experience but from related structures, those of the Hebrew language and biblical narrative.[71] In its function of interpreting the "hidden" aspect of existence and a text in which it reads the unsaid and the unwritten ("the white space between the words"[72]), it certainly resembles psychoanalysis.

We shall see later, however, that these relationships do not authorize (neither in this case nor in that of Far Eastern traditions) the confusions that characterized the Cordoba colloquium.

## Maimonides and Nachmanides

One example among many will allow us a brief glimpse at how kabbalistic discourse expresses a concern for rationality that is more stringent than that of ostensibly rational theologians. Our example involves Nachmanides'[73] commentary on Genesis 46:1, a long dispute with Maimonides' theses concerning anthropomorphisms in the Torah, according to which, *grosso modo*, one cannot accept any material representation of God. One of the cruxes of this discussion involves the content of the concepts of *kavod* and *shekhinah*, translated as "glory" and "presence." The context of certain verses that employ these notions have material implications; for example, "The glory of God filled the tabernacle." These implications led Maimonides to consider the content of this *kavod* and *shekhinah* as created, and therefore as external to God. Nachmanides showed that this conception leads to a contradiction, because other verses designate this *kavod* or *shekhinah* as the object of the Hebrews' worship, leading to the result that they should be considered idolators no different from the others in the Bible. Nachmanides examines the Maimonidean theses and their implications and highlights the contradictions, both internal and with the plain sense of the biblical verses. Finally, he demonstrates that the error lies with the radically scholastic and vivid idea of God as pure spirit. This, he says, is not the manner in which the Torah speaks; instead, it employs a number of ideas that differ from one another, expressed by various names—such as *Elohim*, the Tetragrammaton, *Kavod*, *Shekhinah*. The contents of these are not to be deduced from a priori conceptions about God, for example, but from the teachings of the Kabbala, whose purpose is precisely this. These ideas are perfectly accessible to reason and noncontradictory, so long as they are considered in the context of this kabbalistic formalism and the particular language associated with it and are not reduced to certain representations that one would make of man's relations with God and nature.

Similarly, Maimonides rejected physical anthropomorphisms—the hand of God, the eyes of God, God hears, God descends, God sees, God lives, and so forth—as human idioms, again because God does not have any material attributes. Nachmanides, on the contrary, observes first that, if by God one designates an infinite transcendence, there is no more reason that this transcendence be spirit rather than matter. Nachmanides proceeds to show that it is not a case of the Bible "speaking in human language," but rather of a description of levels of existence (worlds) and of the interactions among them: these expressions designate general categories (hand, eye, etc.) that refer to a single form traversing all of these worlds, of which our common corporeal experience thereof is one particular case.

This dispute between Maimonides and Nachmanides, who lived a century after him, and whose commentary on the Pentateuch is considered to be one of the first kabbalistic texts, is particularly significant. Situated at the height of the Middle Ages, it clearly demonstrates the contrast between two conceptions of Torah study: one claims to be rational, but begins with a number of a priori postulates concerning God and revelation, thereby proving itself to be pseudo-rationalism; the other sees the Torah as precisely the demystification of these a priori postulates and thereby proves itself truly rational to our eyes.

Thus we see how things are turned upside down: the truly rational expressions of traditional Judaism are to be found in kabbalistic thought because its formalism, abstract but rational, provides us with a language that can carry forward its teachings without calling articles of faith into play; whereas the ostensible rationalists cannot do without them. To recognize such an inversion, however, we must discover that reason can have a different and broader form of expression, which is also more rigorous than that of scholasticism or of classical nineteenth-century rationalism.

## Kabbala and Alchemy as the Midwives of Modern Science?

Reflecting about science can assist us in this task. From this perspective, the contemporary scientific context makes it easier to penetrate this form of thought. But there is a more direct route as well, from within traditional thought itself, on condition that it be steered with no preconceived judgment as to a possible "mystical"—in fact theological—content of the object of study. In other words, we are not dealing with a forced and artificial rapprochement with a recent phenomenon in the history of physics. To persuade ourselves of this, we need only read texts such as that of Nachmanides already cited, as well as works in which kabbalistic rabbis endeavored to persuade their ostensibly rationalist adversaries by demonstrating the limited character of the latter's use of reason. Prominent among these are books already referred to, such as Moshe Hayyim Luzatto's *Hoqer Umequbal*, which takes the form of a dialogue between a kabbalist and a philosopher-theologian, and *Vikuha Rabba*, an exchange of letters between a hasid and a mitnagged.

Finally, let us highlight a perspective that holds that the rapprochement with modern physics is quite unjustified. Whereas for scientific thought classical rationalism, although broadened in the new forms of rationalism, retains its value for many problems, this pseudo-rationalist religion has no such value and appears to be the heir of medieval theology. In classical science reason was associated with elements derived from a world neither rational nor irrational, that of the images and representations of sensory experience. Sensory experience, taken as access to reality by the paths of sense perception, is not itself rational. (If it were, this would mean that sensible reality is itself rational—precisely the illusion dismissed by modern physics; not that this physics asserts that sensible reality is irrational, but rather that the former can exist without having to postulate the rationality of the latter. As A. Regnier put it: "The illusion held by some that reality is rational derives from our obligation to make rational models of this reality. We must understand that if these models must be rational, this is because they are abstract objects and not because they are models of reality."[74]) However, this experience remains that of material reality directly accessible to the senses, about which a consensus of intersubjectivity—if not of objectivity—can be easily obtained. On the contrary, every "rational" theology associates with reason elements that are untransmittable and dogmatic, expressed in its articles of faith.[75]

All the same, for our purpose here it is more important to realize in what way not only theology, but also a mystical rationality such as that of the Kabbala, must be distinguished from scientific rationality, even if both are forms of rationality.[76] This is all the more important because it seems that Kabbala, through the intermediacy of Christian mystics and alchemy,[77] overflowed the banks of Jewish tradition and influenced the Renaissance philosophies from which classical science emerged,[78] marked by its origins despite its break with them.

It is in these philosophies of the sixteenth and seventeenth centuries that mystical rationality, quite different from the scholastic and prescientific age in so many aspects, appears most clearly. Before Kepler and Newton, who mark the pivotal rupture, Paracelsus[79] is a good representative of this extraordinary compound of intuitions that presage nineteenth-century science with magical and alchemical thought, rationalized in a natural philosophy whose explanatory power, in the absence of technical efficacy, is extremely seductive.

For example, it affirms the primacy of experience over literary revelation, but only to better justify alchemical and astrological practices through which "everybody" was supposed to be able to experience reality. Another example is the magical action of the imagination working through images, which makes it possible to explain action at a distance and thus appears as a manifestation of a human omnipotence characteristic of magic in an enchanted world peopled by elves, angels, and the like. (This power of the image, which H. Corbin finds among Islamic mystics, was taken over and brought up to date, as the *imago*, by Jung and the new alchemists of the twentieth century. We shall return to this later.)

These examples, when examined more closely, demonstrate that it is not irrationality that characterizes this thought, nor even the flight into mystery and the refusal to accept the verdict of experience. Quite the contrary is the case. (Reciprocally, it demonstrates to what extent the so-called experimental method of modern science is conditioned by a certain manner of exploiting reason and by a particular vision of the world accepted as the point of departure and possible source of acceptable hypotheses. It cannot be reduced, as is so often stated, to a simple acceptance of the verdict of facts and experience, as if these could be perceived in some "pure" fashion, independent of a conceptual framework imposed a priori, within which they must in fact find their place.)

Experience and facts were received on the basis of certain a priori postulates, set in the framework of thought that typified the Renaissance, and more precisely the enlightened researchers and philosophers of the Renaissance. Today we rightly view this context of thought as antiscientific; then, however, it opened the road to scientific thought, as alchemy did for chemistry. It was an animistic and magical thought, but it claimed to be rational and critical. It differs from the scientific thought that succeeded it in that it involves a panvitalism in which the most obvious experience, which serves as the paradigm and point of departure for all thought, is not taken from mechanics—pendulums or other movements of massive bodies—but from the evolution and development of living beings, of which we all have immediate experience, *in our own life and from the inside.* From this follows a whole series of consequences that render it inaudible and incomprehensible if one wants to understand it in the conceptual framework of contemporary science. As Alexandre Koyré wrote of Paracelsus: "For him, more than for any of his contemporaries, the dissolution of medieval science had provoked a renaissance and reanimation of the most primitive superstitions."[80] Unlike his scholastic predecessors, Paracelsus did not seek knowledge in the codexes of the tradition; it was "in the world, in reality, in life and nature that he wanted to find his lore and his masters."[81] But this nature, like that of the philosophers of the Renaissance, is first and foremost alive and animate, as we sense and "experiment" it[82] ourselves. "What is most characteristic of this entire school of thought [is that] it is animated through and through by the belief that the processes of the external world, of the physical world, merely repeat and symbolize those of the soul."[83] The difficulties with which it collides are those of any thought about life that stumbles against the question—which we shall rediscover for ourselves—of the "reality" of the possible, of the mode of being of the potential. For

the organicist conception of the world and of evolution yields
with difficulty to logical frameworks. The concept of the germ
contains a circle, vicious for thought, a circle that it cannot
understand, but which it is child's play for life to resolve....
[Living beings] evolve because they are living and every living
being is at the same time what it is not yet, and is not yet what,
fundamentally, it is.[84]

These difficulties were surmounted by a sort of escape permitted by
mystical thought, in which, for example, the idea of the imagination, "a
magical intermediary between thought and being, an incarnation of
thought in the image and position of the image in being,"[85] led to this
unlimited credulity of which Koyré speaks, where experience serves to
ground all superstitions because nothing is posited as impossible for this
vital nature. On the contrary, we know that modern science, both chemistry and physics, truly began after alchemy, with the establishment of principles of impossibility: chemistry with the conservation of mass, physics
with the impossibility of perpetual motion. By virtue of the possibilities of
quantification and calculation they allowed to develop, these limiting principles and others added later proved to be most fruitful in the enterprise of
transforming and mastering matter—even if it must repress the role of
imagination to the domain of inner life and a metaphysical organicism that
later characterized the philosophy of romanticism.[86]

## A Word about Gnosis:
### Rationality, Strangeness, and Cunning

L ong before the Renaissance and alchemy, however, one of the most
ancient forms of mystical (and mythical) rationality was that of the
gnostics. The latter is perhaps the source of the former, in the Christianized
Europe of the Middle Ages, despite its dualism and pessimism, which
clearly contrast with the monism and unlimited optimism of alchemy, from
which ultimately emerged the scientific optimism that recognizes and
makes use of bounds and limits. Our knowledge of the different gnostic
systems comes to us, most often, through the texts of the Church fathers,
who denounced them as heretical and sought to demonstrate their absurdity. Nevertheless, scholars can recognize them as explanatory systems
with relatively well-articulated structures, even if the constitutive elements
seem to have been drawn from a syncretism of Greek mythology, ancient
Judaism, and primitive Christianity. The study of the few extant original

gnostic texts[87] and of the gnostic heresies analyzed and denounced by the Church fathers can be supplemented by study of the most ancient writings of the Jewish Kabbala to unveil the mythical and symbolic significations in the light of which it is no longer possible to speak of absurdity or even of irrationality. The relations of filiation and community of origins between Kabbala and gnosis have long been recognized.[88] As Tardieu put it, though, "each form of gnosis has its own logic"; whereas for H. C. Puech,

> every gnostic system, however disconcerting it may be at first because of its strangeness, its apparent incoherence, obeys a common motif that constitutes it as an organic whole, determines its ordering, articulations, internal finality, and, by connecting the parts with one another and with it, grounds its cohesion and explanation. Whence the originality and specificity of the traits presented, in their structure and mechanism, by all systems of the gnostic type.[89]

Without entering into textual analysis, which would lead us too far astray, we must ask why these systems are strange and disconcerting, why they seem to be incoherent, if analysis discloses that they express their own logic, which we can even discern on a second examination. This is posing, by another route, the question of multiple rationalities, some of which appear more *immediately* rational than others. There is no doubt that this sometimes deceptive *appearance* of rationality or irrationality is sometimes influenced, as we have seen with regard to the Kabbala, by an element of habit, of familiarity with the terminology and the types of argumentation, which yields the sense of nonstrangeness so often confounded with rationality. We often confuse 'familiar-in-the-Western-tradition'[90] (Christian or post-Christian) with 'rational', and this confusion works in both directions: an uncommon but intelligent and profound thought will often be considered irrational;[91] whereas a banal, dogmatic, and impoverishing or even false thought, but one that reassures by its habitual and familiar character, will sometimes be viewed as rational.

Compared with the scientific and philosophical tradition, gnostic systems clearly evince uncommon traits, also found in most myths of origin and in the mystical cosmogonies that have incorporated such myths. The reality that serves them as the foundation and point of departure for abstractions and grandiose frescoes functioning as explanatory systems is not that of the surveyor and geometer, or even of the astronomer, but first of all that of the living world, and more precisely that of the world of the family and of parental relations; not, of course, the living world of modern biology, physicochemical and molecular, but rather that of an uncontested vitalism that extends throughout the universe. The world is the result of normal or abnormal births; the dynamic of history, both physical and human, is viewed as that of vital processes in which sexuality, pregnancy, and childbirth serve as paradigms, even if the myths generalize these processes into forms of sexuality and generation that are mythical, that is to say monstrous, or in any case never seen concretely in the living world described by the life sciences.[92]

On the other hand, the goal of these systems is not disinterested knowledge, but an ethic that simultaneously states the law, good, and evil (generally life, fertility, and happiness on one side, death, destruction, and suffering on the other[93]) and grounds this natural law, described and narrated by the cosmogony in question. In other words, its object is to describe the world or, more precisely, our experience of it in our daily life, by means of a genesis in which the elements of this experience are ordered in a manner that grounds in reason the judgments about good and evil that the law in any case makes us render. The myths and cosmogonies of different traditions contain numerous common themes, so that it is relatively easy to pass, for example, from Indian traditions to Jewish mystical traditions, whether directly or by way of Greek myths and gnostic systems. Nevertheless, these traditions differ profoundly with regard to what they consider to be good and evil and the laws that regulate conduct in the societies where they evolved. The idea that these laws can be deduced from the cosmogony and explanatory system that characterize such traditions is probably false. It is rather a case of hindsight, where these laws already exist and characterize a particular society as the result of slow processes of maturation conditioned by complex interactions, both conscious and unconscious, among history, geography, culture—in brief, by the "social imaginary"[94] of a given society; they are then rationalized, recovered from it, and integrated into a global vision of the universe.

Here the constitution of such a global vision of the universe is at the very root of the thrust of elaboration and expression of these explanatory systems. These systems claim to be both total and absolute "knowledge" ("gnosis") of "forces" and "powers" revealed to initiates and a means of salvation; that is, liberation from evil, suffering, and the exigencies of a world of limitations. They also present two aspects: a totalizing intellectual structure, on the one hand, and a reference to the opening of mystical escape on the other (with its origin by means of revelation and its goal of ultimate liberation).

Unlike the case of modern scientific knowledge, here these two aspects coexist perfectly, because the paradigms of knowledge are not objects postulated outside the human subject, but the human subject itself, perceived from the inside. The ultimate reference is not geometric but organic: the world is perceived through the metaphor not of space-time, the locus of being and of phenomena, but of a living organism. The point of departure is the acute and overwhelming perception of the unity of All in the inner and daily experience of the "I" of day-to-day life, as well as in that extended to the "you," to the "it," and to the "world" of ecstasy and mystical experience in all its forms.

When it is a matter of explaining and rationalizing, the form molds itself around the content, such that, here too, the form of the reason used for this must be unified with other affective and corporeal modes of apprehending reality. This is the form of reality so admirably described by M. Detienne and J.-P. Vernant in their study of Metis (cunning intelligence) in Greek thought.[95] It is also that of the wisdom and cunning of the serpent in all the phallic myths. And it also that of both biblical Knowledge and biblical Wisdom (*hokhmah*), as these appear in the Bible[96] and as they are viewed by the kabbalistic tradition,[97] the source at once of life and of intelligence. There too, as for Athena among the Greeks,[98] ambiguous relations still exist with the serpent and with sex; one of these is that of cunning-nudity—in Genesis the same Hebrew word (*'arum*) designates both the cunning and the nakedness of the serpent.[99] These relations are present in the legends and myths that haunt all the major texts of the kabbalistic tradition, from *Sefer Yetzirah* to the *Zohar*; they were analyzed at the beginning of this century, with a wealth of detail, in one of the last major works of the post-Lurianic Kabbala, the *Book of Knowledge* by S. Heikel-Eliashoff.[100]

In all these cases we observe discourses that, as Detienne and Vernant say with regard to Metis, the crafty wisdom of the Greeks, "embody the action of genesis on two levels, cosmic and mental."[101] What we have to deal with here, in this "proper logic of myths" or "rationalized cosmogonies," is not separatory, classifying, and ordering reason, the ideal of "pure reason" of Western science and philosophy. It is rather what Yehuda Elkana calls, in another context,[102] "cunning reason";[103] or that wielded by Hermes, Eros, and of course Athena, and especially by her mother Metis. For Detienne and Vernant, Metis, daughter of Ocean, is opposed point by point to Themis, daughter of the Earth and another spouse of Zeus, taken to wife after he had swallowed Metis, pregnant with Athena, so as not to be her victim. As opposed to Themis, whose omniscience relates to

> an order conceived as already inaugurated and henceforth definitively fixed and stable.... Metis, by contrast, relates to the future seen from the point of view of its uncertainties.... She tells of the future not as something already fixed but as holding

possible good or evil fortunes and her crafty knowledge reveals the means of making things turn out for the better rather than for the worst.[104]

Themis represents "the aspects of stability, continuity and regularity in the world of the gods: the permanence of order, the cyclical return of the seasons,... the fixity of destiny."[105] On the side of Metis there are mobility and flux, obscurity, contradiction, uncertainty, but also that which makes it possible to triumph over them—cunning or the intelligence that "operates in the realm of what is shifting and unexpected in order the better to reverse situations."[106] At the same time "a power of the waters, fluid and polymorphic, who promotes fertility and nurtures growth, like her sisters, the other daughters of Ocean, Metis remains extremely close to her mother Tethys who, according to one ancient tradition for which Homer provides evidence, was herself *genesis pantesi* and thus gave birth to all things both divine and human."[107] It is in this association of genesis and practical intelligence (the ruses of fishing and the hunt) that we find "on two levels, cosmic and mental,"[108] sexual and intellectual, what is designated in certain Stoic texts by the definitive shortcircuit expression "seminal reason" or *logos spermatikos*.[109]

It is remarkable, and rather ironic, that we fall back on this "practical reason," simultaneously crafty and creative (creative because crafty, cunning and even deceitful in that it must deal with the unforeseen, the disorderly, and the random), when we endeavor to characterize scientific creation itself: although all attempts to rationalize the history of scientific discovery and invention in a rational and unitary (metascientific) theory of scientific knowledge have failed, the reason at work in science as it is practiced appears to be the reason of the craftsman, a sort of tinkering (quite different from Lévi-Strauss's tinkering of savage thought, but tinkering all the same)—what Yehuda Elkana analyzes as "cunning reason." It is all the more ironic that science gives the appearance of trying to go beyond this craftsman's reason and generally asserts the purity of its rationality inasmuch as it aspires to unity and universality. It is as if the craftiness of Metis had won out over itself, taking the form of its contrary, in order to attain the most effective possible mastery of that segment of reality in which regularity, stability, and assurance are, pragmatically, most appropriate. Cunning reason appears as the operational mode of scientific reason despite itself; and if Hermes[110] with his craft could reappear as the founder of the modern science of fluctuation and creative disorder, this is still despite that rationality. For it is recognized as cunning reason only in epistemological, and therefore extrascientific, reflection on the scientific method, which we attempt to rationalize within a unifying discourse about science. The invocation of this craftsman's and tinker's reason is no more than the recognition that such a discourse is impossible. This is why R. Thom was to some extent justified when he qualified these attempts at a theory of creative disorder as nonscientific; but only to some extent, because he confounded the metascientific and indeed metaphysical level with that of scientific practice itself, in its rational use (in the sense of Themis) of statistics and calculation of probabilities.[111] In fact, this use, like all applications of reason in scientific discourse itself (and not in discourse *about* science) is that of a reason that *vaunts itself* ideally "pure" and universal, devoid of contamination by the contingent, the subjective, the unforeseeable, if possible the incalculable, and certainly the nondeducible. The object of the computation of probabilities is just that: mastering the contingent, to the extent possible, by rendering it calculable and predictable.

It would be interesting to analyze the role played conjointly by the fathers of Greek philosophy and the fathers of the Church, at the dawn of this purification, in the creation of this pure and Western reason—distinguished from "seminal reason"—the only one familiar to us and thus the only one that can be "rational" for us. M. Serres[112] has demonstrated the influence of war and death at the origin of mathematical reason. A reading of the Church's denunciation of gnostic heresies also teaches us about the process by which the head was severed from sex, by which the straight, regular, and identical was divorced from the crafty, the unforeseen, and the paradox of life-death,[113] by which metaphysical, theological, and pure reason was insulated from the creation of the living, seminal, and practical. It seems to be a process of desexualizing the sacred, whereby sex is banished from the company of the paradigmatic experiences of knowledge—those of divinity, metaphysics, and language. The *creative* verb of theology cannot be understood except as the transfigured (and desexualized) relic of the primordial wisdom that acted in its dual register of procreation and mind. As a result, the function of language in Western rationality could be established only by being devitalized (desexualized) in what are today called "formal languages" (at risk of finding the subtle eroticism of logical mathematical structures and games relocated to another level). The logos of understanding has replaced the *logos spermatikos* and usurped its entire domain; while the spiritualized Holy Family has replaced the active sexuality of the Olympian gods and of the Indian pantheon (or indeed of the figures of the Kabbala). Ultimately all of this leads to philosophy's peremptory judgment that a gnostic myth is "only a lucubration that makes man's fate depend on the domestic squabbles of a metaphysical household."[114]

But this process of separation, distinction, and delimitation, initially excluding the entire obscure world of chaos and "black mud"[115] and subsequently effecting its recovery by reason become "universal" (thanks to the missionary monotheisms and then to the humanism of the Enlightenment and its successor ideologies[116]), has been most effective and continues to be so. This process made it possible to construct the grandiose edifice of thought and of the human capacity for tinkering known as Western science. In addition to successful techniques of mastery or transformation of matter (from which little by little chaos was or rather tended to be eliminated, making way for the transparent order of equations), this structure has introduced the experience and habit of an *open rigor* currently found nowhere else in such *institutionalized* form. We seem to have a contradiction in terms here, and twice over, because the rigor of the critique and exclusion, far from walling off and limiting scientific discourse, opens it to constant renewal, despite all the dogmatic tendencies that would prevent this. On the other hand, the institution of science, in universities and research centers, despite its heaviness and the natural tendency of all institutions to stagnate, has finally and in despite of everything (not without battles and scuffles between ancients and moderns, and new moderns reviving the ancients, or new ancients reviving themselves, and the corrosive influences of the extrascientific stakes, conscious and unconscious, that characterize the spirit of each age) been placed at the service of the opening to creative innovation, without sacrifice of the emphasis on rigor and criticism. This is probably merely one last trick by Metis, on the crooked path of the serpent's wisdom become straight so as to better master the straight and the regular.

Perhaps this is the origin of the insatiable temptation to build science into a global system and means of salvation, into gnosis—precisely the fate against which it must always be on guard if it is to remain effective. Parallel, and equally ridiculous, is the temptation to scientize mystical visions and experiences of the universe, whereas the original gnostic revolt claimed to be liberating thought from the Greek science of the ineluctable and necessary.[117]

## Notes

1. The same applies to *mythic*. See M. Detienne, *The Creation of Mythology*, trans. Margaret Cook (Chicago: University of Chicago Press, 1986); "Le mythe, plus ou moins," *L'Infini*, no. 6 (1984), pp. 27–41. The relations between mystical and mythological are complex, with both overlaps and differences (see, for example, Mircea Eliade, *Patterns in Comparative Religion*, trans. Rosemary Sheed [New York: Sheed and Ward, 1958]; and Gershom G. Scholem, *On the Kabbala and Its Symbolism*, trans. Ralph Manheim [New York: Schocken Books, 1965]). For reasons that will be apparent later (see Chapter 7), we would see in myth a collective

expression that corresponds to the content of the mystic experience for the individual. In other words, supposing that these two types of discourse refer to the same types of experiences, the mythological is to the social and collective what mystical experience is to the individual.

2. The Catholic monk Henri Le Saux, who became an Indian swami long before these developments, was a pioneering witness to the difficulties and rents provoked by this sort of encounter for those who live it profoundly; even if, of course, it is an inexhaustible source of riches. See M. M. Davy, *H. Le Saux, Swami Abhishiktananda, le Passeur entre deux rives* (Paris: Cerf, 1981)

3. The influence of poet-philosophers like Alan W. Watts (*The Wisdom of Insecurity* [New York: Pantheon Books, 1951]; *The Book, on the Taboo Against Knowing Who You Are* [New York: Vintage Books, 1966]) on the Beat Generation and the (counter) culture that came in its wake is undeniable. Too much poets not to be mystics (even independent of psychedelic experiences), but too marginal and controversial for the institutionalized forms of mysticism and religion in the West (i.e., the so-called Judeo-Christianity commonly referred to, which is much more Christian than "Judeo"), it was only normal for them to find in Far Eastern traditions what their native theistic culture could not give them.

4. See C. Jambet, *La Logique des Orientaux: Henry Corbin et la Science des formes* (Paris: Le Seuil, 1983).

5. Gershom Scholem, *Major Trends in Jewish Mysticism* (New York: Schocken Books, 1954); *On the Kabbala and Its Symbolism*.

6. *Doctrine de la nondualité (advaita-vāda) et Christianisme. Jalons pour un accord doctrinal entre l'Église et le Vedānta, par un moine d'Occident* (Paris: Dervy-Livres, 1982).

7. Ibid.

8. Scholem, *Major Trends*; *On the Kabbala and Its Symbolism*; Henri Atlan, "Niveaux de signification et athéisme de l'écriture," in *La Bible aujourd'hui*, ed. J. Halperin and G. Lévitte (Paris: Gallimard, 1982), pp. 55–87.

9. J. H. M. Beattie, "On Understanding Ritual," in Bryan R. Wilson, ed., *Rationality* (Oxford: Basil Blackwell, 1970), pp. 240–268; T. Settle, "The Rationality of Science versus the Rationality of Magic," *Philosophy of Social Sciences* (1971), pp. 173–191.

10. Note that *turned on* in this sense was evidently coined to describe the psychedelic experiences of the 1960s.

11. Mishna *Avot*, Chapter 1. The type of exegesis referred to here is *midrash*, which explores and spurs on the text (see Atlan, "Niveaux de significations"). Rabbi Shimon's statement is attenuated, but not contradicted, by another talmudic dictum, where, in response to the question of whether study or action is more important, the answer is "study, because it leads to action" (BT *Kiddushin* 40a).

12. Raymond M. Smullyan, *The Tao Is Silent* (New York: Harper and Row, 1977).

13. The Tao is the source of things and words, but is neither thing nor word, like the *Qodesh* and *Hokhmah* of the Kabbala, the source of every thing and every word that is neither thing nor word (see Rabbi Abraham Isaac Kook, *Orot Haqodesh* [The lights of holiness], vol. 2 [Jerusalem: Mossad Harav Kook, 1964] pp. 283–286, based on the Zohar, II 121 and III 61a) [see the English anthology of his works, *The Lights of Penitence...,* trans. Ben Zion Bokser (New York: Paulist Press, 1978)]: the different traditions experienced the same paradox; although it is neither thing nor word, we have only the words made for speaking about things with which we cannot not speak of it; and it is by living among things and with things that one is supposed to live it. Of course, silence is the simplest solution to this paradox, recommended by all (although this too is a paradox, as we have seen, since you have to *write* a book to *say* that the Tao is silent, just as Rabbi Shimon had to use words to praise silence). But beyond this silence, the various traditions differ in how they express this experience. It may be merely a difference of emphasis, with Oriental mystics stressing the beyond of discourse, the unity of the All beyond and through the multiplicity of appearances, whereas—although many received ideas run counter to this—Jewish monotheism accented the experience of language and its structures and the multiplicity of reality, despite the possible experience of unity.

The mutual fascination of East and West probably embodies the search by each side for something felt lacking in itself. When Smullyan writes that "the Sage...is vacuous and stupid like a newborn infant" (*The Tao Is Silent*, p. 32), this has a positive connotation vis-à-vis his own experience as a "Judeo-Christian" Westerner; that is, of that medley of silly catechism with elegant science and philosophy. Vis-à-vis the limitations of the excessive sophistication and arrogance of omnipotent scientistic discourse his statement has a positive connotation. On the other hand, taken in and of itself, it can only impel those in India, China, and Japan who were raised exclusively in the context of such teachings to seek enlightenment (if not illumination) in the West, in its science, philosophy, and technology.

14. Davy, *Henri Le Saux.*

15. Henri Le Saux, *Gnânânanda,* pp. 42f., cited by Davy, p. 35.

16. In fact, there are already significant differences of expression in the descriptions themselves. Mystic revelation is frequently compared with a recollection, with the memory by which you remember what your true self knew in another time and place from which day-to-day life has distanced it. But this theme is found in Jewish tradition, too, in a somewhat socialized form, when Judah Halevy, in the *Kuzari* (eleventh century), speaks of revelation as a memory of events that our ancestors witnessed; and we are taught, conversely, with regard to ritual practices, that all that individuals can discover in the depths of their practice is what they themselves saw and heard, in a mythical past, when they were present at the collective Sinaitic revelation (Henri Atlan, "La mémoire du rite, métaphore de féconda-

tion," in *Mémoire et histoire*, ed. J. Halperin and G. Lévitte [Paris: Denoël, 1986], pp. 29–49).

17. Emmanuel Levinas, *De Dieu qui vient à l'idée* (Paris: Vrin, 1982), p. 9.

18. A. Rifflet-Lemaire, *Jacques Lacan* (Brussels: C. Dessart 4d., 1970), pp. 855–877.

19. Lacan, "La Science et la verité," *Ecrits*, pp. 855–877.

20. R. Y. H. Ashlag (author of a commentary on the Zohar) in an anthology entitled *Matan Torah* [The giving of the Torah], 2d ed. (Jerusalem, 1977), pp. 9–15.

21. BT *Megillah* 18a. This passage follows the account of the establishment of the canonical text of the Eighteen Benedictions by "120 Sages, among whom were many prophets," after which it was forbidden to add further praises of the infinite God to it. For prayer can be only finite, hence partial and inadequate. Only those who can state them exhaustively should be allowed to recite the praises of the Infinite ("Who can tell the might acts of the Lord, proclaim all His praises?" [Psalms 106:2]). It is with regard to this impossibility of uttering everything that R. Judah glossed the second verse of Psalm 65: "Silence is praise for You" with the definitive aphorism, "The [best] drug of all is silence." This expression, astonishing for classic religious commentary, simultaneously expresses the experience of the world of ecstasy and drug-induced hallucinations at the origin of the "praise of the Lord" and the rejection of this experience as a goal in itself, the search to go beyond it because of its ineluctable limits, all the more dangerous in proportion as its fascination and refinement are greater (see Chapter 8).

22. As is known, the Zohar was not published until many centuries after his death, by the Spanish kabbalist Moshe de Leon, who was probably its real author (Scholem, *Major Trends*).

23. The Hebrew original uses the words *sefer* 'book' and *sofer* 'author', which are derived from a single root meaning to count or recount.

24. A perversion of the same type, but even more dangerous because of its collective dimensions and political implications, is that of the Sabbatean form of false messianism. There too resides a danger of the literal realization, this time in concrete political life, of aspirations that apply mainly to the inner life and whose realization can be only indirect and through the distancing effects, barriers, and transpositions of the law in practical life. This temptation is always rampant in periods that follow great catastrophes in Jewish life, as is demonstrated by Gershom Scholem in *Sabbatai Ṣevi, the Mystical Messiah, 1626–1676*, trans. R. J. Zwi Werblowsky (Princeton, N.J.: Princeton University Press, 1973).

25. In a chapter entitled "In Your Light We See the Light," a contemporary hasidic rabbi (R. C. N. Berzovski, *Netivot Shalom* [The pathways of peace], [Jerusalem: Yeshivat Beit Avraham, 1982]) quotes and comments on excerpts from particularly expressive ancient kabbalistic texts. From the twelfth-century R. Abra-

ham Ben David: "A man should know, before all, the one who formed him and should recognize his creator.... For even if he is hidden from the sight of all living beings, he is nevertheless in their hearts and disclosed in their thoughts.... And you, son of man, listen with your ears and open your eyes, and you will see the image of your creator who is before you, opposite you." From *Keter Malkhut*, by the eleventh-century poet-philosopher Solomon Ibn Gabirol: "You are the light of the world, and the eyes of every sensible person behold you. Such a person does not have blinders that hide the light of the world from him. His sensibility makes him merit the illumination of knowledge and he sees the creator (may he be blessed) in every creature. 'The heavens declare the glory of the divine, and the sky proclaims its handiwork' (Psalms 19:2). The sun and moon and the heavenly hosts prostrate themselves before you, as well as the earth and all that are on it, from the mountains to the valleys. Everything becomes transparent and manifests the creator, who animates and gives being to all things. And all things bear witness and recount that being is one and his name one, and that there is no other beside him. With his own eyes he will behold God (may his name be blessed); with his own ears he will hear and his heart will understand the voice of the being that calls to him from all creation and all events."

Berzovski goes on to explain how, in view of this illumination we have received aids, "sources of light," namely the Torah and the commandments, especially the Sabbath. The province of the Torah is to make human knowledge luminous and to enlarge it. As the Baal Shem-Tov said (referring to *Midrash Tanhuma* 58), "those who study the Torah are the people of whom Isaiah spoke (Chapter 9), who walk in darkness and have beheld a great light, the light of the first day of creation, which filled the entire universe from one end to the other, and which the creator stored away for those who observe the Torah."

Although the language of creator-created dualism is preserved in this text, along with the celebration of the face-to-face revelation without fusion that is characteristic of Jewish mysticism, there are also elements of what hasidim call the annihilation of the "what is" in the unity of light. This is explained by Berzovski , who compares this illumination by knowledge to the enlargement of the personality of an individual, previously sealed up in his house, who uncovers the world in ever broadening and new circles. "When his knowledge is contracted to the four corners of his house he sees only himself and his desires; but when he merits the illumination of knowledge and the world that is all light is disclosed to him, there is no longer any place in it for any material interests, because everything is "'what is not' and null."

It is easy to see how these texts are compatible with the hypothesis to be presented in Chapter 8 concerning the origin and meaning of rituals as the (re)presentation of the *reality* of the world of dreams, hallucinations, and mystic illumination.

26. Atlan, "Niveaux de signification."

27. Thomas Cleary, ed. and trans., *Time-less Spring, A Soto Zen Anthology* (Tokyo and New York: Wheelwright Press, Weatherhill, 1949), p. 35.

28. D. T. Suzuki, in D. T. Suzuki, Erich Fromm, and Richard De Martino, *Zen Buddhism and Psychoanalysis* (New York: Harper and Row, 1960), p. 48.

29. Aristotle, *Sophistical Refutations*, 164$^b$20, trans. W. A. Pickard-Cambridge, in *The Complete Works of Aristotle*, ed. Jonathan Barnes (Princeton, N.J.: Princeton University Press, 1984), p. 278.

30. Suzuki, in *Zen Buddhism and Psychoanalysis*, p. 49.

31. Hofstadter, *Gödel, Escher, Bach*, pp. 39, 233, 254.

32. Ibid., pp. 252f.

33. Ibid., p. 259.

34. Compare the teachings of the twentieth-century rabbi A. I. Kook. Although he can hardly be accused of anti-intellectualism, he nevertheless warns intellectuals of the danger of being cut off from human reality as it is generally lived, spontaneously and without any sophisticated logical elaboration, including its spiritual and esthetic aspects (*Orot Haqodesh*, vol. 2, pp. 364f.). As did Plato, it is in a balance between "reason and the hidden depths" (ibid., vol. 1 [1963], p. 105), between the "wonders of mystery and the rigor of natural intelligence" (ibid., p. 106), between "the imaginary and the intellect" (ibid., p. 238), checking and limiting each other, that he finds the antidote to the dangers of deviation (inhumanity on the one side, nonsense and childishness on the other) that characterize them. "Reason has its successes in the general and fails in the particular. By contrast, mysticism as the unveiling of the hidden penetrates the particular, without recoiling from a single detail. But it faces the danger of being closed up in this pettiness and sinking into obscurantist childishness" (ibid., p. 105).

35. Suzuki, in *Zen Buddhism and Psychoanalysis*, pp. 50–51.

36. C. Vigée, *L'Extase et l'errance* (Paris: Grasset, 1982).

37. R. M. Pirsig, *Zen and the Art of Motorcycle Maintenance* (New York: William Morrow, 1974).

38. "Since the destruction of the Temple, prophesy has been taken from the prophets and given to fools and children," according to R. Yohanan in BT *Baba Batra* 12b.

39. R. D. Laing, *The Politics of Experience* (New York: Pantheon, 1967); F. Roustang, *Un Destin si funeste* (Paris: Minuit, 1976.

40. Yves Bonnefoy, "'Image and Presence': Inaugural Lecture at the Collège de France," trans. John T. Naughton, in *The Act and the Place of Poetry: Selected Essays*, ed. John T. Naughton (Chicago and London: University of Chicago Press, 1989), pp. 156–172.

41. It is in this same loyal combat that we, for our own part, would oppose

scientific knowledge and mystical rationality. The Image lies, as is demonstrated by criticism and disillusionment. But it is also what the "young reader" finds in his intuition of the Intense. The loyalty of the combat, for the poet, the poet's concern to face it, to confront this aporia, lead him or her to a dialectic of dream and existence, illusion and reality, the third term of compassion at the height of passion and desire, which does not fail to recall the playing field, the intermediary between reality and illusion for Winnicott and Fink (see Chapter 7). This makes the poet accept *together* two laws of literary creation. One, the closure of the written word, demystifies the naivete of the subject who would speak: "Hemmed in by the words he does not understand, by experiences whose very existence he does not suspect, the writer, and this is the element of chance which so distressed Mallarmé, can only repeat in writing that strictly limited particularity which characterizes any given existence" (Bonnefoy, ibid., pp. 163f.). But the second "law" of literary creation bars him from staying there, because "the world which cuts itself off from the world seems to the person who creates it not only more satisfying than the first but also more real" (ibid., p. 164). The lie of the Image is only this impression of reality: a lying impression, in fact, if it designates some particular pseudo-reality erected into Reality, a particular Image absolutized and become Image. In the background, though, its truth, the "second level of the idea of poetry," is truth struggling against the abolitions, the closures—the "presence which opens"—of "this first network of naiveties [sic], of illusions in which the will toward presence had become ensnared" (ibid., p. 171). On this level, poetry "has denounced the Image, but in order to love, with all its heart, images. Enemy of idolatry, poetry is just as much so of iconoclasm" (ibid., p. 172). "These images which, if made absolutes, would have been its life, are nothing more, once one overcomes them, than the forms, the simply natural forms, of desire, desire which is so fundamental, so insatiable that it constitutes in all of us our very humanity" (ibid., p. 171).

42. Dan Sperber, *Rethinking Symbolism*, trans. Alice L. Morton (Cambridge: Cambridge University Press, 1975).

43. Atlan, *Entre le cristal et la fumeé*.

44. Sperber, *Rethinking Symbolism*, p. 79.

45. C. Vigée, *Les Artistes de la faim* (Paris: Calmann-Levy, 1960), p. 149.

46. D. Oster, *Monsieur Valéry* (Paris: Le Seuil, 1981), pp. 106 and 160.

47. Atlan, *Entre le cristal et la fumée*.

48. Ilya Prigogine and Isabelle Stengers, *Order out of Chaos: Man's New Dialogue with Nature* (Boulder, Colo.: New Science Library, 1984).

49. "To think it is [a defect] would be like saying that the light of my reading lamp is no real light at all because it has no sharp boundary" (Ludwig Wittgenstein, *The Blue and Brown Books* [New York: Harper and Row, 1965], p. 27).

50. Ibid., pp. 17–18.

51. The question posed here is evidently that of the relations between philosophy and mysticism, whereas elsewhere those between science and philosophy are at stake. Perhaps Wittgenstein, again, can guide us by locating philosophy, as specializing in the meaning of words and aiming to resolve the contradictions that it creates itself by requiring natural language to have a rigor and generality it is not designed to have (ibid., pp. 17–29), in a quite specific hollow between science and mysticism. Like every hollow, it separates at least as much as it unites. This seems to be what one (lost?) philosopher tried (but without great success) to state at Cordoba, lost in the All of spiritualist physicists, mystic predicators, and Jungian psychoanalysts (C. Jambet, in *Science and Consciousness*).

52. The entire exoteric Jewish tradition (the Talmud) is grounded on the search for and constantly refined definition of the correct path (*halakhah*) to be followed in daily life, far from illuminations, but not without the presence of some traces thereof.

53. Aurobindo Ghose, *The Life Divine* (Pondicherry: Sri Aurobindo Ashram, 1955); *The Message of the Gita: With Text, Translation, and Notes*, ed. Anilbaran Roy (Pondicherry: Sri Aurobindo Ashram, 1977). See also Swami Siddheswaranda, "Introduction à l'étude des ouvrages védantiques," in *Comment discriminer le spectateur du spectacle?* trans. M. Sauton (Paris: Librairie d'Amérique et d'Orient, Maisonneuve, 1977).

54. Plato, *Timaeus* 71e–72b, trans. Benjamin Jowett, in *The Collected Dialogues of Plato*, ed. Edith Hamilton and Huntington Cairns (Princeton, N.J.: Princeton University Press, 1961), pp. 1194f.

55. Cited in *Science and Consciousness*, pp. 3f.

56. See Solomon Ibn Gabirol, *Fons Vitae*; the introduction to the French translation of this work by Jacques Schlanger (*Livre de la source de vie [Fons Vitae]* [Paris: Aubier-Montaigne, 1970]) clearly depicts the links between the mystic poet Ibn Gabirol, whose Hebrew *Keter Malkhut* has entered the canon of traditional texts, and the "Arab" philosopher Avicebron (none other than the same Ibn Gabirol), whose *Fons Vitae* was quickly translated into Latin and practically ignored by Jewish readers.

57. Traces of this can be found in general writings of kabbalists, such as *Vikuha Rabba*, an exchange of letters between a hasid and a mitnagged, or Moshe Hayyim Luzatto's *Hoqer Umequbal*, which pits a philosopher and a kabbalist discussing the accusations of incoherence and irrationalism made by the former against the latter, who clearly manages to refute them and turn them back against their maker.

58. What Maimonides himself thought constitutes the object of scholarly studies on a putative esoteric doctrine that Maimonides ostensibly concealed behind the surface meaning of the *Guide for the Perplexed*. Whatever the case, and without having to invoke such a hidden doctrine, it is clear that an extraordinary

inversion concerning the articles of faith occurred between the time of Maimonides and the generations of religious philosophers who followed him. For him, the existence of God, His unity and His noncorporeality, were certainties demonstrable on the basis of propositions in Aristotle's *Physics* and *Metaphysics*, which he considered to be incontestable scientific truths (*Guide for the Perplexed*, part 2, Chapters 1–5 and 33). Faith involved only what was in the domain of opinion and was taught by tradition, dealing essentially with the rules of conduct that aimed at perfecting people by bringing them closer to God. Thus theological dogma as religious tenet did not exist for Maimonides. It appeared only later, among those who wished to continue to accept his teachings and interpretations but could no longer accept the existence, unity, and noncorporeality of God as scientific verities, once the Aristotelian foundations on which Maimonides had established his "proofs" thereof had crumbled away. These foundations, which he accepted only because he considered them to have been irrefutably demonstrated, include the impossibility of a real infinity, the impossibility of atoms and vacuums, the existence of the ether, and the living nature of the celestial bodies, endowed with souls, intellect, and awareness, and governing thereby events on earth (*Guide for the Perplexed*, especially part 1, Chapter 73, and part 2, Chapter 4).

Echoes of an interesting aspect of the controversies provoked by Maimonides' writings can be found in a thesis on the history of mathematics dealing with a fourteenth-century rabbi who opposed him in the name of the philosophic rationality of his time, while adhering to the Nachmanidean tradition to be discussed later: T. Lévy, *Mathématiques de l'infini chez Hasdaï Crescas (1340–1410): un chapitre de l'histoire de l'infini d'Aristote à la Renaissance* (Paris: Université de Paris-Nord, 1985).

59. On the history of the relations between Kabbala and rabbinic orthodoxy, see Scholem, *On the Kabbala and Its Symbolism*.

60. See on the role of kabbalistic commentaries such as *Sod*, the hidden meaning that is at the same time the most remote and abstract from the plain meaning of the biblical text and the deepest "interiority" of that text, in Atlan, "Niveaux de significations," pp. 55–58.

61. For example, the basic book of the Safed Kabbala (sixteenth century) by a disciple of R. Isaac Luria, R. Hayyim Vital, *Etz Hahayyim* (Tel Aviv, 1961–1964).

62. In the previous chapter we saw that the scientific method proceeds "bottom up," from the particular to the general, although it does not forbid itself recourse to logico-mathematical deduction. Similarly, we shall see in Chapter 5 that the discourses of traditional knowledge proceeded in the opposite direction ("top down"), even if, in symmetrical fashion and as the formula indicates, some of them did not forbid themselves recourse to generalization and abstraction. In fact, it was not really a matter of induction, but of generalizing projections that flowed from the correspondence posited a priori between macrocosm and microcosm, characteristic of these traditions, and that later became totally extrascientific. The result is nevertheless quite interesting with regard to the possible relations between ethics and

knowledge. Unlike scientific knowledge, whose object could become only more and more estranged from that of behavioral ethics (see Chapter 8), the traditional disciplines, even in their abstract and rationalized form, lie at the origin of rules of conduct (ritual, social, moral) that are an integral part of their scope of knowledge. It is only with difficulty that the rules can be separated from the knowledge where one of the functions of the latter is to enunciate the law—both moral and natural. We can easily understand that it is the correspondence between macrocosm and microcosm that makes this possible: the traditions of mystical knowledge can justify themselves, a priori, by a certain (albeit relative) pertinence to the affairs of our daily subjective affairs, because they form one source of its experiences.

63. See p. 123.

64. S. Heikel-Eliashof, *Sefer Hada'at Leshem Shevo ve-Ahlamah* (Jerusalem, 1908), p. 12.

65. *Mitnagged* = "opponent" (of the hasidim).

66. *Maggid* = a "teacher" bearing a personal message, received by an individual in a vision.

67. *Bat qol* (pl. *benot qol*) = "voice," less strongly personified, and thus of more general import, understood as originating "above."

68. See the preface to Rabbi Hayyim of Volozhin, *Nefesh Hahayyim* (Vilna, 1824).

69. BT *Baba Batra* 12a.

70. This is the term used in psycholinguistics to designate the abstract character of propositional forms, which remain constant through various paraphrases that give them multiple concrete meanings (applications).

71. Atlan, *Entre le cristal et la fumée*, Chapter 12.

72. Heikel-Eliashof, *Sefer Hada'at*; see Atlan, "Niveaux de signification."

73. Nachmanides, the thirteenth-century biblical commentator, one of the most important in the rabbinic tradition, drew much of his inspiration from kabbalist sources.

74. A. Regnier, *Les Infortunes de la raison* (Paris: Le Seuil, 1966), p. 103.

75. The question may arise of the role of faith in the Kabbala. Understood as belief in a dogma and as a priori mysterious knowledge, it may be considered to occupy a negligible place in the systematic texts of which we are speaking, even if they draw on experiences of personal revelations and inspirations whose *existence* is reported by their authors, but not the *content* of the mystical experience. What these texts call *emunah*, frequently translated as "faith," refers to the question of confidence in a possible unity of the abstract and the concrete, posed on two levels.

On one level it is a question of praxis, that is, of the relations, never cognitively demonstrated and always problematic, between knowledge and ethics or between knowledge and behavior. The *act* of faith, in the strict sense, thus consists of the decision to activate concretely what is otherwise only abstract knowledge. (Rabbi Joseph Ibn Giqatila, a contemporary of Moses De Leon, in *Sha'arei Orah* [Gates of light], Chapter 2, points out the relationship between *emunah*, in the sense of reliability, true because worthy of confidence, something on which one can rely, and the words *oman* 'artist' or 'craftsman', and *amon* 'pedagogue'. The common denominator, beyond their shared linguistic root, is the fulfillment of a promise, whether that of the creative work or of the child who grows up.)

The same question appears on another level, in the form of a priori confidence in the possibility of effective relations between the abstract and the concrete, despite the experience of the difficulties that these relations pose. This confidence can certainly be assimilated to a priori scientific optimism, without which scientific research could not have existed (especially in its infancy), because the latter also consists of an a priori confidence in the potential of abstract reason to account for and grasp concrete reality.

76. We shall see later, à propos of Wolfgang Pauli's study of Kepler, that this distinction came to the fore at least twice, precisely in ages when the danger of confusion is most evident: at the dawn of classical science in the seventeenth century, and today, when the problems of interpreting quantum physics are leading some to search for the key of a new scientific rationalism in a neoalchemy.

77. Michel Caron and Serge Hutin, *The Alchemists*, trans. Helen R. Lane (New York: Grove Press, 1961).

78. See below about Kepler (Chapter 5, p. 172), as well as about Newton's roots in alchemy (Chapter 8, p. 346). In seventeenth-century England, figures like Francis Bacon, Robert Fludd, Henry More, and Robert Boyle represent, along with Newton the alchemist, the brand of natural philosophy in which occult, alchemical, and Rosicrucian-hermetic doctrines coexist alongside elements that, once freed from the former, would become the experimental method (see B. J. T. Dobbs, *The Foundations of Newton's Alchemy* [Cambridge: Cambridge University Press, 1975]).

79. Paracelsus is commonly presented as a "precursor of the rational science of the nineteenth century,... a genial erudite physician,... one of the greatest minds of the Renaissance," or as "a late-born heir of the mysticism of the Middle Ages,... a pantheistic kabbalist and adept of a vague stoicizing Neo-platonism and natural magic," or finally, as a heterodox Christian ultimately faithful to Catholicism (see A. Koyré, *Mystiques, spirituels, alchimistes du XVIᵉ siècle allemand* [Paris: Gallimard, 1933, 1977]). Koyré analyzes these different aspects in Paracelsus's works and demonstrates, at the end, their rationality.

80. Ibid., p. 80.

81. Ibid., p. 81.

82. Whereas in French *expérience* means both "experiment" and "experience," leading to a certain confusion between the two, the differentiation that English makes between the concepts accurately locates the contemporary barrier (which did not exist in the Renaissance) between what can be approached scientifically and what cannot, even though the latter does not thereby cease to be real and perhaps even the object of rational and critical thought.

83. Koyré, *Mystiques*, p. 114.

84. Ibid., pp. 113–115. Modern biology faces this problem all the time, and resolves it, for better or worse, by invoking cybernetic concepts such as feedback and program, which themselves pose new problems (see Atlan, *Entre le cristal et la fumée*).

85. Koyré, *Mystiques*, p. 99

86. Ibid., p. 99.

87. R. Stadtlender, "Gnose et hermétisme," *Encyclopédie des mystiques*, ed. M. M. Davy and M. Berlewi (Paris: Laffont, 1972), pp. 135–156.

88. Scholem, *Major Trends*.

89. H. C. Puech, cited by M. Olender, "Le système gnostique de Justin," *Tel Quel*, no. 82 (1979), pp. 71–88.

90. Along with other mystifying aspects of the incantatory function of reason, M. de Dieguez (*Le Mythe rationnel de l'Occident* [Paris: Presses universitaires de France, 1980]) has also denounced this confusion (see Chapter 5, p. 203).

91. The examples of the revolutions in mathematics and physics, "irrational" numbers and classical mechanics, said to be "rational" in comparison with its modern successor, indicate the extent to which this confusion is anchored in scientific practice itself, at least on the linguistic level; because, in the final analysis, the new theories represent so many victories of reason, albeit over modes that are always new and strange vis-à-vis the previous ones.

92. Certainly, mystical experiences, in the strict sense, those of "modified states of consciousness," to use the expression of the American neomystics of the psychedelic revolution, provide reference points and bases for descriptions of reality using terms like *mental, supramental, ego, cosmic consciousness,* etc., which constantly recur in Western attempts to translate the traditional systems of the Far East—whether vulgarizations or profound and illuminating syntheses like that of Sri Aurobindo. But the "vital," and especially the cosmic male-female sexual, is always there, in India and in ancient China and Japan, as well as in Greek mythology, gnosticism, and the Kabbala.

93. See Atlan, "La vie et la mort: Biologie ou éthique," Chapter 13 of *Entre le cristal et la fumée*.

94. Cornelius Castoriadis, *The Imaginary Institution of Society*, trans. Kathleen Blamey (Cambridge: Polity Press, 1987).

95. Marcel Detienne and Jean-Pierre Vernant, *Cunning Intelligence in Greek Culture and Society*, trans. Janet Lloyd (Hassocks, Sussex: Harvester Press, 1978).

96. See, for example, Exodus chapters 28, 31, and 36; Job; Ecclesiastes; and Proverbs (especially chapter 8, in which personified wisdom speaks of itself in the first person as associated with the Creator and as antedating the creation of the world [see further, n. 103]).

97. Kook, *Orot Haqodesh*, vol. 2, Chapter 1.

98. Detienne and Vernant, *Cunning Intelligence*.

99. Genesis 2.

100. Heikel-Eliashof, *Sefer Hada'at*.

101. Detienne and Vernant, *Cunning Intelligence*, p. 137.

102. Namely, the context of Western science; but science that is done and not the ideal image one frequently has of it (Yehuda Elkana, "A Programmatic Attempt at an Anthropology of Knowledge," in E. Mendelsohn and Y. Elkana, ed., *Sciences and Cultures* [Dordrecht: Reidel, 1981], pp. 1–76).

103. This cunning reason is also that of artists who create and shape their work not like an architect-planner, but rather in the way that one educates a child, through play. This is how *Genesis Rabba* (1, 1) interprets Proverbs 8:30–31, where Wisdom is speaking about itself: "I was with [the Creator before the Creation] like a child to be raised [or, according to alternative readings proposed by the Midrash, like a teacher, a craftsman, or an instrument providing the plans for building the world], a source of delight every day, rejoicing [or playing] before Him at all times, rejoicing [or playing] in His inhabited world, finding delight with mankind." Wisdom was already there, as the Torah, before the creation of the world: active like the artist of creation, or like a child growing up with the creator—depending on how the Hebrew word *amn* is vocalized and interpreted (see n. 75); but in any case "finding delight with mankind" (which did not yet exist!). Certain aspects of this cunning reason correspond to what the kabbalistic tradition calls the "Wisdom of the left side." This is mentioned, inter alia, in the *Zohar* (Genesis 32a), where it is described as "the light that emerges from the darkness," as well as in Aschlag's commentary on this passage and in his commentary on other passages in the Zohar (Genesis 52a, 68a–b; Exodus 34b), where the hidden meaning of sacrifices in the Bible, especially the rite of the scapegoat, is explicitly related to the cunning of the serpent, which must be turned against itself, by means of greater cunning (see Henri Atlan, "Violence fondatrice et référent divin," in *Violence et vérité*, ed. P. Dumouchel [Paris: Grasset, 1985], pp. 434–449).

104. Detienne and Vernant, *Cunning Intelligence*, pp. 107f.

105. Ibid., p. 107.

106. Ibid., p. 108.

107. Ibid., p. 137.

108. Ibid., p. 137.

109. M. Olender, "Phallus," in *Encyclopaedia Universalis* (Paris, 1985), pp. 379–382.

110. M. Serres, *Hermes—Literature, Science, Philosophy*, ed. Josué V. Harari and David F. Bell (Baltimore: Johns Hopkins University Press, 1982); *La Naissance de la physique dans le texte de Lucrèce* (Paris: Minuit, 1977).

111. R. Thom, "Halte au hasard, silence au bruit," *Le Débat*, no. 3 (July–August 1980); Henri Atlan, "Postulats métaphysiques et méthodes de recherche," *Le Débat*, no. 14 (July–August 1981), pp. 83–89.

112. Serres, *Passage du Nord-Ouest*; *La Naissance de la physique*.

113. Atlan, *Entre le cristal et la fumée*, Chapter 13.

114. E. Brehier, *Histoire de la philosophie* (Paris, 1948), cited by M. Olender, "Le système gnostique de Justin."

115. See Chapter 5.

116. See Henri Atlan, "Un peuple qu'on dit élu," *Le Genre humain*, no. 3–4 (1982), pp. 98–126.

117. H. Jonas, "Gnosis und spätantiker Geist," cited by R. Stadtlender, "Gnose et hermétisme," *Encyclopédie des mystiques*.

*Chapter Four*

# Intermezzi

## Unicorns, Electrogenic Demons, and Parapsychology

"Even if archaeologists or geologists were to discover tomorrow some fossils conclusively showing the existence of animals in the past satisfying everything we know about unicorns from the myth of the unicorn, that would not show that there were unicorns."[1]

This is how Saul Kripke defined the subject of his lectures on linguistics and philosophy, whose goal was to revive the distinction between the referent and the signification of a noun. I should like to use this observation to introduce some remarks on demons and parapsychology; the reader is referred to Kripke's work for an appreciation of the full profundity of his insight.

My first remark concerns the existence of electrogenic demons. What was the reaction of most individuals who received unexpected shocks of static electricity before the discovery of electricity?[2] They almost certainly invoked the action of demons, all the more mysterious and at the same time all the more manifest, because the phenomenon was generally nonreproducible, neither by the subject-victim nor by any witness who might have wished to verify the reality of the phenomenon perceived by a third party. If we put ourselves in that situation, the question of the existence of such demons tends to get mixed up with the question of the real or illusory nature of the phenomenon itself. Our belief—or disbelief—in such demons would depend on whether we have had the experience, on whether we believe in the experience of others or even our own experience. The controversy would rage between those who believe in them and those who do not, with strong arguments to support those who had suffered the effects of these demons, and other strong arguments put forward by those who invoked illusion, fraud, or mystification—until electricity was discovered and these phenomena recognized as a static electric discharge. But what is discovered no longer has anything to do with demons, for it depends on the context in which it is described and, perhaps, explained. The discovery of electricity does not confirm the existence of the demons. In one sense, on the contrary, it denies their existence, even while it gives a more solid (because uncontested) status to the very phenomena that had formerly "demonstrated" the existence of the demons. Taken to the extreme, as with Kripke's unicorn, even if what is discovered has all the *properties* attributed to the object of the initial belief, this, once named, relates to a different referent than the sum of its properties.

Thus just when the existence of demons seems to be "scientifically" confirmed, it is on the contrary definitively undermined (at least with regard to these demons, whom we shall call "electrogenic"), because their effects are recognized and placed in a quite different theoretical context, one where electrogenic demons have no role. The same would apply to the unicorn were manifestations thereof to be discovered in a context (paleontological, archaeological) quite different from the mythical context where it has been hitherto located. The same remark was made by J. M. Lévy-Leblond[3] with regard to quantum nonseparability and its relationship—or rather lack of relationship—with the nonseparability of the mystics of the All. This lack of relationship is clearer in proportion as nonseparability is formulated in the language of physics, which particularizes it and differentiates it from the nonseparabilities of mystical traditions.

With regard to parapsychology, psychokinesis, and extrasensory perception, in the best of cases we are currently at the stage of electrogenic demons before the discovery of electricity (that is, of course, before they could even have received the name *electrogenic* demons!).

It is most likely that these phenomena, were they to be integrated into and labeled by a scientific theory, would disappear qua parapsychology, psychokinesis, and extrasensory perception. They would still require some authentic label, rather than the remote analogies with quantum mechanics of which the Cordoba colloquium provided a number of examples. In this case, too, the criterion would be the pertinence of the level of description and the continuity of a scientific discourse that, begun on a particular level of organization, cannot be extended to other levels except progressively, in small steps, without skipping over intermediate stages, while attempting the maximum reduction of what can be reduced and the maximum coverage of the interstices between neighboring disciplines.

One apparent exception merely confirms the rule: acupuncture. The discovery of a neurophysiological significance for the application points of the acupuncture needles taught by Chinese tradition seems to provide "scientific" confirmation for the reality of the traditional schemas and the teaching of the Tao on the balance of *yin* and *yang*. In fact, this is a case of an empirical reality viewed through two different lenses, two totally variant theoretical interpretations. The conceptual framework of traditional acupuncture, with its flows of male and female "energy" in meridians endowed with cosmological significance, has nothing in common with that of neurophysiology and its physicochemical and molecular foundations. Even if the empirical consequences, analgesia or disappearance of symptoms, are the same, different phenomena are involved, because the phenomenon cannot be detached from the explanatory framework in which it is perceived. Another example is that of the ritual use of plants (cacti and mushrooms) by Amerindian shamans and the phenomena of mystical revelation and participation, with possible therapeutic applications, such as one of them has described.[4] This is an autobiographical account concerning a Mexican shaman, Maria Sabina, who relates facts that a French naturalist and specialist in hallucinogenic mushrooms, R. Heim,[5] witnessed during an expedition on which he encountered her. Along with his English colleague Watson, he participated in divination and treatment seances under the influence of psilocybin-containing mushrooms, on which he reports in his works. Here too the effect of "little gods who speak" and their revelation of the "cosmic language"—Maria Sabina's description of the effects of these mushrooms—has very little in common with the botanical classification of the mushrooms, the chemistry of psilocybin, and the modifications in neuronal excitability and synaptic transmission that these drugs probably produce.

We are dealing with two quite different classes of phenomena, even though they correspond to a single empirical reality. The problem is that it is impossible to perceive this reality outside some conceptual framework; the language that describes it, always interpretive, helps to construe it and thereby to create different classes of phenomena: one a matter of spirits and demigods; the other of membrane receptors, neurotransmitters, and ionic fluxes across neuron membranes. It would certainly be an error to believe that only the latter class of phenomena is real, whereas the former is illusory. The subjective experience of the hallucinogenic trip—or of the mystic or poetic trance—is just as real as the modification of membrane permeability, even though physicochemical and neurophysiological language cannot account for it. To guard against this error, however, there is no need to unify and confound the two classes of phenomena and the levels of organization and interpretation to which they correspond. That is the easy way out, adopted by those who do not want to sacrifice the multiple experiences of reality—and in this they are quite right—but still want to discuss it in the context of a global and unitary theory.

## The Undecidability of Noncontradiction

The principle of noncontradiction is the foundation of our logic. Even so-called contradiction logics submit to it, because they stretch out contradictions in time and thereby resolve them; or find some property that makes it possible to differentiate the two terms of the contradiction so that it vanishes. In any case, the discourse that expresses these contradictions and attempts to expound these logics always itself obeys the principle of noncontradiction, according to which A cannot be A and not-A at the same time and in the same relationship. This applies equally to logics of the included middle.

This principle, along with the principle of causality (viz., effects follow from causes, and like causes produce like effects), is fundamental to both action and reasoning, without which one cannot even imagine a reality other than delirious or dreamlike. What is more, the effectiveness of these principles grounds the belief in the intelligibility and rationality of reality: simultaneously principles of reason and of effective action, they attest that reality is comprehensible and that reason is the tool by which we comprehend it (even if we accept the statement, attributed to Einstein,[6] that the fact that the world is comprehensible is itself incomprehensible). This belief is so deeply rooted at the basis of every discourse that even counterculture, antiscientific, or simply mystical discourses cannot totally renounce explanation and rationalization in phrases that do not wish to be considered "mad" and that therefore proceed by the rules of logic—even if their goal is to denounce logic, reason, and "Cartesianism."

Nevertheless, if we reflect on the two sorts of possibility, we encounter, exacerbated, the problem of *superposing without confounding* these two modes of existence: existing in logical discourse and existing in objective reality. These two modes are distinguished even more clearly when our task is to prove, not the existence of an actual phenomenon, but rather its possibility. The first step is to investigate its theoretical and logical possibility, because demonstrating its logical impossibility (i.e., its internal contradiction or contradiction of facts or laws considered to be true) entails its real impossibility as well. Only subsequently does the opposite result, its logical possibility, its noncontradiction, lead to the admission, not of its reality, but only of its possible reality; that is, to its existence as one possibility among others of the same class. This possible existence is not opposed to impossibility, because it is already existence, *possible* existence, to be differentiated only from *actual* existence, without necessarily *being opposed to it*. Thus a heavier-than-air pyramidal mass may rest on a pedestal on its base or on one of its sides. The fact that at any given moment only one of these is realized renders the others unreal although possible. On the other hand, the impossibility that this pyramid could rest suspended immobile in the air, above the ground and without support, renders this situation unreal in quite another fashion: this is the result of a logical impossibility that we derive theoretically from its implied contradiction of the law of gravity, which we accept as true. Proving the impossibility of a phenomenon simultaneously denies it both logical existence and real existence. But proving the possibility of a phenomenon does not ipso facto entail that it is real: it merely proves the logical existence of its possible existence. Its actual existence must be established by empirical methods (or perhaps by further logical proofs of its theoretical necessity).

In these last cases, the experimental verification of theoretical predictions acquires its full triumphant value, as noted previously, because it is one more demonstration, quasi-miraculous, of the correspondence between experience and reason—a demonstration that never comes on its own, even when one seeks it, expects it, and postulates it. On the one hand, we must postulate some rationality of nature when we use language to describe it as objective or at least as intersubjective reality. On the other hand, we always have the feeling that nothing compels nature to behave in accordance with the rules of our logic and our discourse,[7] even if we rationalize everything and reassure ourselves by declaring that these rules themselves are produced by nature.

It was only normal that Wittgenstein played the role of provocateur,[8] at the very frontiers of madness, when he endeavored to "demonstrate" in the *Tractatus* that the distance between things and the words of logical discourse is irreducible, that precisely there is the locus of what he called the "mystical element,"[9] and that "belief in the causal nexus is *superstition*."[10]

Nevertheless, self-confessed mystics attempt to rupture this presupposed or constructed harmony between reason and reality by attacking the rationality of language itself. Although we are accustomed to broken chains of causality (multiple, circular, inverted), the use of the *unresolved* contradiction is much more astonishing. As we have seen, it abounds in the *koan* literature of Zen Buddhism, and among the poets and mystics of the Orient, Christianity, and Islam; it is also to be found, albeit in a less overtly provocative fashion, in the Talmud and Midrash of Jewish tradition.

All of these discourses, rejecting the postulate of science that reality is rational, are based on the idea that reality is contradictory, and that logical noncontradiction is only a structure imposed by our thought, adapted to the exigencies of short-term action and of mastering the superficial and illusory layers of reality.

Of course, every time science succeeds in unveiling more deeply hidden aspects of reality, which obey rational laws, it is contradicting this a priori assumption. It is false and illusory to imagine that the two methods can work together, even though both aim at uncovering the hidden truth behind the appearances of reality. One can, however, still ask about the *reality of this contradiction* that opposes the scientific method, grounded (inter alia) on the principle of noncontradiction, to intuitions or illuminations of a species of ultimate reality that can be only contradictory. In fact, if "ultimate reality" is contradictory, perception of a contradiction is merely the result of the limitations of our logic; this would also be the case, of course, of a perception of a contradiction between the scientific method founded on noncontradiction and the mystical traditions that reject it.

As the reader may have gathered, I am going to try to show that there can be no answer based on logical discourse to this question of the reality of noncontradiction (or the noncontradiction of reality) because it quickly leads to a variant of the paradox of the Cretan liar and encounters the limits formalized by Gödel's theorem.[11] This is why the approach I shall propose—clearly not based on logic, but then neither is its opposite—consists of weighing pro and contra in each context of discourse, so as to evaluate the advantages and disadvantages of positing or rejecting the principle of noncontradiction as describing reality. This means that, with regard to the particular case of the scientific method (noncontradictory) versus the mystical traditions (non-noncontradictory), one must also make an ad hoc decision concerning the criteria of utility and fruitfulness to be applied. But the verdict that these two modes of discourse only *seem* to contradict each other leads in fact to eliminating the specificity of scientific and logical discourse, which itself rests on the reality of the principle of noncontradiction. In other words, it is a verdict whose consequences with regard to the metaphysical fusion thereby obtained between science and mysticism are not symmetrical; it is a fusion in which science disappears. This has some advantages, as we shall see when we attempt to analyze what needs the proponents of this fusion are endeavoring to satisfy. But since the scientific method, with its specificity, produces irreplaceable results, both on the plane of knowledge and thinking and on that of their technical applications, the disadvantages of this fusion carry the day over the advantages. This is the pragmatic approach that the present volume proposes, again taking into account the knowledge of the specific contributions of these two processes of knowledge that move in opposite directions: scientific method and the mystical traditions. This approach, which cannot be grounded in pure logic (for that is impossible), nevertheless derives a certain coherence—beyond the benefits it procures—precisely from the undecidability, in both directions, of the noncontradictory nature of reality, seen in some sort of objective manner, independent of the logical categories of thinking and speech.

Such undecidability can be demonstrated in a relatively simple fashion, on condition, of course, that the very terms of the question not be rejected—although this would be perfectly justified.[12] We have, however, found sufficient justification for accepting these terms: what is it in some of our experiences of reality that renders the principle of noncontradiction effective, while other experiences disclose its limits, circumscribed in a mode of thinking and speaking that, for all we can know, does not exhaust the totality of existence? Or, more schematically, is the principle of noncontradiction a property of objective reality or rather merely an interpretive projection onto our perception of reality of properties pertaining to the logic of our discourse?

Our demonstration (which clearly does not escape the categories of logic yet makes them shatter into paradox) consists first of all of observing that negation is not the symmetrical counterpart of affirmation; if the latter can directly describe what exists, the former cannot be seen except through thinking about what does exist. This property of negation has been noted numerous times and in different ways by logicians since Wittgenstein, who observed that "nothing in reality corresponds to the sign '~' [negation]."[13] The result is that every proposition containing a negation is already the result of an operation of thought and does not describe reality as it is. In particular, the statement of the principle of noncontradiction—that A cannot be simultaneously A and not-A—like every statement including a negation, does not describe reality. Thus we seem to have proven that this principle is only a projection of our thought and does not necessarily describe reality, with the implication that reality can itself be contradictory. But *in constructing this proof* we have used the principle of noncontradiction! Hence if this principle does not describe reality, neither does the proof founded on it. We are trapped by the classical paradox whose archetype is that of the Cretan who says that all Cretans are liars, a paradox whose logical structure is that of the self-referential negative propositions at the origin of proofs of logical undecidability.[14] More precisely, if our proof does not describe reality, it loses its force; hence the principle of noncontradiction *can* describe reality. If, however, we suppose this to be the case, then the proof that relies on it *does* describes reality, which proves that the principle of noncontradiction does not describe reality, which contradicts what we have already posited, and so on. Our proposition is thus proven to be undecidable.

But we are not done yet. This *proof of undecidability* does not concern reality unless we admit that the principle of noncontradiction does describe reality. If we suppose otherwise, then the proof of undecidability does not describe reality, so that whether or not the principle of noncontradiction describes reality *is not really undecidable!* On the contrary, if we suppose that this principle describes reality, then whether or not this principle describes reality truly is undecidable! In consequence, the question, "Is the undecidability of our proposition concerning the reality of the principle of noncontradiction really undecidable, or is it only the result of the operations of our thought?" is itself undecidable. And so on, regressing infinitely from one level of undecidability to another.

But these levels never appear except inside a metalevel with its own metalanguage, in which the reality of the principle of noncontradiction—the basis of the proof of undecidability—is admitted. Outside this language, nothing is undecidable any more: you can "decide" that reality is contradictory and describe it in accordance with this verdict. This is what some mystics, inter alia, do. And this provides an unusual insight into the special status of limiting principles, whose fruitfulness in science is so well known.

The principles of the conservation of mass and energy, which established the impossibility of ex nihilo creation and the destruction of matter and energy, the Carnot principle, which grounds the impossibility of perpetual motion, as well as Gödel's principle of undecidability, which states the impossibility of a complete formal metalanguage based on its own axioms—these are limiting principles that establish physical or logical impossibilities. Far from putting a damper on scientific knowledge, these principles, by determining the contexts within which relations can be established, are extremely productive. But it must be clearly seen that this fertility derives precisely from the demarcation of the frameworks within which rules of truth can be generated and that, by construction, it concerns only those domains of reality and experience thereby dissected out and delimited. For example, the principle of the conservation of energy loses all of its fecundity when extended, through misuse or abuse, to forms of "energy" such as psychic and sexual "energy," whose quantitative relations with physical forms of energy (mechanical, thermal, electrical, chemical, nuclear) have never been established—and for good reason, since the psychic and sexual phenomena they are supposed to propel are described only at levels of organization quite different and separate from those to which physical descriptions can apply directly. Similarly, Gödel's principle of incompleteness and undecidability loses its pertinence if you try to extend it to a reality that you are willing, like mystics and certain artists, to accept as contradictory.

Here we have hit on the characteristic trait of the scientific method, whose fruitfulness depends first of all on its analytic nature, on the fact that it dissects reality into separate domains within which partial truths, relative to the mode of dissection, can be found. We also see how rupturing the limits of these dissections to generate a single amalgam that abolishes the differences among them leads to the collapse and sterilization of this method, even if something of this unifying tendency is always present in any explanatory process. This is why scientific research is more productive in its effects of mastery and operational manipulation than in its effects of explanation. Dogmatic scientific explanations are doubtful and inferior, unavoidable as temporary way stations, but threatening to arrest and sterilize the progress of the method that produced them. By contrast, traditional mythical explanations, which often lead back to mystical experiences, have quite a different function, because they are posited a priori, by tradition or by illumination. Only after the fact do they serve as an occasion (in the best of cases) for scaling down the infinite grids projected on reality that must be adjusted and readjusted as the action requires. Here the explanatory framework is posed a priori, but extends to infinity, so as to take into account whatever could happen; this is quite different from the framework of the scientific disciplines, constructed step by step as the result of the process and method of its disciplines themselves.

## About "Possibles"

What is the mode of being of the possible? How does something exist that is merely possible? It probably has less existence than something that is real, even if we do not truly know what reality is, but more existence than something that is impossible. What, then, is this mode of existence of the possible? *Where* do "possibles"[15] exist?

Consider the two types of possibility contained in the definition of a number by an algorithm that permits its computation. Pi, for example, is perfectly defined by a number of algorithms, such as the division of the circumference of a circle by its diameter, or the limit of certain convergent series. But although the infinite decimal sequence of pi cannot *actually* be written, it is given *potentially* by the algorithm.[16] What does "potentially" mean here? In what world of possibles is this potentially infinite series that cannot be written to be found?

Biologists, too, have formed the habit of speaking of possibles and potentiality. François Jacob's "set of possibles"[17] describes the living world as a realization in nature of a multitude of possibles, one combinatory out of an a priori infinite abundance, which is restricted at the same moment it is realized, conditioned by the constraints of natural selection. The "potential" existence of unrealized (and thus not observed in certain conditions) properties of living beings has even acquired a molecular reality, now that they have been observed in other conditions. The discovery that genes capable of determining physical traits can be blocked by repressor mechanisms that inhibit their expression and thereby prevent the realization of the trait in question has led biologists to speak of the potential existence of these traits or of an unexpressed genetic potentiality. But this is clear and intelligible only when there are circumstances in which this trait is effectively observed, due to the derepression of the genes that determine it. In other cases, especially theoretical extrapolations about evolutionary mechanisms with the appearance of new properties—such as the evolution of species, undirected adaptive learning, or the development of language—employing the notion of biological potentiality poses the same questions concerning the bizarre and (necessarily) unreal mode of existence of these potentialities. As Jean Piaget said in response to a remark by J.-P. Changeux about the phenocopy, which exists as a "copy" only in the mind of the observer: "All this exists only in the mind of the observer, but I would say the same about the notion of potentiality, which is the most dangerous of notions. This is an Aristotelian notion which is of the 'dormant property' type and which acquires significance only when one has measurement (potential energy, for example)."[18]

Jaako Hintikka,[19] a linguist and philosopher who has followed and renewed the Kantian search for the conditions of possibility, has devoted several works to this question. But he has considerably simplified his task by viewing possibility as logical possibility only; that is, what exists in a noncontradictory discourse. From this starting point, the real or unreal character of these possibles is confounded with the true or false character of all such noncontradictory propositions; and this character is determined by the quest in the world of sensory experiences—more or less mediated (this is certainly a source of numerous problems)—for examples or counterexamples that tend to demonstrate the falseness of negative or affirmative propositions, respectively. This process of logical empiricism is also that spontaneously used in scientific proofs. Hintikka demonstrates its richness and does a good job of explaining the processes we use spontaneously, without, in fact, really knowing what we are doing. Thus, in particular,[20] he proposes one way, quite natural in his formalism, of understanding how a mathematical proof adds a new item of information about the world, even if this information was already contained in its premises and even if, as is often asserted (a bit too facilely), mathematics is merely an immense tautology.[21]

However, this entire approach clearly supposes that reality is necessarily noncontradictory, which is indeed possible—but which, as we have seen, is merely one of the two options of an undecidable proposition. The other attitude also remains legitimate, because it corresponds to the other possibility. In that case, sensory experience comes first, and is not informed a priori by the logical discourse that *ab ovo* restricts the possible to the noncontradictory. This restores the possibility of experiencing a contradictory reality; more precisely, of experiencing a nonlogical reality, one that is neither contradictory nor noncontradictory. This is the experience claimed by mystics and artists, even if, subsequently, some of them deem it important to translate the experience into the terms of rational discourse. In this approach, reality is initially postulated as arational: neither rational nor irrational. As such, it can be seen and experienced straightaway, in an instant or in eternity, in the vision of the mystic and in that of the artist. Reason is then sometimes used, secondarily, as one means of speaking of reality and of sharing the experience of it. Poetic discourse is another arational means of speaking about it, continuing on to song and then to music, which, according to the quip of Vladimir Jankelevitch, "like consciousness with its subconscious reservations and its unconscious ulterior motives…, is unaware of the principle of contradiction."[22]

We see once again how two forms of discourse, each of them rational, are incommensurable, cannot be superimposed and even less confounded, and are like trains on parallel tracks moving in opposite directions: that of an a priori rationality moving toward reality, and that of an a priori unlimited sensory reality moving toward the reason of discourse.

## Notes

1. S. A. Kripke, *Naming and Necessity* (Cambridge, Mass.: Harvard University Press, 1980), p. 24.

2. Although Classical Antiquity knew that light bodies were attracted by a piece of amber (*elektron* in Greek) that had been rubbed with a cloth, the effect was ascribed to the action, inter alia, of a living soul. Only in the seventeenth century did "electric force" begin to be studied on its own and become the subject of theories based on various experimental devices and on other natural phenomenon, such as lightning.

3. J.-M. Lévy-Leblond, personal communication.

4. Alvaro Estrado, *Maria Sabina, Her Life and Chants*, trans. and commentaries by Henry Munn, with a retrospective essay by R. Gordon Wasson (Santa Barbara, Calif.: Ross-Erikson, 1981).

5. R. Heim, *Les Champignons toxiques et hallucinogènes* (Paris: N. Boubée, 1963).

6. See Chapter 6, n. 84.

7. Gregory Bateson has remarked that it is quite difficult to suppose that nature can distinguish correct from incorrect syllogisms, something that is nevertheless implicit in our normal manner of thinking about nature (Bateson, *Men Are Grass*; see also Chapter 7, p. 299).

8. In fact, these difficulties have never stopped haunting philosophical thought, from the birth of logic down to contemporary philosophers. They depend, inter alia, on the almost ineffable and certainly arbitrary nature of the relations between logical necessity and necessary existence. See, for example, N. Rescher, "Aristotle's Theory of Modal Syllogisms and its Interpretation," in *The Critical Approach to Science and Philosophy*, ed. Mario Bunge (London: Collier-Macmillan, 1964), pp. 153–157, especially the discussion he cites by Lucasiewicz concerning Aristotle's principle of necessity that unduly confuses logical necessity and necessary existence. See also Jaako Hintikka, *Logic, Language Games, and Information* (Oxford: Clarendon Press, 1973). We shall return to this question of the mode of existence of possibles later in this chapter and again in Chapters 5 and 7.

9. Ludwig Wittgenstein, *Tractatus Logico-Philosophicus*, 6.522: "There are, indeed, things that cannot be put into words. They *make themselves manifest*. They are what is mystical." See also 4.121: "What expresses *itself* in language, we cannot express by means of language. Propositions *show* the logical form of reality."

10. Ibid., 5.1361.

11. The same form of the paradox of the Cretan liar is used by Popper with regard to a question, analogous to the one we are posing here, about rationalism as an ideology that is the source of beliefs and behavior: "A rationalist accepts *only* positions that can be rationally justified" is itself untenable and contradictory, because the position cannot itself be defended rationally (Karl R. Popper, *The Open Society and Its Enemies* [Princeton, N.J.: Princeton University Press, 1966), vol. 2, p. 230).

12. One way of rejecting the terms of the question consists of denying the existence of objective reality and taking refuge in an absolute subjectivist idealism. We leave aside, for the moment, the question of knowing what it means to be real, as posed, for example, by W. Yourgrau, "On the Reality of Elementary Particles," in *The Critical Approach to Science and Philosophy*, pp. 360–381. We need merely observe that the question we are asking is one consequence, among many, of the fact that the reality of physical reality is no longer so immediate, due to the mediation of theory. The conclusion of this paragraph can only reinforce this questioning about what reality is, while getting even farther away from any possible definitive answer.

13. *Tractatus* 4.0621. Wittgenstein goes on to observe that "the propositions '$p$' and '$\sim p$' have the opposite sense, but there corresponds to them one and the same reality" (viz., that either '$p$' or '$\sim p$' is true). We should also cite his remarks on the

nonexistence of logical objects, implying that a negation, $\sim p$, is already a propositional sign carrying with it all possible truth functions and does not designate a negative reference to some object that is symmetrically opposed to $p$ (see *Tractatus* 4.431, 4.441, 5.02, 5.44, and 5.512). See also Russell's discussion of phrases that denote something that does not exist but nevertheless bear possible meanings within certain propositions (Bertrand Russell, "On Denoting," *Mind* 59 [1950]; reprinted in T. H. Olshewsky, ed., *Problems of the Philosophy of Languages* [New York: Holt, Rinehart and Winston, 1969], pp. 300–311). Finally, we should note what Vuillemin has to say about the negation of performative statements such as "I promise to come." They are transformed into declarative statements ("I do not promise to come") in which the difference is that the former have a direct relation to the action they involve, whereas the latter have lost this relation: thus the effect of negation does not bear solely on the content of the statement, but also on its relation toward the action envisioned ("Remarques sur le 4.442 du *Tractatus*," in *Wittgenstein et le problème d'une philosophie de la science* [Paris: Centre national de la recherche scientifique, 1971], pp. 153–167).

14. See, for example, Hofstadter, *Gödel, Escher, Bach*.

15. "Just as the only necessity that exists is *logical* necessity, so too the only impossibility that exists is *logical* impossibility" (Wittgenstein, *Tractatus* 6.375). But what about possibility? *Can* we say the same thing about it? We shall see later (Chapter 7, p. 306) that the possible, like negation and totality, poses difficult problems for the author—and reader—of the *Tractatus*, at the limits of the world and of logic, playing the role of pseudo-concepts that condition language without being speakable by it. On the basis of these problems, but continuing them despite everything, the "second" Wittgenstein, accepting natural language just as found, makes the famous somersault represented by his theory of language games, in which "there must be perfect order even in the vaguest sentence." Ludwig Wittgenstein, *Philosophical Investigations*, trans. G. E. M. Anscombe (New York: Macmillan, 1968), I.98, p. 45.

16. For the moment we leave aside the question of the problematic links, not devoid of circularity, between the possible and the infinite (see Chapter 7, n. 24). Many philosophers have wondered about actual versus potential existence. Aristotle already distinguished within the second of these two sorts of *dynamis*, potential *as such* (a source of change or power to effect change), that is, a specific potentiality, and potential *in general* (the capacity a thing has of passing to a different state), in the sense that "bronze is potentially a statue" (*Metaphysics* 1065$^b$5– 1066$^a$7). The former implies the existence of a temporal process of construction or of becoming, such as growth, aging, etc. (an algorithm?), which he calls, generally, a "motion." But the mode of existence of this potentiality (that of the statue, for example) is defined by means of the category of entelechy of motion. In this category, hard to understand today, we can read, if we wish, a prefiguring of both vitalist biological finalism and physico-mathematical finalism (see Chapter 5), depending on whether we are more sensitive to the designation of the final state of the

motion-process or to that of the process per se, in its finality. Nevertheless, this distinction remains important in that the possible designates a process that "seems" already to be more real. But the question is merely displaced to the *manner* in which we acquire *knowledge* of this process (see Chapter 7, n. 70).

17. François Jacob, *The Possible and the Actual* (Seattle and London: University of Washington Press, 1982).

18. Massimo Piattelli-Palmarini, ed., *Language and Learning: The Debate between Jean Piaget and Noam Chomsky* (Cambridge, Mass.: Harvard University Press, 1980), p. 64. The controversy surrounding Piaget and concerning the very definition of the concept of the phenocopy, which lay at the bottom of this exchange, can be settled, in principle, by experiments on the structure and mechanisms of expression of the genome of the species in question. Only in these conditions, and if the experiment confirms it by giving it, in addition, a precise content with regard to the mechanisms regulating the expression of the genes in question, would the idea of genetic potentiality retain its molecular meaning.

19. Hintikka, *Logic, Language Games, and Information*.

20. The question of what is logically possible but does not exist in reality, until experience demonstrates otherwise, is represented in mathematics by the classical debate whether it is discovery or construction (see, for example, G. G. Granger, *Langages et Épistémologie* [Paris: Klincksieck, 1979]; and the *Actes d'un colloque internationale sur Langage et Pensée mathématique* [Luxembourg: Centre universitaire de Luxembourg, 1976]). To this classical alternative between mathematics as a great tautology, in which the mathematician merely discovers entities and necessary relations that were always there, and construction-invention, in which the proof of a theorem adds something truly new but contingency seems to be able to make the bed of the arbitrary, Wittgenstein proposed a third term. See Ludwig Wittgenstein, *Remarks on the Foundations of Mathematics*, ed. G. H. von Wright, R. Rhees, and G. E. M. Anscombe, trans. G. E. M. Anscombe (New York: Macmillan, 1956); also S. A. Kripke, *Wittgenstein on Rules and Private Language* (Oxford: Basil Blackwell, 1982); C. M. Lich, "Creation and Discovery: Wittgenstein on Conceptual Change," in *The Need for Interpretation*, ed. S. Mitchell and M. Rosen (London: Athlone Press, 1983), pp. 33–53. For Wittgenstein, mathematics and psychology share the defect of associating a "confusion of concepts" with effective technique: that of proof, in the former case, and of the measurements of experimental psychology, in the latter (*Philosophical Investigations*, part II, xiv, p. 232). Although his attempts to clarify psychological concepts take up a large part of his reflections on language games, in mathematics they permit him to maintain the possibility of innovation at the same time as he reduces that of the arbitrary. He shows how the development of mathematics implies an activity of renewal that remains rigorous and obeys the rules that guarantee its rationality, but which is nevertheless a renewal in that it bears on the very concepts that mathematicians invent and modify as they go along constructing. We shall encounter this question again on several occasions (in Chapters 5, 6, and 7), along several different routes. In par-

ticular, we shall see in Chapter 7 how considering knowledge to be games opens the world of possibles by giving it a particular mode of being, that of play.

21. Hintikka, *Logic, Language, Games*. See in particular "Are Logical Truths Tautologies?" (Chapter 7) and "Information, Deduction, and the A Priori" (Chapter 10). This theory repeats a result established by S. Winograd and J. D. Cowan (*Reliable Computation in the Presence of Noise* [Cambridge, Mass.: MIT Press, 1963]), who, following von Neumann, studied the properties of computational networks whose reliability in the presence of noise was greater than that of their components. Extending Shannon's theory to noisy computational channels, they showed how the computation destroys information, in Shannon's sense, in that it reduces the a priori uncertainty concerning the result of a test about the sensible world (see Atlan, *L'Organisation biologique*).

22. Vladimir Jankelevitch, *La Musique et l'ineffable* (Paris: Le Seuil, 1983), p. 94. Like the possible, which, I would suggest, is to be found in a world of elsewhere, "one who looks for music somewhere will not find it" (ibid., p. 138).

## Chapter Five

# Interpretation, Delirium, Black Mud[1]

### The Interests of Reason and the Interpretive Impulse

We have seen how mystical elements are naturally present in scientific rationality. Not only the processes of discovery (doubtful analogies, intuitions, illuminations in obscure metaphysical or religious contexts, such as Newton's alchemical writings), but also those of scientific theorizing are often imbued with a concern for a comprehensive unitary explanation, for discovering Ultimate Reality and the Golden Number; this concern, for all its rationalizing and mathematical form, associates them with mystical traditions. Materialist metaphysics is no better protection against these dangers than the metaphysics of the Cosmic Mind.

We have also seen that certain mystical traditions, or certain currents within these traditions, developed a rationality that is quite "reasonable," shielding from the light (at least explicitly) only the means of revelation; the contents of the revelation, however, are subsequently expressed in coherent and independent discourses that have their own value and life not necessarily referred to some ineffable content of mystical experience. In other words, Newton, the alchemists, and the kabbalists seem to belong to the same party as today's spiritualist quantum physicists.

I shall try to demonstrate that this impression is false and works to the detriment of both sides; it is not enough that two different discourses are rational for them to have the same *explanatory aim*. In other words, what is

159

important here is not that both deal with reason (once this has been admitted and recognized), but that reason can be applied in many fashions. These processes, and others, are characterized and differentiated by their different uses of reason, by their spoken or unspoken presuppositions about the relations between reason and reality, rather than by the intrinsic rationality of one and irrationality of the other. This is where the question of delirium is introduced or confusion reappears (one surmises), because, on the one hand, delirious thoughts are the archetype of thoughts that have "lost their reason," whereas, on the other hand, rational delusions certainly exist.

Here too we confound reason (as opposed to unreason, as the corrupted operation of the logical faculties, or to antireason, as their systematic rejection) with the various ways of *using reason*, determined by what Jürgen Habermas, following Kant and Fichte, designates and analyzes as the *interest* of knowledge.[2] Habermas applies the notion to the distinction between the natural sciences and the social sciences: different interests lead to different ways of using reason. The former have a technical interest of instrumental mastery and accumulating know-how; the latter are typified by a practical interest of intersubjective communication, symbolically mediated by the social tradition. He resolves the problem he finds in Kant, namely, that pure reason is necessarily governed by the interests of practical reason, by searching for a critical thought that is self-reflecting, as the self-production of reason, in a living context of the self-production of the species. This distinction between two different uses of reason, one governed by the technical interest in mastery, the other by a practical interest in communication, is not the only one possible. It partially overlaps the distinction we have been led to establish between a formal usage, bearing only on abstractions detached from any sensible content, and the common usage of reason, directly applied to sensory representations. To the extent that the former has become increasingly dominant in the natural sciences, it has helped separate the scientific usage of reason from disciplines with ethical or social applications. In effect, the *abstraction* of scientific discourse leads to a discipline that has few points of connection with lived experience, which for its own part remains governed by the directly sensible. Today its interest is seen more clearly as being limited exclusively to the effectiveness of operational and instrumental mastery; this has always been the case, but formerly it was less blatant, hiding behind theoretical and metatheoretical pretensions to a rational explanation of the universe.

But we can—and must—extend these distinctions to intellectual enterprises other than those of the sciences as they have developed in the West. We can recognize differences in the employment of reason, governed by different interests, not only within the positivist sciences (between the natural sciences and the *sciences humaines*), but also between the sciences and nonscientific traditions, whether Western (poetic, esthetic) or not, for all that they do not willingly and systematically think themselves irrational. Although these differences lead to discourses that, as we shall see, are properly "incommensurable,"[3] they nevertheless stand out against their common background, which should first be located: our apparently irresistible need to explain, to make order among things, to discover in them (or to give them) a meaning, by seeing (or establishing) relations among them that make a disparate aggregate of diverse sensations into an organized fabric, unified in space and, perhaps most of all, in time. To get to that point we expend the full assets of our ingenuity, patience, and efforts, sometimes consciously and collectively, in those institutions that have assumed the traditions of research and knowledge, and sometimes unconsciously and almost automatically, so great is the difficulty of confronting unexplained phenomena.

Following Freud, we can consider this need to originate in what he calls "the impulse for knowledge and investigation,"[4] which spurs the child's "theories" about birth, sexual relations, and sexual differentiation. For M. Neyraut,[5] these theories are the first example of unconscious thought characterized by its own logic, which is different from that of conscious thought.

Nevertheless, in conscious thought, in our different ways of consciously reacting to events, we are dealing with a similar impulse, even if civilizations consisted of transforming the unconscious, the subjective, and the ineffable into institutions, customs, interminable discussions, and narratives until the Western invention of objective discourse and its logic.

## Interpretands

Let any event occur, common or unheard of, and our almost immediate reaction is a discourse, explaining it in one fashion or another, integrating it with the already known that makes us what we are, individually and as members of a linguistic community. These explanations, whatever they are, can be only interpretations, projections of preexisting schemes on what we perceive. This process is so immediate, so "natural," so automatic, that a posteriori it is extremely hard for us to separate the raw event perceived by our senses from its interpretation and the meaning it thereby acquires. Let us call "interpretands" these events that our senses make us perceive, but which seem to be only elements offered ineluctably for us to interpret them. Only by extremely elaborate critical reflection can we sometimes and with great pains manage to separate what may be given by the senses from the logical discourse about these data.

In practice, though, it is as if we had at our disposal a relative diversity of explanatory schemes, accumulated in different frames of reference or strata of our cognitive apparatus, based on the sociolinguistic groups to which we have belonged, simultaneously or successively: family, school, religion or ideology, country, linguistic community and the culture or tradition associated with it, and finally this language of reason and science that claims to be—and sometimes is—universal. Depending on the interpretand that calls us, a scheme deriving from one of these strata that compose us will impose itself, more or less strongly, sometimes in indistinct rivalry with another scheme that rises, *simultaneously*, from some other stratum.

## An Attempt at Classification

An event takes place before us: a stone works itself loose, a man dies, a child is born, someone dreams and the dream comes true, a radioactive substance decays and emits radiation—or many other things. Once we perceive it (directly or via some witness), the event "naturally" triggers associations with other events that do—or do not—constitute its explanation or possible explanations.

### Regularity and Physical Causality

In the simplest case, we recognize an event as being superposable on another event that is already known and integrated into a chain of causes and effects. It is then explained as the effect of its cause, itself linked to another cause, and so forth, the full causal chain being furnished by scientific, physical, and cosmogonic theory. In the final analysis, Schrödinger's equation and the Big Bang theory provide the explanatory scheme, with, closer to home, the efficient cause that produced the event in question.

Often, though, it is not so simple: the event is not readily perceived as repeating some similar and familiar event, such that the principle of like causes producing like effects could be applied to it. The event appears to be unique, or almost so, and a priori quite improbable, on the basis of what we already know. Or it may involve the repetition or conjunction of causally independent events, and it is precisely their repetition or conjunction that seems to be unique and improbable. The cause is far from clear; in such a case we speak of chance or coincidence. This opens the door to all sorts of interpretations, because, even in cases of this type, we nevertheless endeavor to integrate the event into some explanatory scheme—so unbearable do we find it to leave things in a state of total nonmeaning. Even the invocation of mystery plays an interpretative role and provides a meaning, by associating the event with all others that seem to require the same invocation.

Pushing the analysis a bit further, we can try to distinguish various sorts of possible explanatory schemes. The one we have considered previously can be designated "physical-causalist": an event is explained by its physical cause. But even in this case, interpretation has already made its presence felt. When we explain that a stone falls *because of* gravity, the latter is not another event perceived directly, like the fall of the stone it was invoked to explain. Gravity, as Bateson remarked[6] through the humorous bent of the teacher of a gifted little girl, is (just like an instinct) an explanatory principle that is explained by nothing in its turn. Even without speaking of the Schrödinger equation or the Big Bang, it is no longer the case of one phenomenon caused by another phenomenon, but of an aggregate of phenomena already integrated into an explanatory scheme from which it is difficult to extract them, a scheme furnished by schools and the teaching of scientific laws and theories.

### Abstract Causality in Physics

In daily life, in our latitudes, these explanatory schemes are considered to be the solid pedestal of our objective knowledge, grounded on the principle of causality. This is why impersonal causalistic explanation and physical causalistic explanation are confused in practice. But for someone who reflects on the fundamentals of physics, the abstraction of explanatory schemes, which has increased regularly throughout the history of that science, makes it difficult to maintain this confusion. For such a person, physical explanation appears clearly as what it is: an interpretation *by* physical science. It is no longer a causal explanation, but integration into a more general abstract framework, making it possible to successfully predict, by means of computation, classes of events that have not yet been observed. There is a vast distance between direct sensory observation of events and the abstract mathematical form of the physical law. The latter, unlike an event that causes another event, lies at quite a different level of abstraction, where its relations with reality pose formidable problems. It is hard to consider physical laws to be the cause of the phenomena that they can be used to predict. Their effectiveness itself becomes a phenomenon to be explained, a sort of interpretand whose own cause must be found! The physicist Wolfgang Pauli, whose exclusion principle in quantum physics is among those most marked by this character of efficacious abstraction, wondered about this. His answer invokes Jung's theory of archetypes, unconscious images and structures present in all of us from all eternity.[7] As we shall see later, this invocation is not devoid of ambiguity. In effect,

Pauli merely observes this a priori harmony, because its unconscious and unknown character rules out giving it an objective and causalist description. On the contrary, these archetypes, even unconscious, serve Jung as an explanatory scheme whose causal status remains ambiguous. Even though the 'acausal orderedness' effectuated or observed in a meaningful coincidence is constantly stressed, it is the archetype that is supposed to *produce* this coincidence of meaning. In this sense, for Jung, it is the cause, especially to the extent that one uses it to explain the occurrence of the coincidence.

Jung eventually came to speak of a "transcendental cause" that is not a cause, or of the contingency of the archetype as "psychic probability," an act of creation, "contingent to causal determination"[8]—all of which are problematic concepts or pseudo-concepts. We shall return to them later.

### Physico-Mathematical Finalism

Another sort of explanatory scheme, it too provided by the physical sciences, can be called "physical-finalist": a phenomenon is explained because it obeys a law of evolution, whereby a given system passes from one state to another in accordance with a law that specifies the final state it must attain. Heat diffuses from the hotter to the colder in a conducting body to equalize the temperatures, "because" this phenomenon is regulated by the second law of thermodynamics, which stipulates that the final state of the conductor must be one of maximum entropy, precisely that realized by the equalization of temperatures.

The character of explanatory principles represented by physical *phenomena* themselves appears here too when we realize that the falling stone can be explained by the same gravitation, viewed this time as a physical finalism, such that the fall of a body is explained by the fact that it attains a final state of minimum potential energy. It is important to stress that this physical finalism, unlike its biological counterpart, is in no way offensive and is perfectly acceptable as a scientific explanation. This follows from its inclusion of two properties always missing from biological finalisms: as A. Lautman discerned,[9] it is distinguished from nonscientific finalism by being expressed in a mathematical formalism (in the form of the evolution of a potential function to a maximum or minimum); and this in turn permits predictive calculations with a more general scope than mere observation of directly perceived evolutions and histories.[10] Above all, these laws of extremum of mathematico-physical functions do not entail the existence of any conscious will that decides, in the manner of a person or god, in what direction and toward what goal the phenomenon should or must develop. The metaphor of the genetic program, accepted with such enthusiasm by biologists, undoubtedly constitutes an attempt to extend a form of physical finalism to biology. Even though it is not formulated mathematically, it has become scientifically acceptable because it does not invoke a divine or cosmic mind, unlike classic vitalist (teleological) finalism, and because it uses the computer as its model of a "non-purposeful, end-seeking system," to quote the anticipatory definition of Pittendrigh, father of the distinction between teleonomy and teleology.[11] The fact that this notoriously inadequate metaphor has nevertheless been accepted straightaway as the principle explaining the development of the embryo, because of its nontheological character and the long antivitalist and antispiritualist struggle of modern biology, clearly demonstrates the role of the consensus of the society of scientists in the production of scientific interpretations. We also see how this consensus, like every interpretive scheme, is profoundly marked by the history of the successive explanatory schemes that gave birth to it and of which it marks the most recent avatar.

However, this detracts not a whit from the explanatory power of science, *unless we begin by making it into an absolute.* Once we have recognized its operation as an interpretive system, the latter must observe the rules of the game imposed during its history, on pain of vanishing, denatured and transformed into other interpretive systems (mythical, poetic, mystical, religious). Each of these systems offers its own advantages and disadvantages, which disappear in such a fusion. This is why biology's rejection of conscious and divine finalisms and acceptance of teleonomy, in the form of the genetic program, are justified, despite the latter's relatively feeble explanatory virtue. This weakness has been recognized many times, among other reasons because it involves a program without programmers, unless the work of natural selection is considered to be the writing of computer programs, which poses difficulties[12] at least as great as those encountered in comprehending myth. Still, this lame interpretation of the directed development of every living being is preferable to the invocation of a divine will or cosmic mind, which is always the endpoint of vitalist theories— preferable not from the perspective of absolute explanatory value, but from that of the rules of the scientific game and of success and effectiveness as judged from within the context established by these rules. Practically speaking, the physicochemical and cybernetic explanation has facilitated and continues to permit an unprecedented proliferation of new experiments and manipulations, sparked by the questions raised by this explanation in each particular case, which themselves lead to new questions. By contrast, the explanation that invokes God or the cosmic mind departs from the context established by the rules of the scientific game and thereby halts the process of discovery and scientific manipulation of things.

## The Probabilistic Explanation

The invocation of *probabilities* constitutes a third type of explanatory scheme. When what I have called an "interpretand" cannot be reduced to a known physical cause or physical principle expressed by an extremum law, we can still integrate it into scientific knowledge if it can be given a probabilistic treatment. It is viewed as an element in a class of events with which we associate, theoretically or by observation of frequencies, degrees of probability. The occurrence of any particular event within this class (i.e., of the interpretand in question) is not explained any better, but part of its mystery is eliminated by being *operationally* related to chance. Here chance plays an interpretive role that is neither trivial nor tautological, because it has a predictive power derived from its quantitative expression in a law of probability. Even if this, once again, does not explain the details that make the event unique, it reassures and fully plays its interpretive role by integrating the unknown into the known, the occurrence of the novelty into a preexisting explanatory scheme. An apparently unique and inexplicable event has nevertheless been "explained" when we can accord it a degree of probability, small but nonzero: hence it *must* occur at least one time, and the interpretand in question realizes this one time—it just happens that I was there, directly or by mediation of some observer, when it occurred.

## Starting to Wander off the Path:
## The "Law of Series" and Jung's Principle of Synchronicity

A more subtle probabilistic interpretation with greater "explanatory" (perhaps we should rather say "demystifying") power consists of showing that the event in fact had a greater probability than was previously believed, so that its singularity was less than it seemed to be. An interesting historical example is provided by the so-called Law of Series in medicine. Every physician has noted that cases of rare diseases tend to cluster together in series within relatively short periods, separated by long intervals in which not a single case is observed. Such a disease, of which a physician may see only a few cases in his or her entire professional career, is detected in several patients, one after another, during a relatively short period, on the order of several months. Because these involve noninfectious diseases and unrelated (familial or otherwise) patients, these cases seem to be totally independent, so their occurrence in clusters is always astonishing. Since their observation is due only to chance,[13] one would expect that observations of several causally independent successive cases should be dispersed, separated by time intervals on the order of a mean interval estimated as the inverse of the mean number of cases observed per unit time. The fact that this is not true and that these cases tend to occur in groups is well known; physicians are regularly astonished, because they have no explanation for it. Instead of explaining it, Kammerer[14] gave it a name, invoking a "Law of Series" whose mechanism remains quite obscure. It is as if the physician observes coincidences, but coincidences that recur rather more than would be expected on the basis of the common intuition about the chance occurrence of events.

With this and several other observations, Jung[15] began an article in which he wondered about the coincidence of causally independent events and proposed his principle of synchronicity, as an explanatory principle in addition to the principle of causality. To this principle of synchronicity Jung assigned the status of the particular explanatory principle characteristic of mythic thought and of non-Western traditions.

This principle makes it possible to conceive of the existence of relations among events in circumstances where not only can no causal relationship be recognized among them, but where one is even unthinkable, because, inter alia, a temporal inversion or spatial separation rules out any exchange of energy or communication. These relations are called "acausal"; underlying them is a common meaning, all the more striking because the events that convey this meaning cannot be causally dependent. For example, a patient tells Jung of a dream she had had the night before, about a golden scarab; at the same moment a golden beetle bumps into the window, attracting Jung's attention to the point that he opens the window to let it in (thereby triggering scientific astonishment and curiosity in himself, and an affective shock necessary to the therapeutic progress of his patient, previously closed up in the rationalism of her Western philosophical culture). Jung also made much of Rhine's ESP experiments, which seemed to demonstrate, on the basis of statistical analyses subsequently contested,[16] the reality of phenomena related by some "unconscious knowledge" despite a spatiotemporal distance that excluded any possibility of causal relations by exchange of energy or information.

At the time Jung did not know about "quantum nonseparability," but the use he would have made of it to provide a physical grounding for his theory is quite apparent, and his disciples have not failed to do so. For him, the discovery of quantum discontinuities and the laws of radioactivity, seen as "acausal" (because susceptible only to statistical description) relationships between physical phenomena, was enough. Aware of the calculation of probabilities, Jung does admit the possibility of fortuitous events and coincidences, which can be evaluated by computations that measure the probable character, where only the effect of chance (defined as the absence of causal—or any other—relations) is taken into account. But his process rests on the capital distinction he establishes between meaningless and meaningful coincidences. Only the latter express the reality of these acausal relations and make it possible to integrate, in a coherent vision of things, the biological and archetypical structure of the unconscious, particle physics, extrasensory perception and psychokinesis, and even astrology and traditional techniques of divination such as the *I Ching*. To establish this distinction he analyzes, *a contrario*, what physicians, following Kammerer, call the "Law of Series," which seems to belong to the family of meaningless coincidences. For Jung the observation of several cases of a rare disease, clustering with no apparent reason, is an example of coincidence concerning which his principle of synchronicity *could* be invoked. He refuses to do so, however. We shall see later how, with regard to astrology, Jung (in a manner that is at the very least open to dispute) applies the negative results of a statistical test to "ground" astrology on this principle. In the case of medical coincidences, however, he reproaches Kammerer for having gotten onto the wrong track and contradicting himself by invoking a "law of series" as an additional principle of explanation. What is more, Jung proposes a solution to the problem by suggesting that perhaps computing the probabilities would provide an adequate account of these clusters of cases.

In fact, a probabilistic treatment clearly demonstrates that commonsense intuition is wrong: the "laws of chance," as computed probabilities, can indeed "explain" the phenomenon. The probability that these occurrences of a rare disease are separated by equal intervals is much less than the probability that the intervals are different; if one imagines all the various possible ways of distributing the dates of these occurrences over a given period of observation, equal intervals represents only one possibility, clearly less probable than all of the others with unequal intervals. It can be demonstrated[17] that this remains the case even if we accept only approximate equality of intervals (within a certain margin); the incidence of cases separated by quite different intervals remains more probable than that of cases at approximately equal intervals. Hence clustering is merely the realization of the most probable phenomenon, contrary to what commonsense intuition initially told us.

Thus this phenomenon of the Law of Series, which always intrigues physicians, loses its mystery at the same time that we are reassured that it has been "explained." Nevertheless, this explanation leaves behind an aftertaste of inadequacy, like any probabilistic explanation. This is because the Law of Large Numbers, which establishes a convergence between a calculated probability and an observed frequency, is itself the result of observation and not causally explained. If you explain to a child that at least one person must necessarily pass through the door of a certain building during the next hour *because*, taking into account how many people live in the building and their presumed habits of coming and going, the mean probability can be roughly calculated and estimated that around ten persons per hour will pass through the door during the day, the child would be flabbergasted to see that it really works out that way. And there is no satisfactory answer to the question, "Why is it this way?" since of course the "because" of the previous sentence does not imply a causal relationship.[18]

### Probabilities and Spiritualist Physics: The Jung-Pauli Misunderstandings

This may be why probabilistic explanations give rise to interminable debates and controversies as to their scientific status and legitimacy. The central role of the calculation of probabilities in quantum physics greatly facilitates the task of those whom we have called the "spiritualist physicists." Their encounter with Jungian psychoanalysis did not have to wait for the Cordoba colloquium in 1979; it goes back to the very origins, if one may say so, as attested by a 1952 volume co-authored by Carl Gustav Jung and the physicist Wolfgang Pauli.[19] This is the book in which Jung expounded his principle of synchronicity[20] and Pauli[21] raised the question (which remains open) of abstract-concrete relations in physics.

Pauli found it more appropriate, however, not to directly analyze the new problems posed by quantum physics, which he had helped develop, but rather to examine how the question was posed at the dawn of classical physics, in the work of Kepler. He saw the effectiveness of Kepler's laws, mathematical formulas that make it possible to describe planetary motion, as the first example of what later became the rule in physics: systematic use of a mathematical formalism, abstract and nonempirical in origin, in the scientific explanation of reality. This process, which began with Kepler, culminated in the quantum physics that Pauli had helped found. For him, though, Kepler represented a pivot point, simultaneously a break and a continuation with the prescientific, magico-symbolic and alchemical age, which also postulated a harmony between abstract forms and concrete reality, except that the former were not expressed via a logico-mathematical apparatus.

For Pauli, the continuity through Kepler is just as instructive as the discontinuity, and he uses it to propose elements of an answer to the question—still the same question, but even more obsessive for modern physics—about the basis of the efficacy of abstract forms of nonempirical origin as applied to the explanatory and predictive description of concrete phenomena. Confronted by the abstractions of quantum physics and the problem of their relationship with reality, Pauli finds in Jungian archetypes a means of identifying the origin of scientific theories. In this way he endeavors to resolve the problem of the relationship between mathematics and physics by reducing it to a particular case of psychophysical parallelism. As an example he cites Kepler's method, showing how it is rooted in a Platonic idea very close to that of the Jungian archetypes. Today we could perhaps conduct similar exercises based on Newton's alchemical writings.[22] But the misunderstanding would be just as total as that between Jung and Pauli.

The first misunderstanding is that for Pauli the rupture between scientific method, on the one hand, and alchemy and magic and symbolism, on the other, is real. For Jung, if there is a difference, it is the greater generality of the symbolic, the incorporation of the scientific method into a discipline that is at the same time more general and more profound, access to which is provided by the psychology of depths and mythical lore.[23] For Pauli, by contrast, the reversal of the role of mathematics and computation, considered to be minor and not very dignified before Kepler, signals an irreversible break, propelling mathematics to a central place in the new—and henceforth only scientifically acceptable—expression of the relationship between the abstract and the concrete.[24]

The most flagrant misunderstanding between these two coauthors regards the calculation of probabilities. Jung considers it important to establish the existence of what he calls "meaningful coincidences," which must be carefully distinguished from "meaningless" coincidences. Habitually, every association of events that the calculation of probabilities accepts—with a high probability of not being mistaken—as the result of chance, with no need to invoke a hidden link (causal or not) between them, is considered to be a meaningless coincidence. Any highly improbable association that nevertheless occurs regularly sparks questions about the existence of hidden causal relations between these events. Jung is not content with this classic use of the calculation of probabilities, however. He begins by admitting that if the frequency of coincidences does not significantly exceed the probability computed for them exclusively on the basis of chance and excluding hidden causal relations, we certainly have no reason to suppose the existence of such relations. On the other hand, such a coincidence, even if it occurs only once, reveals for Jung the existence of an acausal relationship that is meaningful; as if, because the basis of the coincidental association cannot be either causal or *probabilistic*, it must *necessarily* involve meaning. In other circumstances, however, Jung utilizes the calculation of probabilities in a more classic fashion to "prove" the existence of these very same meaningful acausal relations. If the frequency of observed associations appears to be higher than chance alone would allow us to predict, the existence of a relation between the coincidental elements seems to be required. If this cannot be—physically—causal, it must be acausal(!).

Jung applies this type of reasoning to the Rhine telepathy experiments, whose positive results seemed to be statistically established in the absence of any causal relation; but when it comes to astrology, he has recourse to the previous, paradoxical mode of using probabilities (as too, *a contrario*, with regard to medical series). In fact, his attempt to provide astrology with a statistical foundation by a search—correctly conducted—for correlations between the result of the marriages of 200 couples and their prediction on the basis of astrological themes of conjunctions ultimately fails. But it is precisely this failure that allows him to consider such an association, when observed, as a meaningful coincidence! The observation of medical series, on the contrary, cannot be considered to be very significant if it is possible to account for it by statistical probabilities (which, as we have seen, seems to be the case).

Thus, according to the needs of the cause (or rather of the *acause*), the calculation of probabilities serves either to prove the existence of statistical correlations without causal relation or, on the contrary, to establish the nonexistence of such correlations, implying all the same that such correlations, devoid of any statistical basis, are nevertheless the best expression of the reality of these acausal relations, meaningful coincidences(!). For Jung, these calculations are not very important; what is important is to demonstrate the unity of meaning of causally independent events. Ultimately, whether or not statistical probability can account for this is secondary, once the subjective human meaning is an element of reality and makes it possible to establish a relationship between events that would not otherwise have one. (If one accepts this method, it is hard to see why the medical Law of Series should not receive the same treatment: these different cases, causally independent, could also be related by the unique meaning that joins them in medical observation and diagnostics. This seems to be what Kammerer meant when he spoke of a "Law of Series," and what Jung contests precisely because the incidence or reality of the series could be explained by a calculation of probabilities.)

For Pauli, on the other hand, calculation of probabilities merely eliminates or establishes, in the absence of any immediate knowledge, a direct or indirect causal relation between events that are associated in one fashion or another. This is why, quite naturally, in the most classical and least Jungian manner possible, he concludes from the negative result concerning astrology and marriages that he sees "no reason to concede to horoscopes any objective signification independent of the subjective psychology of the astrologer."[25] It is clearly here that the misunderstanding resides. For Jung, the "subjective psychology" of the observer has just as much "objective signification" as what he observes. In particular, his principle of synchronicity postulates such an indissociable unity between observed reality and the psyche (especially unconscious but sometimes conscious) of the observer. Meaningful coincidences are labeled by the archetypes of the unconscious of the observing subject and correspond to "the simultaneous incidence of two different psychic states." They play the role of "acts of creation,"[26] in which "the archetype represents psychic probability," because "the meaningful coincidence, or equivalents of a psychic state and a physical state that do not have a causal relationship, in general signifies that there exists a modality without cause, an 'acausal orderedness.'"[27] As he explicitly states, this modality postulates that *psychic reality and objective reality are perceived and treated as one and the same reality*:

> Synchronicity is not a philosophical view but an empirical concept which postulates an intellectually necessary principle. This cannot be called either materialism or metaphysics....It seems to show that there is some possibility of getting rid of the incommensurability between the observed and the observer. The result, in that case, would be a unity of being which would have to be expressed in terms of a new conceptual language—a "neutral language," as W. Pauli once called it.[28]

What is more, this postulate creates problems with regard to the nature, acausal or not, transcendent or not, of synchronicity, as we have seen previously. From certain aspects, it seems that despite everything the archetype produces effects as if it were a cause! And this is most definitely the problem that interests Pauli as a physicist—the problem of the relations between classic causality and the abstract-concrete relationship as it appears in mathematical physics. But the abstract, for him, is not the subjectivity of the observer. Unlike Jung, all his efforts initially tend to evince, as compared with nonscientific or prescientific traditions (and notably alchemy), the evolution and change that are represented by the modern science that began with Kepler, in which the abstract in question is henceforth exclusively that of mathematics.

### From Fludd to Kepler:
### From Alchemy to Computation as the Principle of Interpretation

Kepler, for his part, still displayed the Neoplatonic "animistic" attitude of his age, whereby the agreement between observations and the deductions of abstract thought results from a sort of resonance between the soul of the world and the human soul; the physical world is the realization of archetypical images that have existed since the origin of things, common to observed objects and the human soul that observes them. On the other hand, these archetypical images, this efficacious abstraction, can be expressed "objectively" only through the rigor of mathematical reasoning and the manipulation of quantities, to the exclusion of the true images of traditional qualitative symbolism. For Pauli this is where the break between scientific thought and what preceded it is located.

To illustrate his thesis, he quotes abundantly and comments on the long controversy between Kepler and Fludd, an alchemist-kabbalist-Rosicrucian, which clearly depicts the disagreement concerning the type of abstraction to be accepted or rejected. For Fludd, these archetypical images can be only those taught by alchemy and the Hermetic lore; their nature can be only that of figures or forms, in the proper sense, with which are associated symbolic meanings that permit a unifying illuminating knowledge. Mathematics as we know it is qualified as vulgar, because it deals with dividing and enumerating quantities, an activity traditionally considered to be demonic.[29] Fludd's own mathematics, the only kind acceptable, is qualitative and permits a unifying knowledge that allows access to the core of things, to the true mysteries hidden behind appearances, to causes and not to effects. This controversy, as Pauli stresses, has lost none of its interest, because of the multiple dialectic reversals in which, to a contemporary reader, now Kepler and now Fludd seems to be the more remote from the modern scientific conception. For Kepler too remains attached to the divine harmony of the world, revealed to him by the music of the spheres, in his quantified (by his famous laws) observation of planetary motions. "Quantities are the archetype of the world." "Mathematical reasoning is innate to the human soul." This permits and at the same time expresses the "harmony of the world"[30] of the abstract and concrete, which science discloses and makes it possible to observe. Thus, Pauli avers, "for the purpose of illustrating the relationship between archetypal ideas and scientific theories of nature Johannes Kepler (1571–1630) seemed to me especially suitable, since his ideas represent a remarkable intermediary stage between the earlier, magical-symbolical and the modern, quantitive-mathematical descriptions of nature."[31]

As for Pauli himself, his interest in these matters (and ours too) does not mean that it is a question of "revert[ing] to the archaistic point of view that paid the price of its unity and completeness by a naive ignorance of nature."[32] The question remains and returns with even greater force due to the methods and discoveries of particle physics: "A purely empirical conception according to which natural laws can with virtual certainty be derived from the material of experience alone," does not take account of "the development of the concepts and ideas, generally far transcending mere experience, that are necessary for the erection of a system of natural laws.... There arises the question, What is the nature of the bridge between the sense perceptions and the concepts?"[33] The elements of an answer that he finds in a theory of archetypes that goes back to Kepler, and through him to Plato and Pythagoras, of course brings Pauli close to Jung.

But when we read about the Fludd-Kepler controversy in Jung and Pauli's coproduction we cannot fail to sense the methodological divergence that, beneath their common vocabulary, separates the latter pair: where Jung unifies (like Fludd), Pauli (like Kepler) counts and distinguishes. Both can agree that "the natural sciences are only a part" of a "unified conception of the entire cosmos."[34] But Jung finds this unified conception in Oriental lore and alchemy, reinterpreted by his psychology of depths, whereas Pauli maintained his guard against a transposition of what he views as only a necessary presupposition into an explicitly formulated corpus of ideas. For Jung, the distinction between scientific method and the method he proposes also bears on the partial character of the knowledge acquired by the former, due to experimental conditions: "There is created in the laboratory a situation which is artificially restricted to the question and which compels Nature to give an unequivocal answer."[35] The total knowledge to which the principle of synchronicity would allow access he finds in the model *already constituted* by the divinatory practices of the *I Ching*, where "Nature in her unrestricted wholeness...answer[s] out of her fullness." "In the intuitive or 'mantic' experiment-with-the-whole, on the other hand, there is no need of any question which imposes conditions and restricts the wholeness of the natural process.... [In its practice of divination], an unknown question is followed by an unintelligible answer."[36] So that this will nevertheless lead to knowledge, an "equivalence of meaning" is postulated between a psychological state and a physical process, following the teaching of two Chinese sages (the *I Ching*), who moreover drew up a list of symbols and established a method for interpreting the meaning of each of the possible combinations of the oracle's figures. Despite this opposition, Jung's thought does not renounce a scientific character; this is where it becomes confused, because it *thereby* seems to pretend to a warranty of greater truth. In a fashion not devoid of circularity, this scientific character is asserted, inter alia, on the basis of the usage that a Pauli—followed by many other more enthusiastic and much less inspired physicists—can make of Jungian terminology. For what truly interests Jung in this essay—as his association with Pauli bears witness—is to advance subjective human *meaning* as an element of "objective" reality that makes it possible to think the psychophysical relation and thereby to answer the questions that quantum physics asks about the abstract-concrete relationship.

On the contrary, Pauli's questions, still relevant, stay far away from the interpretations of the divinatory arts, alchemy, and astrology. It is merely that the conceptions of the last century on psychophysical parallelism fail to satisfy him, as do the purely empiricist ideas of this century. The relations of subject-object, observer-observed, mind-matter are different for modern physics than what they were for classical physics. The concept of wave-particle complementarity,[37] which implies that two different aspects of a single reality can appear to the exclusion of each other, depending on the experimental apparatus arbitrarily chosen by the observer, suggests to him the possibility of a similar complementarity between *physis* and *psyche*. On the other hand,

> microphysics shows that the means of observation can also consist of apparatuses that register automatically; modern psychology proves that there is on the side of that which is observed introspectively an unconscious psyche of considerable objective reality. Thereby the presumed objective order of nature is, on the one hand, relativized with respect to the no less indispensable means of observation outside the observed system; and, on the other, placed beyond the distinction of "physical" and "psychical."[38]

Finally, the situation of the researcher, henceforth included in the object of his or her research, and the feedback effect on the researcher's cognitive system of the knowledge acquired about the world lead Pauli to recognize a similarity between the cognitive process and religious experience; the example of Kepler allows him "to prove the existence of a symbol that had, simultaneously, a religious and a scientific function."[39] But this similarity of experience and function by no means implies a confusion of content, as he warns his readers at the outset:

> As *ordering* operators and image-formers in this world of symbolical images, the archetypes thus function as the sought-for bridge between the sense perceptions and the ideas and are, accordingly, a necessary presupposition even for evolving a scientific theory of nature. However, one must guard against transferring this a priori of knowledge into the conscious mind and relating it to definite ideas capable of rational formulation.[40]

Here we are far from Jung and the "incomprehensible response" given to an "unknown question," which the analysis of meaningful coincidences make it possible to rationalize, while making Nature speak in its totality.

This warning against the danger of transferring the a priori into the conscious mind seems to refer explicitly to the attempts at rationalization, repeated with even greater intensity by some of Jung's disciples, that inspire the tide of neoalchemists, scientific astrologers, and other spiritualist physicists. This is why we have reviewed the Jung-Pauli dialogue at length; although seeming to prefigure Cordoba it reproduces, despite the appearance of agreement and community of thought, some aspects of the Kepler-Fludd, science-alchemy controversy, which Pauli comments on in the same text. His dialectical reversals and his deft steps with two extremely brilliant minds allow us to touch the depth and difficulty of the questions raised by the use of the calculation of probabilities, whereas statistical interpretations of quantum physics have accumulated problems: the still-existing problem of abstract-concrete relations ("concept–sensory experience") is supplemented by the approximate character of probabilistic explanation, even less satisfying than the ideal of simple linear causality, which seems to have totally disappeared.

### Probabilities and the Status of the Possible

One way of feeling how probabilistic explanations leave us hungry, while nevertheless reassuring us by their role as interpretative schemes habitually integrated into scientific rationalism, is to realize that they involve the manipulations of "possibles." The calculation of probabilities is based on taking account of unreal but possible cases, or at least of a certain category of possible events—those that resemble events actually realized in every point except that the actual events are real and the others could be real! In fact, these events can be distinguished by some property that makes it possible to label those that are real and those that are merely possible. But this property—time or place of occurrence, color, the number on the face of a die, and, more generally, the rank on a scale—is considered to be contingent rather than expressing the intrinsic nature of the event! Hence an attempt to understand the status of the possible cannot avoid a discussion of the contingent or necessary character of the events considered.

Now the status of the possible is not always very clear, despite the efforts of the philosophers. The distinction between logical possibility and empirical possibility, which we have already mentioned, does not eliminate the problem of the mode of being of the possible. In the attempt to conceive of that mode we encounter and go beyond the traditional questions of philosophy concerning the necessary and the contingent, where the latter is distinguished from the former as a logical but nonnecessary possibility; that is to say, as something that has merely been proven to be not impossible. Similarly, questions about the conditions of a priori and a posteriori, analytic and synthetic knowledge (where the former call into play only the principle of noncontradiction, while the latter are at least in part empirical), do not exhaust the issue of the possible, despite the interesting revival represented by post-positivist philosophy, of which Saul Kripke[41] is perhaps the most important representative.

Kripke's description of an 'a posteriori necessity' that can be discovered by scientific knowledge is a way of reconciling the empiricism of the scientific method with the ontological truth that this philosophy would recognize in it. As we shall see, it is difficult to go all the way down the road with Kripke, because it is hard to distinguish at any price, as he does, epistemic possibility from metaphysical possibility.[42] All the same, the possibility (at once logical and empirical) of an a posteriori necessity remains interesting and enriching (even from the epistemic point of view), because its impossibility can certainly not be proved: it has the advantage, inter alia, of saving the reality of an entity even when it can be approached only through probabilistic descriptions. We are dealing then with an asymptotic reality, that designated by the extension to infinity implied by the Law of Large Numbers.

Perhaps this question of the status of the possible, intermediate between the real and the imaginary—which we shall encounter again, with reference to playing and games—links up with the question in which the query vanishes in the circularity[43] of the indefinite back-and-forth oscillation between the dualism of our immediate experience and the monist identity that we are compelled to entertain by the effectiveness of rationality on matter and by the reductionist postulate of the scientific method. The immediate experience of the abstraction of thought, vis-à-vis the concrete nature of sensory perceptions, leads to renewed astonishment when we observe the effective adequacy of the latter.

The idea of a unique nature that produces these two types of worlds or realities, but to which we always have only indirect access—whether by thought or by perception—allows us to imagine in a purely theoretical manner that, taken to the extreme, has no empirical content whatsoever, their original unity, responsible for the encounters between them that we sometimes observe and provoke. Perhaps the reality, despite everything, of the possible—which is not real but not imaginary either—is to be prospected for in this place that, for us, is no place, the unique origin of what can be unveiled only by these two paths, our thought and our body; and we are so made that we cannot perceive their realms as other than different and irreducible.

Moreover, this irreducibility leads us, even if we profess the most reductionist materialism, to employ different interpretive schemes than those we have already seen, whenever the exigencies of daily life and our relations with other human beings push us to do so. These schemes involve animist explanations that entail the existence of wills, desires, intentions, and, generally, phenomena related to relatively autonomous persons.

## Animism as Inevitable Pragmatism

Certain interpretands "naturally" trigger in us explanations that may be called "animist-causalist" and "animist-finalist," in that a person is held to be responsible for them, causally or teleologically. The former consist of reducing the incidence of a phenomenon to the intervention of an individual, viewed in his or her complex totality, with no attention paid to any of the determinants that may drive this individual. The cause of an event is not identified—certainly not directly—with some other physical event, but with the action of an individual who is postulated, a priori, as having a status identical with my own: this event was triggered by so-and-so, in a causal process still to be analyzed, but in any case of a type identical to that by which I would myself have produced the event. "Animist-finalist" explanations, too, consist of associating an event with an individual, but more directly with that person's will or intention or even unconscious desire; in brief, to a purposeful intentional process that posits the final objective at the beginning and serves as a conduit for the process by which the interpretand appears to have taken place.

Of course we all use these types of interpretive schemes in our daily life when the individuals in question are human beings, even if, in other circumstances, we maintain the reductive physicalist philosophical position that person and psyche are illusions stemming from our ignorance and that, in the final analysis, molecular motions bear exclusive responsibility for these events. These interpretations permit, inter alia, the recognition or acceptance of the notions of civil and moral responsibility, with the (derived?) notion of "legal person." One can hardly see how law would be possible without them, which means that the implicit philosophy of our daily life, as well as any philosophy of law, must be in some fashion dualist (unless it is a monist idealism that treats matter and the scientific descriptions thereof as no more than figments of the mind!).[44]

This means that, whatever our temptations to unify knowledge on the basis of scientific materialism, we must suspend making a definitive judgment—because our life is at stake—about the mind-body problem. As Wittgenstein put it: "The kernel of our proposition that that which has pains or sees or thinks is of a mental nature is only, that the word 'I' in 'I have pains' does not denote a particular body, for we can't substitute for 'I' a description of a body."[45] Kripke, at the end of his critique of the theory of identity (i.e., of materialist monism), without opting, however, for Cartesian dualism, put it this way: "I regard the mind-body problem as wide open and extremely confusing."[46]

This having been said, it is important to see that these same animist explanatory schemes are at work in pre- or parascientific, magical or mystical interpretations, where an interpretand is reduced to the action or intention of some nonhuman person: a demon, angel, god, animal, social class, society, people (even if the last three are *also* human, insofar as they are constituted *by* human beings). Of course, here there is a shift that tends to be categorically rejected by every discipline influenced by scientific tradition, with regard to demons, angels, and gods; there is much more discussion when it comes to certain animals and human groups. The process involves extending the domain of legitimacy of a projection we make on the basis of the experience of our own "I." If our life in society inevitably leads us to accept, at least pragmatically, this projection onto our experience of other people (we allow that each of them can say "I" as legitimately as we can), the scientific tradition impels us to refuse to extend this projection to other experiences. Here, of course, lies the problem of the *sciences humaines*, with their hybrid and problematic status[47]—which does not mean, as we shall see, that they are devoid of value.

## On the Relativism of Knowledge and the Reality of Interpretands

In a more general fashion, it is interesting to try to situate the different modes of knowledge (and the different traditions in which they are expressed) in relation to these five types of explanatory schemes that allow us to assimilate events in the world (and to reassure ourselves about them) by taking them as interpretands, data to be interpreted: physical-causalist, physical-finalist, probabilistic, animist-causalist, and animist-finalist. Only the first three have the right to be cited in scientific explanations, whereas the last two provide labels and models for traditional mythical and mystical explanations. In these traditions, even if no person is clearly responsible for an event, and even if the immediate physical cause is known, one is not satisfied unless the event is linked to some hidden personage, whether particular (mythological being) or general, such as the Cosmic Mind, the World Soul, or a personal god, to mention only the most current expressions.

Yet it cannot be denied that scientific interpretations enjoy a privileged status, at least in our society, with regard to their relationship with "truth." For many people, only scientific explanations are "true" or correspond precisely to "reality"; the others are not only approximative but also illusory, even deranged. In all cases we are dealing with interpretations; that is, with projections of abstract explanatory schemes onto sensory perception so as to give us a unified representation in which the unifying relations are produced by reason. The common idea that delirium is an inadequate projection of our thought on reality, whereas nondelirious (because "rational," hence true) thought is the direct expression of this reality, is extremely naive and cannot withstand analysis by any theorizing process,[48] scientific or otherwise. We always employ abstract and generalizing projections, with a difficult and hard to identify origin, certainly not imposed by "the facts," because the latter simply are not there except as data to be interpreted, if they are not already *perceived* through the lens of preexisting interpretations.

Most contemporary epistemological studies[49] have only reinforced this tendency to relativize scientific theories vis-à-vis one or several a priori criteria, universal "truth," or reality per se, always belied by counterexamples from the history of science as soon as any philosopher thought he or she could identify them.[50] If we would distinguish delirious from nondelirious (i.e., "rational" or at least "reasonable" or "appropriate to reality," whatever that means) discourse—and we certainly can use such a distinction in our daily life—we need other criteria, different from those that permit us to distinguish between the discourse of reality itself, "imposed by facts," and a rationalizing projection of our mind on these facts. According to these criteria, all theories, scientific and otherwise, are delirious, because they all involve interpretive projections, and any rational discourse about facts always invokes rationalization. Elsewhere[51] I have suggested a criterion for delineating the delirious, bearing not on the content of a discourse but on the use made of it. This means that here, too, it is the use made of reason and experience, and not the rational or irrational character of a discourse, that is most important, as the experience of rational deliriums or delirious rationalizations may already have taught us.

All this leads us to a corrupting relativism about the "truth" and the "reality" to which scientific knowledge gives access. This relativism can turn into skepticism if we note that the explanatory power of animist interpretations is often just as powerful, if not more so, than that of scientific interpretations. Especially when it comes to natural phenomena, the scientific interpretation frequently adds very little to what the animist interpretation provides; that is, attaching the event to a causal (or teleological) chain: lightning and thunder, whether interpreted as an electrical discharge or as the wrath of a divinity, remain what they are, in both cases integrated into a causal chain and thereby "explained." It is only if we desire to act on certain of the phenomena that constitute (or accompany) the occurrence of "thunder" that the former interpretation becomes more efficacious, notably with regard to its electrical properties. Note, moreover, that from the perspective of the effects of thunder on the mind or a social organization, the second interpretation is not devoid of effectiveness, at least in an animist society.[52] In any case, and leaving aside their effectiveness for mastery, the explanatory power of these two types of interpretation is the same, if one considers them from the point of view of the consensus of the human communities that produced and accepted them.

Yet we find it hard to resign ourselves to such a relativism. Science seems to us, despite everything, to be more "true" than superstitious and animist beliefs, and we regularly witness attempts to ground this sentiment on a realist philosophy of knowledge. Among those of recent date, that of Saul Kripke is probably the most interesting, although it too is open to dispute, as we shall see. We can perhaps attribute these attempts to the need to be a "philosopher," in Bachelard's sense of the term;[53] that is, to the impossibility of totally renouncing comprehensive reflection on the content of knowledge and its criteria of truth. This reflection leads to a unitary vision of things in which the "true" cannot be separated from the reality of what is. If this is the case, however, this need would seem to be commonly shared by nonphilosophers, both scientists and nonscientists. In any case, any analysis leading to a pragmatic relativism about the question of the real, even if it too is the product of philosophers, appears to be a new challenge to the power of our knowledge, a gauntlet we seem unable to prevent ourselves from picking up. This relativism always leads down the slippery slope of a disincarnate idealism, perilous to the mental health of each of us, which raises the question of the very existence of a reality outside the knowledge we can have of it. It is crucial that we be able to brake our descent of that slope and rescue this existence, or we shall suffer total dissociation between what we think (say, write) and the very conditions of our own existence as human beings acting and interacting with our material and social environment.

## The Reality of the Real, According to Kripke

Kripke's merit is that he rescued this existence by as it were turning nominalism on its head. The philosophies of language designated "logical positivist" and especially "post-positivist" reinforced the nominalist tendencies of most physicists who pondered about their discipline, following the path of the Copenhagen school, after quantum mechanics had proven its efficacy. The abstract character of the ultimate explanation in physics (the solution of an equation with its probabilistic interpretation) and perhaps especially its dependence on the conditions of observation led those who did not want to be seduced by the charms of spiritualist physics to a nominalist attitude,[54] rather classical and finally quite healthy: we never have direct access except to the names that we give things and to the discourses we carry on about them, the indispensable lenses through which we know things and act on them. The relative effectiveness of these lenses is the only indication that a relationship must exist, despite everything, between these discourses and these things. Whether one holds to Wittgenstein's "mystical element" of language,[55] or goes back to the apparently arbitrary relationship (but one that evokes Kripke's "a posteriori necessity"[56]) between name and thing of the book of Genesis (2:19)—"And [God] brought [all the animals] to the man to see what he would call them; and whatever the man called each living creature, that would be its name"—the very mode of existence of reality, outside of discourse about it, remains in question. It is this reality of the thing behind its arbitrary name that Kripke saves with great adroitness.

Analyzing the function of proper nouns in language as "rigid designators" (of someone or something), Kripke distinguishes the conditions in which the name is given, always relative and contingent, from the "rigid" character, that is, necessary and not arbitrary, of the function of designation. Doing this, he slips in the notion of "a posteriori necessity," thanks to which some empirical knowledge, the conditions of which are a priori contingent because they "could have been" different, *can* nevertheless be necessary a posteriori, because it designates something in the real world as it is by its "nature" and could not have been otherwise (on pain of not existing at all) in any imaginable counterfactual situation (any other "possible world"). By using the categories of modal logic that allow possible worlds to be formalized (at least under certain conditions), as well as by invoking the intuition of the man in the street who employs natural language (as opposed to "the perverse intuition of bad philosophers"), Kripke rescues the reality of what is designated by a proper noun, and with the same stroke by a description, too, if we understand that the latter, like the proper noun, is used to name the referent and not to define it. The referent remains what it is in all "possible worlds," although the manner of "naming" it, the description contingently used to do so, could have been other.

Thus he opposes the common idea according to which "whether an object has the same property in all possible worlds depends not just on the object itself, but on how it is described."[57] His most convincing argument invokes the intuition of natural language, for which someone's name (and perhaps description) serves to designate without defining the person, beyond or short of any definition, that is to say, *without confusion between the meaning of the definition and its referent.* It is of course this distinction between the signification of a word and its referent that serves as the basis for this rescue of reality. The gap between the word and the thing (the meaning of words and what they designate), and thus in the final analysis *the fuzziness of natural language*—into which "possibles" (ad infinitum, and different for various interlocutors) always creep in surreptitiously—saves the existence of the reality of things. But Kripke goes further and endows scientific descriptions with a particular status by virtue of their function as "theoretical identifications,"[58] so that the defining function of these descriptions—that is to say, their *meaning*—allows them to designate the nature of things *as they are* in reality:

> In general, science attempts, by investigating basic structural traits, to find the nature, and thus the essence (in the philosophical sense) of the kind. The case of natural phenomena is similar; such theoretical identifications as "heat is molecular motion" are *necessary*, though not a priori.[59] The type of property identity used in science seems to be associated with *necessity*, not with a prioricity, or analyticity.[60]

Another example of theoretical identification that reveals (a posteriori) the true nature (necessary) of something, despite the contingent manner in which it was perceived and named, is contained in the statement: "Lightning is an electrical discharge." Assimilating the a posteriori necessity of the content (meaning) of scientific knowledge to the necessary existence of the object designated by its name or by a description, independent of the (contingent) fashion in which it was named or described, certainly makes it possible, this time, to rescue not only the existence of the reality of things but even the identity between scientific discourse and this reality. The advantage is that it gives a logical, or at least philosophical, grounding to our intuition, which feels that "lightning is an electrical discharge" has a "truer" ring, or at least another kind of truth, more real, than "lightning is the anger of a god." But is this really persuasive?

In the case of proper nouns, the existence of the referent is saved by the fuzziness of natural language, the gap between what the noun designates (rigidly) and its meaning. Here, curiously, this existence is itself designated by the *meaning* of a particular content of knowledge (which is, moreover, privileged by this very fact), that which is *revealed* by science. For all practical purposes, at the level of the scientific description of an object—"molecular motion," "electrical discharge"—the meaning and referent get mixed up. This evidently is not the case at the level of the words used to name these "realities," such as *heat* and *lightning,* the meaning of which, being contingent on "epistemic conditions," is different from the referent. Thus science makes it possible to find the referent in the meaning of what it says; in other words, it truly speaks the language of real things, without any gap or fuzziness or infiltration by possibles and the imaginary.

There is a curious inversion here, because only *formal* language has this transparency, but precisely because there are no more effects of meaning in it, because it is merely an abstraction where the meaning of terms and of relations is univocal, because devoid of referent. In fact, it is perfectly true that science aspires[61] to this transparency of formal language; it is precisely when science attains it, however, in mathematical physics, that the question of the reality of the content of knowledge it describes is asked with the greatest force, due, inter alia, to the abstraction of its discourse. For Kripke, evidently, science says "heat is molecular motion" in the same way as ordinary intuition has us understand "Aristotle is Aristotle" or "the star Hesperus is the planet Venus," designating thereby a reality independent of the contingent conditions used to name and describe it.

But this, too, is hard to accept.[62] We need merely ask questions such as, "What is molecular motion?" or "What is an electrical discharge?" and try to answer them for this certainty to be shaken. The relationship between heat and molecular motion cannot be comprehended except in the context of statistical thermodynamics, which is itself a mechanical and statistical *interpretation* of physical phenomena. These latter are described in other ways in the language of macroscopic thermodynamics, where heat is viewed as a particular form of energy. This interpretation is far from being trivial, notably with regard to the problem of the *irreversibility* of changes accompanied by the production of heat, which must be related to *reversible* microscopic motion. This relationship, at the origin of the concept of entropy and of the second law of thermodynamics, classically calls into play[63] the degree of ignorance of the microscopic states of a material system by the ideal physical observer, the standard by which these magnitudes are defined. Kripke, in a note, recognizes that these problems arise but prefers "to leave such questions aside in this discussion."[64]

Similarly, the "electrical discharge" of lightning can be defined as a rapid displacement of electrons in a nonconducting medium, under the effect of an intense electrical field accompanied by the cascading ionization of the atoms of this medium. This definition itself requires clarification of the concepts of electrical field, conductor, ionization, and electrons. These clarifications lead slowly but surely to difficult questions about the status of scientific knowledge such as are posed about the abstractions of quantum mechanics, because they lead to a description of ions and electrons in terms of (probabilistic) functions, solutions to equations whose material physical meaning is just what is at issue.

One of the obstacles to accepting Kripke's thesis about theoretical identifications derives from the fact that it too jumps from one level of organization to another—a problem that underlies the difficulties of reductionism, as we have already seen. His demonstrations of the identity of the designators, that is, of the reality of the referents, effective for proper nouns, do not have so much force when it comes to scientific descriptions. The latter, too, have meanings that are themselves contingent, in some fashion, on the conditions of production of scientific discourse and thus on the conditions of their own production. What is more, these meanings act not only as designations and identifications, but also, in essence, as explanations; and they play this role in the physicalist-reductionist context where a phenomenon is considered to be explained better in direct proportion to its reduction to phenomena described in terms of physics. In other words, "molecular motion" is not on the same level of organization and description as "heat," which designates it, nor "an electrical discharge" vis-à-vis lightning. Hence it is more difficult to accept the identification of the latter member of each couple by the former than it is to accept that of Hesperus by Venus or of Aristotle (the name) by Aristotle (the man).

It is interesting to note that Kripke's train of thought inevitably leads him to raise the (ultimate?) question of reductionism, namely, that of mind and body, from his own perspective of looking for the real identity beyond the conditions of cognition: this time it involves identifying a person with his or her body, or a *particular* sensation with a *particular* state of the brain, just as heat is identified with molecular motion. But there he halts in midstream, observing quite correctly that "there is of course no obvious bar, at least (I say cautiously) one which should occur to any intelligent being on a first reflection just before bedtime, to advocacy of some identity theses while doubting or denying others."[65] In other words, Kripke has a tendency to locate the barrier between scientific identifications, which he accepts (along the line of identifications by proper nouns and by the descriptions of natural language), and mind-body identifications, which he rejects. My own tendency would be to place the barrier elsewhere: between identifications of natural languages (accepting his demonstration that names are rigid designators) and scientific identifications, for which too many arguments support separating meaning from referent.

We can clearly understand that, having rescued reality from what is designated by the nouns of ordinary language, one is tempted to employ the same method to rescue the reality of our scientific descriptions and ground them on a universal truth beyond the conditions of the emergence and production of scientific discourses. But aside from the fact that nothing prevents us from erecting the barrier in one location rather than another, the feeling of ordinary reality that is rescued in this way is much less pregnant when it is a question of scientific descriptions rather than of names or expressions that designate someone or something at the same level of observation as that of the description itself (as in one of Kripke's examples, "the star Hesperus is the planet Venus").

Of course we may also have this feeling of simple and essential truth and of ordinary reality—which the philosophers' discussions seem merely to obfuscate—when facing established and certain scientific descriptions that are certainly "true," as compared with mythical descriptions, illusory beliefs, or previous philosophical or theological descriptions. Kripke's attempt is meritorious in that it endeavors to rescue, philosophically, this feeling from the all-around relativism in which the material reality of things seems to vanish. But we must admit that not all scientific theories procure this feeling, and even less so when we have access to them from the inside, as it were, when we participate in their elaboration and discover the new problems they pose and the "research programs"[66] they constitute for scientific communities.

Certain examples do indeed seem to justify the idea that science discovers and reveals what is necessarily and ontologically true (even if this is a posteriori and the means of revelation are empirical and not analytical). The ancient idea of a flat earth covered by the celestial vault, like a cloak spread out above it, seems to be definitively false, and the revelation of the spherical nature of the earth does seem to be that of an a posteriori necessary truth concerning the reality of the nature of the earth. "The earth is round" seems "more true" to us than "the earth is flat": more true in itself, from the perspective of the reality of what the earth is and not only from the perspective of the rules of the scientific game. But leaving aside the fact that one can always invoke a subjective and local truth, that of our immediate perception of the horizontal nature of every not particularly large expanse of ground around the place where I find myself, numerous other examples do not provoke this sense of immediate reality.

This probably occurs when the theoretical description is too abstract, too remote from sense data and hard to represent in sensory images. The spherical nature of the earth, by contrast, can be easily modeled by a globe that we can perceive directly. Similarly, direct experience of circumnavigations of the earth has become relatively common. This explains how the theory has largely overflowed the limits of the scientific community and become the only acceptable description of reality concerning the shape of the earth. We shall see later, in connection with the special status of causal explanation, the same effect of proximity to sensory experience that gives theoretical descriptions a factual evidential character, even if this always involves interpretations by means of abstractions.[67] It must be noted, what is more, that the nature of the excessive abstraction that inhibits a sensible representation is itself relative to individual variations and the habits of cultural or specialist communities. Training in the operative manipulation of abstract concepts eventually gives them a reality almost as immediately perceptible as is the spherical nature of the earth. We shall see later[68] how this phenomenon is taking place for a new generation of physicists with regard to the abstractions of their field.

Taken to the extreme, moreover, the question of the existence or absence of an object in mathematics indicates the degree to which the abstract-concrete distinction is relative to each discipline and should be seen as a correlation rather than as a true opposition: a concretion is perceived as such in comparison to an abstraction, and vice versa. The question of the mathematical object leads to replacing this correlation with that between language and object or between form and content. For Granger, the concept of formal content,[69] paradoxical at first sight, makes it possible to recognize the existence of objects that play the role of the "concrete" in mathematics. These objects are constructed by the operations that act on them and that are thus primary with regard to them; in a "dual" fashion, however, one can postulate them first and only then define the operations on these objects. This duality is apparently found in the natural sciences, even if imperfectly. On the other hand, the idea of formal content as a mathematical object can be seen as a mode of rendering the logically possible "real."

## Physical Science as Interpretation

Nevertheless, these effects of habit and training, reserved for the moment to a community of specialists, do not obviate the problem of the distance between macroscopic physical reality (classical physics) and quantum reality. They can even, paradoxically, lead to questions about the reality of classical physics,[70] once that of quantum entities has been integrated and assimilated. Hence, as we have seen, for quantum physics the abstraction and remoteness of concepts from sensory data have become largely incompatible with a sense of immediate reality that has no need of being theorized, to the point of serving as the occasion for the spiritual physicists' shifts in meaning that we have already encountered.

To avoid these shifts, the ontological reality of quantum physical objects must be rescued, and this is precisely what Kripke attempts. It is the same dilemma exposed, with great rigor, by Bernard d'Espagnat in *In Search of Reality*; even if one does not share his metaphysical conclusions, it is hard to reject the terms of the problem of a "veiled reality."[71]

Every open inquiry about quantum physics, free of preconceived ideas, leads to arguments in favor of two contradictory hypotheses, each sufficiently convincing that the other cannot eliminate it. What is described by physics concerns the reality of matter, objective and independent of the properties of the human mind. At the same time, however, the interactions between empirico-logical knowledge and the object of this knowledge are so intricate and the process of knowledge is so deeply integrated with the manner of describing reality that one cannot consider the latter to be truly attained and known as it is in itself, objectively (with "strong objectivity"[72]), by virtue of the description that physics gives of it. Hence the idea that, although reality cannot be totally unveiled through scientific knowledge, the latter is nevertheless a privileged mode of access, albeit not the only one.

One can make this same objection to Kripke: the discourse of physics need not explicitly disclose—"reveal"—reality itself, even though it is a discourse about that reality. Wittgenstein's idea that it is a matter of laying a mesh over a surface covered with irregular black spots remains viable.[73] We might also cite a metaphor coined by J.-M. Lévy-Leblond, which, seeming to go in Kripke's direction, actually moves the other way. To explain his view of wave-corpuscle duality, Lévy-Leblond[74] uses the metaphor of a cylindrical object that we cannot, without previous training, perceive globally as it is, but only in one of its aspects: either as a circular base, or as a side seen in projection as a rectangle. The quantum object, by analogy, is one that we can perceive only via experiments that show only one of its aspects, wave or particle; but in itself it is neither one nor the other, just as the cylinder is neither circle nor rectangle. Our incapacity to perceive it globally, other than as the solution of an equation, certainly poses a problem for our mode of physical knowledge; fundamentally, though, nothing forces us a priori to hold that submicroscopic objects, which are never perceived directly but only through experimental devices interpreted by mathematical models, must be representable by the objects heretofore studied in classical physics, themselves abstract and idealized.

Lévy-Leblond in fact lobs the problem back to classical physics, expressing his astonishment that its approximative representations, of waves or particles, are satisfactory on the scale of most macroscopic objects, when they are manifestly no more than false approximations that quantum physics teaches us to jettison. The latter "reveals" to us the nature of reality in itself no more than the cylinder is revealed by the perception of circles and rectangles. As for the quantum object itself (the "cylinder"), it is attained only through those means of observation and theory through which we become aware of it and describe it. But if the physical theory does not *reveal* its reality, this does not mean that the reality does not exist or that physics denies its existence. It is only that its perception by our sense organs, even extended by analytical and technical tools, remains limited, despite the spectacularly successful operational mastery *of* this reality permitted by such perception.

Another example of the oscillation between sense perception and the abstraction of quantum reality involves the new methods of medical imaging, using x-ray tomography, nuclear medicine, or nuclear magnetic resonance. This example is interesting because here it truly is a case of a back-and-forth movement in which one leaves behind the macroscopic reality of human anatomy, long familiar through dissection and anatomical sections, to enter the quantum reality of the interactions between various types of radiation and the atomic and subatomic structure of the matter composing the organs of this body. Then one returns from the mathematical analysis of these interactions to the computerized reconstruction of images, in which the macroscopic structures can be recognized by our immediate visual perception, which compares them with anatomical sections obtained directly from cadavers. The successful realization of these reconstructions is evidently proof that the mathematico-physical theory of the quantum interactions between radiation and matter does indeed concern the reality of the material composing the human body and these machines, which thereby allow us to undertake nontraumatizing explorations. This is all the more stunning in that we leave the macroscopic realm directly perceivable by the senses (that of an anatomical section) to return to the same macroscopic realm perceived by the same senses (the image after its computerized reconstruction). Between the two, unlike what one might believe, the excursion into the domain of quantum interactions does not involve knowledge of the ultimate, "essential," and "ontological" reality of matter. The success of medical imaging methods demonstrates only the operational power of microscopic physics (associated with computers), without augmenting its explanatory power in the slightest: the nature of the quantum object is not elucidated in any way, and physics' description of it is not given independent of the means, experimental and mathematical, by which this description acquires its meaning. The technical success demonstrates that the scientific description speaks of the material reality of things (and not of mere projections of our imagination), because it enables effective action on that reality; but to convince ourselves of this we need not allow, in addition, that the meaning of this description is independent of its conditions of production and thereby confused with its referent. The latter remains a "veiled reality," whatever the technological successes to which scientific constructions may lead us. This is why, rather than the disclosure or revelation of reality, it seems to me more precise to speak, with Jerome Rothstein,[75] of the organization of reality by scientific laws, while allowing this notion to retain its ambiguity as to the origin of organization: whether organized reality itself, the physicist observer-theoretician who organizes this reality, or the varied interactions between reality and this physicist, armed with measurement devices and a theoretical framework for interpreting their measurements.[76]

Have we thus returned, despite the effectiveness of technology, to that relativism in which physical law (and scientific law in general) has the same ambiguous status vis-à-vis "reality" and "truth," and the same function of organizing reality, as myths are today recognized as having in non-Western civilizations?[77]

## Causality as Proximity

Nevertheless, we cannot or do not wish to rid ourselves of the idea (or feeling) that "the earth is round" is more "true" (more "real") than "the earth is flat"; that "spontaneous generation is impossible" is more "true" than "decomposing flesh produces vermin and rats"; that Darwinian evolution is more "true" than creation in six solar days of twenty-four hours each (even if the *mechanisms* of evolution are the subject of dispute among specialists, due to theoretical difficulties that have not been overcome), and so forth.[78]

Where and how can we locate the origin of this idea or this feeling, which resists our analyses and our inability to demonstrate that in all cases it is merely a matter of the interpretation that we project on interpretands? Perhaps we must return, after all, to the special status of causal interpretation, which gives scientific explanations greater persuasive force than other types (including probabilistic explanations). It may be that, instead of science disclosing the ontological reality of things, this special status, and the greater persuasive force that accompanies it, are sufficient to account for the attributes of scientific knowledge as it relates to reality. Perhaps the causal relationship between things can be itself interpreted as an abstraction based on the perception of time as a succession of events. Events directly perceived by the senses are memorized in such a fashion that their succession in time seems itself to be directly perceived. This succession, with its irreversible direction, is transformed into a causal relation, by abstraction and generalization to a class of events. The effect of the transformation is to suppress the unpredictable character of temporal succession and thus ultimately to suppress the disquieting, even anguishing—because unmasterable—character of our perception of time. Time is transformed from a source of the unpredictable and the new into an ineluctable and logical sequence, thanks to which—if everything goes well—it is mastered. But this transformation, although it leads to a thought-abstraction of what was perceived, *does not excessively distance us from it.* The causal relationship remains relatively close to the immediate perception of things; perhaps this is why it appears to be itself "manifest" and just as "real" as the things that it links: two directly perceived events are causally associated by the intermediacy of the *perception* of their succession in time.

Certainly, causal relation is an abstraction of this perception of succession,[79] but it is the *closest* abstraction, because it permits an immediate return to the perceived experience, thanks to its predictive power: the "same" cause reproduces the "same" effect; that is, the "same" succession of events can be imagined and predicted and will thereafter be *effectively perceived* by the same individual or by another individual in communication with the first one. Of course, it is not the same event that is reproduced, but a different event assimilated to the first by a distinctive characteristic that serves as a criterion (most often the "interest of reason," in the sense meant by Habermas) for classification.

What is more, this persuasive force becomes strongest when the correlation has recourse to numbers: the elaboration of quantitative causality probably began with geometry and is found in science today. The measurement that associates a number with a perception makes it possible, in the simplest and most effective manner, to abstract a generalizable character from this perception and at the same time to associate it computationally with other measurements (effective or imagined). These latter measurements, thereby predicted, permit an immediate return to direct perception of things where they are found, thus "verifying" the "reality" of the detour into abstraction and computation that seemed to have distanced us from it. In other words, whatever Wittgenstein may say in the *Tractatus*,[80] and even though there is little that can be rigorously opposed to it, causality seems to be more than an interpretive grid applied to things; the causality of things, *as relation*, seems to be more real than other abstract interpretative relations between things. Even if this is an illusion or "superstition,"[81] it has its own persuasive force, which the scientific method has inherited. In other words, the latter derives its special status from the proximity[82] of its processes to immediate perceptions, even when it employs abstract detours and interpretive projections of its theories. Its persuasive force derives from the fact that causal interpretation has a less "interpretive" air than other forms of interpretation, to the extent that the success of its predictions permits a rapid and *effective* return to the world of perceptions (i.e., to "concrete reality").

## Explanation is a Bonus in the Sciences

This is why the true power of this method is fundamentally not one of explanation but of prediction; and, as Popper understood, this makes it much easier to disprove a theory than to verify it, because the success of one prediction does not prove that another prediction based on the same theory will succeed in other circumstances.[83] Hence, the scientific praxis of those who devote themselves to the discipline of the same name has become more and more frequently dissociated, and rightly so, from the search for total and definitive explanations supposed to give an account of the whole of reality. Taken to the extreme, we have learned to renounce the explanatory value of a theory, which we accept despite its inadequacies, or of theoretical approximations or even paradoxes, if they seem to be fruitful as a source of new experiments, new demonstrations, new structures, and, ultimately, new technical successes. This is how specialists estimate the value of a scientific theory today, much more than by its ability to explain natural phenomena, in which most laboratories evince less and less direct interest. Artificial, laboratory-built objects[84] ("frictionless" inclined planes, machines, pure lines of genetically identical animals, synthetic compounds, new cellular species produced by biotechnology), based, of course, on natural systems but involving idealizations or simplifying transformations, are the true objects of laboratory research. This is understandable, because the physical-causalist interpretive schema is most effective when applied to them; that is, when it can rigorously associate its predictive power with its explanatory power.

In the case of natural events, by contrast, scientific interpretation adds little more, fundamentally, than does magical animistic interpretation, *from the perspective of its explanatory power*, that is, of attaching the event to a causal chain. Lightning remains what it is, whether interpreted as an electrical discharge or as divine anger: in both cases it is integrated into a causal chain and thereby "explained." As we have seen, only if one seeks to *act* on some of its aspects (precisely those linked to the electrical properties that can be recognized in it) *to the exclusion of certain others* (its effects on a mind or social organization conditioned by animist interpretations) does the scientific explanation prove more effective. It is just as if, in one of Wittgenstein's language games, we could establish no distance between the explanation and the effectiveness of this explanation: "[One player's] carrying out the order [given by the other player] is now the criterion for [the first player's] having understood."[85] In other words, a scientific interpretation is superior to others by virtue of its effectiveness (in the domain of effectiveness that it circumscribes and that defines, moreover, the field of technology) and not by its "pure" explanatory power, that is, what invokes the inner experience of a "feeling of relief"[86] after the effort to comprehend, in cases where this experience can be dissociated from "objective" observation of technical efficacy.

The scientific community as a whole, however, is increasingly less accepting of the pertinence of such a dissociation. The sciences have evolved such that the technical or at least operational interest has more and more become the determining element of the intersubjective consensus on which the experience of what constitutes an acceptable explanation is based. The confusion between the two types of experience and explanation—objective technical effectiveness and the internal feeling of comprehension—occurs more readily with regard to the physical-causalist interpretations that are most directly applicable to artificial structures and laboratory objects. This is why artifacts have increasingly become the ideal objects for the application of the scientific method. At the same time, the content of scientific theories has become more and more distant from "animist" experiences of personal life, increasingly circumscribing its domain of reality while eliminating whatever is not suited to it. Not every question asked about our experience of reality by means of our perceptions is necessarily scientific, even if nothing demonstrates its inutility or illegitimacy. To be scientific, it must also be treatable by a scientific method, especially the experimental methods, and, in any case, must be amenable to statement in the language of contemporary science. In parallel, what is important in scientific praxis, beyond what it says on the subject of science, hardly has to do with explaining reality, but rather with an empirico-logical praxis of constructing reality.

Scientific explanation no longer exists. The only explanations that are scientific are local explanations directly plugged into experimentation and the assembly of new instruments. *The need for an explanation of reality is, fundamentally, antiscientific.*[87] The satisfactory explanation is a bonus, the esthetic pinnacle that accompanies and sometimes completes—not necessarily, but only when possible—the result truly sought: technical performance. For the practitioners of the contemporary science of laboratories and factories, operational and analytic, simultaneously modest and triumphant, the need for explanation is merely a relic of metaphysical, indeed religious, wonder. The latter is still active, overtly and surreptitiously, in the subjectivity of each individual, and especially of many scientists, for all that it has been repressed and circumscribed by the scientific and technical culture of the West. Bachelard noted this opposition between the operational and constructivist character of the practice of the "new scientific spirit" and the conviction that, despite everything, it involves a process of explaining reality. For him, this opposition lay at the core of the fruitfulness of science, because this conviction, although no more than a conviction produced by the psychology of the scientist-subject, is in fact the *motive force* of research, animating from within the individuals who devote themselves to this praxis. In addition, a sort of guarantee that this a priori conviction is not illusory, even if the history of the sciences seems to disprove it more and more a posteriori, can be found somewhere in the special function of mathematics.

## On the Reality of Numbers

The purely operational and nonexplanatory conception of the sciences seems to be totally reversed by the success and efficacy of mathematics in physics. There we seem to have a deductive explanatory apparatus for which reality is first of all that of mathematical theory, of which physical assemblages provide only models.[88] This deductive and totalizing function, by furnishing general and global, although abstract and mathematized, theories of the material universe, appears to contradict the local, limited, and pragmatic character of scientific explanation. This is why spiritualist physicists tend to be recruited from among the ranks of theoretical physicists directly in the grips of this experience, whether they are idealists or materialists, united by their conviction that physical science reveals the "ultimate reality" of things.

It is nevertheless easy to see that this reversal is merely apparent, when one takes into account that mathematical language is itself constructed. Nothing is more opposed to natural language than mathematical language, which means that the latter is not so natural as the practice of arithmetic and Euclidian geometry might have led us to believe. In fact, it associates at least two properties that make it a language apart, a language whose construction and learning frequently do violence to the linguistic usages of the languages known as natural because they are spoken "naturally" after an almost unconscious learning period. These two properties—the central role of the use of numbers and the quest for discourses that are perfectly univocal and transparent, thanks to the rigor and generality of contradiction-free causal relations between perfectly identified elements—lead to a language without referents. The meaning of its signs is solely that given them by its syntax, that is, by the rules of association, to the exclusion of any reference to any semantic content whatsoever—neither the content directly designated by the perception of an object nor (and even less) that, perhaps different, accumulated in a fuzzy and ambiguous manner by the in-part unconscious use of language. It seems to be this absence of referent that makes possible the transparence and rigor of a perfect contradiction-free causality linking perfectly identified elements; whereas numbers, both as a system of numeration (that is, of static order) and as a system of computation (that is, of generative dynamic relations) always retain the possibility of referring back to a content:[89] that of hypothetical objects in a situation where they are enumerable or mensurable. This means that the question of the real or unreal character of mathematics reduces to the twin questions of the real character of relations (of causality and noncontradiction), on the one hand, and of the reality of numbers, on the other.

We have already encountered the first of these questions and have decided (if that is the word) for its undecidability, with regard to the reality of both noncontradiction (whose undecidability can be "demonstrated"[90]), and causality (which we viewed as merely an abstraction of our perception of time): which merely reinforces the question. The second question remains: are numbers real or not? Of course, we are not talking about the technical distinction between real and imaginary numbers found in the mathematics of complex numbers, but about so-called natural integers. Do numbers exist as an objective reality, or are they a production of the human mind? The history of systems of numeration and of number theory[91] clearly shows, however, that the distinctions between different sorts of numbers imply, at least in the eyes of the mathematicians who discovered or invented them, a character that is progressively less real or natural; from positive integers to "complex" and "imaginary" numbers, passing by way of "irrational" numbers, "transcendental" numbers, and "real" numbers.

This is not merely a case of the conventional use of words, as is often the situation in mathematics, where a technical definition has absolutely nothing in common with the meaning of a term in daily or philosophical language.[92] It is important to remember that in physics, when one has completed a computation and returned to measurement, that is, to what the senses can directly perceive of reality, one keeps only the results that are positive numbers. The negative or imaginary roots of equations that are supposed to describe reality are most often discarded as not corresponding to "physical reality." Probably one of the difficulties of the problem posed by quantum mechanics concerning the relation between formalism and reality derives from the fact that a physical magnitude (the wave function) is represented by a complex number.[93] In fact, this difficulty and this abstraction are already to be found in the incommensurability of the diagonal, which is the origin of so-called irrational numbers. This difficulty and abstraction are also found in inequalities such as $(a + b)^2 \neq a^2 + b^2$, or, if $a$ and $b$ are complex numbers, $|a + b|^2 \neq |a|^2 + |b|^2$. It is as if there were a frontier, movable but nevertheless always there, between the mathematical "realities" that are acceptable for representing physical reality and those that we meet up with in calculations but must part company with at the end of the path, because they "do not correspond to anything physical." The mathematical nature of a physical entity is *given* in advance (usually a positive real number, but sometimes a complex number, for example to represent an oscillatory phenomenon with its amplitude and phase); at the end of the computation we reject whatever does not conform with it. Again, and whatever use is made of numbers in physics, it is extremely difficult to provide a definitive answer to this question, because so many arguments plead for the natural character of numbers (which mathematicians *discovered* in nature) rather than for their being *invented* constructions.

## The Dualism of Access Paths

On this question, as in general on the question of the adequacy of the (abstract) theory to the (concrete) reality, the wise position (trivial for anyone who rejects dogmatism) still consists of admitting the existence of a unique but indescribable objective reality that cannot be attained directly. This is another sort of veiled reality that can be uncovered only by two separate paths, and thus only partially—the path of our sensory perceptions and that of our logical and imaginative thought. In other words, the abstract-concrete division results from the existence within us of these two different paths of access, which we experience separately.

This attitude has the advantage of accounting for or, more exactly, of making it possible to accept simultaneously the unity of what exists, which we experience whenever there is a correspondence between the theoretical and the perceived, or between the abstract and the concrete, alongside its duality, which we also experience whenever, despite everything, the gap between the concrete and a theory too abstract to be "real" (for all that it is effective) strikes us as irreducible. This attitude permits us to accept the contradiction between these experiences: neither the experience of unity nor that of duality is illusory, but each, on its own, cannot pretend to contain the whole and even less to reveal some "ultimate reality."[94]

## Animism as the Explanatory Absolute; Ethics and Monotheism

Despite the appearance of a top-down sequence from mathematics to physics (Bachelard's "descending rationality"[95]), scientific research remains a structure cobbled together haphazardly from interpretations. From this perspective, it is no different from other interpretive traditions: beyond its aspiration and pretension to explain the totality of things, it in fact arrives at local explanations directly associated with action. On the other hand, it is characterized and distinguished by the unique place that the physical-causalist scheme of interpretation occupies in it, to the almost total exclusion of others: probabilistic "explanation" is the only other type of interpretation to which it has recourse, when all else fails.

The result is an even stronger focus on effective action and more evident distancing from the initial need for explanation, relegated to metaphysics or to a subjective psychology that is highly receptive to metaphysics. The particular role that mathematics plays there can lead to the same result by stripping[96] ("explanatory") theoretical discourse of the maximum of meanings that refer to what is directly perceived by our experience of the world. The perceptible reality to be explained is limited to that of laboratory artifacts because this is the reality on which the method works most effectively. To the extent that this reality is constructed by the scientific method, its explanation is confounded with its construction, and the value of the former with the success of the latter.

By contrast, the mystical traditions are deliberately animistic, with all the accruing advantages and inconveniences. We are not necessarily referring to the primary animism conventionally attributed to so-called primitive peoples, if indeed such a thing truly exists outside the minds of bygone ethnologists. There is no reason, in effect, why the explanation of a phenomenon by a soul (divine or human, ancestral or otherwise) incarnated in an animal, plant, or some other natural phenomenon should necessarily imply that these cultures entertain a naive belief in such an incarnation, directly and in the literal sense, rather than an interpretive attitude of a symbolic order. Dan Sperber's book on symbolism[97] provides examples and a persuasive argument supporting the idea that the animist interpretation takes place at another level and does not contradict the immediate perception, to some extent nonsymbolic, of natural phenomena; just like enclosing certain phrases in quotation marks classifies them as having a different level of meaning (metaphorical, hypothetical, etc.) in a discourse where they would be absurd without quotation marks.

However this may be, an animist explanation, whether literal or symbolic, implies that an event is referred to a person; the inner experience (what makes us say "I") is at the core of every explanation. The inner experience is the paradigm projected on the interpretation of every event: just as "I" (or my "soul" or the "soul" of a stranger who has taken possession of me, but, in any case, someone, an "I" like my own) am at the origin of the phenomena that I trigger, so too someone must be (causally or intentionally) at the origin of phenomena I have not triggered but which I observe. If this someone is not visible in the form of a person like me, with whom I may be able to communicate in some language, I attribute these phenomena to an invisible being and look for the traces of personal action; just as seeing footsteps in the sand leads me to attribute them to a person who passed that way rather than to the rearrangement of the grains of sand by an impersonal natural phenomenon or by chance. Throughout history, such interpretations have proven themselves to be on the whole much less effective than scientific interpretations; from the perspective of their explanatory power, however, they have a plus side as well. If their effectiveness is extremely doubtful when it is a question of mastering and manipulating physical events—nonhuman natural phenomena or machines—they are often much more persuasive when human events are to be explained. It is only natural for the latter to be perceived straightaway as personalized and even intentional, despite the most materialist positions that we can defend theoretically.

As we have seen, our daily life, especially our relationship with the law (and ethics), implies that we take seriously the reality of the responsibility of individual and legal persons. As a result, the interpretations that invoke this responsibility always have a more immediate and more "natural" aspect than do "scientific" ones, in which this responsibility is replaced by physicochemical or other laws (even thought these latter are also called "natural" laws). It seems clearer to explain that I was struck on the head by a rock because someone, attacking me or defending himself, threw it at me, than to invoke a succession of physicochemical determinations leading to the mechanics of the arm and ballistics of the rock and originating in the motion and interaction of the molecules that constitute a human body and, ultimately, as always, to equations of quantum mechanics! In this context, the status of psychological and sociological "laws" and of the *sciences humaines* in general remains ambiguous, as we shall see.

Yet when global explanations are sought, mystical interpretations, however little they are rendered plausible by a cultural context, traditional or otherwise, seem to correspond more closely to our immediate inner experience than do physical-causalist interpretations, which always have an artificial aspect, leaving a taste of a long-winded and quite irrelevant rigmarole. In effect, what was peripheral and indeed illusory for reductionist materialism takes center stage in mystical traditions: the experience of inner life, of the me and the I, of consciousness, of liberty and will, of duration and creative time, of feelings and subjectivity. This is equally true of certain Western philosophies that are fairly close to the preoccupations of the *sciences humaines* (to which we shall return) and of existential philosophies in which the questions of ethics, responsibility, and liberty are taken seriously.[98] Some even find mystical accents in them, as does Vladimir Jankelevitch in some admirable pages of his *Le Je-ne-sais-quoi et le presque-rien*: "Since contradiction is the mystery *par excellence*, inasmuch as it cannot be conceived, but is lived each moment in the irrational continuity of time, it is undoubtedly true to repeat quite simply, with Schopenhauer and Malebranche: Liberty is a mystery."[99]

For contemporary Western philosophy, however, only scientific knowledge can rationally speak about objective reality, and it has no rivals on its home ground. It is from the viewpoint of the rationality of this knowledge that "liberty is a mystery." Even Bergson could pretend only to a division into spheres of influence, *grosso modo* physical and metaphysical, leaving the "mechanical" to science while claiming for philosophy the rights to the "living." It is in their vocation or pretension to encompass everything in a single explanatory whole that mystical traditions differ from these philosophies. They assert the same vocation as the sciences do (this is why, unlike philosophy, there can be a rivalry between them and science—a rivalry that the spiritualist physicists erroneously resolve in a syncretism); but *their point of departure is different*. Also different is the initial experience around which the interpretations are constructed—precisely the experience that scientific method demands be ignored. In mysticism, the experience of reality is first of all my experience of myself; generalized and extended to everything that exists, this then functions as a principle of interpretation with multiple ramifications and refinements. For it is true that, to use the expression consecrated (if we may use the term) by militant atheism, man creates God in his own image; but this creation is not necessarily always less rational than the productions of scientific theory. It is not a matter of a single image, but of several: not only that of the Father, the best known in Western religions, but also, as in paganism and in kabbalistic tradition, of other human figures— mother, wife, daughter, grandfather and son, the developing embryo—or of more abstract images, that of language in its relations with the body and thought, and of course that of sex, the "fundament" of all structures in the universe. But I am always experiencing the image of a person, whether my own, extended to the universe of nature and other human beings and to everything that exists in the great Cosmic Self and Universal Soul; or whether, first of all, the image of the other person, the encounter with whom (asserts Emmanuel Levinas[100]) grounds the ethical experience in a need for transcendence. The person always remains the reference, even if in his otherness vis-à-vis myself.

In all cases where these experiences are lived and analyzed not only in the mode of the ineffable, but also in the references of an interpretative discourse (such as the "doors of intelligence," "tree of life," and "tree of knowledge" of the Kabbala), they ground logical and structured discourses of which Far Eastern cosmogonies and the kabbalistic tradition are among the most remarkable examples. Another apparent point of contact with science, in addition to the unity and universality of knowledge, is the rational character of the discourses of these mystical traditions, which refuse to take refuge in the ineffability of the initial experience. Unity is postulated: that of the All, of moral law and natural law. But in these traditions the point of departure is moral law, which mysticism and magic extend to the natural world; whereas the symmetrical temptation exists among scientists, and especially among those who would listen to them, of an opposing process that "deduces" moral law from natural law. This postulated unity is in all cases monotheism, whereas the multiple experiences of different images constitute an initial polytheism. The traditions are distinguished by the subtle dialectics and different emphases they place on each aspect of the relations between monotheism and polytheism. In particular, a gross monotheism (to be met with in the East as well as in the West) postulates this unity as already there, fully realized and the object of our discourse and descriptions, whereas a more refined monotheism takes seriously the experiences on which it is grounded, including their multiplicity, so as not to end up in the illusion of disembodied spirit.[101]

Whatever the elegance and rigor of certain products of these traditions, they do not feature a central role for the physical causalist interpretations that characterize science, even if such interpretations are invoked from time to time. On the other hand, the "descending" animist interpretation (moving from top to bottom, from the general to the particular, from the whole to the part) reigns here almost without rival. We have seen that, in certain circumstances, when we are dealing with human phenomena involving persons, the explanatory power of these interpretations can be superior to that of scientific interpretations, even if, in general, the contrary holds for effectiveness in transforming nature. Another way of looking at this is to observe that the postulated unity of moral and natural law can have greater legitimacy in the mystical than in the scientific tradition—at least a legitimacy internal to the tradition that postulates it. How, in fact, can ethics be based on physics, when the latter begins by circumscribing its own domain and excluding ethics from it? Despite the incongruity of the product, the need for a unified law seems to be so great that we have never stopped witnessing prodigies of ingenuity in the attempt to establish such a unity. On the contrary, this unity flows naturally from a process that posits it from the outset because it does not circumscribe its object, extended from the beginning to the All (perhaps opening, what is more, onto an infinity that goes beyond it, at least for the Jewish Kabbala, which sees this opening as what distinguishes it from pagan mysticisms).

Thus we see the mixtures of genres constituted by the syncretism of spiritualist physicists and scientific moralists. On the pretext that mystical traditions, the origin of the moral laws that humanity has adopted, can conduct rational interpretative discourse and that scientific theories have attained a degree of abstraction that brings them close to these traditions, it is hoped that the technical effectiveness of the latter can guarantee the truth of the moral law to be received from a particular tradition. In fact, however, *the points of departure are different* (objectifiable sense data in one case, subjective experience in the other), *the processes move in opposite directions* (bottom to top versus top to bottom),[102] and the *interpretive methods are different* (physical-causalist and probabilistic in one case, causalist-animist and finalist-animist in the other).

Only a vulgar monotheism's need for unity at any price can explain these jumbles, which merely sterilize both methods, whose value consists precisely in the coherence of the rules that characterize each. We shall return to this point later.

## *The* Sciences Humaines *and the "Rational Myth of the West"*

There is one domain, however, that of the *sciences humaines*, in which this necessary separation is even more difficult to maintain. Psychology, sociology, history, ethnology, anthropology, economics, and political science study and try to understand and explain phenomena that are specifically human. These sciences set as their objects domains of reality in which human beings, as subjects, are the main factors, so that causal explanations cannot ignore them. Even if a reductionist stance is posed once and for all as a matter of principle, as a way to put everything right with scientific orthodoxy, the praxis of these sciences takes place at a level of organization on which the phenomena proper to the human *mind* can neither be ignored nor reduced to molecular interactions, as we have seen. Whence the old familiar squaring of the circle: how can scientific objectivity be comfortable with objects of research from which subjectivity cannot be banished? How can scientific rationality be comfortable with objects in which the irrational, claimed and experienced as such (passions, delirium, inventions of the arts and mysticisms of the irrational), is an inevitable and sometimes decisive part?

Here, too, scientific method manages to ride out the tide—even if in a less spectacular fashion than in the natural sciences—by segregating and circumscribing its object in such a way that the latter is adapted to it, made to order, as it were. The art of psychological, historical, sociological, and other schools is not so much to explain mental, historical, and social phenomena as to define and circumscribe the mind, history, or society in such a fashion that scientific methods of observation, of reproducible measurement, of classification, and of predictive theory can, as far as possible, be applied to them honestly and rigorously, with no ideological or religious a priori, with no other metaphysics than, perhaps, that of a mysticism of science.

Of course this is also the case, as we have already seen, with the natural sciences; but there the consequences are quite different. The natural sciences wind up by constructing a reality of artifacts that is readily accepted: the reality of technology (mechanical and electronic machines, chemical products, and, now, the creations of bioengineering). By contrast, the reality of artifacts constructed by the different schools of the *sciences humaines* can hardly gain acceptance outside the circle of adepts of these schools. In the former case, technical success and the construction of new devices and substances imposes a new reality whose material existence is just as objective and irrefutable as is unretouched natural reality. Even the theoretical disagreements, the divergences between schools concerning imperfections and unresolved problems, do not keep this technical reality from thrusting itself on everyone. In the case of the *sciences humaines*, people are loath to allow themselves to be conditioned and reconstructed to make them conform to the ideal of scientific rationality. The theoretical disagreements and conflicts between schools concern the very reality that is to be construed and not merely some speculative aspect thereof. This means that the scientific ideal is itself scarcely attained, to the extent that a more or less conscious voluntarist "project of transformation"[103] always *directly* interferes (or threatens to interfere) with the "project of knowledge." This engenders the accusations often made against different schools of being or not being "scientific"; whereas the scientific or nonscientific character of the professional output of a physicist (or chemist or biologist) is not usually contested, even if it involves a theoretical context whose full details have not yet won the consensus of the community of specialists. To escape these disputes, the tendency is always to circumscribe and delimit the object of research even more, so that the method applied to it, empirico-logical and, if possible, quantitative and mathematical, approaches as close as possible to that which dominates the natural sciences.

But the scarcely pertinent character of this method—hardly applicable to the reality of human beings, and ultimately hardly usable—soon appears and throws a spanner into the works, due precisely to the criterion of productivity and effectiveness. And the dilemma crops up again, this squaring of the circle that is sometimes used to characterize the "soft" sciences as opposed to the "hard" natural sciences.

One question demands an answer, of course, at least in passing: why does all of this exist? That is, why do we see all this activity and effort, educational and research institutes, so many tons of books, articles, and essays? The hard sciences defend themselves by their technical effectiveness, their utility—and use—in a context of production and of transforming our natural environment. This programmatic context constitutes the basis of the broadest social consensus, albeit not discussed and scarcely conscious, on which the different forms of power in our society rest.[104] The technical "imperatives" imposed by the construction of new machines and new electronic and computer tools and by the discovery of new chemical, biochemical, and pharmacological syntheses are accepted as inevitable, just like natural phenomena, by both rulers and ruled. The "progress" constituted by the pursuit of research programs leading to these applications comes automatically: it is the only good, the only value that our societies accept as transcending all ideological and religious differences. The tiny minorities who oppose such progress are marginalized in various forms, of which consignment to a park bench and commitment to a psychiatric hospital are the most common. Twenty years after it was denounced by Marcuse,[105] the one-dimensionality of which this consensus is both the witness and guardian has preserved intact its recuperative force and capacity to survive by integrating and swallowing up any potential contradiction. This consensus is sufficiently broad to provide the social infrastructure required for scientists to work. Their inner motives (the passion to know, intellectual enjoyment of knowledge, the creative joy of the builder, recognition by one's peers and others, with the glory, money, and finally the power that accompanies them) are of minor importance: they are accepted as the necessary ingredients for making the wheels of the machine of progress and productivity turn.

All of this is much less clear for the *sciences humaines*. In the light of the productivity of the natural sciences, the former frequently have the air of a luxury that is scarcely less gratuitous and useless, indeed parasitical, than philosophy is. Yet they are nevertheless more than tolerated: they are encouraged, subsidized, enjoy their share of recognition in glory and money, even though their contribution to technical progress is almost nonexistent and their utility, therapeutic or prophylactic, in the organization and management of human affairs is far from manifest. Here we have more than one indication that the criteria of productivity and technical utility are not sufficient and that, just as for the recognized practice of the arts and philosophy, the social motivations that propel the development of the soft sciences, despite (or because of) their softness, are to be sought at a different level. Here I welcome the hypotheses and even the curses of de Dieguez[106] concerning the "rational myth of the West," because they place the accent on the character of the belief (not necessarily justified but nevertheless omnipotent) in causality as the only means of establishing a reassuring order in the otherwise disquieting reality of unpredictability, in human phenomena above all. The belief, never called into question, in the *truth* of the causal relations established between things leads to a uniformity in the accepted explanatory schemes of a particular era; the result is the confusion we have already noted[107] between the rational and what is *commonly* accepted as true—*between the rational and the usual*. The operation of this belief, like any unifying and comprehensive belief, is in large measure irrational, or, at least, involves the rationality of myth: because it is understood that only a rational method can lead us to truth, what we habitually believe to be true gets confused with what we deem to be rational. Conversely, what appears to be new, unusual, and questionable seems at first glance to be irrational.

In all cases, the rational is confounded with the usual (habitual, common). When reason is valued as a source of explanation and means of discovering the truth, there is a lightning shift between what is rational, in the sense of conforming with the principles of identity and noncontradiction, and what, in general, serves to "explain," that is, to integrate the unexpected, the new, and the unknown into the old order, even at the price of denaturing them. We have seen that the same phenomenon is sometimes encountered in non-Western religious traditions: trends are considered to be rationalist because they use daily forms of discourse, even if it is interlarded with contradictions or at least with mysteries that make it possible to paper over these contradictions. Others are considered to be irrational because they invoke uncommon relations between reason and experience, although these relations are more satisfying from the perspective of the needs of unbiased reason. Of course one can reproach de Dieguez for himself falling into an interpretive trap, this time in the name of the "apophatic intelligence" postulated as transcendent or of "critical anthropology," the science of sciences, supposed to make it possible to unmask rationally (and scientifically) the rational myth of the West, which he denounces as the unconscious heir of Christian sacrificial theology.

The belief in the transcendence of his own intelligence makes him think he can escape the myth, but the exercise of this critical intelligence cannot avoid using one form or another of interpretive, ordering reason. The latter makes him construct a new theory, that of a "second-degree rationality in which politics reveals the unconscious of the theological."[108] Here we shall not discuss this theory, which is seductive and illuminating despite its inevitable simplifications,[109] but only contest this belief in the transcendence of critical intelligence or take it all the way to its logical conclusion, namely, to criticism of its own analyses, those to which critical thought has led it. This is what de Dieguez himself recommends, moreover, in several pages,[110] but without being diverted from writing others[111] in which the study of ancient myths is rationalized in the name of the same commonsense "evidence"[112] whose mythical and illusory character he has already demonstrated.[113] At the same time, his critical reading of these ancient myths, especially those of the Bible (not to mention the Talmud),[114] does not prevent de Dieguez from seeing in them no more than a primitive and barbaric prefiguration of the New Testament. In other words, his reading remains enclosed in the enlightened "Judeo-Christian" Western tradition, which is in fact none other than that of the classical Christian theologian that he remains, even when, an atheist as regards the Christian God, he denounces the interweaving of totalitarian politics with sacrificial theology via the Idol of the Causality and Determinism of nature.

This does not necessarily deprive his denunciations of all value, of course! But it is preferable, if one would denounce the false rationalizations of monotheistic theology, not to believe that one can escape myth, to recognize its inevitable and not valueless, but multiform, role in *every* exercise of thought and discourse, and thereby to *relativize it*. In this way one avoids making it the only idol and permits the multiplicity of idols to neutralize their idolic effect, while preserving their functions in economy, history, and the life of thought.[115] This type of trap, into which de Dieguez falls[116] even as he warns against it,[117] threatens every attempt at a sociological or psychosociological interpretation of the history of science; for the key to this interpretation, whatever it may be once theorized, is also to be found in the same history of science whose hidden motives it pretends to unmask. It must then invoke a meta-metainterpretation to unmask its own hidden motives. And so on ad infinitum.

This does not prevent—quite the contrary—the belief in the a priori, global, and unifying truth of scientific rationality from functioning as the foundation of the minimum (or maximum, depending on the society and regime) social consensus that permits the *sciences humaines* to exist. For this belief does not need to be justified. It is nourished by the technical successes attributed to the scientific method and by the failures of traditional interpretive systems, which are not suited to the changes of life and society produced by these same technical successes. It works by displacement: technical effectiveness serves to ground the belief in the truth of the results of the same method when applied to human phenomena. The successful technical mastery of the material world (constructed at the same time as it is mastered, and mastered even better insofar as it is constructed) "proves" the truth of the scientific method. This same method (or a method that resembles it enough to be taken for the same), applied to another object, guarantees the truth of the theories thereby elaborated and of the beliefs they induce. The result of this displacement is a *belief that believes itself to be true*; that is, a vision of the world that is to be believed in because one has reasons to believe it true ("scientifically"), instead of the illusions of myth (of "primitive" or "underdeveloped" or "ahistoric" civilizations) and religion (from the past of our own civilization). Freud, in the *Future of an Illusion*, holds that reason will dissipate the illusions of religion, but never imagines (at least in that text) that it might subsequently be necessary to dissipate the illusions of reason.

I am not trying, in turn, to unmask the hidden motives of this belief, but only to note that it exists. By no means does this observation devalue scientific praxis, neither that of the *sciences humaines* nor that of the natural sciences. It merely invites us to recognize the value of this praxis *in itself*, a value based on its efforts and on the results that it can produce locally, whatever they may be (usable or not, whether concepts and ideas or a methodological discovery, like those, at the limit, of a game of mind and society), without our having to believe in the absolute, because "scientific," truth of its products. Or, alternatively, it lets us recognize in this belief the same illusory and mystifying character possessed by belief in the God of universal monotheistic religion.

## Disinterest: The Price of Entry into Scientificity

A curious situation results from this attitude of "positive" (as opposed to "nihilist") skepticism or skeptical engagement in the practice of these games. The sciences are exact in inverse proportion to the degree that they imply the subjects they study. The odds that a given scientific discipline will be rigorous decline when the knowledge it produces leads to direct implications for the subject who practices it. Conversely, the more a science is exact and produces indisputable results, the less do its theoretical consequences have manifest and immediately predictable implications for our life. The *sciences humaines* have direct consequences on the vision of human affairs: in them, the consequences of a theory are not at all indifferent, at least in principle, for the life of the individual subjects of a study. At the other extreme, mathematics (if one considers it a science) or theoretical physics has only the most indirect (and in any case unpredictable) consequences on human affairs: it is quite indifferent, from the perspective of our *immediate* experiences in our daily lives, whether an algebraic or topological hypothesis is demonstrated or refuted, or what properties of spin or charge a new elementary particle is discovered to have. It is customary to oppose the ("soft") *sciences humaines* to the ("experimental," "hard") natural sciences, on the grounds that in the former it is extremely difficult to generate reproducible experiences in well-defined experimental conditions. But this other aspect, related to the nature of the object-subject, is at least as important. Classically, detachment from human affairs is a guarantee of scientific truth, in that it constitutes a guarantee of objectivity. By contrast, the manifest implications of what is at stake in the critiques and controversies of the *sciences humaines*, for the lives and interests of their practitioners, call into question precisely their disinterestedness and thus the (objective) scientific truth of their results. In fact, we know quite well that matters are not so neatly cut and dried. The levels at which research takes place can also be differentiated in history, sociology, psychology, and so on, such that researchers can circumscribe a particular and well-defined domain as the object of their "scholarly interest," which can thereby remain objective and distinct from their interests as living, feeling, and acting human beings.

On the other hand, the natural scientists' interest in their topic, for all that it is esoteric and ostensibly detached from the objects of their life, is probably determined by individual and collective personal motivations linked with their lives, at least unconsciously, or perhaps[118] with cultural stakes, more or less hidden in the history of ideas, that plunge directly into the a priori of metaphysical, religious, or political beliefs. Many psychoanalytic exercises aim at unmasking these unconscious motives (though they too are exposed to the critique directed above against sociological interpretations, namely, the need for meta-metainterpretations to unmask the hidden motives of the metainterpretations, and so on ad infinitum). From this point of view, the guarantee of truth based on objectivity is undermined in the natural sciences as well and the loop is closed, with studies of the conscious and unconscious psychosociological origins of scientific paradigms spiralling indefinitely in the vortex of meta-meta-...-interpretations.

Nevertheless, in conscious scientific discourse the distinction between the hard and soft sciences remains, initially based on the technical success of the former and the degree of reproducibility of their conditions of observation and experimentation, but reinforced, as we have seen, by the degree of manifest disinterest and direct subjective nonimplication in the results of what is being studied.

Moreover, in the *sciences humaines* (and this is perhaps what makes them "soft"), the criterion of scientificity is in some way dissociated from the criterion of truth—of a certain type of truth, of course, that which concerns the relevance of a theory or a model for our experience of reality. As we have seen, in the hard sciences this relevance is to a large extent constructed at the same time as the theory itself, in the reality of the laboratory, a technical reality built to order so that the theory will apply to it. This artifactual reality, in its own turn, can appear as a simplified model of our experience of natural phenomena or ancient technicity, traditional and empirical, even if the explanation of the latter by the former often poses difficult problems. The exercises of Faraday, who, to explain a candle flame, had to invoke the most advanced theories in different branches of physics and chemistry, demonstrate the difficulty of such transpositions. The same is true of the test that few apprentice physicists (not to speak of their veteran colleagues) pass successfully; namely, explaining a particular physical phenomenon occurring around them (the play of colors, equilibrium sets, multipart pendulums, etc.), not to mention the paradoxes or open problems with which only the physics of these last few years has started to deal, such as Olbers' paradox[119] or the particular forms taken by liquid vortices or seafoam.

Nevertheless, despite the difficulties, the transition can still be made, even approximately, from physical theory to our daily experience of nature.

In the case of the *sciences humaines*, on the contrary, where there is hardly any possible link through the artifactual reality of laboratory and technique,[120] there remains a vast distance between the reality of our experience of life (both objective and subjective) and the domain of reality circumscribed and abstracted by the conditions in which a model is validated. What is more, to the extent that a theory seeks to be rigorous and satisfy the criteria of scientificity, it chooses its object precisely by circumscribing and defining the domain that lends itself to reproducible experimentation and predictive modeling. In general, this domain represents only a very particular situation, or even an a priori abstraction, which bears only a remote relationship with our experiences of daily life. The result is that one knows at the outset, while devising the theory, that its predictions will be applicable only in a limited or nonexistent domain of our reality and that, ultimately, the odds that the knowledge thereby produced will satisfy the criteria of empirical truth are in inverse proportion to the odds that it will satisfy the criteria of scientific truth! Chomsky explained this in his critique of the psychological schools that represent behaviorism: "Much of their [the "behavioral sciences"] scientific character has been achieved by a restriction of subject matter and a concentration on rather peripheral issues." (Chomsky admits, incidentally, and quite rightly, that "such narrowing of focus can be justified if it leads to achievements of real intellectual significance," but he believes that in this case "it would be very difficult to show that the narrowing of scope has led to deep and significant results."[121] This introduces another criterion of utility in the process, in addition to applicability and direct effectiveness, and brings it closer to a philosophical process than to a technological and scientific one.) The snag is that his own work, philosophical in any case, has not removed the misunderstanding; quite the contrary. He has merely contributed to the general movement of strong physicalist reductionism by pretending to give a nontrivial biological basis to his linguistic theories.[122]

Thus we reach the sort of paradox announced above, namely, that there are more reasons to have confidence in the truth of a science that involves us less. At the extreme, a science dealing with man is the most suspect,[123] because it involves us the most. On the other hand, a truth that does not involve us does not involve us in the sense that it has no importance for us, that it has every reason for appearing useless to us. The so-called crisis of science, with the reactions of antiscientific skepticism rehabilitating more or less obscurantist irrationalisms, certainly derives, inter alia, from this ever-widening gap between what can be accepted as scientifically "true," but does not concern us, and what concerns us but is suspect of comprising interested and not "scientifically established" opinions. Here we can see, moreover, a special case of a more general crisis in the circuit of meaning between individual and collective: individuals, whose actions, compounded with those of others, constitute the social reality, do not recognize themselves in the constraints and the image of themselves that this social reality reflects back to them.[124] Similarly, the subjects of objective knowledge contribute to the production of an established, collective knowledge that reflects back an image of themselves that does not concern them: that of an abstract theory of general value, in which their subjectivity has no place. From this perspective, religions are much more effective, because the global meaning they propose concerns a priori the subjectivity of each of us: each of us can have the experience of its truth, if we are truly willing to (and can) believe in it. But religions, in the West, have become precisely objects of belief and are thereby separated from science. In "exotic"[125] societies, symbolic and mythical thought, which seeks out the true reality at the deepest level of human subjectivity, was at the same time "an instrument for knowing" reality in all its forms and allowed no "illusory" aspect to be separated from it; in the West, however, only science has a legitimate right to the status of instrument of "true" knowledge. From this springs the desire, indeed sometimes the irrepressible need, for synthesis, unification, and reconciliation between science and religion; or at least, if this is not possible for the Western "Judeo-Christian" religions, which are too far compromised, then between the Western world and exotic traditions.

## Freud versus Jung and the Scientificity of Psychoanalysis

In this search to unite a demystifying critical truth ("true" because scientific and demystifying) with something (a discourse or praxis) that concerns us as human beings, as individuals in our full life, psychoanalysis occupies a special and in certain respects exemplary place. Its various schools have attempted to get around this alternative of scientifically true and uninvolved versus involved but suspected of interested illusions. Even if it has not succeeded (when it deals with individuals and acts on them, it is hardly scientific; when it would be scientific it is scarcely human), the manner in which the confrontation has been staged has great bearing on our discussion. It is not happenstance that the Jungian school was so well represented at Cordoba.

As a therapeutic practice, it shares with medicine the special and fascinating status of a technique that is supposed to be scientifically grounded and that concerns us directly, because its domain of application is first and foremost our own person, even if only in circumstances, in principle exceptional, of disease. In many minds, medical truth combines the two aspects of scientificity and effectiveness for our own life; even if the scientificity of medicine can sometimes be contested and even if, as is now being realized more and more, the problems of life cannot be reduced to problems of health.[126] Above all, however, medicine and therapeutic techniques in general are a domain where inferring the truth of a theory on the basis of technical (therapeutic) success is scarcely justified. The disease and the cure constitute complex systems characterized by a large number of parameters; information circulates through many levels of organization, from that of biochemical and molecular disturbances through that of the somatic or psychological symptom in its sociological context. The models we can construct to represent the sequence of events leading to the symptom and its elimination include so many ad hoc hypotheses and so many holes at the transitions from one level to another that the manifest success of a given therapeutic protocol can usually be explained in the context of many such models, quite different one from another. This is why the therapeutic success of a method cannot generally serve as "experimental proof" allowing us to "scientifically establish" its value. In the domain of therapeutics, empiricism is king: if a cure (or a particular cure that both patient and therapist can agree on as the desired objective) has been obtained with sufficient frequency that we can reasonably persuade ourselves that it is the result of a certain course of treatment, it becomes easy to include this technique within a general theory of man and the universe, whether it invokes what the physical and biological sciences teach us in each generation or some traditional mythological lore or another.

Studies of alternative forms of medicine and healing techniques regularly lead to the observation of undeniable therapeutic successes, at least for certain types of diseases, although each of these techniques rests on a more or less elaborate theoretical corpus, with its own pseudo-scientific jargon located somewhere between that of science and that of myth. Of course, these comprehensive theories often exclude those that official medicine accepts, and are even mutually exclusive, whereas *each of them* holds its therapeutic success to prove its own truth. Certainly the domains of psychosomatic illnesses, functional disorders, and, in particular, common emotional and neurotic symptoms are privileged loci of *successful* application[127] of all sorts of therapeutic methods (all the various psycho-bio-mystico-therapies); but these successes cannot pretend in the slightest to demonstrate anything about the methods concerned. One of the (many) misunderstandings about psychoanalysis derives from the fact that its founder explicitly desired to integrate it into the movement of established scientific knowledge, while, as a nonconventional therapeutic method, it soon came to share the fate of all sorts of healing techniques and occupied the place left vacant, for the patient, by magic and religion.

It is not only as therapy that psychoanalysis has acquired a special place, but also, and especially, as a psychological theory creating the object and method of a new science of man, for those who accord it the status of science, or as an unpassable horizon of all philosophy and all science, for some of its adepts, or even as a metapsychological (and thereby metaphysical?) theory that indelibly imbues the spirit and language of our age—even if, like many, one denies it the status of science and, along with Wittgenstein, considers it to be "a powerful mythology."[128] And that is precisely the question that concerns us here: is it science or is it myth? Lacan for his part, and probably with justice, sees it as a discipline in itself, with its own particular truth values, an original instrument of exploration and knowledge to be added and juxtaposed to science, magic, and religion. In this way he attempts to get around the contradictions between the Freudian vocation or desire to establish it as a science and the evidently insurmountable difficulty of building up an objective science of the subject. Calling the linguistic sciences to the rescue, as a means of definitively grounding psychoanalysis as a scientific discipline, should not delude us; nor, to judge by a reading of his essay on science and truth,[129] does it seem to have deluded Lacan himself, despite his (incantatory?) reminder that he has no doubts concerning the scientific status of psychoanalysis.[130]

For Castoriadis,[131] the question is decided more simply and more radically by denying that psychoanalysis has a true vocation for knowledge and seeing in it chiefly a vocation of transformation. The inadequacies of Freudian theory on the mechanisms of sublimation, in which he sees the effect of what he calls the "social imaginary," allow him to perform this operation. This has the incontestable advantage of rescuing psychoanalytic practice as *oriented* exploration and knowledge, without any need to establish the scientific and objective truth of the theory that supports it.

But what preoccupies us here is different and much more limited. The history of psychoanalysis has revealed the hidden ambiguity of the relationship between science and mysticism, of which we have already seen several aspects, from the perspectives both of the physical and biological sciences and of certain forms of mystical and mythological expression. This should not surprise us, because its chosen object of study is the hidden depths where the psyche, as the object of scientific knowledge, quickly links up with myth (and dreams) as the product, privileged expression, and means of investigation of this psyche. This ambiguity, along with the desire not to be enclosed by it and the wish to maintain an attitude toward its own process that is "correct," "rational," perhaps even "ethical," seems to me to constitute the connecting link among Freud's differences with some of his disciples, such as Jung, Groddeck, and Ferenczi, with whom he ultimately broke over the question of the "black tide of mud…of occultism."[132] What interests us here is to note the extent to which, opposing his rivals-disciples, Freud is indefensible and incomprehensible when it comes to the content of the theory, although we must follow him if we would maintain the method and the rigor of the process. In effect, from the point of view of content, the barriers that Freud would erect between the rational and scientific psychology he wishes to develop and the mystical "deviations" he denounces in Jung, for example, seem to be quite arbitrary. The latter had no great difficulty in showing that he was merely continuing and extending the method of exploration instituted by Freud in his *Interpretation of Dreams*; in other words, that Freud is sinning through cowardice, as if afraid of his own discoveries.

Some have sought to locate the point of rupture in fidelity to the emphasis on sexuality as the exclusive central node of the structures of the unconscious. On this question, too, Jung easily demonstrated how this exclusivism is arbitrary, even from the perspective of the Freudian approach, if one understands it narrowly—apparently a necessary condition if it is to be employed as the line of demarcation of an antimystical Freudian orthodoxy.[133] This is what Mircea Eliade, for example, does when, carried away by his Jungian enthusiasm, he accuses Freud of unknowingly being one of the last positivists and treating sexuality in a superficial and narrow fashion, instead of making it say more than it does, as was always the case when it was "everywhere and always a polyvalent [symbolic] function whose primary and perhaps supreme valency is the cosmological function."[134] Jung, for his part, reproached him from the other side for giving sexuality a numinous character, but unknowingly, manifesting his materialist prejudice and religious and nonscientific attitude in his exclusive and passionate attachment to sexual theory.[135]

Later we shall attempt to show that Freud's main concern in rejecting the mysticism of mythological traditions, understood literally, was not to hold fast to a "pure" sexuality, as Eliade reproaches him, but rather to find a mean term between the latter and a traditional mythical signification, in which, "saying more than it does," it would *mean* something specific, expressed in its own language, that of a "science of the unconscious," and not in the language of mythology. Whatever the case may be, Eliade's accusation is clearly false, as is shown by the developments, stimulated by Freudian theories of sexuality, made by Freud himself and many of his disciples who wanted to guard and continue his orthodoxy. Of course these are the same developments that make it possible to attack Freudian psychoanalysis on its other flank, asserting that it too, despite fighting against it, is a mythology, indeed neither more nor less a mysticism than that of Jung—and denying it at that! But this merely revives the question of the why and how of the barriers that Freud wanted to erect. We know that for some people[136] the response to this question is to be sought in a psychoanalysis of Freud and his relations with his successive disciples in the history of the psychoanalytic movement; for others,[137] in his lack of comprehension of unconscious but nevertheless fundamental phenomena (which he was unable to unveil because of his own unconscious conditioning in his role as a creator), such as Rank's myth of the hero or Jung's collective unconscious.

Perhaps today, with the perspective of several generations, when the value of the Freudian enterprise no longer needs to be proved, whatever the truth of his theories and their scientific, poetic, or mythical status, it is possible to tackle this question with more serenity, no longer having to justify the defense of an orthodoxy or heresy, neither of which really needs one. It is rather a matter of finding the stake, *not in the content of knowledge*, but in *different attitudes of process and method* applied to a difficulty that, today and a posteriori, may appear insurmountable and in any case sanctioned by failure. Any judgment we might make of these protagonists no longer concerns, of course, the truth or error of their theories, but rather the fruitfulness of their respective failures. Let us say at once that this judgment will in general be favorable to Freudian orthodoxy, even if—and because—the temptation is great, as for Eliade,[138] to find in favor of Jung from the point of view of a possible—but illegitimate—judgment of the content of the theory.

Freud wanted to ground psychoanalysis as a science and have it recognized as such by the scientific community. This is hard to contest, for it emerges from explicit statements. What is more, everything in his method expresses his concern to deviate as little as possible, despite the originality and irreducibility of his discoveries, from a method on which the consensus is that it is not only rational but also scientific. By preference, he relies on physical causalist interpretations, not only to interpret phenomena previously considered to be insignificant—or meaningless—such as dreams, slips of the tongue, witticisms, and ancient myths, but also to assemble into an explanatory theory psychological facts built up from these phenomena, after having himself postulated them, in an original manner, as what we have called "interpretands." In effect, determinist causalism traverses his entire method because, a priori, everything can be explained, and the role of interpretation and theory is to discover the hidden cause that must exist behind every behavior or discourse, even if it seems to be fortuitous and meaningless. Moreover, the cause to be discovered can always be reduced, by right, to a physical mechanism, even if only through the byways of successive psychological and metapsychological models. Despite the fact that these different models (unconscious-conscious-preconscious, id-ego-superego, Oedipus complex, Eros-Thanatos) belong properly to psychoanalytic theory and despite their exclusive application to the theory of psychopathological observations, extended perhaps to the psychosocial, they are by right physical models, because, on the one hand, they function as mechanisms and, on the other hand, the presupposed substrate of these mechanisms is of a biological nature, and biology itself can be reduced to physical chemistry.

This postulate of physicalism appears most clearly in the use of the concept of psychic energy, in the so-called economic theory wherein this energy, as in physics, is a conserved magnitude (and is neither lost nor created).[139] But if this concept, which designates "an energetic substrate postulated as a quantitative factor in the operations of the psychic apparatus,"[140] was needed to anchor psychoanalysis in the natural sciences, it was not sufficient. This is clear in the use made of it by Jung, who reshapes the physical analogy for his own purposes by giving it an even broader extension, reproaching Freud for his "materialistic prejudice" that prevented him from recognizing "the seriousness of parapsychology and...the factuality of 'occult' phenomena."[141] There is nothing astonishing in this when one recognizes that in Freud this physical analogy already has an ambiguous, eminently contestable, and pseudo-scientific nature. He too makes an immediate jump from the physical to the psychical. No mechanism for the *quantitative* transformation of this psychic energy into any of the known forms of physical energy (heat, work, electricity, chemical energy, etc.) is proposed, or even imagined, that could justify the direct linkage of psychic phenomena and physicochemical phenomena, in their energetic aspect, to some invariant quantity.[142] Nor does the controversy with Jung hinge on Freud's scientifically ambiguous use of this notion. It centers rather on sexuality as the biological intermediary—necessary for Freud, impoverishing for Jung—between the physical and the psychic: in effect, the central role of the sexual can easily be understood as due to its being the most obvious locus of articulation between the biological and the psychic (along with language,[143] but closer to the biological than the latter is) and not as a bizarre pansexualist obsession on Freud's part. Of course, this did not prevent Freud from remaining attached to the energetic theory of the libido and the impulses, in its successive avatars. Quite the opposite, because, in the context of the science of his time, it was his warrant of mechanicism and physicalism, indeed of materialism, which safeguarded his scientific orthodoxy, at least on the verbal level.

Today, however, it is what seemed to be the most scientific aspect of his work, superficially and on the level of content, that has largely lost its interest, whereas what suggested the numinous and the mythological—sex as source of fantasies, nocturnal life, the other side of things, the world of dreams, negation, and contradiction, the world of the nontemporal—has stimulated two generations of researchers and practitioners. Thus the breadth of the Freudian oeuvre has prevented it from being prisoner to that pseudo-scientific orthodoxy; and his disciples, like himself, have always been able to find something to get around it and nurture much broader modes of thought, including, notably, the symbolic, the poetic, and the mythological. This is how he won his match with Jung, who considered him to be "bound within the confines of a biological concept."[144] But he won the match without being able to avoid conceding that his opponent was right, a posteriori, concerning the content of their theories and the arbitrary character—from the point of view of this content but not of the a priori metatheoretical attitude—of the barriers he erected between what was and was not acceptable.

In effect, why should one reject the use of mandalas[145] or the *I Ching* as privileged modes of investigation and not that of dreams and slips of the tongue, if not because of an attitude that is a priori opposed to the direct use of existing extrascientific traditions of thought? Similarly, why should one accept the principle of the atemporality of the unconscious and the theory of denial, which to some extent defy the causalist and noncontradictory logic to which we are accustomed, but reject the principle of "synchronicity" as an acausal relationship between meaningful events, which permitted Jung to provide a "basis," albeit in a rather curious fashion (as we have seen), for the reality of astrology.

Freud was torn, in a moving fashion, between his reactions of rejection and his desire to go further in his exploration of virgin territory. With regard to Ferenczi's experiences of thought transmission, he wrote to him: "I am afraid you have begun to discover something big," whereas he announced to Jung: "In collaboration with Ferenczi I am working on a project that you will hear about when it begins to take shape."[146] But a little later, to Jung who requested authorization to explore the occult and astrology,[147] Freud responded ambiguously and invoked the risk of tarnishing Jung's scientific reputation.[148]

At the same time he preserves his own distance, writing to Ferenczi: "Jung writes to me that we must conquer the field of occultism and asks for my agreeing to his leading a crusade.... I can see that you two are not to be held back. At least go forward in collaboration with each other; it is a dangerous expedition and *I cannot accompany you*."[149] From these exchanges it seems that Freud has no genuine persuasive reasons for opposing his disciples' attraction to the occult; he can base their different attitudes only on differences in impulses. In fact, what reasons can be invoked that will not seem arbitrary and of the same type as those that his detractors opposed to his own researches? We can understand Jung in his evolution and in his later reactions to Freud, after the rupture was consummated. As against what must have appeared to him as mere dogmatism without scientific justification, he holds fast to giving psychological explanations, as witness his report of the conversation in which Freud warned him against the black mud of occultism.[150]

It is true that, considering only the riches of the domains to be explored and the abundance of expected harvest, we must yield, as Mircea Eliade does, to Jung's arguments. We are no longer persuaded by Freud's—delayed—reaction to the episode of the bookcase,[151] when he wrote:[152]

> I therefore don once more my horn-rimmed paternal spectacles and warn my dear son to keep a cool head and *rather not understand something than make such great sacrifices for the sake of understanding.*[153] I also shake my wise gray locks over the question of psychosynthesis and think: Well, that is how the young folks are; they really enjoy things only when they need not drag us along with them, where with our short breath and weary legs we cannot follow.

Yet the italicized phrase indicates the true stakes: the value of comprehension, that is, the *nature* of the explanation, its method rather than its content.[154]

In the same letter Freud proceeds to give an example of demystification of what might have seemed to be a superstition, a demystification itself so acrobatic as can be truly justified only by the humorous tone of the entire letter.[155] Before concluding this history of the creaking bookcase and phantoms by declaring that, in consequence, his interest in what he calls Jung's researches on "the spook-complex" will be "the interest one has in a lovely delusion which one does not share oneself," he offers this parting shot: "Here is another instance in which you will find confirmation of the specifically Jewish character of my mysticism."[156]

If one does not—or cannot—see here anything more than an unimportant sally of wit,[157] one must seek Freud's reasons elsewhere. They can be found without difficulty in his attitude to mythology and its possible relations with science. In his cautionary notes to Groddeck we encounter his concern to maintain an *analytic*, that is, differentiating, method: "Why do you plunge into mysticism, suppress the difference between the spiritual and the corporeal?... I fear that you are also a philosopher and that you have a monistic inclination to despise all the lovely differences to the profit of the seductions of unity. Does that clear us, despite the differences?"[158] For Freud, this concern seems to coincide with that of being not a "philosopher" but a scientist. The only possible criterion of scientific identification and demarcation, for him, is the social criterion of recognition by the scientific community of his time. This is evinced with the greatest possible clarity by his approach to mythology. On the one hand, he was delighted that Jung shared his "belief that we must conquer the whole field of mythology."[159] On the other hand, however, unlike Jung, he understood this conquest as applying only within the prevailing consensus of historical criticism, as the only scientifically acceptable attitude to myths. He indicates this to his correspondent in his justification, through analysis of a biblical myth, of his "objections to the most obvious [i.e., noncritical] method of exploiting mythology."[160]

Unfortunately, this attitude quickly turns against itself, from the perspective of the content of the historical theories on which he deems it imperative to base it: in effect, with the rapid evolution of the knowledge and theories that at any given moment represent the consensus of specialists, it soon becomes clear a posteriori, and almost ineluctably, that the theories on which he based himself are eminently contestable. Mircea Eliade correctly noted this with regard to Atkinson's hypotheses about the primordial horde and Robertson Smith's on totemic sacrifice-communion, on which the theses of *Totem and Taboo* rest.[161] With the passage of time, we see that many Freudian hypotheses and theories have little more scientific grounding than do those of Jung. As a result, a posteriori, the latter's arguments are buttressed and Freud appears to be the authoritarian and bourgeois father, prisoner of limited ideas and an outdated science, whereas his disloyal and rash disciples are his true heirs. But for those who adhere to the value of the method rather than of the theories, this simply will not wash. For us, the rigor of the Freudian method appears quite simply in its adherence to the rules of the social game of scientific research, in which one speaks only in the recognized language of the community or in a new ad hoc language invented for the occasion and continuous with its predecessor.

This constitutes both the grandeur and the (from a certain perspective inevitable) failure of the Freudian scientific enterprise. Had Freud truly succeeded in incorporating his theory into science, it could have been only in the physics, biology, and history of his time. Today practically nothing of it would remain. What this science of the nineteenth and first quarter of the twentieth century held to be the most contestable aspects of his theory today appear to be the most interesting and richest, even if, much later, significant efforts have been invested in *translating* them into the language of contemporary science: that of signaling and information theory (Hartmann) in place of energetics, that of mythological symbolism in linguistic theory and structuralism (Lacan), that of the mechanism in system analysis (Green), that of the problematic of life and death in biocybernetics (Green, Canguilhem). But these efforts ineluctably collide with the insurmountable difficulty that they must ultimately apply not to a system that has been artificially isolated in the objective conditions of the experimental laboratory, but to human subjects in the fullness of their lived experiences (even if these are apprehended only through the artificial structure of psychoanalytic therapy). It has also proven necessary to invent ad hoc theories, such as those of transference, difficult to render scientific for all that they are indispensable; whereas the new attempts at a formalism of "tangled hierarchies"[162] in artificial intelligence and biocybernetics could perhaps serve as a basis for attempts at contemporary scientific translation of these same theories.

Furthermore, the most original discoveries, whose fecundity is never called into question, may concern not successive models of psychic organization, but rather phenomena themselves, posited and perceived as privileged means of observing this organization. And these phenomena are those that traditionally nourish mythology and mystical experience: dreams, coincidences or apparently unexplained fortuitous events, myths themselves.

Thus we have already found at least two reasons why the enterprise of guaranteeing the scientificity of psychoanalysis must be confessed to be extremely perilous and to constitute one of the stumbling blocks of the psychoanalytic movement, which is condemned to oscillate unceasingly between sacrificing rigor to richness or richness to rigor. On the one hand, the interest of scientific rigor and adherence to physical-causalist determinism is associated with the use, as tools of investigation, of phenomena previously the province of traditional nonscientific cultures. What is more, to the extent that the complete human subject is implicated by a praxis that is, inter alia, therapeutic, the "project of transformation"[163] (cure, the "liberation of pathological or religious alienations," the "lifting of the Illusion," the attainment of the "truth of the subject," etc.), with its voluntarist and even ideological side, is not sacrificed (sometimes quite happily) on the altar of an objective "project of knowledge." We readily understand that the ambiguous scientificity of psychoanalysis redounds to its benefit, because for many (perhaps even for Freud himself, in his innermost being?), these nonscientific aspects are its most original and most interesting elements. Hence there was a great temptation to leapfrog over all the barriers and find the great fusion or union between the new psychoanalytic science and nonscientific traditions. This would seem to be following the program, always implicit in scientific theory, of searching for economy and elegance by means of the most general and most unified theory possible, and thereby rediscovering the never-disproved teachings of the mystical traditions about the fundamental unity of the universe, disclosed in its "ultimate reality."

At the same time, however, the concern to remain within the tradition of Western thought, marked by the science of the nineteenth and twentieth centuries, made it possible to give these discoveries a connotation and finally a meaning different from what the Eastern traditions could attribute to them; simply because of the different cultural contexts and their feedback, in this same context, on philosophic and scientific thought itself. This is why, although it was difficult to justify the establishment of barriers and the rejection of a unified theory from the perspective of the discourse that Freud, Jung, Groddeck, and others shared, we can understand and vindicate, from the methodological point of view, the panic-stricken fear of allowing oneself to sink into the black mud of occultism. Such a submersion would make this fruitful ambiguity disappear just as surely as would the opposing attitude, the restriction to a scientism cut off from the experience of life, relevant only to a handful of specialists in Man, with few links to living human beings and their bodies, affects, thoughts, and communities.

To maintain this fruitful ambiguity it was necessary to keep asserting a scientific character while forging new concepts. Even if the latter were later declared bastards of the evolution of science ("disorganized id," "psychic energy," etc.), they permitted the discipline to continue to develop in the shelter, as it were, of this ambiguity. Sensitivity to this bastardy of concepts, considered from the perspective of the biology and physical chemistry of today, leads one to speak of the failure; whereas the success is patent if one considers the fecundity that the school has evinced.

To attain that fecundity, Freud's wager, opposed to that of Jung, was to sacrifice an apparent and immediate richness in favor of rigor, hoping—and therefore leaving open some door—that a greater richness would later emerge from this rigor. The difference between Freud's and Jung's attitudes toward myth makes it possible to locate clearly the nuance that becomes a gulf once the rupture is consummated: it is one thing to say that psychoanalysis is a science not reducible to the biological and physical sciences, even though it is based on them (as one can say of any particular science[164]), and that its objects and tools of investigation are, inter alia, those of mythology and traditional nonscientific cultures; it is quite another thing to say that it is a science that unlocks the deep truth of these traditions and thereby rehabilitates them, endowing them with the "scientific" character that seems indispensable in our society for acquiring letters patent in the pretension to truth.

It is on account of this wager of methodical rigor and differentiation that Freud was a man of science, more than on account of the physicobiological details of his theory, which are certainly the less interesting elements today; even though, to support his wager, he had to maintain the strictest possible contact with these same elements, at least as linguistic phenomena.

## The Scientific Wager in Modern Psychoanalysis

It is interesting to see how Freud's disciples continued this wager. In our own generation, the work of A. Green[165] is exemplary, because it sets itself the task of formalizing what seems a priori to be the most recalcitrant to any scientific approach, the world of emotions or affectivity in its entirety, that is, a world where the irreducible elementary unit, the "affect," is seen as an integrated psychosomatic phenomenon in which symbolic mental aspects and physiological corporeal ones cannot be separated, even though nothing in our theoretical tools lets us think about them together. This same insurmountable contradiction was also noted and analyzed by P. Marty,[166] one of the founders of the French psychosomatic school.[167]

If we compare Green with another psychoanalyst, Erich Fromm, we encounter the same divergence of these two tendencies: the interest in scientificity versus the unhesitating willingness to follow the paths of the mystical traditions of the Orient.[168] But here the contrast is even more radical and epitomizes the divergence. In the first place, these two authors belong to the next generation, after the rupture, and have already and definitively chosen their camps: Green is a Freudian, which, for him, means scientific, as we shall see; Fromm considers himself a humanist psychoanalyst, violently criticizing Jung,[169] but going even further than the latter in his search for the total "truth," including religious, of the "accomplished man," who is liberated thanks to psychoanalysis.[170] What is more, these authors, addressing themselves to what can be considered to be the stumbling block of scientific psychoanalysis—the lived experience of the inner transformation produced by psychoanalytic therapy, located beyond an intellectual phenomenon of a "sudden awareness"—derive antithetical developments from it. Both come after Freud himself recognized the inadequacy of conscious awareness of hidden motivations and unconscious desires, which implicates only the intellect and discursive reason in the interpretation. Any effect, therapeutic or otherwise, can be produced only if the interpretation is accompanied by a profound affective transformation—whence the successive reworkings of his theory that Freud had to undertake, leading, inter alia, to the theories of transference and countertransference.

The experience of the irreplaceable role of the affects and emotions in therapy was also the occasion for Jung to posit and reinforce his theory about the "objective" existence of "subjective" meanings.[171] But the Freud-Jung debate, as repeated by authors of the next generation, is no longer really a debate. Debate is no longer possible, because the successor generation has no room for hesitation about methodological postulates.

For A. Green, psychoanalysis can be only scientific, even when it deals with the lived experience of transference and of the affect in its totality, and even if it is clearly prohibited from considering that experience exclusively from the outside, from the perspective of its effects on behavior, in the manner of the behaviorists. For him, renouncing this demand for scientificity because of its difficulties (which he is very careful not to underestimate) can lead only to the renunciation of psychoanalysis itself:

> The empathy that is so necessary for the analyst soon became the easy prey of affects that the analyst projects on the patient, and the beyond of the speakable, of the intelligible, of the representable, can easily take on a mystical allure in which scientific truth runs the risk of foundering.... Taken to the extreme, the question that is posed ruins in advance any process of knowledge. Can one speak of the affect? Doesn't what we say concern the margins of the phenomenon, the propagation waves farthest from the center, which remains unknown to us? The same question is posed concerning the unconscious. Allowing oneself to be fascinated by this enigma, however haunting it may be, would imply the renunciation of psychoanalysis.[172]

For Fromm, by contrast, taking account of affective phenomena and their irreducible role in the therapeutic experience leads immediately to rejecting the subject-object separation and the central role of the intellect and reason that characterize the scientific method. This produces his enthusiastic encounter with the Eastern traditions, especially Zen Buddhism, where he finds all the advantages of a process based on a lived mystical experience, *satori*,[173] without the latter's entailing the discord and theoretical complications caused by theology and the invocation of the God of Western religions. For Fromm, the question soon arises of the relations or affinities to be established between the experience of the "illumination" of Zen and that of the "transformation of character" that accompanies a subject's discovery of his or her unconscious and "derepression." Whatever the degree of proximity of this relation, one thing is certain for him: here the paths of intellectual research and discursive reason, as known in Western science, are inappropriate, just as they are inappropriate to someone who seeks a profound understanding of Zen. "The importance of this kind of *experiential knowledge* lies in the fact that it transcends the kind of knowledge and awareness in which the subject-intellect observes himself as an object, and thus that it transcends the Western, rationalistic concept of knowing."[174] Citing and borrowing for his own use the teachings of the Zen master Suzuki, he stresses "the difference between intellection and the affective, total experience which occurs in genuine 'working through,'" because "to be aware of my breathing does not mean *to think about* my breathing. To be aware of the movement of my hand does not mean to think about it. On the contrary, once I *think about* my breathing or the movement of my hand, I am not any more aware of my breathing or of the movement of my hand."[175]

From this starting point, Fromm joins Suzuki and the traditional teachings of Far Eastern mystics in their a priori distrust of intellectual reflection and logic. The latter are no more than a makeshift, necessary when we cannot do without them in practical daily life, of which the sciences seem to be part: the flowering and liberation of the whole person, thanks to the emergence "into the light" of the unconscious, are obtained at the end of a practice in which "*man* must be trained to drop his repressedness and to experience reality fully, clearly, in all awareness, and yet without intellectual reflection, except where intellectual reflection is wanted or necessary, as in science and in practical occupations."[176]

Once again, the interesting point in this alternation between Green and Fromm—which, given the vast difference between these authors, might well seem incongruous—is that for both the point of departure and chief object (if one may use the term) of investigation is at the core of the problem in psychoanalysis and in the *sciences humaines* in general: affectivity and unreason as fundamental, irreducible elements of human reality. But whereas Fromm, going further than Jung, seeks a key to these difficulties in Zen techniques of illumination, Green, staying within the Freudian tradition, obstinately seeks to forge ad hoc concepts while refusing to compromise with richer but bastard notions, bastard because derived from other traditions, resting on other presuppositions, in other contexts. Finally, continuing the Freud of the early years and gleaning in passing what he can find among the "orthodox" disciples, he attempts to build a model.

Comparing the two attitudes, as we did with Freud and Jung, we can understand how rejecting the richness of everything that the mystical traditions can add seems both arbitrary and ridiculous for those who consider content more important than method. On the other hand, it is the very condition of a certain ethic of research for all those for whom present rigor, even at the risk of amputation and impoverishment, is a condition of future fecundity. Even if Green's model is open to dispute—and it certainly is, if for no other reason than that its content relies excessively on the conservation of psychic energy, a concept that can with difficulty be integrated into the modern, physicochemical vision where it is supposed to find its place—his method is the only proper one for preserving "the process of knowledge"[177] as a process, beyond its content. Once again we encounter the divergence between the process that dissects and differentiates, even at the risk of amputating and curtailing, while endeavoring to protect itself and remain lucid about what it is doing, on the one hand; and the process that has attained the ultimate truth where everything is brought together and unified, in the light of illumination, on the other.

In fact, Green is no dupe in his attempt at analysis and modeling. Recognizing that "the true attainment of psychoanalysis is...psychoanalysis, that is, the possibility of analyzing mental activity,"[178] he leaves it to humor or to games to suggest what this psychic maturation might be, the culmination of psychoanalytic work on the subject delivered up to it. It is no longer a question, of course, of definitive human accomplishment or of illumination, but of "the limits of psychoanalysis";[179] likewise, and in an even more critical fashion, when it is a matter of rendering the closest possible account of the double corporeal and physical, or energetic and symbolic, character of the Freudian concept of instincts and impulses. Speaking of the "psychization of stimuli,"[180] or again, "even when it is merely a case of transcribing the demands of the body," of an "energetic transformation [that seems] to make the demand intelligible," he arrives at the "notion of the limiting concept," just as all of Freud's versions of the id designate, for Green, an "unthinkable concept."[181] He sees clearly that here it is our instruments of analytic knowledge that are faulty, poorly suited by their structure, as we have already seen, for the transition from one level of organization to another.[182] Superficially one might say that there is no difference between invoking a limiting concept and invoking the ineffability of the experience of illumination. This is perhaps true from the perspective of the content of these expressions; but from the perspective of method they are separated by all the difference in the world: everything that exists between circumscribing, closer and closer, in a negative fashion, and postulating the ineffable as a positive. Only the former method leaves room for something that can be disputed, for a possible opening, for a yet-to-be-said unsaid—what the model leaves aside—thanks to which the process continues and is not halted in the unifying ecstasy of a "truth" that, for all its ineffability, is none the less posited as revealed once and for all. Only the former maintains the presence, to use the expression of M. Olender (in a stunning passage on the "absence of narrative"), "of mental categories to be infringed,"[183] indispensable to the pursuit of any discourse, word, or thought whatsoever.

Wolfgang Pauli concluded his commentary on the Kepler-Fludd con-

troversy by distinguishing between "two types of mind, a differentiation
that can be traced throughout history, the one type considering the quantitative relations of the *parts* to be essential, the other the qualitative indivis-
ibility of the *whole*."[184] The latter, among whom he ranks Plotinus, Goethe,
and of course Fludd (and we can add Jung, Fromm, and other contemporaries, scientific or religious, who are searching for ultimate reality), would
reject the amputation of reality produced by the dissection into parts and
the perturbations that our (artificial) instruments introduce into their
appreciation of "natural" phenomena. Pauli, in a position to know that
these perturbations are an integral part of our knowledge of these natural
phenomena, to the point that the latter cannot be conceived without them,
clearly could not recognize this form of spirit in himself. But he did see in
it the expression of the psychological divergencies between "the feeling or
intuitive type" and the "thinking type," the former able to relate only to the
qualitative, the latter to the quantitative: "two aspects of reality" that Pauli
confounds with the mental and the physical, respectively. His encounter
with Jung allowed him to search for what was for him, "unlike Kepler and
Fludd, the only acceptable point of view [which] appears to be the one that
recognizes *both* sides of reality—the quantitative and qualitative, the physical and the psychical—as compatible with each other, and can embrace
them simultaneously."[185] We have already seen the nature of the spiritualist
or rather parapsychic misunderstandings to which this encounter gave rise,
in which Fludd and alchemy triumph in the end, where the quantitative
and anatomizing reason are ranked alongside the vulgar tools that are good
only for managing in our daily life.[186]

Thus, in the Freud-Jung contest, Freud's attempt to anchor psychoanalysis as a scientific discipline against the "black mud of occultism" was
probably not merely the caprice of an authoritarian old man, nor one of the
bad jokes that his unconscious played on him, but rather a fundamental
element of a process with multiple stakes that required, to steady itself, the
consensus of a particular human society, however limited and bounded,
like any society: that of the scientists and philosophers of his time. This
attitude can be seen as perhaps more fruitful than Jung's, even though, as
far as content was concerned, the latter was probably right. From that perspective, Jung was right to find no justification for the barriers artificially
erected in the unconscious between the fruits of psychoanalytic discovery
and those of the Tao, astrology, and spiritualism. From a strategic point of
view, however, Freud's feeling was more correct, even if he found it hard to
justify himself other than by asserting his authority: it is through his
research method that psychoanalysis could assert a certain scientificity, and
this is clearly how it had to oppose itself to its own orthodoxy of content,
that is, to any attempt to freeze it as a true and definitive corpus of teach-

ings; and to that end instituting an orthodoxy of method that cannot but appear arbitrary to those for whom the only objective is the attainment of the Truth of Ultimate Reality.

## Notes

1. Freud warned Jung against the danger of letting himself be submerged by the "black mud of occultism." This famous dispute will provide us with an example of the problem of the barrier that we must erect, if only to preserve our sanity, between scientific and animist explanations, even though we know that (1) we cannot do without the latter in our daily life; and (2) the location of this barrier is always relative to some interest of knowledge and thus always arbitrary from a perspective that claims to be unique and absolute.

2. Habermas, *Knowledge and Human Interests*.

3. Paul Feyerabend, in *Against Method*, uses this term to designate the relations between scientific theories that replace one another in the history of science. The incommensurability here is even stronger, as we shall endeavor to show.

4. Sigmund Freud, "Infantile Sexuality," in *The Basic Writings of Sigmund Freud*, trans. and ed. A. A. Brill (New York: Modern Library, 1938), p. 594.

5. M. Neyraut, *Les Logiques de l'inconscient* (Paris: Hachette, 1978), p. 42.

6. Gregory Bateson, *Steps to an Ecology of Mind* (New York: Ballantine Books, 1972).

7. C. G. Jung and W. Pauli, *The Interpretation of Nature and the Psyche* (New York: Pantheon Books/Bollingen, 1955).

8. C. G. Jung, "Synchronicity: An Acausal Connecting Principle" (trans. R. F. C. Hull), in ibid., pp. 42 and 137–138.

9. A. Lautman, *Essai sur l'unité des mathématiques* (Paris: UGE, 1977).

10. See Wolfgang Yourgrau and Stanley Mandelstam, *Variational Principles in Physics and Quantum Theory*, 3d ed. (New York: Pitman, 1968). Not all extremum principles in physics necessarily express a finalism. The principle of least action makes it possible to determine a priori a trajectory, that is, the series of states through which a moving object must pass from its initial to its final state. This is a nonfinalist but quite deterministic description in which the entire series of states in time is given at once by the equations of motion. Yet neither is it a simple causal sequence of events produced one by another in a temporal series of causes and effect. In fact, computation of the trajectory makes it possible to eliminate time by giving the sequence of states straightaway. This appears clearly in the reversible

nature of the equations of mechanics, which remain invariant when the time variable changes sign; that is, when the direction of time's arrow is reversed. By contrast, the principles of evolution that minimize or maximize a function when it characterizes the final state (and not the trajectory), such as minimum free energy, maximum entropy, and so on, do exhibit this character of physical finalism. In all cases, however, the explanatory virtue of these descriptions is located in the mathematical formalism employed and the physical meaning of the functions used to describe the dynamics of the system. We are well aware, of course, that when we say this we have not explained very much about this explanatory virtue. We are rather reopening the Pandora's box of questions posed by mathematical physics, which deal precisely with the famous physical meaning of mathematical formalisms. We should note in passing that these questions were not born with quantum mechanics, but were already asked by classical mechanics and thermodynamics. See J.-M. Lévy-Leblond, "Physique," *Encylopaedia Universalis*; Prigogine and Stengers, *Order out of Chaos*; Atlan, *L'Organisation biologique*, Chapter 9; Atlan, *Entre le cristal et la fumée*, Chapter 2).

11. C. S. Pittendrigh, "Adaptation, Natural Selection and Behavior," in A. Roe and G. G. Simpson, ed., *Behavior and Evolution* (New Haven, Conn.: Yale University Press, 1958), pp. 390–416. See also Atlan, *Entre le cristal et la fumée*, Chapter 1.

12. See Atlan, *L'Organisation biologique* and *Entre le cristal et la fumée*; see also Hofstadter, *Gödel, Escher, Bach*.

13. Here chance is taken with its least compromising, from the metaphysical perspective, sense of the conjunction of two independent series. In the present case this conjunction involves the causal series that produces an illness in a given subject and the causal series that places the physician in a position to observe the patient.

14. Cited by Jung, "Synchronicity," pp. 11ff.

15. Ibid.

16. See especially the report and critique by Martin Gardner, *Fads and Fallacies in the Name of Science* (New York: Dover, 1957).

17. One way of doing so involves the diagram below, suggested by M. Milgram (personal communication). Let $t_1$ and $t_2$ be the times of incidence of two such independent cases $x_1$ and $x_2$, represented on two perpendicular axes by a point between O and T, where T represents the total duration of observation. The probability that $x_1$ will take place at some time $t$ between O and T is the same, whatever the value of $t$; the same applies to $x_2$. The probability that $x_1$ and $x_2$ take place at the same time is represented by the line $t_1 = t_2$, which is the diagonal of the square in the diagram.

The probability that $x_1$ and $x_2$ take place at times separated by a relatively small interval is proportional to the shaded area in the diagram. By contrast, the

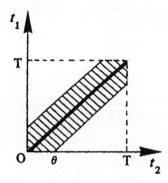

probability that $x_1$ and $x_2$ will be separated by an interval larger than $2\theta$ is proportional to the unshaded area of the square. This part is larger than the shaded area for $\theta < 0.3T$. This can easily be established by finding the value of $\theta$ for which the two areas are equal; i.e., unshaded area $(T - \theta)^2$ = shaded area $[T^2 - (T - \theta)^2]$, which yields $2\theta^2 - 4T\theta + T^2 = 0$, true for $\theta = T(1 - \sqrt{2}/2) \approx 0.293T$, for $\theta < T$.

The probability that $x_1$ and $x_2$ will occur within an interval less than $0.3T$ is thus greater than the probability that their occurrence will be separated by a larger interval; hence the odds are greater that such events will be clustered, relatively speaking, than separated. (It can also be shown that the mean value of $|t_2 - t_1|$, i.e., the most probably value for the interval between these two times, is $1/3T$, and not $1/2T$, as naive intuition would expect.) For three cases, an analogous calculation can be made on a cube with side $T$, instead of a square; and, in general, on a cube in $n$ dimensions for the incidence of $n$ cases.

18. The observation that a physical phenomenon (such as radioactive decay) can be described only by a probability law has been used as an illustration of the acausal order invoked by Jung with his principle of synchronicity (H. Reeves, M. Cazenave, P. Solié, K. Pribram, H. Fetter, and M. L. Von Franz, *La Synchronicité, l'âme et la science: Existe-t-il un ordre acausal?* [Paris: Payot, 1985]). But there is a clear shift of meaning here. For an imposition of order that does not invoke a habitual causal relation, there is no indication of the objective existence of the meanings we can ascribe to coincidences. But it is just this, the existence of meaningful coincidences outside of the interpreting subjectivity, that constitutes the more-than-debatable crux of Jungian synchronicity.

19. Jung and Pauli, *The Interpretation of Nature and the Psyche.*

20. Jung, "Synchronicity," in ibid.

21. W. Pauli, "The Influence of the Archetypal Ideas on the Scientific Theories of Kepler" (trans. Priscilla Silz), in ibid.

22. B. J. T. Dobbs, *The Foundations of Newton's Alchemy.*

23. Jung, "Synchronicity," p. 50.

24. See later on the controversy between Kepler and the alchemist Fludd, which Pauli discusses at length.

25. Pauli, "Influence," p. 190

26. Jung, "Synchronicity," p. 140. Two events *observed* at the same time may not actually occur simultaneously. This is why Jung speaks of "synchronistic events" (i.e., events that obey the principle of synchronicity, where the simultaneity is mental and the relationship among events their common meaning) and not of synchronous events.

27. Ibid., p. 138.

28. Ibid., p. 133. Jung's own language, by contrast, is not always "neutral," as is evidenced by the rapprochement he makes between meaning, which plays the central role in the experience of synchronicity, and the Chinese Tao, with its multiple, theological translations, which he rejects in favor of rendering it as "meaning"! (p. 96)—yet another misunderstanding, because this idea of meaning is itself one of the philosophically most obscure and he makes no effort to state it more precisely.

29. Pauli, "Influence," pp. 196ff. See also the theses of Michel Serres, *Le Passage du Nord-Ouest*, on the origin of mathematics in war and diabolism.

30. The title of a five-volume opus by Kepler, which Pauli discusses at length.

31. Pauli, "Influence," p. 154

32. Ibid., p. 208

33. Ibid., pp. 151f.

34. Ibid., p. 209

35. Jung, "Synchronicity," p. 50.

36. Ibid.

37. We shall see later how contemporary physicists' increased familiarity with these quantum objects, after a half-century of use, has led them to relativize this complementarity and see it as merely a shortcut formulation and not as the expression of some ontological reality.

38. Pauli, "Influence," pp. 210f.

39. Ibid., p. 212

40. Ibid., p. 153

41. Kripke, *Naming and Necessity*.

42. Kripke seems to define as epistemic only what can be known by the

sense organs, whereas scientific knowledge leads *directly* to what is, and thereby extracts its truth. This would be a return of sorts to a scientific neorealism whose motives are clear—saving what is from the all-around relativism in which philosophies of language seem to have drowned—but which all the same is not persuasive, because of the large number of counterexamples the physical sciences provide us by their formalism (see the example of heat, later), not to speak of the *sciences humaines*.

43. This is the same circularity we encounter when we think of thought as being simultaneously a phenomenon in nature and what permits us to know, by means of abstraction and imagination, this same nature.

44. In one of the last major attempts to found "natural law" on "natural science" (J. G. Fichte, *The Science of Rights*, trans. A. E. Kroeger [London: Routledge and Kegan Paul, 1970]), we can clearly discern the role played by these different forms of interpretation. For there to be law, there must be a responsible and free person; for there to be natural science, there must be rationality founded on causality. The union of the two is effected in the rationality of a person's concepts, which have a causal capacity; and this is tantamount to defining persons as rational beings. This rationality (or reasonability) consists of a rational adaptation of means to the ends set out by the person's will. These ends determine the activity of the material body, because the latter "is posited as *the sphere of all possible free acts of the person*," who in turn becomes a cause "only and merely through his will...; for, to trace out a conception of an end is, to will" (p. 91). On the basis of these "deductions," inter alia, Fichte proves "theorem four": "The finite rational being cannot assume other finite rational beings outside itself, without positing itself as occupying a determined relation toward them, which is called the Legal Relation" (pp. 62f.) Note that even this does not allow Fichte to derive natural law from moral law; the two remain separate and distinct (pp. 80f.). Today, however, the evolution of the natural sciences and the success of their weak reductionism no longer allows us to value this type of synthesis. In effect, it disassembles persons into physicochemical or impulsive mechanisms in which hardly any room remains for liberty and free will (except in indeterminacies viewed as holes in the fabric of scientific knowledge, which does not—yet—cover them). Even the least-reductionist psychoanalysis merely deepens the unreasonable, if not irrational, character of what is superficially reported about human will. In other words, we discover that positing this union implied by the idea of a "causal person" in fact presupposes a finalist science. The living body is seen as "an organized product of nature" (p. 116) and clearly differentiated from the organized "product of art," in that its ends are interior to itself, whereas those of the latter are external. But a (natural) science of these natural purposes (here assimilated to the will of rational beings) still seems to be possible. This confidence is hard to justify today, when the physical and biological sciences have progressively eliminated conscious purposes (souls) from their field of study.

45. Wittgenstein, *Blue Book*, in *The Blue and Brown Books*, p. 74.

46. Kripke, *Naming and Necessity*, p. 155, n. 77.

47. "Y a-t-il des sciences humaines?" Colloque de la Fondation Hautvillers (Paris).

48. F. Roustang (*Un Destin si funeste*) links these processes (and thereby "explains" them) to a "natural" struggle against psychosis, which leads precisely to psychotic ravings when it does not succeed. This takes account of the frequently observed rapport (or even coexistence in the same individual) of genius and folly.

49. Bachelard, Lakatos, Feyerabend, Castoriadis, Agassi, Holton, Elkana, and Schlanger, to cite only a few of the authors who have contributed to this.

50. Some attempts (like that of Karl R. Popper, *The Logic of Scientific Discovery* [New York: Basic Books, 1959]) to define the criteria of scientificity, in the wake of the problem known, since Hume, as the problem of induction, can relate only to the operation of rules for verifying theories (which Popper, as is well known, shows to be merely rules for falsifying them), to the exclusion of the mechanisms for the origin and production of theories, inevitably traced back to metaphysics or, in the best of cases, to psychology or a yet-to-be-realized metapsychology. In addition, this separation between rules of verification and rules of production cannot long resist the analysis of the history of how science is conducted. Hence the rules of verification themselves do not seem to furnish an a priori criterion of scientificity, valid in all cases (see, for example, Yehuda Elkana, "A Programmatic Attempt at an Anthropology of Knowledge," in *Sciences and Cultures*, pp. 1–76).

51. Atlan, *Entre le cristal et la fumée*, pp. 144–149.

52. On the mechanism of self-fulfilling prophecies, see the chapter on mimesis and morphogenesis in J.-P. Dupuy, *Ordres et désordres* (Paris: Le Seuil, 1982).

53. Gaston Bachelard, *The Philosophy of No: A Philosophy of the New Scientific Mind*, trans. G. C. Waterston (New York: Orion Press, 1968).

54. On this, see, for example, Regnier, *Les Infortunes de la raison*.

55. Wittgenstein, *Tractatus*, 6.522 and 4.121.

56. Kripke, *Naming and Necessity*.

57. Ibid., pp. 40f.

58. Ibid., p. 99.

59. Physical *theory* (statistical thermodynamics) *identifies* heat with the disordered agitated motion of molecules or, more precisely, with the mean kinetic energy of this motion. Whence this curious statement, whose difficulty will become clear later.

60. Kripke, *Naming and Necessity*, p. 138. He goes on to note that, according to the point of view he is defending, "scientific discoveries of species essence do not constitute a 'change of meaning'; the possibility of such discoveries was part of the

original enterprise. We need not even assume that the biologist's denial that whales are fish shows his 'concept of fishhood' to be different from that of the layman; he simply corrects the layman, discovering that 'whales are mammals, not fish' is a necessary truth. Neither 'whales are mammals' *nor* 'whales are fish' was supposed to be a priori or analytic in any case."

61. Elkana, "A Programmatic Attempt," p. 37

62. The very existence of fringe groups in science, who have defended theories like a cold sun and hollow earth, clearly shows that the referent designated by the temperature of the sun or the shape of the earth is not as immediate as is a person designated by his or her name. This holds a fortiori with regard to rival scientific descriptions that, in the current state of knowledge, are equally plausible and equally acceptable in the context of the specialist consensus, so that neither can win out over the other. This merely highlights the "epistemic contingency" recognized by Kripke.

63. See T. H. Hill, *Statistical Thermodynamics* (New York: McGraw-Hill, 1956); K. Denbigh, *The Principles of Chemical Equilibrium* (Cambridge: Cambridge University Press, 1971); and Atlan, *Entre le cristal et la fumée*, Chapter 2.

64. Kripke, *Naming and Necessity*, p. 129, n. 67.

65. Ibid., p. 144.

66. Imre Lakatos, "History of the Sciences and Its Rational Reconstruction," in *Boston Studies in the Philosophy of Science* (Dordrecht: Reidel, 1973).

67. For Gaston Bachelard (*The New Scientific Spirit*, trans. Arthur Goldhammer [Boston: Beacon Press, 1984] and *The Philosophy of No*), the idea of a *construction* of reality, which always follows a deconstruction (a "realization," by the effect of a "descending rationality" or a "surrationality," the conjunction of mathematical modeling and experimental and technical demonstration), took precedence over that of a simple disclosure of reality in modern science. It is interesting to note that he illustrated this idea with a detailed analysis of the evolution of the concept of heat (*Étude sur l'évolution d'un problème de physique: La propagation thermique dans les solides*, 2d ed. [Paris: Vrin, 1973])—the same example cited by Kripke without further analysis. Today, following in Bachelard's path, we would have to envision, for this practice of scientific construction or "realization," not only mathematical modeling per se, but also every type of logical modeling associated with technical demonstrations. In fact, the advances of biology during the past four decades have involved the association of new techniques of enzymatic biochemistry and biophysics with cybernetic rather than mathematical models.

68. See Chapter 6.

69. Gilles-Gaston Granger, "La notion de contenu formel," in *Information et Signification*, International Colloquium on the Philosophy of Science (Brest: Université de Bretagne occidentale, 1980), pp. 137–163.

70. J.-M. Lévy-Leblond, "The Picture of the Quantum World: From Duality to Unity," *International Journal of Quantum Chemistry* 12, supplement 1 (1977), pp. 415–421; "Classical Apples and Quantum Potatoes," *European Journal of Physics* 2 (1981), pp. 44–47.

71. Bernard d'Espagnat, *In Search of Reality* (New York: Springer-Verlag, 1983).

72. Ibid.

73. Wittgenstein, *Tractatus*, 6.341. See also 6.342, where he remarks that the "possibility of describing the world by means of Newtonian mechanics tells us nothing about the world: but what does tell us something about it is the precise *way* in which it is possible to describe it by these means. We are also told something about the world by the fact that it can be described more simply with one system of mechanics than with the other." Finally, after having defined mechanics as "an attempt to construct according to a single plan all the *true* propositions that we need for the description of the world" (6.343), he notes, *nevertheless*, that "the laws of physics, with all their logical apparatus, still speak, however indirectly, about the objects of the world" (6.3431). It is still a matter of choosing a middle term, of not being forced to select between the naive realism of total objectivity and full relativist idealism.

74. Lévy-Leblond, "The Picture of the Quantum World" and "Classical Apples and Quantum Potatoes."

75. Jerome Rothstein, "Information and Organization as the Language of the Operational Viewpoint," *Philosophy of Science* 29, no. 4 (1962), pp. 406–411.

76. Henri Atlan, "Signification de l'information et complexité par le bruit," *Information et Signification*, pp. 1–29.

77. See, for example, P. Smith, "La nature des mythes," in *L'Unité de l'homme*, vol. 3, *Pour une Anthropologie fondamentale*, ed. E. Morin and M. Piatelli-Palmerini (Paris: Le Seuil, 1978), pp. 248–265; T. Settle, "The Rationality of Science versus the Rationality of Magic," pp. 173–194; the critique of the theses of anthropologists such as Frazer, Evans-Pritchard, Lienhardt, and Beattie by I. C. Jarvie and J. Agassi, "The Problem of the Rationality of Magic," in *Rationality*, ed. Bryan R. Wilson, pp. 172–193, and the response by J. H. M. Beattie, "On Understanding Ritual," ibid., pp. 240–268. In all this literature, no one dreams of identifying scientific rationality purely and simply with that of myth, ritual, and magic. On the contrary, it is a matter of underlining the differences, it being understood nevertheless that the old "naïve view of science as an accumulated mass of empirical observations from which theories have somehow to be squeezed" (Jarvie and Agassi, "The Problem of the Rationality of Magic," pp. 178f.) had to be abandoned. Science should be seen instead as "a highly articulated system of explanatory theories which may be tested against the facts" (ibid., p. 190). The discussions found throughout this collective production, *Rationality*, bear on the precise diagnosis of these differences, and are

nourished by the differences, sometimes semantic, concerning what should be designated as rationality of beliefs or of behavior, strong or weak rationality, etc.

Similarly, the entire oeuvre of Claude Lévi-Strauss (including the series *Mythologiques* [Paris: Plon, 1962, 1967, 1968, 1971] and *The Savage Mind* [London: Weidenfeld and Nicolson, 1972]), who contributed to creating the trend of thought, implies recognition of myth as a form of mental exercise aimed at organizing reality, even while distinguishing it from scientific activity essentially by its comprehensive character of universal explanation. The isomorphism he establishes between the relations of science and myth, on the one hand, and those of technique and tinkering, on the other, do not exhaust the subject when one notes the "tinkering" nature of scientific construction, too. Among other differences we shall find later, often mentioned in these texts, the incompleteness of science, which allows it to be evolutionary and advance, as opposed to the completeness of mythic and magical explanation, in which everything is explained once and for all.

But this difference may perhaps be more of degree than of nature, if we are sensitive to the capacity for evolution and reintegration presented, in varying degrees, by the great mythological and religious traditions. As we shall see, at base it is just as much a question of different interests and objectives as it is of different methods. Thus in the enterprise of knowledge and legislation composed of the Talmud and Kabbala, the search for innovative interpretations, associated with the contrary affirmation that every new explanation, past and future, was already contained in what Moses received "from" Sinai (Mishna Avot 1,1), constitutes a species of compromise by paradox, in which one loses nothing of the sacred and atemporal nature of the lore nor of the effectiveness of reason as the source of infinite meanings and renewed mastery (see Henri Atlan, "Niveaux de signification et athéisme de l'écriture," in *La Bible aujourd'hui*). For M. de Dieguez, rationalism is merely the "rational myth of the West," the title of his provocative work that resumes other studies to be added to the file of this relativism of scientific knowledge (see in particular his article "Progrès," *Encyclopaedia Universalis*, vol. 13 [Paris, 1977], pp. 628–632).

78. A public debate has raged recently, especially in the United States, between "creationists" and "evolutionists," concerning the right (and duty) to teach both schools symmetrically, as two equally valid theories—creation as reported in the Bible and the neo-Darwinian theory of the evolution of species. This dispute is typical of the confusions we would condemn here. As we shall see in connection with other examples, it does not involve objective knowledge, despite appearances, but rather two myths of origin locked in a struggle, not in the name of the quest for scientific truth, but instead on account of the ethical, religious, and even political consequences derived from them—and rather erroneously at that. It is not in the name of the conceptual difficulties of neo-Darwinism, apparent in the wake of new discoveries in molecular biology and paleontology, that the theory of evolution is opposed. These problems are real—for example, those that stem from the selectively neutral character of mutations observed at the molecular level (Kimura). Sometimes one hears of the "crisis" of neo-Darwinism, but in fact it is a case of technical difficulties that give rise to new models, such as that of punctual equilibria, or models of nonlinear determination of phenotype by genotype (Stephen J.

Gould, "Is a New and General Theory of Evolution Emerging?" *Paleobiology* 6, no. 1 [1980], pp. 119–130; R. C. Lewontin, *The Genetic Basis of Evolutionary Changes* [New York: Columbia University Press, 1974]; G. Weisbuch, "Un modèle de l'évolution des espèces à trois niveaux basé sur les propriétés globales des réseaux booléens," *Comptes rendus de l'Académie des Sciences* [Paris] 298 [1984], pp. 375–378; H. Atlan, "Molecular vs. Biological Evolution and Programming," in E. Ullmann-Margalit, ed., *The Kaleidoscope of Science* [Dordrecht: Reidel, 1986], pp. 137–145). In this controversy, on the contrary, these problems are exploited, not without a certain bad faith, to make it appear that the evolution of species as a whole has been called into scientific question; they are used to discredit any theory of evolution and to rehabilitate, as at least plausible, a "theory" of creation in six days, as is defended by certain religious fundamentalists. In fact, what is being fought here is not one scientific theory by another, but one myth of origin by another. Bad faith is not the only villain of the piece; the vulgarization of science and the naive belief in the truth of its theories have also played their part. Neo-Darwinism has been vulgarized as an element in a grand cosmogonic fresco recounting the origins of our humanity as if we were eyewitnesses, and explicitly contradicting religious catechisms by placing itself at their own elementary and dogmatic level. Some have felt this vulgarization to be dangerous for the moral and religious underpinnings of society; for one section of the population and of those responsible for education, defense of morality *must* go by way of elimination of evolutionary theories as accepted scientific truths. This confusion of types clearly derives from the fact that the biblical tradition is read only on the level of a simplifying catechism in which its function as a myth of origin and founding myth is confused with that of an objective discourse on what took place, in truth and literally, during the first days—or even first few seconds—of the universe.

In parallel, evolutionist thought is not in competition with creationism unless it too is caught up in a similar catechism involving the same confusion, but in reverse: between what is initially only a synthetic arrangement of paleontological and biological observations, on the one hand, and a new myth of origin that would reveal an ultimate reality about what we are, by telling us where we come from, on the other. We must recognize, however, that these confusions may have some semblance of justification. First, it is a historical fact that evolutionary theory came to the fore, thanks to Darwin and others, in a climate of violent opposition to revealed religion and not in one of totally disinterested serene scientific research (without speaking of the well-known sociological motives aimed at providing a "scientific" foundation for Malthusianism and Social Darwinism). There too we must distinguish between the motivations of the discovery, with stakes that were not always "pure," and those for the acceptance of the theories by a community of specialists. On the other hand, it is also a fact that the polysemic and metaphoric character of mythological discourse, which provides its abundant richness that goes far beyond the literal meaning of the catechisms, allows anyone who wishes to do so (and has the intellectual capacity) to read this discourse through a new lens that may have been inspired by a scientific theory.

This was realized, with regard to an evolutionist reading of biblical texts, by

Teilhard de Chardin, or by A. I. Kook in his new understanding, it too evolutionist, of a kabbalistic reading of these same biblical texts (*Orot Haqodesh*, vol. 2, pp. 535–552). The frequent error is to believe that these are scientific discourses, when they deal rather with the infinite renewal of the metaphors of myth.

79. Note that, in contrast to the philosophical tradition, Whitehead wanted to consider "causal efficacy" to be a mode of direct perception, just like sensory perceptions per se, and, in association with them, constituting the symbolic references thanks to which we perceive and objectify the reality that surrounds us (Alfred North Whitehead, *Symbolism: Its Meaning and Effect* [New York: Macmillan, 1927]). If the idea of causality as proximity of experience can lean on this conception, it is nevertheless important that we not confuse this "causal efficacy," which interconnects objects perceived at the same level of observation and abstraction, with a different sort of causality, much more problematic, in which a theory with a different level of observation and greater generality explains phenomena and thereby seems to cause them. There is a great difference between "event A occurs *because* of event B, which preceded it in time and produces it as a cause produces an effect," and "event A occurs *because* of phenomenon B, which is itself a fixed phenomenon, a law of nature (like gravity or electromagnetism) and does not 'produce' A but makes it possible to explain its occurrence." If causal efficacy has some proximity to the direct perception of things, there is still nothing that implies an elaborate interpretive and theoretical activity. The confusion between these two uses of "because of" facilitates a belief in the objective reality of the interpretations by displacing the objectifying effect of one form of causality onto the other. This displacement is at the root of many naive beliefs that eventually lead, sometimes after many refinements, to a belief in an objective description of Ultimate Reality.

80. Wittgenstein, *Tractatus* 5.1361.

81. Ibid.

82. See also, in a different context, the distinction introduced by Clifford Geertz between "experience-near concepts" and "experience-distant concepts" (cited by Elkana, "A Programmatic Attempt," p. 39).

83. J. Agassi ("The Nature of Scientific Problems and Their Roots in Metaphysics," in *The Critical Approach to Science and Philosophy*, ed. M. Bunge [London: Collier-Macmillan, 1964], pp. 189–211), reviewing and commenting on Popper, assigns significant explanatory force only to scientific theories, whereas pseudo-science and metaphysics have a very great interpretive power but a weak explanatory power. This judgment is merely the consequence of the fact that Popper could not steel himself to abandon the a priori belief in scientific explanation as the only process able to lead asymptotically to truth; even if (and, for him, because) the inscription of this type of explanation in a process of searching for errors that frequently leads to its rejection distinguishes it from other interpretive activities, where everything can always be explained because nothing can be falsified. The attempts to measure the explanatory power of theories by their information con-

tent, itself a function of the number of ways to refute them, have been unable to withstand the critical confrontation with the history of science (Lakatos, "History of the Sciences"; Feyerabend, *Against Method*)—providing an example of a (meta)theory that, although certainly not scientific (because *about* science), is falsified by historical counterexamples in which we see scientific explanations carrying the day without obeying Popperian schemas.

Popper himself, incidentally, goes further (*Realism and the Aim of Science* [London: Hutchinson, 1983], pp. 265–278) and denies that science involves any explanatory activity, in the sense of providing, rather than demanding, explanations. Only the solution of specific problems, removing contradictions encountered in the course of scientific research itself, is legitimate. Everything else follows from an essentialist illusion that one can find the definition of a word that would be, in itself, "the most exact," independent of any particular problem to be resolved. He links this illusion with metaphysics (Platonic as well as Aristotelian), and, on a deeper level, with our fundamental animism, which rests on the omnipotence ascribed to words and thought, as Freud has shown for the child.

Popper also finds this tendency among quite a few philosophers of different stripes, including Berkeley, Wittgenstein, Husserl, G. E. Moore, Carnap, and even Freud. He designates as animist the concern for giving a name to things and thereby acquiring a power, initially explanatory, and subsequently of mastery, over them. This extreme attitude, in which every explanation would be rejected, is hard to maintain in biology, where the object of study is an integrated system that performs particular functions, just like a machine. In Chapter 2 we noted the problems associated with understanding functional meanings in biological organizations. Nevertheless, taking apart a machine and determining the relationship among the functions of its elements with their interconnections, on the one hand, and the observed functions of the machine as a whole, on the other, certainly plays the role of explanation; even if the distance that must always be maintained between the explanatory model of a naturally organized system and the system itself prevents us—as long as we resist the temptation to decrease this distance—from taking the explanation for the reality itself. Nevertheless, it is in this explanatory function of science that one can find the origin of these mystic deviations, whether embodied in a discourse that is scientist, merely materialist, or explicitly spiritualist.

Among the nonsciences mentioned previously, Agassi's distinction between pseudo-science and metaphysics is interesting in that both are characterized by the same nonfalsifiable (and hence, by Popper's criterion, nonscientific) interpretive activity; but the former vaunts itself established knowledge, whereas the latter can serve as a research program. Thus, for example, Agassi accords Freud's work the status of pseudo-science, secondarily transformed into metaphysics/research program (it being understood that all science has metaphysical roots). As is known, Lakatos extended this idea of research program to scientific theories themselves, with their scientific character deriving, ultimately, only from their recognition as such by a community of specialists. Thus, despite the possibility of their being falsified (or because of it), their explanatory power is not thereby increased as compared with other interpretive activities.

As Jacques Schlanger puts it, at the end of his "Théorie descriptive de l'expli-cation" (*Revue de métaphysique et de morale* 85, no. 4 [October–December 1980], pp. 468–488): "The explanation of an event, however tiny, is never finished.... It had to be inserted into a context that gives it a meaning. But this context itself demands an explanation, in the context in which it is inserted; and so on.... Every meaning is based on an idea of the whole; every meaning has a metaphysical foun-dation.... [What is more,] the explanatory procedure satisfies only the explainer's desire to understand and perhaps to manipulate. It is the explainer, and not the explained, that feels the impact of the explanation." See also the same author's "Expliquer," in *L'Activité théorique* (Paris: Vrin, 1983), pp. 19–50; and the idea of "explanatory relativity" in A. Garfinkel, *Forms of Explanation* (New Haven, Conn.: Yale University Press, 1981).

84. It is true that we are also observing a (timid) return to some more "nat-ural" research objects, as in ecology and field ethology, or in some problems of clas-sical physics, neglected because considered to be nonfundamental and overly com-plex, such as turbulence and other forms of foam. This marginal curiosity nevertheless opens new paths, for example, the study of *natural* complexity, which, it must not be forgotten, also benefits from the fallout from the study of artificial and computational complexity. See Henri Atlan, "Natural Complexity and Self-Cre-ation of Meaning," in *The Science and Praxis of Complexity*, ed. S. Aida et al. (Tokyo: United Nations University, 1985), pp. 173–192; F. Fogelman-Soulié, ed., *Les Théories de la complexité*, colloque Cerisy, 1984, autour de l'oeuvre de Henri Atlan (Paris: Le Seuil, 1991).

85. Wittgenstein, *Brown Book*, in *The Blue and Brown Books*, p. 132.

86. Ibid., p. 129.

87. This conclusion matches that of T. Settle ("The Rationality of Science") concerning explanatory incompleteness as a characteristic trait that differentiates science from magic. This explanatory incompleteness explains (*sic*) the growth of scientific disciplines as opposed to the stagnation of magical cosmogonies. The incompleteness is manifested in various ways, such as the absence of an immediate causal explanation when the only possible scientific representations are statistical (magic is then invoked to fill the gaps and designate the cause) and the proliferation of disciplines that cannot be reconciled in a single grand unified theory. But this opening is not as general in scientific practice as is believed, and we also find it in magical thought and practices (Elkana, "A Programmatic Attempt"). Even this cri-terion cannot by itself realize the great division between scientific and nonscientific explanations (see Chapter 8, n. 60). Perhaps, as we have suggested, the demarca-tion should be shifted so as separate disciplines that are not totally explanatory but are predictive and effective—the state of the natural sciences today—from disci-plines that provide explanations in terms of first causes or Ultimate Reality, which remain mythological, even if they borrow in bulk from various scientific theories.

88. See Chapter 2, p. 64.

89. Granger, *Langages et Épistémologie*. In another article, Granger asks about the possible existence of a formal content despite its paradoxical aspect (at the same time form without content and nevertheless content); he tries to give an affirmative answer, endeavoring to grasp what is, despite everything, not merely tautological in mathematics (Granger, "La notion de contenu formel").

90. See Chapter 4.

91. A. Warusfel, *Les Nombres et leurs mystères* (Paris: Le Seuil, 1980).

92. Michel Serres's essays on the origin of mathematics, in *Le Passage du Nord-Ouest*, clearly demonstrate the violence represented by the discovery of numbers called for that very reason "irrational" and its exorcism by their integration into number theory. There too, as with causality versus temporal succession, reason makes it possible to exorcise the anguish caused by what does not fit in.

93. See Feynman, *Lectures on Physics*, vol. 3, Chapters 1 and 3. The probability that an electron is found at a particular point in space is the square of the absolute value of the wave function at that point, $P = \Phi^2$. Because electrons are described as waves whose amplitude is equal to the wave function, also known as the "probability amplitude," when two electrons are copresent in an experiment, their wave functions—complex numbers—must be added. The result is that the probability of the presence of two electrons at two points, 1 and 2, in an electron-interference experiment is equal to the square of the absolute value of the sum of the two wave functions, $|\Phi_1 + \Phi_2|^2$ and not to the sum of the two probabilities, $|\Phi_1|^2 + |\Phi_2|^2$.

See Feynman's resigned comments on the impossibility of truly reconciling the mathematical formalism that successfully describes the observations with some underlying (behind the law) physical mechanism that would "explain" the phenomenon better than the formalism does (Feynman, *Lectures on Physics*, vol. 3, Chapter 1, pp. 10f., and Chapter 3, p. 1).

94. It is significant that the discovery of Hindu nonduality by the Christian monk Henri Le Saux was accompanied by rents between, on one side, this nonduality and, on the other side, the dualistic Christian tradition. It is too bad that this conflict pushed him to ascribe the blame for it to the existence in Christianity, alongside its Greek origins, of a "Jewish anthropomorphism"! To accuse Jewish tradition of anthropomorphism, with regard to the divine, is certainly going too far for a Christian and can be attributed only to ignorance (see in this context the discussion in Chapter 3 of the Nahmanides-Maimonides controversy). But such ignorance is hardly rare, even if it does not fail to astonish when it appears in circles that elsewhere are not satisfied with superficial knowledge. A particularly striking example is that of the Hindu sage Ramana Maharshi, who, we are told (*Doctrine de la nondualité*, p. 99), liked to remark that "I am what I am" is the only sentence in the Bible printed in capital letters, clearly unaware that Hebrew has none (and leaving aside the fact that the Hebrew verbs are actually in the future—"I shall be what I shall be"; it is true that the mistranslation into the present tense is found in almost all translations, but any yeshiva student knows that this is erroneous and in

fact distorts the meaning of the text). (See Atlan, "Niveaux de significations.") The attempt at evasion by means of a scapegoat to which Le Saux succumbs here, blaming the impossibility of a unity between Hinduism and Christianity on the Jewish sources of the latter, certainly calls to mind Simone Veil and her own self-lacerations, as was noted, incidentally, by M. M. Davy (*Henri Le Saux*, p. 69). This is another snare set by the love of Love, by the search for doctrinal Unity, which merely deepens the division, exclusion, and anathema where, in principle, it is only a question of perfect Unity. It seems that the Western monk referred to previously, and probably also Ramana Maharshi, whose remark he reports, are more serene on this score.

95. Bachelard, *The New Scientific Spirit.*

96. Only in the shelter of this stripping, and the rigor that accompanies it, has the physical-finalist interpretation any right to be accepted, as we have seen.

97. Sperber, *Rethinking Symbolism.*

98. Emmanuel Levinas, *Totalité et Infini: Essai sur l'extériorité* (The Hague: Martinus Nijhoff, 1981); *L'Humanisme de l'autre homme* (Montpellier, France: Fata Morgana, 1972).

99. V. Jankelevitch, *Le Je-ne-sais-quoi et le Presque-rien*, vol. 3: *La Volonté de vouloir* (Paris: Le Seuil, 1980), p. 32.

100. Levinas, *Totalité et Infini* and *L'Humanisme de l'autre homme*; see also his *Difficile Liberté* (Paris: Albin Michel, 1963).

101. Thus we read (Psalms 62:12): "One thing God has spoken, two things I have heard," extensively cited and commented on in the talmudic tradition (see Chapter 6, n. 62).

102. This difference can, in addition, be inverted, depending on the meaning one attributes to *top* and *bottom*. For some, scientific knowledge proceeds from top to bottom, because of the deductive aspects of its empirico-logical method, its structuring of reality by what Bachelard called its "applied rationality" (see Chapter 2, n. 71)—unlike mystical initiation, which moves from the bottom to the top, from revelation to revelation until full illumination is achieved. But in their discourses about reality, to which these traditions try to give a rational structure, they proceed in opposite directions. Mystical traditions take as known ultimate reality, that of Unity and the All, which is given in illumination, and deduce from it judgments and modes of conduct concerning specific experiences. By contrast, the scientific tradition works in a step-by-step fashion, building pieces of what seems to be a reality hidden behind the phenomena, because it permits assembling them, as far as is possible, into a chain of causes or at least into one that is calculable and predictable. Science constructs, little by little, a truth of mastery that is very different from the truth of illumination, even if the latter can sometimes play a role in the process of discovery by which scientific knowledge is generated. The *goal* of science is explanation;

as such, it appears to be engaged in a quest for illumination, invoking a unified theory that, in the simplest fashion possible, can account for everything. But its *practice* is pragmatic elucidation, in which the true criterion is effectiveness of mastery, and this requires merely local and partial explanation. For Bachelard, this goal of total explanation falls within the province of the scientist's psychology. But are we not falling here into the trap of pschologism, just as the sociology of science makes us fall into that of sociologism? Who will investigate the psychology of the scientist-psychologist who studies the scientist, or the sociology of the scientist–sociologist of science? For Bachelard this was evidently the role of the (nonscientist?) philosopher.

103. C. Castoriadis, *Crossroads in the Labyrinth*, trans. Kate Soper and Martin H. Ryle (Brighton, Sussex: Harvester Press, 1984), pp. 3–45 and 46–115.

104. Until some new "order" ensues. Perhaps the ecology movements in Europe and various more or less utopian alternatives in the United States are putting together the elements of a valid debate. But how far is it possible to go without regressing into an even less-desirable barbarism?

105. Herbert Marcuse, *One-Dimensional Man* (Boston: Beacon Press, 1964).

106. De Dieguez, *Le Mythe rationnel de l'Occident; L'Idole monothéiste* (Paris: Presses universitaires de France, 1981).

107. See Chapter 3, pp. 116 and 123.

108. De Dieguez, *L'Idole monothéiste*, p. 67

109. The question of the sense or nonsense of material objects is quickly swept aside by the demands of demonstration. Thus de Dieguez falls again into the trap that he himself denounces as the common foundation of "two magics" (logical projection in nature and theology): the "desire to proclaim as true what makes it possible to obtain the sought-after result" (ibid., p. 121). A distinction that is open to dispute, to say the least, is established between, on the one hand, the nonsense of "inert" objects, in which the regularities observed and used by scientific and technological rationality are only a "mute monotony" that only "physical theory abusively forces to 'speak rationally'" (p. 107); and, on the other hand, "the breath of life" (p. 255) of intelligence, iconoclastic and creative, which, despite what it may say, leads too to giving a sense to nonsense, even if that meaning is the tragic sense.

Even if the "listening" for the mute silence of the inert is based on what is, incidentally, an extremely interesting analysis (*Encyclopaedia Universalis*, vol. 13 [Paris, 1977], pp. 682–632), de Dieguez is here firmly enrolled in a philosophical tradition that is just as Western and mythological as what he denounces: that of the romantics and of certain texts of Nietzsche (although even in *The Antichrist* Nietzsche avoids the stereotypes about the "Judeo-Christian" and the "barbarous and primitive tribe" from which Christianity is supposed to have emerged, and in the *Birth of Tragedy* he illuminates and criticizes the critical process itself). This tradition has nothing transcendent about it; it too is part of the history of Western thought, one of "the avatars of human consciousness" and "the existential condition of reason," of which de Dieguez writes: "The transfigurations of the monotheist idol are seen to be intimately bound up with the existential condition of reason, and it becomes evident [sic] that the internal mutations of the sacred image are faithfully copied onto the avatars of human consciousness" (p. 203). Why should we see only monotony and dereliction in the nature of things, if subsequently we merely join the ranks (aristocratic, true, but also religious) of iconoclastic thinkers and tragic choruses—those with the capacity to partake of the sacrament and indeed to sacrifice themselves in their turn on the altar of this intelligence "capable of rising in a single bound to a higher critical transcendence and elaborating a problematic of the politics of signs; a problematic that can encompass the scientific myth of *meaning* and the religious myth of *meaning* in an understanding of the common magic that grounds them" (p. 203)? This is an illustration of the fact that, as J.-P. Dupuy puts it so well in his knight-errantry after sense and nonsense, "critical and demystifying thought have never moved ahead except by reproducing new universal principles and making new myths out of them" (*Ordres et desordres*, p. 275).

110. See particularly the end of de Dieguez, *L'Idole monothéiste*, pp. 253–257.

111. For example, ibid., pp. 125–139.

112. For example, ibid., p. 122.

113. Ibid., p. 80.

114. Ibid., p. 256.

115. According to the Talmud, the rabbis were asked, "'Why doesn't God destroy the idols?' They replied: 'If they were of no use, He would; but the idolators worship the the sun, moon, and stars. Why should the world be destroyed because of fools?'" (BT *Avoda Zara* 54b).

116. "Scientific research henceforth passes under the Caudine Forks of the psychological criticism of so-called rational knowledge" (de Dieguez, *L'Idole monothéiste*, p. 25). This "henceforth" suggests that *this time* the illusion is vanquished, knowledge is truly rational, and the theory produced by this quest is, finally, "true."

117. "A Buddhist said: 'If you meet God, kill him; it is not He.' Critical philosophical said in its turn: 'If you meet intelligence, kill it, for it is not yet it'" (ibid., p. 168).

118. Judith Schlanger, *L'Enjeu et le debat* (Paris: Denoël, 1979). "Even more than the history of scientific thought, that of para- or pseudo-scientific thought should teach us the need of a permanent critical operation of the representations that accompany the elaboration of concepts. Nothing is harder to perceive and hold steady than clandestine rationalizations: too remote from us, we no longer perceive them and declare the speculations they support to be absurd; too close to us, and we accept them immediately and scarcely perceive them as implicit evidence." With

regard to Fabre d'Olivet's *La Langue hébraïque restituée*, which she takes as an example in the analysis of which the previous lines form the conclusion, Schlanger notes: "Historians of language have abandoned this book to the historians of mysticism, who send it right back to them. For Fabre, the authority of science and the authority of Genesis, individual judgment and primitive inspiration, reinforce each other. But it may not be possible for us to obtain in the same pages, by the same process, in the same movement of the spirit, both knowledge and wisdom" (ibid., p. 93f.). One of the purposes of the present volume is to demonstrate the relevance of this remark.

119. For two very different presentations and discussions of Olbers' paradox see Benoit B. Mandelbrot, "Why Is the Sky Black at Night?" in *Fractals: Form, Chance, and Dimension* (San Francisco: W. H. Freeman, 1977); and Hubert Reeves, *Atoms of Silence: An Exploration of Cosmic Evolution* (Cambridge, Mass.: MIT Press, 1984).

120. Computer simulation models could perhaps play, little by little, this role of an intermediate reality between theory and raw experience.

121. Noam Chomsky, *Language and Mind* (New York: Harcourt, Brace, Jovanovitch, 1972), p. xi.

122. Piattelli-Palmarini, *Language and Learning*.

123. Whether because, if it deals with mankind, it can scarcely be scientific; or because, to be science, it can scarcely deal with mankind.

124. See the reflections and discussions concerning von Foerster's hypothesis in Dupuy, *Ordres et désordres*; and M. Koppel, H. Atlan, and J.-P. Dupuy, "Complexité et aliénation: formalisation de la conjecture de von Foerster," in *Théories de la complexité*.

125. Mircea Eliade, *Images and Symbols: Studies in Religious Symbolism*, trans. Philip Mairet (New York: Sheed and Ward, 1961).

126. See, for example, N. Bensaïd, *La Lumière médicale: Les Illusions de la prévention* (Paris: Le Seuil, 1981).

127. This is because the number of unmasterable independent variables and the number of levels of organization to be crossed in both directions are greatest here.

128. Ludwig Wittgenstein, "Conversations on Freud," *Lectures and Conversations*, ed. Cyril Barrett (Berkeley, Calif.: University of California Press, 1966), p. 52.

129. Lacan, "La Science et la verité," *Ecrits*, pp. 855–877.

130. Ibid., p. 870.

131. Castoriadis, "Epilegomena to a Theory of the Soul Which Has Been Presented as a Science" and "Psychoanalysis: Project and Elucidation," in *Crossroads in the Labyrinth.*

132. C. G. Jung, *Memories, Dreams, Reflections*, recorded and ed. Aniela Jaffé, trans. Richard and Clara Winston (New York: Pantheon Books, 1973), p. 150.

133. Eliade, *Images*, pp. 14f.

134. Ibid., p. 14.

135. Jung, *Memories*, pp. 146–155.

136. F. Roustang, *Un Destin si funeste.*

137. E. Becker, *The Denial of Death* (New York: The Free Press, 1973).

138. See Eliade, *Images.*

139. See H. Atlan and B. Kohn-Atlan, "On the Transposition of Scientific Concepts in Psychosomatic Terminology," *Fifth World Congress of the International College of Psychosomatic Medicine* (Jerusalem, 1979); and the critical history of this concept, Yehuda Elkana, "The Borrowing of the Concept of Energy in Freudian Psychoanalysis," in *Psicoanalisi e storia delle scienze* (Florence: Leo S. Olschski, 1983); as well as D. Widlöcher, "Quel usage faisons-nous du concept de pulsion," in D. Anzieu, R. Dorey, J. Laplance, and D. Widlöcher, *La Pulsion, pour quoi faire?* (Paris: Association psychanalytique de France, 1984).

140. Jean Laplanche and J.-B. Pontalis, *The Language of Psycho-Analysis*, trans. Donald Nicholson-Smith (New York: W. W. Norton, 1973).

141. Jung, *Memories*, p. 155.

142. What is more, we can recognize today that the conservative character postulated for the libido, by analogy with physical energy, often proves to be more burdensome than useful when one has to account for psychic phenomena in which something is created or at least grows (when a psychic activity, far from dying out when it runs out of gas, keeps itself going and even grows stronger), or when something disappears without being reinvested elsewhere. From this point of view, if one absolutely demands an analogy drawn from the natural sciences, the concepts of information and negentropy, more recent and unknown to Freud, would certainly do the trick better—while we wait for something else to come along.

143. See Chapter 2.

144. Jung, *Memories*, p. 154.

145. Ibid., pp. 195–199.

146. *The Freud/Jung Letters*, ed. William McGuire, trans. Ralph Manheim and R. F. C. Hull (Princeton, N.J.: Princeton University Press, 1974), p. 255, and n. 8 (#158).

147. "Occultism is another field we shall have to conquer—with the aid of the libido theory, it seems to me. At the moment I am looking into astrology, which seems indispensable for a proper understanding of mythology. There are strange and wondrous things in these lands of darkness. Please don't worry about my wanderings in these infinitudes. I shall return laden with rich booty for our knowledge of the human psyche. For a while longer I must intoxicate myself on magic perfumes in order to fathom the secrets that lie hidden in the abysses of the unconscious" (ibid., p. 421 [#254J]).

148. "I am aware that you are driven by innermost inclination to the study of the occult and I am sure you will return home richly laden. I cannot argue with that, it is always right to go where your impulses lead. You will be accused of mysticism, but the reputation you won with the *Dementia* will hold up for quite some time against that. Just don't stay in the tropical colonies too long; you must reign at home" (ibid., p. 422 [#255]; also in *Memories*, p. 363).

149. Ibid., p. 421 n. 6 (emphasis mine).

150. "I can still recall vividly how Freud said to me, 'My dear Jung, promise me never to abandon the sexual theory. That is the most essential thing of all. You see, we must make a dogma of it, an unshakable bulwark.' He said that to me with great emotion, in the tone of a father saying, 'And promise me this one thing, my dear son: that you will go to church every Sunday.' In some astonishment I asked him, 'A bulwark—against what?' To which he replied, 'Against the black tide of mud'—and here he hesitated for a moment, then added—'of occultism.' First of all it was the words 'bulwark' and 'dogma' that alarmed me; for a dogma, that is to say, an undisputable confession of faith, is set up only when the aim is to suppress doubts once and for all. But that no longer has anything to do with scientific judgment; only with a personal power drive.

"...What Freud seemed to mean by 'occultism' was virtually everything that philosophy and religion, including the rising contemporary science of parapsychology, had learned about the psyche. To me the sexual theory was just as occult, that is to say, just as unproven a hypothesis, as many other speculative views. As I saw it, a scientific truth was a hypothesis which might be adequate for the moment but was not to be preserved as an article of faith for all time.

"...There was one characteristic of his that preoccupied me above all: his bitterness. It had struck me at our first encounter, but it remained inexplicable to me until I was able to see it in connection with his attitude toward sexuality. Although, for Freud, sexuality was undoubtedly a *numinosum*, his terminology and theory seemed to define it exclusively as a biological function. It was only the emotionality with which he spoke of it that revealed the deeper elements reverberating within him. Basically, he wanted to teach—or so it seemed to me—that, regarded from within, sexuality included spirituality and had an intrinsic meaning. But his concretistic terminology was too narrow to express this idea. He gave me the impression that at bottom he was working against his own goal and against himself; and there is, after all, no harsher bitterness than that of a person who is his own worst enemy. In his own words, he felt himself menaced by a 'black tide of mud'—he who more than anyone else had tried to let down his buckets into those black depths.

"Freud never asked himself why he was compelled to talk continually of sex, why this idea had taken such possession of him. He remained unaware that his 'monotony of interpretation' expressed a flight from himself, or from that other side of him which might perhaps be called mystical. So long as he refused to acknowledge that side, he could never be reconciled with himself. He was blind toward the paradox and ambiguity of the contents of the unconscious, and did not know that everything which arises out of the unconscious has a top and a bottom, an inside and an outside. When we speak of the outside—and that is what Freud did—we are considering only half of the whole, with the result that a countereffect arises out of the unconscious.

"There was nothing to be done about this one-sidedness of Freud's. Perhaps some inner experience of his own might have opened his eyes; but then his intellect would have reduced any such experience to 'mere sexuality' or 'psychosexuality.' He remained the victim of the one aspect he could recognize, and for that reason I see him as a tragic figure; for he was a great man, and what is more, a man in the grip of his daimon" (Jung, *Memories*, pp. 150–153).

151. Ibid., pp. 155f.

152. Cited in Jung, *Memories*, p. 362 (also in *Freud/Jung*, pp. 218f. [#139]).

153. Emphasis mine.

154. Here Freud has a remarkable presentiment of what today appears to be the criterion most resistant to attempts to differentiate scientific rationality from magic and myth, after the last two have been conceded their own rationality: the local and incomplete nature of scientific explanation, as opposed to the completeness and universality of mythic explanation (see, for example, Settle, "The Rationality of Science"; Elkana "A Programmatic Attempt").

155. Although, more seriously, he invokes, by way of explaining the formation of superstitious meanings by the unconscious, "the undeniable 'cooperation of chance,'" which plays the same role in the formation of a fantastic idea as does somatic cooperation in hysterical symptoms, or the cooperation of language in jokes. But this sort of explanation may, in the context of the age, appear just as unacceptable—or even less acceptable—as Jung's acausal synchronicity.

156. Cited in Jung, *Memories*, p. 363.

157. Elsewhere (*Entre le cristal et la fumée*, Chapter 12), I have explained what I think was Freud's "Judaism," which could only be negative and devoid of any true theoretical content and was rather a consequence of his status as a "metic between two cultures," to borrow the phrase of Marthe Robert, *From Oedipus to Moses: Freud's Jewish Identity*, trans. Ralph Manheim (Garden City, N.Y.: Anchor Books, 1976). It is notable, however, that this concern for keeping a cool head and rejecting indifferent fusion is one of the traits that Scholem considers to be specific

to Jewish as compared to other varieties of mysticism (Scholem, *Major Trends in Jewish Mysticism*).

158. Cited by A. Green, *Le Discours vivant* (Paris: Presses universitaires de France, 1973), p. 257.

159. *Freud/Jung*, p. 255 (#158).

160. "In all likelihood the myth of Genesis is a wretched, tendentious distortion devised by an apprentice priest, who as we now know stupidly wove two independent sources into a single narrative (as in a dream).... I hold that the surface versions of myths cannot be used uncritically for comparison with our psychoanalytical findings. We must find our way back to their latent, original forms by a comparative method that eliminates the distortions they have undergone in the course of their history" (ibid., p. 473 [#288F]).

161. "At the time when Freud was elaborating his explanation of the religious sentiment, and imagined that he had found the 'origin' of the religion, the two hypotheses mentioned no longer enjoyed any credit among competent ethnologists and historians of religions. But although Freud had read Frazer and knew the conclusions that Frazer had come to—namely, the *nonuniversality* of totemism as a social-religious phenomenon (it is unknown among a number of primitive tribes) and the *extreme rarity* of the 'sacrifice-communions' (only four cases—and those unequally confirmed—out of several hundreds of totemic tribes!), nevertheless *Totem and Tabu* appeared in book form in 1913 and since then has been continually republished and translated into numerous languages" (Eliade, *Images,* p. 23n.)

162. Hofstadter, *Gödel, Escher, Bach.*

163. Castoriadis, *Crossroads in the Labyrinth.*

164. See Chapter 2.

165. Green, *Le Discours vivant.*

166. P. Marty, "Les difficultés narcissiques de l'observateur devant le problème psychosomatique," *Revue française de psychanalyse* 16, no. 3 (1952), pp. 339–357. Marty speaks of Freud's "leap" in transforming the affective into the somatic. He tries to resolve this difficulty by adopting the point of view of the psychoanalytic theorist, which is interesting but remains debatable, like any perspective that claims to be metaphoric. "Psychosomatics deals with invisible functions that cannot be schematized. The invisibility of these functions collides with our bent for schematizing in various forms, without which we find it difficult to accept reality. This difficulty is inevitable, but we must bear in mind its deep meaning, since the spatial and schematic representation of reality is one way by which our narcissism intrudes into our research" (p. 350).

167. See Chapter 2, p. 60.

168. Here this opposition is as stark as possible. But it is also found in various forms in the writings of other psychoanalysts who try to analyze mystic phenomena from their own perspective (see, for example, two special issues of the *Nouvelle Revue de psychanalyse*: "La croyance," no. 18 [1978]; and "Résurgence et dérivés de la mystique," no. 22 [1980]). Finally, under the influence of Jacques Lacan, some French analysts opt for something "intermediate" between scientific and mythic discourse. In effect, their theoretical discourse reproduces the property of the unconscious discourse that sometimes uses negation to affirm and affirmation to deny. The result is an overlapping of levels, in which discourse *about* the unconscious reproduces the characteristics of the discourse *of* the unconscious, and consequently the principle of noncontradiction no longer plays the role accorded it in scientific discourse. In particular, paradox has a very different status: a logical monster to be eliminated from scientific discourse, here paradox is on the contrary a window onto complex processes that cannot be (or have not yet been fully) conceptualized. This is what brings such discourses close to those of myth (and reinforces Wittgenstein's verdict that psychoanalysis is "a powerful mythology"); whereas they are clearly different because produced by contemporary authors who, despite everything, make use of their scientific and philosophical Western culture. A particularly suggestive example of this can be found in D. Sibony, *La Juive* (Paris: Grasset, 1983), in which this type of (meta)discourse is applied to traditional Jewish texts from the Bible, Talmud, and Midrash.

169. Erich Fromm, *The Heart of Man: Its Genius for Good and Evil* (New York: Harper and Row, 1964), pp 43–44.

170. Erich Fromm, *You Shall Be as Gods: A Radical Interpretation of the Old Testament and Its Tradition* (New York: Holt, Rinehart and Winston, 1966). See also Fromm, in Suzuki et al., *Zen Buddhism and Psychoanalysis*, p. 129f.

171. Jung, "Synchronicity," pp. 43–45.

172. Green, *Le Discours vivant*, p. 14

173. Rendered into English as "enlightenment" and into French as "illumination," evoking a quite different play of light than the Enlightenment of the Reason.

174. Fromm, in Suzuki et al., p. 111.

175. Ibid., p. 132.

176. Ibid., p. 133–34.

177. See above, and also Green, *Le Discours vivant*, p. 14.

178. Ibid., p. 213.

179. Ibid., pp. 213–214.

180. Ibid., pp. 228–229.

181. Ibid., p. 262.

182. "Here the notion of the limit concept takes on its full meaning, to the degree that our conceptual instruments do not make it possible to think the *event* that occurred at this psychosomatic or somatopsychic intersection" (ibid., p. 229).

183. M. Olender, "De l'absence de récit," in *Le Récit et sa représentation*, colloque de Saint-Hubert 1977 (Paris: Payot, 1978), pp. 175–180.

184. Pauli, "Influence," pp. 205f.

185. Ibid., p. 208.

186. To crown everything, this rejection receives ethical justification (going as far back as Fludd) from the observation that thought that dissects, measures, and counts is adapted to this world of violence, war, and diabolic possession. There is a great temptation, given the collusion between analytic science and war, to hold the former responsible for the latter. In this vein, the analyses by Michel Serres (*Le Passage du Nord-Ouest*) on the origins of mathematics in war are quite disturbing, but it does not seem that this should provide a critical justification for a Fluddian attitude. There is no doubt that our knowledge is a matter of dissecting and multiplicity, and hence of violence (Michel Serres, "L'homme est un loup pour l'homme," in *Girard et le Problème du Mal*, ed. Michel Deguy and Jean-Pierre Dupuy [Paris: Bernard Grasset, 1982]). In this it is opposed to love-fusion. And this multiplicity is also diabolic (Michel Serres, *The Parasite*, trans. Lawrence R. Schehr [Baltimore: Johns Hopkins University Press, 1982]), in contrast to the symbolic of meaning. But at the same time it is the condition of dialogue, without which there could not even be monologues, but only the "synlogues" of ecstasy. In this fusion, too, there is violence; whence the necessity for a bond that contains and delimits, at least as much as it attaches (see the chapter entitled "The Circle and the Bond" in Detienne and Vernant, *Cunning Intelligence*). Violence cannot be overcome by love-fusion, which merely engenders an even more radical violence, but only by cunning intelligence that can exploit and use it.

## Chapter 6

# Ultimate Reality

The belief in some Ultimate Reality of matter, or of the universe, said to be disclosed in a certain lore or type of knowledge, is one of the most interesting snares to study, because it regularly traps scientists, especially physicists, as easily as theologians and mystics, and, among the former, just as many materialist physicists as those whom we have called spiritualists or idealists.

### Physical Reality and Quantum Representations

The proceedings of the Cordoba colloquium provide us with a particularly suggestive example—Franco Selleri's analysis of the problem of measurement and of the reduction of the wave function in quantum mechanics. In this context, the major interest of the analysis is that Selleri was one of the two physicists at Cordoba (along with J.-P. Vigier) who represented the materialist opposition and rejected the spiritualist interpretations of quantum mechanics that dominated the Colloquium. Nevertheless, neither of them questioned the postulate they share with their opponents, namely, that what physical science discovers and describes is, at least in right if not in fact, reality in itself, the aforementioned "ultimate reality" of matter. This postulate prevented Vigier from accepting the idea that different modes of description are suited to different levels of reality, corresponding to different levels of observation.

This same postulate led Selleri to conclude that "it is impossible to

249

avoid idealism" and even a mystical interpretation of quantum mechanics viewed "from the inside." At the end of his analysis, however, this interpretation, which he deems "absurd and unacceptable because of many 'external' reasons, seems to be a logically consistent description of the mathematical structure of the theory,"[1] and the validity of this theory is not really called into question! It is interesting to follow Selleri's analysis step by step to see how he arrives at this conclusion. We shall attempt to demonstrate that his difficulties stem from the refusal to envision a metaphysics other than those of idealism and materialism, both of which postulate the identity of physical reality and the reality *described by physical science.* By contrast, we shall see how other theoretical physicists have acquired a vision of quantum mechanics that happily escapes this alternative, thanks to an attitude we shall call "operational" or "interactionistic," in which what is described by physical science occupies an intermediate position between the disclosure of the reality of physical objects in themselves and the result of a science [physics] that "would become only the study of the spiritual activity of man" and "the mental state of the observer."[2] This attitude takes into account the *conditions* in which physical science, with its mathematical apparatus and methods of measurement as well as its nonformalized, interpretive language, has "knowledge" of reality: knowledge that can appear only as the result of an interaction between a knowing subject and a known object; however, it does not presuppose the "materialist" or "idealist" character of the interaction itself.

Selleri begins by reporting the disappointment felt by some of the founders, like Schrödinger and Einstein, with the first idealist interpretations that invoked some mysterious role of the mind as part of quantum theory. Schrödinger wrote, for example:

> For it must have given to de Broglie the same shock and disappointment as it gave to me, when we learnt that a sort of transcendental, almost psychic interpretation of the wave phenomenon had been put forward, which was very soon hailed by the majority of leading theorists as the only one reconcilable with experiments, and which has now become the orthodox creed.[3]

In fact, at this stage, transcendental and merely operational interpretation were confused, unlike the situation in the simple materialist tradition of classical physics, which simply transposed the perception of macroscopic objects to the representation of microphysical ones.

But as J.-M. Lévy-Leblond shows clearly,[4] when quantum concepts were first elaborated their fathers could understand them only by reference to classical concepts, even those they were meant to replace. Hence so long as *use* had not given them a relative independence that allows them to be understood on their own, in the context of the conditions where they are employed just as "naturally" as the classical concepts of mass, velocity, inertia, and so forth (those, too, were themselves far from being natural when introduced by Galilean relativity), they provoked debates concerning their relations with the classical concepts of space, time, mind, and matter, rather than about their own meaning. Today most practicing physicists no longer need such a relationship, but it still seems to be self-evident, however little we remain attached to the meta-metatheory whereby the reality described by physics (whether material, spiritual, cosmic, unconscious, phantom, energetic, cybernetic, or what have you) is physical reality itself.

In his analysis, Selleri reviews the possible relations between quantum theory and reality in the form of two hypotheses, $I_1$ and $I_2$ (posited without their converse). The first merely notes the validity of the formalism of the theory, in that no experience or observation has thus far contradicted it; the second expresses the identity between knowledge gained through physics and physical reality.

According to $I_1$, two different degrees of knowledge of the object that an observer has (or thinks he or she has) correspond to two different formal structures (two different state vectors) used to describe this object quantum-mechanically. (The converse may not be true: the mathematical formulation may be richer than necessary, i.e., there is a possibility of redundancy in its representation of our knowledge.) According to $I_2$, two different state vectors "correspond to two objectively different physical objects."[5] These "objectively different physical objects"[6] are also what he calls "the *real* structure and *physical* evolution of the object."[7]

He concludes his presentation of the idealist thesis as follows:

> In this way von Neumann's and Wigner's point of view, according to which a change in the observer's knowledge generates the reduction of the wave-packet, leads to the conclusion that, as a consequence of $I_2$, a change in human knowledge can modify the physical structure of the system under investigation.
>
> In this way, it is clear that the observer does not learn because the interaction with the physical reality generates some alteration of his state of consciousness; it is rather the opposite that is true because consciousness imprints on the reality new features that it has in some way decided to generate.[8]

The interesting point is that, for Selleri, abandoning $I_2$ is inconceivable; when he envisions doing so (the effect would be to exclude the parapsychological effects of the implications of microphysical theory), he quickly rejects the possibility as corresponding to a sort of derealization of the world. We should recall that these two hypotheses have already been softened, in that they do not necessarily imply their converse. Thus, according to the second, one can readily accept that "two different physical situations" do not necessarily correspond to two different state vectors, because the formal description may not be *complete*. But if, conversely, two different state vectors do not correspond to "two different physical states," then, for Selleri, there is no further relationship between the knowledge described by physics and physical reality. As a result, "the 'real world' would become a sort of ghost behind the wall which cannot in any way be known and physics would become only the study of the spiritual activity of man." And, he concludes, "it is impossible to avoid idealism if one maintains that the reduction of the wave-packet is due to the intervention of the observer's consciousness."[9]

It is important to note how the word *physical* is used here indiscriminately to designate objective reality, independent of the observer ("the real structure and physical evolution of the object") and the knowledge of it provided by physics. This makes it impossible to envision a third attitude, operationalist or interactionalist, in which the abandonment of $I_2$, implying that two different formal structures "may correspond to the same identical real system," does not necessarily mean that the formalism "describes only, because of $I_1$, the mental state of the observer." In effect, if one does not insist that the formal structure reveals in itself the *reality* of the world, one can very well accept that it remains not only subjectively or epistemologically valid (because of $I_1$), but also that it remains in a certain relationship of projection and interpretation (but not of identity) with reality, in that it *describes the objective knowledge we have of it*. Now this last, *as it takes place within the rules of the game of the experimental method*, is already an *interaction* that is much more than simply "the mental state of the observer." For the physical observer is not a person, but an ideal system composed of a measuring apparatus and an ideal physicist, that is, an idealized human being capable of objectively detecting the indications of the measuring apparatus *and interpreting them* within the context of physical science. (The real observer, even if not a physicist, transmits his or her raw observations objectively, in the sense that they can be shared without dispute by several observers, independently of their mental states—with the possible exception of what are called modified states of consciousness [we shall return to this]. The real observer transmits them to a physicist and more generally to a group of physicists capable of interpreting them in the context of their knowledge of physical laws and of the experimental set-up.)

One cannot say that the observer, when an interpreting agent, must obey quantum mechanics, which is the content and means of this interpretation. The very question is not pertinent; the fact that the observer cannot be included in the purview of quantum mechanics does not mean that the observer's consciousness (whose nature is mental and subjective) acts directly on a wave function (whose nature is material and objective) and modifies it. The wave function is part of the simultaneously abstract and objective description of matter provided by physics; so is the reduction of this wave function during an observation by the ideal physical observer. The observer's knowledge of physics modifies physical reality inasmuch as it is an interpretative projection of abstract schemes on sensory data. This has always been the case in physics (and in all the natural sciences); quantum mechanics is no exception in this respect.

The projection of the interpretive scheme certainly has an idealist character if one assumes that this projection is totally arbitrary or subjective. But this idealism is counterbalanced by the attitude that underlies the experimental method, which expects a response, independent of the mental condition of the observer, from a macroscopic material system set up for this purpose—the measuring apparatus. The role of this apparatus is to constitute a real system, certainly privileged, but real all the same, that can be described step by step and *without discontinuity* across all its successive levels, from that of the (macroscopic) perception of the matter of the needle on a dial down to its microphysical quantum description. Deferring to the response of the experimental measurement implies a return to the macroscopic material level and its consideration as objective reality (in the classical sense, not called into question in the context of this discussion). This reestablishes the equilibrium while imposing some sort of superiority of matter (macroscopic and "true") over mind (as a possible source of arbitrary imagination and "unreality"), thereby compensating for the hint of idealism suggested by the interpretive projection. Such deference implies simultaneously that one can predict the result by means of theory (the latter is precisely the continuous description that makes it possible in the privileged case of this particular experimental set-up to pass from level to level within a single description) and that one accepts a priori the possibility of having to modify this theory if the "matter" yields a different response.

Here too, as in all cases of successful scientific prediction, the experience of an identity between the observed response and that predicted by theory produces the triumphal joy characteristic of the enterprise of knowledge,[10] even—and how much the more so—if the result was predicted, and thus expected and unsurprising. This enterprise is lived as a reunion of what has been separated,[11] of two paths for gaining knowledge that we normally experience as separate and irreducible: the path of thought and the path of sense perception. Hence one can understand that "consciousness impregnates reality with new characteristics that it has somehow decided to produce" without thereby falling into the trap of spiritualist physics. For these characteristics are new only for the knowing consciousness itself; and reality reacts to this impregnation by limiting the arbitrariness of what the mind of the knowing subject has decided to produce. What physical theory describes is the result of this type of interaction (that instituted by the experimental method) between a reality that is present, rather than discovered in itself, and the interpreting and rationalizing activity of our mind. Nor is this unique to quantum theory. It also applies to all physics when we observe a correspondence between a mathematized formal structure and the result of an experiment: the physical *structure* (i.e., that described by the physical theory) is *not* the matter of physical objects. Rather than revealing the ultimate reality of these objects, the theoretical structure maintains a minimal relationship with them that makes it possible to act on them.

That the physical structure is not "reality itself" does not mean that reality becomes a vanishing phantom and only mental life remains.[12] It means only that the physical structure is a "picture"[13] of the current state of our knowledge of matter, which we have obtained by the particular method that is physical science. Is it because a *picture* is not reality itself that the latter disappears, and the picture does not necessarily have any relationship with it? Is the picture the result *only* of our subjective mental life? Of course we can modify the structure, the picture, at our leisure. But it is the nature of physics that these modifications can be made only in accordance with certain rules, accepted by physicists, who define this mode of knowledge.

Note that it was for the same Wittgenstein who proposed the metaphor of the picture as a theory of theory that the causal relationship could not be part of things. For Selleri, on the contrary, it seems that the fact that the state of human consciousness can develop "in a strictly causal way"[14] must itself be the product of observation of things themselves—or the reality of these things disappears. It is not astonishing that someone who considers causality to be part of the reality of things also views physical theory as part and parcel of this reality; in fact, however, this theory is only the product of a particular mode of knowledge, that of physics. Other modes of knowledge, artistic or mystical, for example, obey different rules and accept the use of certain *individual* and subjective techniques of vision and inspiration as a sufficient source for legitimate modifications of the picture—even if they subsequently try to share these techniques by means of some transsubjective emotion!

It can be objected that in one case the quest is for a "true" picture of reality, whereas in the other it is for a "beautiful" picture or for one producing an esthetic or mystical emotion. But the experience of truth is only a particular case of the more general experience of finding correspondences, of a (sexual?) union of which artistic and mystical experiences are other particular cases. The experience of truth is that of a congruence within the usage of language: the opposite of the true is the false, the opposite of truth is falsehood or error; all of these imply the use of language (or of languages, formalized or not) and are defined only in relationship to it.

Nor does truth in itself, or ultimate truth, exist; no more than ultimate reality, if by this one means a picture, a particular description, the product of a particular mode of knowledge. At most one can qualify as "ultimate" the process of knowledge itself, the process of making pictures and what makes this possible; that is to say, the possibility of an effective relationship (one that "works" in some way or another, at one level or another) between at least one segment of the possible and one segment of the real. It is perhaps this possibility that the first Wittgenstein calls "the limit of the world"[15] that he designates by "I," which, as has been made clear, has no psychological meaning for him.[16]

In this sense, and in this sense only—very different from that of the transcendental interpretation deplored by Schrödinger—one can perhaps speak of the transcendental, in the Kantian sense, that physics could reveal to us. But this transcendence would be that of the possible over the real, rather than a transcendance of the spiritual over the material, and thus not really transcendence at all, one that would transcend experience, because all of us, collectively and even objectively, through the use of language, have experience of the possible in a certain fashion. But of what experience are we speaking? And what is its relationship with experience of reality? How are we to understand the mode of existence of the possible and the relations between logical and empirical possibility? Where and how does the unrealized possible exist? Under what conditions is it possible for the possible to be realized? We have already tried to consider these questions.[17] In any case they are only a few among those that remain to be answered.

In effect, contrary to what is often believed, the operationalist or interactionist attitude that I am defending here does not tend to eliminate questions about the foundations of our knowledge by simply looking away out of a concern for effectiveness. I reaffirm Marcuse's salutary lesson[18] concerning the dangers of operationalism as an ideology even stronger than ideologies, because of its faculty for salvaging everything in an indifferent relativism that excludes negation. On the contrary, this attitude must lead to posing these questions with greater force and not considering them to be resolved a priori, unlike the two enemy sisters, idealist metaphysics and materialist metaphysics. I limit myself to describing our lived experience of scientific knowledge, of separation-union in which the object is postulated and perceived as separate from the subject but the cognitive act creates an interaction and possible union. This description is itself extrascientific, however, and in any case definitely outside the domain of application of physical theory—although the latter has begun attempting to take account of this situation of observation and knowledge, at least through its operational aspect of measurement. We can also understand the attempts by certain physicists to extend physical theory to a theory of knowledge by physics, in which the physico-mathematical formalism is the occasion not for a metaphysics of matter or mind but for an epistemology that is itself, if possible, formalized! This latter, thanks to its formalization, is then no different from theoretical physics itself.

In this process, the attempts of younger physicists who have grown up with quantum mechanics are extremely valuable. For them, in the wake of Feynman,[19] quantum objects have an existence that is just as "natural" (or unnatural) as the objects described by classical physics. We have already seen how Lévy-Leblond[20] expressed wave-particle duality through the stimulating metaphor of a cylinder that can be observed only as a rectangle or as a circle. The question of the nature of the quantum object, as posed *from within* physics, deals exclusively with these cylinders; the circles and rectangles are only limited ways (devoid of any profound meaning and useful only within descriptions that are themselves limited) of representing them. Similarly, the reduction of the wave function can be described not in epistemological and metaphysical terms, as is usually the case, but in the terms of theoretical physics, as the description of measurement in the context of quantum theory itself. Thus one arrives at how "one can give a consistent view of the world, described in fully quantummechanical terms."[21] In this context, the reduction of the wave function appears not as a phenomenon with ultimate metaphysical implications but as an algorithm, a rule for computation, a recipe to be used when one seeks to apply the theory to a *limited* domain of the world.

A quantum description of the totality of the world, however, accepting and comprising the observed system as well as the measuring apparatus, the device for recording the measurement, the human observer, and so on, would have no need of this reduction. Underlying this interpretation, part of a movement developing a new way of considering quantum theory,[22] one finds an essential inseparability, in the order of knowledge, of the world, "the impossibility of an intrinsic description for a part of a system (i.e., for a system in a pure quantum state, no pure quantum state can be ascribed to a sub-system)."[23]

M. Mughur Shächter[24] has attempted to clarify the terminology used in stating the EPR paradox and the problem of the nonlocality of quantum effects. As is known, this problem, too, is at the root of spiritualist interpretations, using terms like 'cosmic consciousness', 'physical foundations of parapsychology', and 'effects at a distance of mind on matter'.[25]

Mughur Shächter shows clearly that the questions about the possibility of instantaneous action at a distance between two elementary particles that interacted once but are now separated by great distances cannot even be *posed* rigorously. Even less rigor attaches, then, to the "answers" that experience is supposed to provide to them. The main reason for this is that existing conceptualizations, expressed in natural language, of time (instantaneity), space (distance), and probabilities, associated with experimental tests of predictions calculated using the formalism of quantum theory, are inadequate for a rigorous definition of what is being spoken of. The experiment involves observing and computing statistical correlations between simultaneous measurements effected by two measuring devices situated at a distance; whereas the application of the computational rules of quantum mechanics predicts a certain result, namely, that certain inequalities ("Bell inequalities") concerning these correlations are not respected. The problem, or the paradox, derives from the interpretation given to the results of these computations, performed on quantum objects, although the interpretation, in natural language, employs a semantics that is still that of classical macroscopic objects.

Put another way, these questions—concerning the locality or non-locality of physical reality and the existence of instantaneous influence at a distance—cannot even be asked *inside* physics. These are extraphysical, extrascientific questions. Physics itself does not include the vocabulary and grammar that allow them to be asked. Its physico-mathematical language, as it currently stands, is inadequate to this: within this language, these questions, rigorously posed, have no meaning. It does not contain the concepts (magnitudes, operators, and so on) that would make it possible to place them in unequivocal relation with other already formalized concepts of mathematical physics. But if these questions cannot be asked *by* physics, they are asked *of* physics, by the layperson who does not wish to renounce natural language as a means for describing reality, despite—or because of— its ambiguities; and also by physicists, who do not want to give up the layperson inside them;[26] and perhaps especially by physics students, before they have learned the rules of the game, namely, that *physicists* may not take these questions seriously.

This is why one generally wavers between two attitudes: that of physicists who reject these questions and agree to speak only in formalized, operational language, and that of those who not only do not reject these questions but even supply answers to them. The attitude of the former is justified from the perspective of physics itself, which, in its current state, works quite well. It is complete within its legitimate domain of application;

there is no need to offer any response whatsoever to these questions, hence no need even to ask them. But they also reject these questions as asked of physics from outside physics. The result is that only formalized scientific questions can be asked, not only by a physicist as physicist, but by anyone. The second, opposing attitude can be justified if it is clearly understood that the answers it gives to these metaphysical questions are themselves metaphysical and metascientific. Unfortunately, these responses all too frequently consist of dressing up metaphysical axioms, materialist or idealist, as apparently scientific propositions. They begin by using the scientific language appropriate to the domain of legitimacy for which it was designed and surreptitiously shift from one level of description to another, from one domain of legitimacy to another.

Both of these attitudes, extreme but common—that of the physicist who acts as if the human condition reflecting on "reality" (including its own) can be reduced to the use of the formalized language of mathematical physics, and that of the physicist who dresses up metaphysical axioms in a discourse that uses and abuses this same formalized language—spring from the same confusion we have already noted between physical reality and the description of reality by physics. For the adherents of the former attitude, the only reality is that described by physics. For the latter group, the physical reality of which they have an a priori metaphysical or even mystical intuition, whether expressed in spiritualism or materialism, can be described *only* by physics. In an attempt to unravel this confusion, we are led to the third path, which accepts that these questions be asked of physics but does not believe that the latter, in its current state, can answer them. Contemporary and future physicists are invited to continue their theoretical work so as to be able—as a beginning, and if possible—to ask these questions inside physics, knowing full well that if this program succeeds, if these problems can be asked and a fortiori resolved inside physics, then, as with the unicorn and the demons,[27] we will no longer be dealing with the same questions!

Once again we encounter, at the limits of scientific knowledge, the difficulties always posed by a change in the level of observation and description. For a contemporary physicist, for whom quantum objects exist naturally, the question of the transition remains, but as a reversal of the usual question concerning the "nature" of quantum objects: it is classical objects that cause trouble, those described by classical physics using macroscopic concepts derived from simpler transpositions of common-sense intuition based on the data of our own senses. If quantum objects correctly describe the reality of things, how can one make the transition to a level of reality (macroscopic) on which classical objects (even as limiting cases of the former) are *adequate* to describe this reality *effectively*?[28] If at its elementary level reality needs "cylinders" to be described correctly, why are "rectangles" and "circles" adequate at another level? This time, however, the transition is not from one discipline to another, but inside physics itself. Better yet, here it is precisely the role of physical theory to make possible the predictive transition from a microphysical phenomenon that can be calculated (but not "described" in natural language) to a macroscopic phenomenon that can be observed and described in natural language. This is why a pure and simple rejection of the problem, taking refuge behind a formalism that has no meaning in natural language—a facile attitude that many physicists are inclined to adopt—is an unjustified capitulation. But the opposing attitude, which ignores the difficulty of switching levels and languages and lightheartedly jumps from computational rules to macroscopic interpretations, realistic or otherwise, materialist or spiritualist, is no more justified. For Mughur Shächter, the legitimate attitude is that of an open quest seeking to clarify, evidently with the aid of new concepts, "the intermediaries between what one sees and what one computes."

For the moment, if we want to specify, with a rigor equal to that of physico-mathematical theory itself, the meaning of the terms currently used to designate these intermediaries, we can only crash into a very large question mark. At the end of a meticulous analysis of questions, currently unanswerable, about the meaning of the concepts of (inter alia) time and space as applied to a microsystem of interacting quantum particles, Mughur Shächter reaches what strikes us as the most reasonable and at the same time the most fruitful conclusion: it is not a matter of a retreat into a meaningless formalism or an escape into some metaphysical interpretation or other, but simply of an analysis of the limits of the theory, which at the same time constitutes an invitation to expand these limits—that is, ultimately, a research program.[29]

## The Reality of Meanings in Interpretation

Another example of belief in an ultimate reality of things to be revealed as it truly is by some (scientific or mystical) lore is the belief in the objective reality of the sense and meanings that appear to ordering and interpreting human thought. We have seen this in connection with Jung and his meaningful coincidences. For him, their unconscious archetypal reality, which he "unveiled" through his interpretations, was evidence of objective reality of the same type as the formal mathematical structures that physics reveals as the ultimate reality of matter. The affinity of brilliant minds for believing in the truth of interpretive systems (called "scientific," although they are derived from gnostic, alchemical, or other prescientific traditions, or from Oriental lore) is derived, when all is said and done, from this belief (shared by "orthodox" scientists) in the objective reality of interpretations that provide meaning. This is why it is so difficult to oppose them effectively.

One of the most recent attempts to demonstrate the nonscientific character of these beliefs, following many others,[30] is particularly illuminating. Produced by Jean-Claude Pecker,[31] it concerns so-called scientific astrology. His extensively documented and closely reasoned analysis reveals contradictions in the desire to ground astrology scientifically, which no means, short of total illogic, can overcome. Nevertheless, as indicated by the debate that has ensued, this analysis, like previous ones, persuades only those who wish to be persuaded. In particular, his discussion of the opposing conclusions drawn by partisans and opponents of astrology from statistical studies supposed to establish the reality of the phenomenon in question clearly demonstrates the role of a priori credence in this reality. He shows clearly how this is an application of Bayesian statistics, in which the results of a test cannot by themselves establish or rule out the reality of a phenomenon, but can only modify the likelihood of a theory about this reality, already postulated a priori. The results of statistical tests lead to a posteriori probabilities concerning the likelihood of theories that are the objects of belief. But once the object of such a belief has been postulated a priori as plausible and accepted as what was to be tested, a bias is introduced, depending on whether one chooses to test a theory or its antitheory. In general, tests of a posteriori probabilities, even when meaningful, are not sufficiently decisive to alter the a priori probabilities to any significant extent. This is why in the final analysis they scarcely modify the original belief, whether in the existence or nonexistence of a phenomenon.

Pecker's argument has little chance of persuading scientists (and even less laypersons) who believe in the "scientifically established" reality of these phenomena; once the statistical argument is exhausted, what remains is the demonstration—incontestable, for that—of the nonphysically causal character of the correlations invoked. But, as we saw with regard to Jung, this acausal character of interpretations, amply discussed at the Cordoba colloquium, does not bother those for whom any abstract coherent interpretation is adequate to explain a phenomenon, even if it be coincidence, by giving it a meaning. In other words, the refutation of "scientific" parapsychology and astrology can be effected only at the level of criticism of the principle of synchronicity; that is, of the belief in the objective reality of the meanings that allow us to interpret and explain things. Any other critique, based on the absence of physical causality or on the clearly subjective character of interpretations, leaves intact the belief in the truth of these phenomena, which rests precisely on interpretations that give meaning even though they are noncausalist and which invokes some sort of objective existence or reality of apparently subjective meanings, such that the subject-object distinction no longer holds.[32] Even more than physical experiments,[33] abstract mathematical structures serve to explain phenomena and integrate them into a global meaning (that of physical theory) without any classical causal relationship inhering in this transition from mathematics to physics.

In any case, the reality of these meanings is posited as all the more "ultimate" in proportion as they are hidden and revealed only to the "initiate," an interpreting analyst or scientist who explains how things are, in the revelation of a grand unification where the diversity of immediate experiences is abolished by the unity of the explanatory theory. Once again, this attitude seems to be perfectly legitimate in physics, where the efforts of several generations of physicists have been directed at finding *the* unified theory that would "explain" (actually describe in a quantitative and predictive manner) all elementary phenomena by means of a single equation. But whereas some physicists are aware that this implies the search for a unification of theory and physical science, others, carried away by their enthusiasm for the esthetics of the theory, tumble into the trap of seeing it as progress toward discovering *the* ultimate and unique reality, thanks to which everything will be explained and find meaning. In this they are merely fulfilling the common view of science as purveyor of great "true" explanations to replace the illusory ones of the religious and philosophical systems of the past.

One example can be offered, out of many, from the "serious" scientific review *La Recherche*. An otherwise well-documented and clearly argued article in that journal begins as follows:

> "Everything that is above is like what is below." This verse from the Emerald Tablet, a fundamental text of the alchemists, curiously resurfaces through recent research in physics. Today, in effect, there is an astonishing convergence at work between two disciplines that are at first sight diametrically opposed: cosmology, whose object is the universe as a whole, and particle physics, which studies the most elementary microscopic structures.[34]

There follows an exposition of the cosmological theory of the Big Bang, questions that it raises, and possible responses that particle physics can offer to them. All of this, according to the authors, permits a "physical history of the universe," something that was still inconceivable a few decades ago, when, "for lack of observations...cosmology was considered to be an essentially mathematical discipline," to be developed at long last. Ignoring the well-known difficulties of circumscribing the "physical," with its connotation of real and concrete, by the "merely" mathematical, this introduction comforts the reader as to the legitimacy of his or her expectation that science be the "scientifically established" substitute for myths of origin.

To put it another way, what animates the belief in scientific astrology, parapsychology, and other fads and fallacies is not only, as Pecker says, vulgar trickeries based on the credulity of people or, as he writes elsewhere,[35] an "almost coordinated enterprise of subversion." For the same sort of credulity, as poorly or as well grounded, also functions with regard to the vulgarized products of familiar and established science. As long as the meaning of the interpretation, whatever it may be, works on some given interpretand, and in the absence of the perspective that allows awareness of the relative and operational character, in some limited context, of every interpretation and every meaning—including those provided by scientific theory—we always run the risk of believing in the truth of a particular interpretive system. Viewed, in such a case, as more than it actually is, the system would be credited with stripping the veil from certain aspects of some ultimate reality, otherwise hidden from the eyes of the "uninitiated" observer.

## Science and Mysticism: Games of Speech and Silence

If we do not want to renounce explanation and interpretation, the best way to avoid this belief in the "established" truth, supposed to be hidden within things, of some explanatory system or other—a belief that must be dogmatic, rigid, and, in the final analysis, sterile—is to accept the need to play the game with a set of several different interpretive systems, with strict limitations on their respective domains of legitimacy. Each system obeys the rules of its *own* truth and errors. The task of defining the domains of legitimacy does not necessarily obey a single system of metarules, which assert precisely how to make the switch from one system to another without interrupting the game. At best we can pass from one system to another[36] by comparing the rules of one with those of the other, *in order to differentiate them*; ultimately, it is these differentiations themselves that demarcate the various domains of legitimate application. To put it another way, we must give up the idea of a single monolithic explanation, *while recognizing* that the ambition of every explanatory system, what motivates and permits its advancement and extension to new interpretands, is always to act *as if* it were the only one possible, to *aim* precisely at the golden number of the single and monolithic "true" explanation.

The ability to play this game of multiple systems implies an awareness of the respective limits of the two types of process, the scientific and the mystical, which make antithetical use of the possibilities of the reciprocal flux of experience toward language and of language toward experience.

The bound of scientific discourse is what it leaves unsaid; yet this "unsaid" is the source of its meaning, of what has not yet been conceptualized and remains in its interstices—both in those interstices that separate disciplines and methods and in those located within speech itself, "the white space between the words,"[37] or perhaps "the semantic mud"[38] that is always there, the unconceptualized intermediary between the observed and the calculated. The power of scientific discourse lies in both the rigor *and* the richness of its conceptualizations as they relate to the results of the experimental method. Not only does the richness not prevent rigor; it is created by the rigor, by the very limitations introduced by rigor and imposed by the objective conditions of observation and measurement.[39]

The bourn of mystical speech is speech itself—what it says—because, by definition, what it has to say cannot be said. This is why religious discourses that claim rationality for their literal meaning are intolerably naive or mystifying.

Of course, each of these types of discourse, which correspond to different practical experiences, constantly endeavors to push beyond its own limits. Science does this with the help of general theories that are sometimes risky and always provisional, and thanks especially to the discovery of new techniques of observation, measurement, and calculation that can provide access to new strata of reality and permit analytical and algorithmic conceptualization to grasp what was hitherto interstice, white space, and semantic mud. Mystics do this by means of linguistic tricks and the systematic interplay of speech and silence. These games are not all alike, but peculiar to the various disciplines and traditions. In fact, these games are probably what distinguishes the traditions from one another, if we allow that the mystical experiences that underlie all of the latter may well be of the same nature. Zen Buddhism, for example, seems to make systematic use of paradox and contradiction in its written and spoken teachings in order to make it abundantly clear that these are no more than a preparation for illumination, which cannot itself be the subject of discourse. Discursive logic and reason are used *a contrario*, alongside the practice of Zazen, to make it possible to proceed from one stage of intellection and rationalization to another held to be superior—a stage of lived experience and unity with nature, where the principles of identity and noncontradiction no longer obtain.[40] Because I have no personal experience of Zazen, my comments about it are the result of abundant reading and conversations. In Judaism, by contrast, which I know from the inside, the practice of the *mitzvot* (injunctions and prohibitions that regulate the daily life of individuals and society) is accompanied by the study of texts and their commentaries. There too what is said serves as a springboard, as pretext and pre-text, for experiencing the unsaid.[41]

None of this implies the absence of rationality, but rather a way of using reason different from that followed by science, because the processes move in opposite directions: from the unsaid to the said for the sciences, from the said to the unsaid for mystics; from experience (transformed into experiment) toward discourse for the former, from discourse (broken down and split up) toward interior experience for the latter. The two processes, although both rational, face in opposite directions.

The uses of spoken and written language that are legitimate (because fruitful) in each case are diametrically opposed. Scientific language strives for semantic rigor and the maximum restriction of meaning to a single literal sense, determined by precise definitions, the absence of ambiguity, and strict application of the law of noncontradiction. Metaphor and analogy are suspect and can be accepted only as a provisional makeshift, to be held at a distance and eliminated as quickly as possible. By contrast, the language of the mystical traditions becomes uninteresting when taken literally. Any rationality to be found there (and a fortiori the bias toward deliberate irrationality sometimes expressed there) is that of a symbolism playing relentlessly on several levels of meaning, ultimately abandoning the literal sense to grasp only the metaphor and the infinite possibilities of using it as a text to be interpreted. These two processes also correspond to different goals and interests:[42] the transformation and domination of nature for science, the domination and transformation of social life, in its relations with interior life and subjectivity, for the traditional disciplines.

Total explanation is mystical. Efficient and reproducible manipulation is scientific. Historically, the dissociation between efficient manipulation and comprehensive explanation took place only gradually, under the press of the desire for manipulation that, to become increasingly effective, had to abandon its explanatory power to an ever greater extent. What remains is the provisional consensus of a community of practitioners of a scientific discipline regarding what can be expressed in a relatively poor but univocal language, one that is universal and operational. This consensus, for all that it is relative, is nevertheless quite effective in practice, even if we scarcely know how to turn it into (meta)theory. The source of its successes is to be found in its own limitations: the elimination of subjectivity and of the more far-reaching and ambitious stakes of the *sciences humaines*, the "soft sciences." The verdict of technical success—going back to the unanimous admiration of early men for their comrade who first succeeded in making a fire, through the common recognition of the indisputable success of the Manhattan Project, the Apollo missions, or chemical and biochemical synthesis—associated with the universality of the logic of noncontradiction, permits the existence of the scientific discourse of the international conference. The language spoken there (a broken English that horrifies native speakers) is an impoverished idiom, but it enables the participants to come to an agreement or, at least, to agree on the points of their disagreement and on methods that will eventually make it possible to overcome it.

In the Western world, where science developed and has been accepted as a criterion of truth, success, and efficiency, what remains of the other process is a set of superstitious beliefs, institutionalized religious observances almost devoid of content, and, most of all, artistic experience. There too expression exists only in order to lead to the unsaid of the esthetic experience—whether through the images of the plastic arts, the sounds of music, or the halting words of literature. The praxis that accompanies this experience is an eroticism that the barriers of Christian morality, within which it tested itself and against which it finally revolted, could not resist—and that in consequence is even less effective.

In the Orient, and in societies where tradition remains the point of reference, the scientific process is seen either as deviltry, a perversion from which one must turn away in horror, indeed which must be fought against, or as an accessory from which one must know how to reap the benefits without being caught in its snares. This latter attitude, which entails a certain relativism, was that of the teachers of the Jewish tradition, dating back to the origins of the natural sciences in Greece and ancient Egypt. It is likely that the numerous encounters and interactions between the Jewish and Greek civilizations, imposed by geography and history, had something to do with this.

The dialogue established in that era between the teachings of science and those of tradition maintains that difference; this is clearly evident in the talmudic discussion in which the question that lies at the heart of our problem is posed.

## Natural Science and the Wisdom of Israel in the Talmudic Tradition

In a celebrated passage of the Babylonian Talmud (*Pesahim* 94b) we find a strange comparison between what seem to be contradictory astronomical theories, attributed respectively to the Jewish and Gentile sages. What is being described is the movements of the sun that are responsible for the succession of light and darkness, day and night. We read there that the Jewish sages held that during the day the sun travels below the firmament; during the night it circles back above the firmament—which, it follows, must be opaque. By contrast, according to the savants of the Gentiles—so we read in this compendium of the Jewish sages (since it is part of the Talmud)—during the day the sun travels, not below, but above the firmament, whereas during the night it sinks beneath the earth, where it warms the subterranean waters. This controversy obviously has meaning only in the flat-earth cosmology of the talmudic era; much later this posed problems for many commentators, and notably for Rabbi Loew, known as the Maharal of Prague, himself both rabbi and astronomer, evidently an adherent of the Ptolemaic, though perhaps of the Copernican, system.[43]

The fact that this cosmology has been discarded and that, in light of our current knowledge of the solar system, both positions strike us as equally absurd, has no importance for our present interest. In fact, only the symbolic import of these visions and their differences are important, even if the divergence of opinions regards a physical theory inspired by the science of two millennia ago. It is this symbolism, of course, and its underlying method, that constitute our interest in studying and pondering these texts, transmitted and reiterated over the centuries down to our own day.

Still more interesting for our purpose is the fact that the talmudic text, that is, the Jewish sages, proceeds by putting into the mouth of one of them the apparently paradoxical conclusion that the view held by the Gentile savants is more plausible than their own, because it coincides more closely with empirical observations of the heating of the subterranean waters during the night. This discussion, with its somewhat curious conclusion, is the clew of the labyrinth for later readers, including the same Maharal of Prague,[44] for whom the text must be understood as juxtaposing, not two realistic models of the universe, but two symbolic ones; one of them (that of the Gentile sages) could *also* be understood, and perhaps accepted, as a concrete model. Thus we are dealing here with a symbolic representation whose pretext is what would today be considered a scientific model, relying on it even while distinguishing itself from it. This being the case, "firmament" must be understood according to its scriptural definition (Genesis 1:6–7); namely, as the locus of separation between the "upper waters" and the "lower waters."[45]

The issue in dispute is thus the role of this separation vis-à-vis our experience of daylight. For the Jewish sages, this light illuminates only the "lower waters," site of the multiplicity of visible objects;[46] whereas the "upper waters" (those above the heavens) remain in the solar penumbra, adequately illuminated by a more potent light—one hidden from us—the light of the First Day, before the creation of the sun, in the mythical narrative of the seven days of Creation. As such, these upper waters are simultaneously the locus of the hidden oneness of things and of the origin of questioning. During the night, according to this view, the sun returns to the upper waters to illuminate them in their turn, or perhaps, on the contrary, to imbibe from them the light it will use to illuminate the earth during the following day. This view is opposed to that of the Gentile sages, for whom daylight is the only light, illuminating with (almost) total clarity all worlds, from the multiple and bounded reality of our own experience to the infinitude of possibilities above the heavens. In this second view night acquires a quite different symbolic value: instead of being a means for renewal from the sources above the heavens, it becomes a sojourn in the netherworld, *beneath* the lower waters and the earth that supports them.

At the same time, however, the firmament acquires a different meaning: it serves essentially as a screen to protect against a surfeit of light and heat during the day, because the sun is considered to emit its radiation from above the firmament. In this conception, moreover, during the night the sun affects the lower waters, too, through a screen, the earth itself, which, although opaque, does not keep the sun from heating the subterranean waters. Thus the succession of day and night takes place on a single level, that of the sun's mediated effect on the lower waters—the world of our terrestrial experiences—with the effects of illumination prevailing over those of heating during the day, and the reverse during the night. For the Jewish sages, by contrast, this function of the screen needed to protect against direct solar radiation is filled by a sort of "sheath" in which the sun, according to this tradition,[47] is normally enclosed; whereas the firmament is an opaque veil separating two different worlds, two separate levels, between which the sun passes directly during the alternation of day and night. In this conception the night, although a period of darkness for the lower world, is a time of light for the upper world, that world "above the sun" where new things can come into being, whereas, according to Ecclesiastes, "there is nothing new under the sun." This supersolar sphere, penetrated by the sun during the night and illuminated from bottom to top, while the moon reigns elsewhere, alludes to the midrashic dialectic of moon and sun, in which the lunar sphere is perceived as being in certain respects superior to the solar, for all that the latter is brighter, precisely because of the capacity for death and resurrection expressed by the phases of the moon.[48]

Thus we see how, starting from an apparent contrast between two cosmological descriptions of the solar system, we attain, among various possible metaphors, a contrast between two experiences of nocturnal life: the renewal of energy produced by rest and sleep ("warming the subterranean waters") versus illumination of the celestial sources in the world of nocturnal dreams and prophetic visions.

Furthermore, this symbolism, in amplified form, spawned an abundant literature, especially in the kabbalistic tradition,[49] where (as for the Gnostics) the universe has the form of the human body, and this screen dividing upper from lower is represented by the diaphragm. The diaphragm separates the upper and lower halves of the body, but not in such a manner as to make the latter merely the seat of "shameful" sexuality. Instead, the lower organs are perceived as being less "alive," in lesser relation with the infinite renewal of life, for all that they are indispensable to it, because they are the site of digestion, which is accompanied by the more obvious act of excretion. The upper half, home to the organs of respiration, circulation, mobility, speech, and thought, is more "noble" and more "refined," because no excrement or obvious "filth" is connected with them.[50] The indispensable functional unity of these two separated realms, that of life in death and that of death in life, is provided by the blood, seat of the vegetative soul[51] (*nefesh*), on the one hand, and, of course, by sexuality, whose organs are located both above and below the diaphragm, on the other. In fact, although the genitals are "below," many "upper" organs are recognized as having a sexual and erotic function—including the brain, described as the organ that secretes the sperm, which then descends through the spinal cord!

Although, depending on the cultural and historical context, many different things could be said about interpretations of this type, their possible proliferation, their richness, and their significance, what interests us here is the attitude of the Jewish sages as found in this talmudic passage. They juxtapose their concept to that of the Gentile sages in order to expound upon the differences between them, but calmly accept that the view upheld by the latter is more plausible from the perspective of what today we would call empirical and scientific knowledge.

Another example of this seemingly paradoxical attitude involves the corpus of medical precepts and theories scattered throughout the Talmud. This has been the object of close scrutiny by the masters of the post-talmudic Jewish tradition, even though its application is forbidden by that same tradition. The medical treatment enjoined by the tradition is that prescribed by the physicians of each particular epoch,[52] whereas talmudic medicine must remain exclusively a subject for theoretical study, because the latter deals with a different human "nature," one supposed to have existed in ancient times but that has vanished today. Talmudic medicine implied an intimacy between objects and the words that express them; or, to put it another way, it posited that symbols have a real existence that, as in magic and shamanic medicine,[53] makes it possible to affect the body by manipulating the symbols. Because this kind of manipulation no longer works for us today, its practical application is banned. But the symbolism on which it is based still has a theoretical interest for the overall world view implied by its study.

Another example of the relativistic and seemingly paradoxical attitude of the talmudic sages, replete with interest in and respect for Gentile science even while distancing and differentiating itself in accordance with their own tradition of knowledge, involves astrology. We should consider this point for a moment. Astrology was an honored and accepted scientific discipline during Antiquity and the High Middle Ages, just like alchemy.[54] As such, the Rabbis respected it and considered it to provide objective knowledge about reality. At the same time, however, they maintained a distance and set a limit to its domain of validity, declaring that "Israel is immune to astral influence."[55] Here, as the context reveals, "Israel" is defined by its submission to an ethico-historical law transmitted and conveyed by a particular pedagogical method, which allows it to overcome the deterministic forces of nature.

This is the majority opinion; but one sage, R. Hanina, asserts that "Israel is subject to astral influence," thereby implying that nothing is immune to the determinism of natural forces. Yet the same R. Hanina proclaims, elsewhere, a relativism even greater than this determinism, in his famous aphorism, "Everything is in the hands of Heaven, except for the fear of Heaven"[56]—that is, everything is predestined except for fear of this predestination. Because this "fear," "the beginning of knowledge and of wisdom,"[57] is in fact proximate to knowledge—it is the *sense of awe*, in the fullest sense of the term, that one feels when confronted by reality and that is at the origin of every question[58]—ultimately the meaning is that natural deterministic forces do not exist and have no effect except for those who recognize them.[59] Celestial determinism appears only for someone who questions the fear of Heaven, and provides the initial impetus to his questioning. Thus, alongside the attitude of those who pretend to want to know the hidden causes of things as they are, we encounter another attitude, composed of openness and freedom, which can escape the toils of this determinism that exists only when recognized. Yet this latter attitude is posited not only as coexisting with the former, but even as in some manner conditioning it.

Thus once again we meet this separation of domains of legitimacy: the wisdom of the nations, of the Greeks or Babylonians (so far as astrology is concerned), a kind of knowledge that in modern parlance would be categorized as scientific; versus the wisdom of Israel, which deals with an ethical program and social order. At the same time, however, this separation is not simply ignorance. For the Maharal of Prague and other traditional commentators (such as R. Baḥya on Genesis 1), Gentile wisdom concerns itself with the study of natural phenomena and their laws, whereas the Torah deals with "supernatural" realities. But this does not mean that the latter—which, strictly speaking, belong to the domain of metaphysics— have no laws or that they do not reflect some rational system. Natural phenomena and the laws that govern them are the province of the nations, of the wisdom of the nations or of one of their sciences; but the pursuit of Israel and its sages is the Torah. The Torah, being a prophetic and ethical discourse, draws its initial authority from the fact that it is inspired, "descended from heaven." But thereafter it is taken in hand and even held in check,[60] to become a subject for meditation and continuous scrutiny by all the Jewish societies that organized themselves around its study throughout the centuries.

However—again according to the Maharal of Prague—science and the wisdom of the nations, particularly of the Greeks, are required in order to understand the Torah, because they make it possible to apprehend the reality of the world for which the Torah legislates. And to the extent that it permits us, in his words, to "comprehend the existence and order of the world," this Gentile wisdom constitutes a "ladder by which we ascend to the wisdom of the Torah."[61]

This division between two types of wisdom, which nevertheless maintains an opening and a dialogue between them, is quite fundamental, for two reasons. First, it makes it possible to sustain a critical attitude—not in the name of some metatheory or of a metaphysical system transformed into the "first science," but simply by the distance that the alternation between two wisdoms makes it possible to maintain toward each of them. Second, it is fundamental because the two modes of knowledge, for all that they are different and incommensurable, still have something to offer each other. Metaphysics, which is influenced by mysticism, can still be the starting point for scientific discovery, albeit in an indirect and obscure fashion, one that is impure from the point of view of an all-conquering epistemology and a history of triumphant science, artificially reconstructed a posteriori. Conversely, there is no substitute for the scientific method—given the rigor of its analytic progression from the bottom up, its efficacy in constructing a material reality (the reality of the laboratory and of technology) transparent to the theory for which and by which it is constructed, and amenable to description in a "universal" language—when it comes to its influence on the recurring experience of rendering the abstract and concrete commensurable with the world of sense perceptions, even if the latter are carefully winnowed (and quite different from those that interest the mystic) so as to make them available to scientific theorizing. Thus the possible union of these two modes of knowledge—traditional mystic knowledge that leads to ethics, and scientific knowledge that leads to technologi-cal expertise—cannot be itself a precisely defined body of knowledge, a metatheory that would encompass both of them; it must rather relate to individual and social experience and to the practices of those who devote themselves to it.

## Moral Law and Natural Law

Those for whom the Jewish tradition can be summed up as a "monothe-istic religion" may find it paradoxical that it defends a sort of epistemo-logical relativism and pluralism. The oneness of God—to employ theologi-cal terms[62]—is pushed aside, either into the transcendent beyond or the eschatological future.[63]

As immanent, this oneness is experienced through that of earthly law—natural law that is at the same time moral law. But what is involved here is a *decision*, an *act* of faith, leading to a program of social construc-tion, rather than a datum of objective knowledge about a reality that already exists. The reality that can be known by objective methods—or merely that can be expressed in words—seems on the contrary to be split in two, insofar as how one experiences it and how one theorizes about it. The hope that moral law and natural law can be conflated is staked in a wager whose success depends on man's desire and skill to rejoin what has been split asunder. This is why natural law, as represented in the sciences, is assigned the highest value—even though, as its truths are progressively unveiled, it is not apprehended as the expression of ultimate reality, but only as the most perfect harvest of the knowledge of nature that those who have devoted themselves to it have been able to reap.

As for moral law, it too is subject to relativization of its literal expres-sion and concrete application, as compared with some theoretical absolute. Although handed down from on high, it is nevertheless expressed in the words of the sages who have dedicated themselves to endowing it with existence.[64] The idea that these two laws might in fact be one is attractive; it certainly underlies Jewish monotheism, although it is deferred to a future constructed by and for the "Just," or to a transmundane ineffability.[65] While we wait, only human symbolic and mythical rituals can recombine in experience, rather than in theory or metatheory, these two domains of legitimacy: that of the God of heaven-descended ethics (who stands apart) and that of the immanent "presence" that can be experienced through doing and knowing.[66]

This, in brief, is the attitude of at least some of the teachers of the tal-mudic and kabbalistic tradition with regard to the possible and desirable relations between moral law and our knowledge of natural determinism. Their attitude involves both a *desire* for oneness, in the unifying conception of an ultimate reality latent in the manifold of our experiences, and a *resistance* to this desire, because it bears within itself the risk of self-destruction. As such it exemplifies the relativism or non-nihilistic skepticism championed here. It is this desire for oneness that leads us to look for "explanations" or "interpretations" that are ever more all-encompassing, whether obtained by the empirico-logical scientific method, where the explanation seems to be obtained as a bonus over and above the main operational goal of mastering nature, or by traditional modes of knowledge that posit this unity a priori, as a function of goals that are at the same time mystical, religious, ethical, and sociocultural, and more or less consciously recognized.

Concomitantly, however, and to the extent that our knowledge is limited—and it must always be limited, both by the multiplicity of its methods and their domains of application and by its openness to infinitely variable experience—we must resist this desire for oneness and refuse to surrender to it. The attempt to make moral law coterminous with whatever knowledge of natural law we have been able to acquire entails the almost inevitable danger of making the foundations on which the legitimacy of these two types of law rest cancel each other out and engage in mutual self-annihilation: concentration on an ethical system, whose domain ought to be that of truth, perverts the lucid and objective search for knowledge of things; conversely, such a search confines moral law within the strait and impassable bounds of "what is" (or rather, of what is thought to exist, according to our current knowledge) rather than within those of what "ought to be," as a function of norms whose origin is elsewhere—the intentional desire for change within the ideology or, in more traditional and more pregnant terms, the in-part unconscious will of the "social imaginary."[67]

## The Normative as a Dialectic of Openness

It is clear that here the normative aspect of moral law (stating what "ought to be," according to some conscious or unconscious goal) engenders openness rather than closure—contrary to what might have been expected—as compared with moral law taken as *identical* with natural law, where its imperatives would be merely the ineluctable consequences of our knowledge of what is.

A formal analysis of these two sorts of interaction between norm and knowledge can be found in an article by M. Bourgeois.[68] Bourgeois analyzes them as two modes of conveying information between agents; inspired in part by E. M. Barrister,[69] he designates these modes as "control" and "power." The former implies the existence, for one of the agents, of an exhaustive descriptive model that endows him with absolute control over the other agent; the second mode, by contrast, implies the existence of reciprocal interactions between the two agents, in which the necessarily incomplete representation that one has of the other is completed and modified by the degree of autonomy possessed by the latter, who can then be perceived by the former only by means of a normative model (because the descriptive knowledge that one can have of another is in part inadequate).

In consequence, the most efficient conditions of closure and blockage exist in the *absence* of an explicit norm. A norm of any sort, associated with a method of knowledge and perhaps clashing with its results, can open it and permit it to evolve by means of cognitive disorganizations followed by incessant reorganizations. By contrast, none of this can take place in the absence of an explicit norm, when the norm is replaced by the data of objective knowledge expressed as a descriptive model—a cosmology or a scientific ideology—that pretends to be complete and exhaustive. One cannot even pose the question of transgressing the norm in these conditions, where the normative has been confounded with knowledge of "what is."

An explicit norm, as a collective blueprint that is more or less internalized by individuals and is distinct from a datum of objective knowledge about the nature of things, can arise only from the mythological, from the symbolic, as Baudrillard uses this term;[70] that is, from activities of social interchange, at once the collective and individual wellspring that defines a common field for a society and for the individuals who constitute it.

By contrast, when the set of reciprocal interactions between norm and knowledge, which have different origins, is reduced to a descriptive model based on knowledge of some human "reality" that is in fact constructed by the theoretical component of this knowledge, the model, soon considered to be all-encompassing and universal, itself establishes the "one-dimensional" norm and proceeds to imprison this frozen reality within the data it expresses. There is no reason why this theoretically perfect state in which norm and knowledge are identified should change, and its possibilities for renewal are extremely limited; until, that is, the tension with reality, which in any event evolves independently of this state of knowledge (which is always of the past) and to a large extent in a manner that cannot be foreseen on the basis of this knowledge, becomes too great. At that point the entire situation falls apart and teeters on the verge of collapse.

Conversely, a normative model posited a priori will always be limited by reality and, by definition, will be in a state of tension with it. In such a case there is no pretense of knowing objective human reality as it is and then caging reality within this knowledge, misnamed "scientific," in order to reinforce its hold; instead, we act on reality in accordance with the blueprint for transformation that the norm, when distinct from knowledge, always implies. This situation liberates the games of knowledge from the need to deal with the norm, while at the same time creating a permanent tension—no longer between an evolving reality and a frozen normative science, but between a norm posited a priori and a critical science that is itself evolving. Only now this tension provides a continual impetus by creating a cognitive openness of constant evolution and renewal, wherein the norm too is modified, though in a different rhythm, and with different reasons and methods, than the data of knowledge are modified—a situation that, in the final reckoning, is more stable and less apt to shatter. The norm, the blueprint—whether conscious or unconscious—guides *action* on human reality, action that is always called into question by its own results and that need not confine the blueprint-reality ensemble in a corpus of knowledge that soon congeals into dogma.[71] This permits continued utilization of this knowledge, but in order to apply its results to continual adjustment of the blueprint to reality (and of reality to the blueprint), rather than in order to constitute a corpus, simultaneously theoretical and normative, in which all are expected to believe and to which all must submit in the name of Truth.

The hypothetical truth of a body of knowledge set up as a dogma can then be replaced by the truth of a passion[72] for knowledge, for the straightforward application of a method that much more nearly resembles the rules of a game, to be followed without cheating, than it does a formal body of knowledge.

Thus the existence of an explicit norm, alongside and in dialectical relation with the exercise of our capacities for objective and critical knowledge, is more fertile than an undifferentiated unity wherein the norm vanishes behind an ineluctable nature, beyond challenge and one-dimensional, in Marcuse's sense.[73] Taken to the limit, any norm is better than knowledge that pretends to be complete because true or true because complete. This is the pretension that hides behind the adjective *scientific* accorded to ideological and political discourse with the aim of asserting that it possesses some sort of objective and unquestionable truth, thereby banishing any opposition to the shadows of an obscurantist or illusory nonexistence, or even to the excommunication of madness. We are only beginning to recognize the extent of the ravages of this incantatory and liturgical use of science as the supposed source of an ethical system ostensibly founded on knowledge of natural law.[74] The zenith of this redoubtable confusion is attained when, with the greatest "rationality" in the world, opposition to the party line—the party that is sole warden of truth and norm—is treated by commitment to a psychiatric hospital. Because the authority that promulgates the law has been appointed guardian and depository of "true"—

because "scientific"—knowledge, those who reject this law can be liable only to the treatment accorded the insane.

Before attaining this refinement in the perversion of reason, similar attempts to establish a scientific ethic as "truth" produced the most murderous totalitarianisms of this century—the heirs, after a gap of several centuries, to those of the Inquisition and the expansion of Islam. The reference, of course, is to Nazi and Soviet genetics; though antithetical in content, they have in common the pretension of ideologies that want to be and call themselves "scientific." It is there, in fact, that the root of the evil is located; namely, that science today, like the missionary monotheism of ages past, is employed only to go surety for a dogmatic imperialism that stamps out every difference and every disagreement. The intellectual ideologues of revolution, massacring their own people in Cambodia in the name of the scientific truth of their Marxism, reproduce, on a different scale, the bonfires once kindled by the Inquisition in the name of the One God of the missionaries, or the devastating Holy Wars preached by fanatical Islam.

But in a certain sense we are going around in circles. After the proclamation of the death of God, and then of Man—the traditional sources of ethics—laws and customs, religion, moral and political philosophy, ideologies, viewed as living wellsprings of ethics, seem to have dried up. Thus we and our conduct are given over to the arbitrary whims of our impulses, of that celebrated "desire" and its no less celebrated discourses, or perhaps to the arbitrary laws of the state, which we cannot see as anything better than conventional and circumstantial. Because this situation is uncomfortable for many, they prefer that law continue to be derived from heavenly truth and consequently no longer trust in anything except science.

The episode of the radio broadcast related at the outset of this volume is an example of this attitude. I hope that I have adequately demonstrated how the demand that ethics be grounded on science is unjustified, despite appearances and despite the misinformation perpetuated by scientific education and by a certain edifying account of the progress of science. It is unjustified for a number of reasons, which we have endeavored to analyze and which can be summarized in two propositions. First, the scientific method can be effective only if its field of action is precisely restricted to the domain to which it can apply. Scientific research is like a game played on the field of a reality, whose boundaries are delineated by the rules of the game. We know the story of the streetlamp, which captures the essence of the scientific process so well: the fellow who had lost something was looking for it under the streetlamp (and not where he had lost it), because that was the only place where there was light enough to see by. The second reason, perhaps connected with the first, is that scientific research selects its objects in the world of artifacts, that is, in an artificial world, constructed in the laboratory, precisely because such objects are easier to study and easier to experiment on. The contemporary case of recombinatory genetics is a flagrant example and of great historical importance. This is the first time that the process of transmuting a natural object into an artificial one, a process already well known in physics and chemistry, has penetrated biology. For the first time, living creatures, the objects of biological research, are not taken from nature, but are created in the laboratory to satisfy the needs of research, technology, and industry, just like machines and plastics in physics and chemistry.

For these two reasons, at least, the demand that science lay the foundations for ethics is unjustified.

## Ethics Comes from Somewhere Else

The question on the agenda is larger, however, and concerns not only science, but also knowledge in general. Ethics cannot be derived from knowledge, because several totally contradictory ethical systems can find an ostensible foundation in the same corpus of knowledge, especially in the sciences. This is due to the fact that ethics comes from somewhere else.

One of the most exhaustive expositions of this question is that by Castoriadis, with his concept of the social imaginary. Every ethical system is a sort of blueprint or purpose rather than a body of knowledge. It expresses itself in the aggregate of desires, needs, and representations, both conscious and unconscious, that take shape in a society in a complex—that is, uncontrolled—manner and thereby constitute what Castoriadis calls the "social imaginary."[75] Only later can ethics be the object of reflection, of knowledge, after it has been imposed as a set of rules and conduct.[76]

It is only secondarily that this social imaginary can be expressed by inspired spokespersons (magicians, prophets, philosophers, and moralists) in the form of moral imperatives, blueprints for society, or ideologies, which always and inevitably contain a certain amount of a posteriori rationalization.[77]

Thus ethics is not born of knowledge. It comes from somewhere else, and this elsewhere is what can be provisionally denominated, following Castoriadis, the "social imaginary." From this perspective, nothing bars us from saying that it "comes from heaven" or even that it comes from God, taking into account that author's remark that the proof of God's existence, for any given society, is the existence in its language of the word God.[78]

Thus, if one can say that knowledge in general cannot be the underpinning for an ethical system, because a number of contradictory ethics can be founded on the same body of knowledge, this holds with even greater force for scientific knowledge because, as we have seen, its domain of application is necessarily restricted to just that segment of reality to which the scientific method can be applied.

## *"Wisdom Is Superior to Folly"*[79]

Still—and all the questions lead back to this—one cannot dismiss knowledge, especially not scientific knowledge, because an ethical system of any sort acquires new dimensions as a function of whether or not it is open to knowledge. Even in that caricature known as a posteriori rationalization this openness to knowledge remains nevertheless openness—all the more so if one is aware of the phenomenon of rationalization and the fact that the openness consists simply in a juxtaposition of languages, in a dialogue between processes that aim at different goals. To repeat what we have said before, for one the goal is knowledge about reality and about ourselves; whereas for the other it is action and the transformation of reality and of ourselves.

These processes have different goals, but they take place, if I may be so bold, within the same individuals—the same "gardens," if you will—because they take place inside ourselves; and we, as individuals, are simultaneously involved in the processes of knowledge and in those of transformation. Perhaps this is how we should read the text in Genesis: "the tree of life [was] inside the garden and [inside] the tree of knowledge [itself at the same time both] good and evil."[80]

It is only in this way, and not at all as part of the attempt to ground an ethical system on the sciences, that dialogue is significant, because then we are dealing with a reciprocal openness between two traditions of study, one of which has the ethical objective of formulating social and moral law, while the other has quite a different objective, cognitive in character; namely, to provide a coherent description of universal laws and the mastery of nature.

In this type of dialogue, though, we must be protected by effective safeguards, because the dangers of confusion, deriving from the two protagonists that we have endeavored to analyze, are great. Each finds in the other what it has undervalued within itself: explanation, in science, and the concern for efficiency, in traditional knowledge. A relativistic pluralism of knowledge, nourishing a (non-nihilistic) skepticism about the truth of theories and the existence of an Ultimate Reality (which science would disclose as well as or better than the mystical traditions), seems to me to provide one of the best anchor points for these safeguards.

Opposing this relativistic attitude is the need to believe in a conceptualizable unity of knowledge and ethics, in the form of an "impassable"[81] Truth-Goodness, which leads to the absurdities of the scientists at the Cordoba colloquium or of scientific astrology.

The issue here is not only the naive credulity of ignorant people, which could be overcome by a well-documented critical report on the latest scientific discoveries. We have already seen how one of the sources of the overlap and confusion between the domains of legitimacy of different methods is our difficulties in navigating the universe of explanations and meanings that objects acquire by virtue of these explanations. All systems of knowledge, whether critical or inspired, are characterized by an ordering and exegetical thought that adumbrates the meanings and sense in the objects and phenomena we perceive. It is most difficult to accept any possible operational value of one explanation or another without also believing in the objective reality of the meanings and sense that it can convey. The case of Jung bears this out, if one thinks of his "principle of synchronicity" and his "meaningful coincidences." But the same question, albeit formulated in a less subtle way than by Jung and his disciples,[82] is encountered in quite a few of these confusions, the illegitimacy of which is exceedingly difficult to prove to those—scientists and/or spiritualists—who allow themselves to be carried away by them.

We have seen in particular that the refutation of ostensibly "scientific" parapsychology and astrology can be effected only by criticizing Jung's principle of synchronicity—for those who are susceptible to such criticism! This is why refutations based on the common sense of causality, regularly opposed to these beliefs, must always be repeated and never seem able to win over the as-yet unpersuaded. Any critique of these convictions, based on physical causality or on the subjective character of interpretation, fails to sway belief in the truth of such phenomena, which depend on noncausal modes of interpretation and invoke the "objective" existence or "reality" of what they mean. Besides, these phenomena are even more "ultimate" in proportion as they are arcane, disclosing themselves only to an initiate. Thus it is a matter not only of the "credulity" of misinformed or malevolent persons, as Pecker believes,[83] but also of the force that impels the quest; namely, the a priori belief in the intelligibility of the universe, which, along with Einstein,[84] we may consider to be a sort of religious creed.

The sane attitude in this domain—though one that even rigorous minds apparently find hard to maintain—is to abandon this belief precisely at the moment when it is justified, when one has "found" the answer, when it is no longer a question of a search to be conducted but of discoveries rendered in forms that can be reported either to oneself or to the public. It is this difficulty, it seems to me, that lies at the origin of the same type of gullibility, which functions equally well for the learned productions of the recognized sciences. As long as the meaning revealed by interpretation is applied literally, without the backward step that permits one to be aware of the relative character of every explanatory interpretation and of every meaning—including those provided by scientific theory—we always face the danger of believing that a particular interpretive system is *true*; of believing that it may be more than an interpretive system because it reveals certain aspects—if not indeed all—of an ultimate reality that is hidden from the eyes of the uninitiated observer.

Here again we encounter the decisive role of the consensus of a community of specialists, or of a claque of fans, or even of the adepts of a sect. When the explanation is one that is commonly accepted by the society of specialists, among whom and thanks to whom the body of knowledge is transmitted and developed, its interpretive character is readily forgotten. This character, however, is much more apparent in the case of a marginal explanation. And it is well known that, in any given period, a not-insignificant part of the knowledge established and recognized by the community of specialists first appeared on the scene in the form of marginal theories that deviated to a greater or lesser extent from the commonly accepted wisdom of the previous era.

## Notes

1. Franco Selleri, "Von Neumann's Measurements and Consciousness: A Critical Review," in *Science and Consciousness*, p. 415.

2. Ibid.

3. E. Schrödinger, in *Louis de Broglie, Physicien et Penseur* (Paris, 1953), cited by Selleri, p. 414.

4. J.-M. Lévy-Leblond, "The Picture of the Quantum World" and "Classical Apples and Quantum Potatoes."

5. Selleri, pp. 414f.

6. Emphasis mine.

7. Selleri, "Von Neumann's Measurements," p. 414; emphasis mine.

8. Ibid., p. 415.

9. Ibid., p. 415.

10. See Chapter 2.

11. As problematic and astonishing, even though expected and "natural," as sexual knowledge?

12. We should recall that for another quantum physicist, Feynman (see Chapter 2, n. 51), the unity of the nature of a glass of wine was to be found beyond the knowledge that the different scientific disciplines provide of it—by drinking it, for example! For these disciplines, including physics, work only by subdividing nature.

13. Wittgenstein, *Tractatus* 2.1.

14. Selleri, "Von Neumann's Measurements," p. 415.

15. Wittgenstein, *Tractatus* 5.641. This is also what lies behind the "still" of 6.341 (see Chapter 5, n. 73).

16. See Kripke, *Wittgenstein on Rules and Private Language*, for a penetrating analysis of what this limit of the world seems to become, for the Wittgenstein of the *Philosophical Investigations*, where it is replaced by the conditions in which various language games are used.

17. Chapters 3 and 5.

18. Marcuse, *One-Dimensional Man*, and Atlan, *Entre le cristal et la fumée*, Chapter 13.

19. Feynman, *Lectures on Physics* and *The Character of Physical Law*.

20. Chapter 5, pp. 64–65.

21. Lévy-Leblond, "The Picture of the Quantum World," p. 419.

22. Ibid., n. 11.

23. Ibid., p. 419.

24. M. Mugur Shächter, "Réflexions sur la problème de localité," *Actes du colloque du centenaire d'Einstein*, pp. 249–264.

25. See Chapter 1.

26. See d'Espagnat, *In Search of Reality*, Chapter 5.

27. See Chapter 4.

28. Lévy-Leblond, "Classical Apples."

29. Mugur Shächter, for her part, sees the orientation of this program as the elaboration of a theory of change and process. Contrary to the concept of object, in the macroscopic sense of the term, firmly embedded within the logic of object

classes and predicates, "a general and specific theory of events and processes, *a logic of absolutely any changes*, with an explicit and unified methodology, has not yet been constructed.... The theory of probabilities, on the one hand, and, on the other hand, different physical theories (Mechanics, Thermodynamics, Field Theory, Quantum Mechanics, Relativity), have managed to overcome this lacuna to different extents. But each for a particular category of facts and by implicit and diversified methods" (Mugur Shächter, "Réflexions," pp. 260–261). One may or may not be persuaded a priori of the fecundity of this path. Only the future will tell. The relevance of the analysis, so far as the present state of physical theory is considered, remains nevertheless beyond dispute.

In effect, "the relations between Quantum Mechanics and the various concepts suggested by the language that it introduces...remain themselves quite obscure. Quantum Mechanics, in fact, indicates strictly nothing concerning these concepts as one might want to imagine them outside observation. Even the probability of presence is only a probability of results of interactive observation; Quantum Mechanics allows one to imagine that a 'system' that makes a mark on a screen at some moment $t$ was itself found as far as one may wish from this mark at as short a time before $t$ as one may wish. Quantum Mechanics leaves quite unconceptualized, within itself, the *reality* whose manifestations, observed through the interactions of measurement, it codifies in so rich and detailed a manner."

The other parts of physical theory or, more precisely, the other physico-mathematical formalisms that constitute it (predicative logic and set theory, probability theory, relativity), present difficulties of the same order. It is as if physical theory placed us "in possession of several constituted syntactic structures" (these formalisms), "each very complex, rich, and rigorous. But these structures are comparable to icebergs emerging from the sea of semantic mud, under whose surface the edges and bases disappear" (ibid., pp. 261–263). We can subscribe to her conclusion, as well: "When no unification yet exists between the discrete, observational, statistical method, oriented toward the microscopic, of Quantum Mechanics, on the one hand, and the realist, continuous, individual method, oriented toward the cosmological, of Relativity, on the other, when everything that has to do with duration and time remains so poorly elucidated, when everything that has to do with the mode of being of those entities called microsystems remains so little explored, what sense can there be to affirming—merely on the basis of tests of 'nonlocality'—that we have found a constraining (i.e., susceptible to contradiction) confrontation, direct or indirect, between Quantum Mechanics and Relativity? Or between Quantum Mechanics and our conceptualization of reality?" (ibid.).

30. See, for example, Gardner, *Fads and Fallacies*.

31. Jean-Claude Pecker, "L'astrologie et la science," *La Recherche*, no. 140 (January 1983).

32. We have previously analyzed the example of astrology, perceived differently by Jung and by Pauli on the basis of their divergent judgments concerning the ("objective") reality of the subjectivity of the astrologer.

33. If one ignores its operational and technical effectiveness.

34. J. Demaret and J. Vandermeulen, "Cosmologie et particules," *La Recherche*, no. 137 (October 1982), pp. 1152–1162.

35. Jean-Claude Pecker, "Entre l'âge d'or et l'Apocalypse," *Le Genre humain*, no. 6 (1983), pp. 115–135.

36. Assimilations of this sort, generally unconscious, take place all the time in our daily speech. This is because so-called natural language is the outcome of a continual evolution in which words and phrases partake of multiple superimposed meanings originating in different domains, with a certain confusion of meaning arising from the actual (not necessarily cognitive) situations in which they are employed. (See, for example, Wittgenstein, *Philosophical Investigations*, part 2, xiii, p. 231, who compares these assimilations to those between two games with different playing fields: "football has goals, tennis doesn't.")

37. See Chapter 2, p. 59.

38. See n. 26.

39. We should recall the joy of reunion after separation, of synthesis after analysis.

40. See, for example, D. T. Suzuki's "thinking with the abdomen." "The one great will from which all these wills, infinitely varied, flow is what I call the 'Cosmic (or ontological) Unconscious,' which is the zero-reservoir of infinite possibilities." "It is more basic than the intellect because it is the principle that lies at the root of all existence" (Suzuki, Fromm, and de Martino, *Zen Buddhism and Psychoanalysis*, pp. 51–52). This does not prevent, as with mystics of other traditions, the intellectual faculties (the *buddhis*) from receiving maximum attention, especially in certain streams where "intellectual yoga" occupies a central role, even if only to teach how to transcend it. See, for example, Aurobindo Ghose, *The Life Divine*; Swami Siddheswaranda, "Introduction à l'étude des ouvrages védantiques"; and *Doctrine de la nondualité*.

41. An analysis of the different levels of traditional Jewish biblical exegesis can be found in Atlan, "Niveaux de signification," in *La Bible aujourd'hui*, pp. 55–58.

42. In the sense meant by Habermas, *Knowledge and Human Interests*.

43. The standard text of the Talmud has the reading: "The Gentile Sages say that during the day the sun travels *below* the firmament and during the night below the *earth*." The text quoted and commented upon by Rabbi Loew (see further), however, is: "The Gentile Sages say that during the day the sun travels *above* the firmament and during the night below the *firmament*" (where the second firmament may well be a copyist's slip—*raqia'* [firmament] for *qarqa'* [earth]).
Rabbi Judah Loew, known as the Maharal of Prague, sixteenth-century

author of numerous philosophical and exegetical treatises, with a kabbalistic bent. In one of his books in particular, *Be'er ha-Golah* [The well of the exile] (Prague, 1598), he sets out to compare a number of dicta of the talmudic sages with those of Renaissance science. To take one example of many, when the Talmud speaks of a solar eclipse, it is impossible to understand it as merely an astronomical phenomenon. Rather, it must be taken in its metaphorical meaning of darkness and the disappearance of the light of day, an "anomaly" contrasted with the regular succession of day and night. If in *scientific discourse* the meaning of a solar eclipse must be reduced to the most literal level and referred exclusively to the celestial bodies involved in it—sun, moon, and earth—as well as to the quantifiable and predictable model with which astronomy provides us, it is impossible to understand any meaning other than the symbolic and metaphorical *in this traditional discourse*, which is concerned with the reverberations of natural phenomena in our inner lives and the ethical value of this life. This is how talmudic discourse, which finds a connection between the incidence of an eclipse and particularly abominable and scandalous human sins, cannot be compared to our scientific knowledge, which allows us to predict and compute in advance when an eclipse will occur, quite independently of human conduct.

As a second stage, the question may arise of possible links between the literal physical meaning and the metaphorical meaning of traditional discourse, with regard to this same phenomenon of a solar eclipse. The same question can be asked with regard to literal and more or less metaphorical uses of such terms as *light* (physical or interior) and *energy* (physical, sexual, psychic, cosmic, etc.). This type of question, which strictly speaking is a mystical one, is dealt with in the rationalist streams of Jewish tradition in the context of ritual and prayer. Prayer and study constitute two different orientations of the mind, which may even be in opposition, as, for example, with the pious ones (*hasidim*) of ancient times, whose excessive prayer was harmful to study (BT *Berakhot* 32b), or in Rabbi Hayyim of Volozhin's kabbalistic work, *Nefesh Hahayyim* (Vilna, 1824), which takes on the modern Hasidim over the same question. In ritual, the attitude is different than in study and knowledge, even of the traditional variety; for it deals with a world in which words possess a utopian transparency to and unity with objects—the characteristic of the sacred realm that ritual is supposed to bring about, by an act of will, and contrasting with our immediate experience of the knowable world of multiplicity.

44. See *Be'er ha-Golah*, §6 (London, 1964), p. 111.

45. See also *Zohar Bereshit*, pp. 17–18.

46. In Hebrew, *mayim* 'water' may be construed as a plural form of *mah* 'what?'. The mystical tradition understands the differentiation of the waters as that of undifferentiated "whats" that lead, by being asked, to "Who?" (see *Zohar*, p. 2).

47. This is quoted and repeated, for example, in the basic text of *Habad* hasidism: R. Schneour Zalman of Lyady, *Liqqutei Amarim* [commonly known as *Tanya*] (Shklov, 1796–1814; Hebrew-English bilingual edition, London: Soncino Press, 1973), part 2, Chapter 4.

48. See Atlan, *Entre le cristal et la fumée*, Chapter 6, and the midrash on the shrinking of the moon (BT *Hullin* 60b).

49. See, for example, the doctrines of R. Yitzhak Luria, as systematized in R. Hayyim Vital's *Etz Hayyim*, the basic text of the Lurianic Kabbala that arose in sixteenth-century Safed, and in the literature derived from it.

50. See Mary Douglas, *Purity and Danger: An Analysis of the Concepts of Pollution and Taboo* (London: Routledge and Kegan Paul, 1966), for one of the best studies of the symbolic significance of filth and excrement in the mythical and ritual organization of Reality.

51. See H. Atlan, "Souls and Body in the Genesis," *Koroth* 8, nos. 5–6 (1982).

52. *Shulhan Arukh Yoreh De'ah* 336, Hilkhot Biqqur Holim, Dinei Rofe, §1, and the commentary of the Maharil, cited by Hiddushei Raaq: "It is forbidden to try any of the medicines of the Talmud, because no man can know what constitutes their essence." This is to be understood either in accordance with Tosephot on BT *Mo'ed Qatan* 11a, and *Keseph Mishneh* on Maimonides (*Mishneh Torah, Hilkhot De'ot* 4), namely, that the context of talmudic medicine is the custom of the ancient Babylonians and is not valid for subsequent ages; or in accordance with Maimonides himself (*Mishneh Torah, Hilkhot Avodat Kokhavim* 11) and BT *Shevuot* 15b, where the use of sayings from the Torah in medical treatment is regarded as blasphemy because they were not given to cure existing wounds and diseases but rather to prevent them and, if necessary, to cure diseases of the soul.

53. See, for example, the autobiographical story of a female shaman from Mexico, and the function of the sacred tongue, made accessible by hallucinogenic mushrooms, in the practices of divination often aimed at healing the sick: *Maria Sabina, Her Life and Chants*, op. cit.

54. A. Koyré, relying on Duhem (*Système du Monde*) and Boll (*Astrology and Religion among the Greeks and Romans*), reminds us that "astrology was a perfectly reasonable and rational system; before Copernicus, believing in the influence of the stars was unavoidable for all who looked for and accepted scientific determinism in nature. Aristotle's cosmology, to consider only one example, necessarily implies astrology" (Koyré, *Mystiques, spirituels, alchimistes*).

55. BT *Shabbat* 156. In addition, the Maharal of Prague, in the sixteenth century, like Rashi and the Tosaphists in the eleventh, rejected the belief handed down from Greek philosophy, and universally accepted during the Middle Ages (even by some Jewish commentators), according to which the celestial bodies have a "spiritual" nature. (See Maharal of Prague, *The Book of Divine Powers. Introductions*, trans. S. Mallin [Jerusalem: Gur Aryeh International; and New York: Otzar Hasefarim, 1975], p. 34 and n. 10.)

56. BT *Berakhot* 33b.

57. Proverbs 1:7; Psalms 111:10.

58. See *Zohar*, Introduction, pp. 1b–2b.

59. Maharal of Prague, *Netivot Olam* (Prague, 1596), Chapter 1 ("Netiv Yir'at Hashem").

60. See the celebrated story of the controversy between an inspired sage, R. Eliezer ben Hyrcanus, and the majority of the Sanhedrin. R. Eliezer cited an opinion from "on high" as his reason for differing from them and managed to produce a miraculous sign (a heavenly voice) that asserted the correctness of his position. None of his opponents cast the slightest aspersions on the authenticity of this voice, nor on the profundity and truth of his inspiration; nevertheless, not only was his opinion rejected, he himself was excluded from the sessions of the Sanhedrin, because "the Torah is not in heaven" (BT *Baba Metsi'a* 59b).

61. Maharal, *Netivot Olam*, Chapter 14 ("Netiv ha-Torah").

62. This is not absolutely necessary, because a nontheological and non-heretical understanding of traditional Jewish doctrine is both desirable and possible. See H. Atlan, "Ce peuple qu'on dit élu," *Le Genre humain*, no. 3–4 (1982), pp. 98–126.

63. See Rashi's commentary on the verse, "in that [future] day there shall be one Lord with one name" (Zechariah 14:9).

64. "The Torah exists only through one who serves as an implement to make it exist," the kabbalistic reading by R. Hayyim Vital (*Etz Hayyim*, 5,9, third gloss on *tselem*) of the talmudic saying, "the words of the Torah exist only in [or through] those who kill themselves for [or over] them" (BT *Berakhot* 63b).

65. "Which no mouth can say and no ear can hear" (BT *Shevuot* 20b); see also Rashi's commentary on Psalms 62:12: "One thing God has spoken; two things have I heard," and on Exodus 20:8.

66. For the kabbalists, the performance of every duty and every action or word that fulfills a precept of the Law is prefaced by an Aramaic formula that can be approximately rendered as "in order to unite God and His presence."

67. Castoriadis, *The Imaginary Institution of Society*.

68. M. Bourgeois, "Control and Power: Two Modes of Information," in *Information and Systems*, ed. B. Dubuisson (Pergamon Press, 1978), pp. 1–10.

69. E. M. Barrister, "Sociodynamics: An Integrative Theorem of Power, Authority, Influence and Love," *American Sociological Review* 34, no. 3 (1969), pp. 374–393.

70. J. Baudrillard, *L'échange symbolique et la mort* (Paris: Gallimard, 1976).

71. On this de-alienating role of action, as opposed to fabrication, see J.-P. Dupuy, "L'information peut-elle sauver le monde?" in *Ordres et désordres*.

72. This attitude may concern not only scientific research but also some types of mystical rationales, as shown by the incident of R. Eliezer ben Hyrcanus (see n. 60) or perhaps certain lines followed by a rabbi of the early twentieth century, the kabbalistically inspired rationalist A. I. Kook, for whom knowledge as truth (and not knowledge *of* Truth) appears more as a desire for knowledge than as a definitive body of information (see Atlan, *Entre le cristal et la fumée*, p. 246, n. 5).

73. Marcuse, *One-Dimensional Man*.

74. See, among others, the superb analysis by Edgar Morin, *La nature de l'U.R.S.S.* (Paris: Fayard, 1983).

75. Castoriadis, *The Imaginary Institution of Society*.

76. The classic *na'aseh ve-nishma*, "First we will do and then we will understand," of Jewish tradition (Exodus 24:7) can be understood not as an enthusiastic act of faith but as a description of an ineluctable progression: individual and social teaching, and the ethical system that flows from them, can start only from practical modes of conduct organized on the basis of preexisting norms and not from the theoretical reasoning by a philosopher who is endeavoring to establish a social order on the basis of reason.

77. All this ultimately leads to the emergence of the judicial norm, a vast question that we lack the means to deal with here, particularly in modern societies where existing laws, inherited from tradition, are continually modified as a result of sociocultural pressure.

78. It would seem that this vision of reality, for all that it may shock a theological and dogmatic mind, is not foreign to kabbalistic thought. We read in the *Zohar*: "God and the Torah are the same thing," and also that the Torah and Israel, as the people who bear it, are one (quoted and commented upon by R. Schneour Zalman of Lyady, *Tanya*, Chapter 5); or again: "God, the Torah, and Israel are attached to one another and do not separate from one another (*Zohar*, 3, 73a, cited and commented upon by R. Hayyim of Volozhin, *Nefesh Hahayyim*, 1, Chapter 16).

79. Ecclesiastes 2:13. Even though the sage is no less deceived than the rest of the world by the vanity of his actions, nevertheless "wisdom is superior to folly," even though "the same fate awaits them both...and [wisdom] too is futile."

80. Genesis 2:9.

81. Whether naively and absolutely or apparently critical, it comes down to the same thing, like Sartre and an entire generation of intellectuals for whom Marxism was the impassable horizon of our modern age.

82. See especially the role of this "principle of synchronicity" in the function of the actual unifying cement employed by the Jungian psychoanalysts at the Cordoba colloquium.

83. Pecker, "L'astrologie et la science."

84. See Yehuda Elkana, "The Myth of Simplicity," in *Albert Einstein: Historical and Cultural Perspectives* (The Centennial Symposium in Jerusalem), ed. Gerald Holton and Yehuda Elkana (Princeton, N.J.: Princeton University Press, 1982), pp. 205–251.

"That the totality of our sense-experience is such that they can be arranged in an order by means of thinking...is a fact which strikes us with amazement, but which we shall never be able to comprehend" (A. Einstein, "Physik und Realität," *Journal of the Franklin Institute* 221 [1936], p. 315, trans. Ilse Rosenthal-Schneider, cited by Elkana in *Einstein*, p. 247).

"The most beautiful and deepest experience a man can have is the sense of the mysterious. It is the underlying principle of religion as well as of all serious endeavour in art and in science.... He who never had this experience seems to me, if not dead, then at least blind. The sense that behind anything that can be experienced there is a something that our mind cannot grasp and whose beauty and sublimity reaches us only indirectly and as feeble reflexion, *this is religiousness*. In *this* sense I am religious. To me it suffices to wonder at these secrets and to attempt humbly to grasp with my mind a mere image of the lofty structure of all that there is." (Albert Einstein, "My Credo," recorded at the "initiative of the German League for Human Rights," Berlin, autumn 1932. German text published by Friedrich Harneck, *Naturwissenschaften* 1 (1965), p. 98; trans. from catalogue of the National and Hebrew University Library Einstein Centennial Exhibition; cited by Elkana, *Einstein*, p. 240).

Chapter 7

# Man-as-Game
## (Winnicott, Fink, Wittgenstein)

> [One of the sages] was in the habit of beginning his
> lectures by telling a joke, and the others would all make
> merry [Rashi: their hearts were opened with joy]. Then
> he would sit in awe and lecture on the Law.
>
> —BT *Shabbat* 30b

### *"Is That Supposed to Be Serious?"*

Accepting that we must play the game of several different interpretive systems—scientific, philosophical, mystical, artistic—while taking care not to confuse their rules: this would be the correct attitude on the paths of knowledge for someone who wished to comply with the need for rigor and rationality and yet not close off the paths opened by different and specific forms of rationality (or of *alleged* irrationality, which comes down to the same thing, because it implies not cheating at the exercise otherwise recognized as rational), each for itself. This is a "correct" attitude not vis-à-vis a metarule derived from an unknown source, but in relation to a concern for fruitfulness, because we perceive that the best way to halt play is to break the rules of a game by imposing on it the rules of another game. But can one really speak of games? Is that really serious?

289

When we learn, by hearsay, of some discovery in a discipline not our own, we ask almost immediately: "Is that supposed to be serious?" The implication is that it could be a joke, a prank, or a hoax, when we are expecting honesty and truth that the seriousness of the information source and of the author of the discovery should guarantee as far as is possible. Is it serious to speak of games[1] when we are searching for serious knowledge? No, of course not, if we deem the seriousness of knowledge to be joyless, excluding humor and any opening toward the imaginary. But yes, of course it is, if we recognize—along with several philosophers, erroneously designated "irrational," of whom Nietzsche is perhaps the most famous if not the best known[2]—that there is no more serious human activity than play; if we do not confound the sense of the tragic with melancholy, if we take seriously—correctly—the tragedy of finite knowledge of an infinite reality, where frustration and limitation do not prevent joy, song and dance, the exultation of knowledge for its own sake.

When asked, "Is that supposed to be serious?" concerning a report of newly acquired knowledge, we should answer "No," if no hoax is involved; for hoaxes and lies are serious. Even if jokes and pranks are not serious, either, about their butts, the distance they establish between things and the words that speak them is the best guarantee against being entombed by a belief in an established theory, frozen into dogma. Inversely, with regard to the metalevel of judging a method, nothing is more serious than laughter if it is tragic laughter, that of someone who knows that he or she is laughing at the seriousness of reality precisely because it is too serious to be locked up in the serious and sad speech of the theoretician who believes in it.

These are not paradoxes. It may be another example of a change of sign along with a change of level.[3] In any case we must note that seriousness is not an a priori warrant of truth. One is tempted to opine just the contrary, given the seriousness of all hypocrites. Nothing is more serious than the games of knowledge, for their stakes are not beliefs—beliefs are not serious and do not require scientific research programs—but our very existence as living beings, members of the human species. Beyond every logical or metaphysical presupposition one can describe the ideas (the stakes of ideological debates and theoretical controversies) in our individual and social life as having the status of entitites with their own life, in symbiosis[4] with other living beings—the individual members of the human species whose brains are their indispensable substrates (just as, for example, bacteria symbiotically support viruses). Their proliferation, modification, and transmission from one human brain to another seem to obey the rules of their own life, different from that of the brain-endowed individuals without whom they cannot exist—a typical relationship of symbiosis between organisms of different species. Nothing is more misleading than to represent them as having a simple causal relationship with us, whether materialist (our ideas are secreted by our brains like the gastric juices by the stomach) or idealist (our ideas determine the reality of what we are by their influence on our beliefs and perceptions). The deceptive character of such representations appears with the experience of the game that effectively underlies all these "serious" activities through which our knowledge constitutes itself.[5]

We see, thus, that ideas do not have to be taken seriously. They are made so that one can play with them without taking them seriously—on condition that we take the game itself seriously. Only on this condition will they not imprison those in whom they have taken up residence so that they can effectively play their role of symbiont with our brains. By making the symbionts of three particular brains—Winnicott, Fink, and Wittgenstein—play a game among themselves we shall endeavor to juxtapose the experience of game-playing, in its relations with the real and the possible, with the superficial belief in the truth of doctrines or theories supposed to express Reality directly.

## Playing and Games

D. W. Winnicott, the child and adult psychoanalyst, has clearly underlined the difference, which English expresses so well, between two sorts of playing: *games*, which follow precise rules, and *creative* play, which obeys only imagination and the inspiration of the moment—children at play, discovering and inventing as they go along, to the point even of surprising themselves. For Winnicott this distinction is fundamental; its practice caused him to discover the irreplaceable function of the second sort of playing in the development of the child's personality, of its individuated self that is distinct from, but related to, the reality that is not it. From a state of nondifferentiation (and total dependence on mother), where world and self are a single whole, individuation takes place progressively thanks to the establishment of an intermediate space, "a third area of human living,"[6] "neither a matter of inner psychic reality nor a matter of external reality."[7] In this space, which Winnicott calls "transitional" space or "the potential space between the baby and the mother,"[8] the normal constitutive activity (which constructs it as a space) is playing, in which a particular object, apparently nothing special but nevertheless privileged (a doll, piece of cloth, stuffed rabbit, blanket, etc.), called the "transitional object," serves as a projection of the self while populating this space outside the body. The constructive function of the playing that makes this space exist, and its irreplaceable role in the development of the creative (and self-creative) faculties by which the child constitutes itself at once in separation from and union with its mother, clearly imply that it cannot be a *game* with preexisting rules, but only *playing*, where (to the eyes of an external observer) everything seems to occur randomly, with no a priori direction.[9] What is important for our purposes is that from here Winnicott was led to propose a theory of culture in which the elaborate activities of the adult as social being (hitherto described by psychoanalytic theory as sublimation activities) are the continuation, on another level, of this playing activity constitutive of the self.

This potential space is described as a "location of playing and cultural experience"[10] in all its aspects. Thus culture, as "an extension of the idea of transitional phenomena,"[11] which designates "that in which we pass, in fact, most of our time when we take pleasure in what we are doing,"[12] has a mode of existence that is neither within nor outside the individual, in the world of shared reality, continuing the critical but relatively long period of progressive separation of the non-I and the I, in which everything rests on a relationship of confidence between baby and mother during the initial stages of the establishment of an autonomous self.

This continuity between children's play and the creative activities of adults has multiple aspects, particularly as it concerns the sense of reality or unreality of what (or who) is created (and self-created) in this way and the positive role of illusion in these processes. For Winnicott, the only difference between children's play and adults' play seems to be the disillusionment about creative "omnipotence" that arises and grows (often not without pain) during the maturation process. But this does not imply that these activities change their locus; they remain situated in that intermediate area between "the reality of the inside and the reality of the outside."[13]

General speaking, in the adult the organization of the self depends on the "resolution of the paradox" constituted by this state of simultaneous separation and union with the nonself, neither within nor without, or perhaps "real-unreal,"[14] which for Fink too, as we shall see, characterizes play. One encounters this paradox in all stages of development. It corresponds to the so-called sense of omnipotence produced in the infant by the appropriate response of the entire environment to expectations projected from within, "because of the mother's extremely sensitive adaptation to the needs of her baby, based on her identification with the baby."[15] It is this same state that is expressed in playing, subsequent to or integrated with transitional phenomena, when the infant constitutes its "self" with the creative faculties that will later permit it to be capable of being alone.

This faculty will appear in the adult to the extent that the child was himself capable of "playing alone under his mother's gaze."[16] It is the sine qua non for a creative attitude toward life, where the creativity of which

Winnicott speaks is not only and essentially, as C. Geets put it, "that of the finite product objectified in a work,"[17] but "creative apperception more than anything else that makes the individual feel that life is worth living."[18]

Finally, this same state of separation-union characterizes effective cultural creation for the adult and takes account of the fact "that in every cultural field *it is not possible to be original except on a basis of tradition.*"[19]

## Playing as the Symbol of the World

This "paradox" is at the heart of our cognitive activity and appears whenever we become aware, by one path or another, of its playful character, more serious than the ostensible seriousness of the learned knowledge that is taken seriously.[20] This activity, not in its results (which are always provisional), but in its dynamism, always amounts to playing with the possible. This is another form of the "game of possibles"[21] that nature plays in the multitude of living species that have appeared over the course of evolution. Here it is still nature that is playing, if you wish, but through the activity of our brains.

We have already encountered several of the logical difficulties posed by the mode of existence of these possible worlds. These difficulties, and the recourse to the experience of playing to describe them, if not to resolve them, is at the heart of philosophical enterprises as different as those of Eugen Fink and, again, Ludwig Wittgenstein.

Fink, a post-Heideggerian philosopher who derives his inspiration from Nietzsche and Heraclitus, sees in play, in all its aspects, especially that of the appearances of theatrical presentations, an object that is at once possible and "worthy of philosophy" even though it is "clearly an affair of childhood."[22] He responds with a resolute "yes" to the question: "Does play have a human reality worth mentioning beyond childhood?"[23] But he, too, does this in what seems to be a paradoxical fashion: the fundamental importance of playing as man's relationship with the world appears precisely in the *unreality* of playing, in its roots in the imaginary—the domain of infinite possibilities—in its gratuitous, useless aspect, which promises nothing, in its subsisting outside the chain of causes and effects and the sequence of purposeful action and meanings, through which we normally perceive the world as real and knowable.

This paradoxical state of play's reality-unreality permits Fink to take seriously the situation, itself paradoxical, of man in the world: playing is very real in the sense that it does exist and we all have experience of it as of one of our activities, fundamental for the child, derivative and apparently unimportant for the adult. But it is unreal in the sense that its content is unreal. It is an unreality—imaginary, an appearance—that is really lived. It is like an irruption—Fink says "reflection"—of something else into the midst of ordinary objects. For metaphysics it is *less* than ordinary sensible objects, indelibly marked by the disreputable place that Plato assigned to the arts and poetry as deformed and deceptive copies. For myth, however, it is *more* than ordinary objects, the realm of the sacred where, in the cultic game of antiquity, the divine epiphany took place as a sort of privileged intercourse with the divine powers, whereby the how of the hidden order of the world is represented and clearly intimated. For Fink, rejoining Heraclitus to discover the intuition of the world as its universal organizing power, this other thing is not an object, but the "totality of the world" (*Weltganze*).[24] For play is at the same time human and "cosmic" or "mundane": human, in that it involves human activity; mundane, in that it is the activity, through human beings and *constitutive of human beings* themselves, of what Fink calls the "world."

This is characterized by an "organizing omnipotence" that includes both what is possible and what is real, the effect of which is what he designates "individuation," that is, the appearance and disappearance of individuals. It is this same organizing power that Heraclitus called "fire, light, time, play, and reason...so many different names for the same cosmic activity,"[25] and of which human play is the "symbol," the "reflection" *in* the world. Thus Fink's work can be seen as a long commentary on the celebrated image of the "child at play" of Fragment 52 of Heraclitus.[26] Some have called it "Nature," or "Logos." Fink calls it the "totality of the world," which is other than an object in the world; and although he speaks of man's "ecstatic relationship"[27] with this totality of the world, he carefully distinguishes it from the gods of mythology, on the one hand, and from the personal God of the Occidental religious and metaphysical traditions, on the other.[28]

Precisely because we are not dealing here with a person—for persons themselves are in the world, real, sources of causal determinations and finalities, creators of meaning—the "reflection" in the world of this organizing power, game-playing, is quite useless, as viewed by "contemporary nihilism," "with a strange and enigmatic uselessness," "without reason and without end, without meaning and without goal, without plan and without value,"[29] gratuitous, light as the dance, "irresponsible," "unreal." The totality, whose symbol is the "reign of the child" at play, is opposed to the personal God conceived as an organizing power, like an adult for whom playing is not serious.[30] But as he attempts to characterize "what attributes of the world determine the playful character of human play," Fink must recognize, of course, that "to say it seriously is extremely difficult, even if only provisionally."[31] From this immensely rich essay we shall borrow here this aspect of real-unreal that characterizes play, due, inter alia, to its relationship with the totality of the world, where "possibles" have their place.[32] Creative play, although active power, appears "unreal" when contrasted with our experience of the reality of objects *in* the world, because playing is an experience not of objects in the world but of what permits objects to become real, to pass from potentiality to reality (whether contingently or necessarily). Thus playing is unreal because it is, in a certain fashion, more than real—surreal, the surrealists would say— by implying, in addition, the possible.

## Reality as a Reduction of "Possibles"

This same relationship between play and creative "organizing" omnipotence, which Winnicott established as a theory of child development, is also encountered down another, mirror-image, path, where the image of the child at play designates the organizing power, the process of "universal individuation":

> Playing becomes a "cosmic metaphor" for the total appearance and disappearance of objects.... The effervescent, intoxicated stream of life, which carries along living creatures in the joy of generation, is mysteriously one with the dark wave that propels the living into death. Life and death, birth and dying, womb and tomb, are intimately related to one another: it is the same active power of the All that produces and annihilates, generates and kills, unites utter joy and deepest sadness.

From the perspective of our experience of reality, however, these unions take place in an "unreal fashion," in the world-game whose reflection in reality is play (theatrical or cultural).

> "Were it not for Dionysus that they conducted the procession and sang the phallic hymn"—we read in Heraclitus Fragment 15—"it would be the most shameless activity. But Hades is the same as Dionysus, for anyone who is struck by the bacchic frenzy." The god of erotic rapture is at the same time the god of death; but he is also the god of the mask and the game.[33]

If we would understand, outside the context of the Heraclitan verses, how this organizing power of the whole, responsible for individuation— that is to say, in a certain manner for the rupture of the whole and for multiplicity as a universal characteristic of reality (the paradox of these expressions is evident)—how this power appears with this paradoxical aspect of real-unreal or of real unreality, we must observe how things become real, how the real emerges through a process of the *reduction and elimination of possibilities*. To the extent that imagination and memory give us access, as thinking and knowing beings, to the domain of possibilities, while with our senses we perceive the domain of the real, we find ourselves in this peculiar situation where we can essay in our life this simultaneously creative and death-dealing reduction.

We encounter this paradoxical state of real-unreal when our sensory experiences and our thought of possibilities intermingle in our life, which we perceive as being *itself* both "self-realization" and "a retrenchment of our possibilities."[34]

## The Opportunities Provided by Modern Atheism

As we see, Fink keeps brushing up against myth and religion, but only to separate himself from them, as a child of the century of modern atheism and contemporary nihilism. For this unreality is a separate precinct within reality, a distinct domain, just like that of the sacred and the symbolic. But whereas the sacred games of the cults of antiquity used the gods as intermediaries, superior to human beings by virtue of their creative and generative faculties, based on their share of the organizing power of the world, the modern "god-vacuum" constitutes the "good fortune"[35] of modernity that we ought to see as the backdrop of so-called nihilist philosophies. For us, the fact that modern culture, scientific, technical, and philosophical, has banished the pagan gods offers the "chance" of de-alienation—but not that proposed by the naive positivist humanism that would replace the gods with human beings. The disappearance of the gods from our environment, progressively less natural and more manufactured, renders the sacred less and less momentous in our industrial and postindustrial urban societies. For this reason, however, play acquires greater importance for those able to engage in it despite the absence of divinity: the play is no longer the epiphany of a god, unquestionably superior to man although sharing his condition of being an object within the world, exalted and personified; it is rather a symbol, in the sense of a reflection of or opening to this cosmic activity that is imperfectly designated by the words "fire, light, time, play, and reason."

If the symbol is a finite object that represents the infinite universe,[36] the need to take account, in some fashion or other (metaphoric, "symbolic"), of the totality of this infinite world, which cannot be experienced as an object can, derives from our situation as individuals endowed with a cognitive faculty, "open to understanding" and provided with reason such that "the thought of the 'All' does not let go of us," because "it is the peculiar destiny of our human reason to be troubled and always overwhelmed by the thought of the totality of everything that exists."[37] For this same reason, and because of this same cognitive faculty, we cannot stop classifying and ordering phenomena; we explain them and interpret them on the basis of prephilosophical projections that institute, for Kant, "the conditions and possibilities of experience," the "hierarchy of things,"[38] according to which "more" or "less" being is ascribed to them and they are perceived and thought as closer to truth and wisdom, farther from illusion and folly, more "worthy" of being the objects of philosophy. But if Kant *posed* the problem of a priori thought of the world, Fink finds his "solution" less important, because, "for Kant, 'world' ultimately becomes something subjective, a 'regulating idea' which we cannot do without in order to direct the course of experience, and which we never know how to 'ransom' and realize in actual experience."[39] Fink finds this ransom in the "game as symbol of the world." Moreover, modern culture, rational, productive, and demystifying, enables us to have a better appreciation of this reflection of the word in play, avoiding the state of alienation in which we were held by divine mediation degenerated into religion. The prospect of modern atheism resides

> in a possible openness to the world, which is no longer "mediated" through some supreme Being and is no longer feigned by that mediation. Profound thought about human play leads to such an openness to the world, if it is totally severed from its cultic origins and—what is even more important—if this severing is not effected as a profanation of the cultic play.... To the extent that the profane belongs to the sacred, like shadow to light, profane play cannot be the reference for the question about the worldliness of human play; only play that is neither sacred nor profane can do this.... The world itself is neither holy, like God, nor unholy, like blasphemous man; it is "beyond" such differences.[40]

In other words, modern culture, founded essentially on post-Nietzschean philosophy and critical and scientific reason, offers us the best chance of liberating ourselves, not so much by profaning and forgetting religion—for these activities still belong to the dimension of the sacred—as by play, which we would be better able to perceive, without mediation and feigning, as in an "ecstatic relationship with the game of the world."[41]

## Language Games:
## An Alternative to the Disclosure of Ultimate Reality

But what kind of playing are we talking about? Theatrical plays, comedy and tragedy, of course; but also backgammon and all other games properly so called, of children and adults; those of art; and, finally, those of science.

Here we have an alternative to the habitual conception according to which our knowledge reveals the hidden order of things. For when one recognizes the fundamental role of play, whether from the point of view of developmental psychology or of some philosophy of being in the world, one cannot avoid finding all the characteristics of ludic activity in our rational cognitive activity. Its relationship with the world of possibilities gives it its aspect of "unreality" or of lesser reality, as compared with the immediate data of our senses. We have seen that the privileged status of causal relations probably derives from their greater proximity to our immediate perception of temporal succession. In other words, our impression that causality exists in reality—*pace* Wittgenstein's aphorism that it is a "superstition"—is justified by the exercise of our memory, which makes us perceive the succession of events in time with *almost* as much intensity and "presence" as pertain to what we perceive directly, in the present, through our senses. But this is only a difference of degree, with combinations of relations, greater and greater abstractions, permitting us to reason with the greatest rationality in the world about unreal data that we can think of only as possible, in both of the senses we have already indicated.

Alongside this aspect of manipulating possibles, it is worth noting that our cognitive activities, rational or otherwise, include the entire gamut of traits that characterize different types of games: ranging from games with precise and rigorous rules[42] that call into play only intellectual faculties of analysis, synthesis, cleverness, and guile, or physical dexterity and skill, or a combination of the two; through games of chance where the rules exist only to "give meaning" (of greater or lesser gain or loss) to the verdicts of fate; and, finally, to games with no rules whatsoever, at least not a priori, where, as in those of children, the players create the world at will, as their imagination moves them, changing the meanings of objects, words, and relations with no restrictions. When one is dealing with forms of knowledge elaborated by means of reason and expressed by more or less formalized languages, it is difficult to imagine that they provide us with any direct access to the reality of things, even if their starting point in observation and their return (and recourse) to experience somewhat attenuate the abstract, imaginary, and "unreal" nature of the concepts they devise. This naive realism, with which we have all grown up and which seems self-evident, is merely the result of adopting what is ultimately an idealist position (even concerning "materialist" theories), subordinating the being of things to our thought, provided the latter is rational.

Gregory Bateson[43] was rightly astonished that we consider it self-evident that nature must be rational. We have seen previously that no a priori logically "decidable" response to this question is possible. This question cannot be asked except implicitly, starting from scratch each time, like a wager, in the process of our rational activity that tries its skill at making contact with what we perceive of the world and endeavors to grasp this reality. The game-playing alternative allows us to escape this question in its explicit, metaphysical form and go around it by demonstrating that it is not inevitable; that it is dependent on a certain metaphysics and becomes irrelevant in the light of a conception of the world—formerly pre-Socratic and mythical—that our culture is today reviving and refining, because of the paradox of its simultaneously "nihilist" and scientific aspects. "Metaphysics could fully realize its world-conception of a rational universal hierarchy of being only by repressing the view that the totality of the world acts like a game. 'Rational order' or 'game'—that was precisely the question."[44]

With regard to the *telos* of a living organism—an anthropomorphic question if there ever was one, but which continues to haunt biology despite its most reductionist aspects—a number of metaphoric answers have been proposed: "A bacterium dreams of becoming two bacteria," said François Jacob, to which Edgar Morin replied: "Why not to enjoy its own metabolism?" I have suggested that its "goal" is neither one nor the other, but rather to attain a state of thermodynamic equilibrium, like any spontaneously evolving physical system.[45] And now it is proposed that this dream might be to "play like a child," such that the dialectic of death and chaos employed by life would be only the imprint of the uselessness and gratuity of this game. This vision of things is opposed to that of a preestablished ("programmed") purposeful harmony that would explain the adaptation of living creatures to their environment. On the other hand, it allows us a better understanding of their capacity for adaptation, just because of the "useless," unintentional nature of the game, which always triumphs as long as the game goes on, even if its rules are modified along the way.

If we absolutely insist on considering that the order of things is the result, or imprint, or reflection of some kind of thought, then analogical and metaphorical thought, logically "incorrect"[46]—that of poets and schizophrenics—is at least as likely a candidate as rational thought.

We are assuming the contrary when we project our rationality on nature, particularly on that of living creatures. We attribute to it a logic and a rationality that make it possible to explain behavior and strategies in which chains of causes and effects are supposed to function "correctly" from the perspective of our rational thought, logically adapting ends and means, in the way we have conceived and built our artificial machines, adapted to their functions.[47] H. Simon's work on "the science of the artificial,"[48] as well as the cybernetic "tradition" that views living beings as natural machines, both by projective analogy and by their *difference* from artificial machines,[49] demonstrates that this projection is effective as a heuristic procedure; that is, as a research method based on taking into account what is not known in the very process of knowledge. But to take this seriously and humorlessly, extending this projection beyond its legitimate domain, which is that circumscribed by the manipulative effectiveness of models that simplify the complexity of reality, inevitably leads to untenable metaphysical positions; untenable because they are merely dogmas that are themselves either contradictory or incomplete when compared with the richness of lived experience, like the bygone "rational" theologies. Rather than seeing this sort of thought at work in nature, either as a "cosmic consciousness" based on our experience of our own voluntary actions or as "a rational order," a "cosmic reason," based on our experience of our rational thought, the theory of game-playing as symbol of the world seems preferable to me, if one absolutely insists on navigating in these waters of generalization and the absolute, where only a sense of humor can save us from drowning and asphyxiation. If we must speak of the creative logos (perhaps because it speaks to us, or because we hear voices), then we should at least see it neither as Reason, nor as Consciousness, but as a game—eminently real—*with* possibles, in which our rational activity itself takes part by inventing rules: those of the multiple games of reason.

Here we again encounter Winnicott's distinction between playing and games, but turned on its head. Our adult activity, unlike the self-creative play of the child, cannot be creative except through the rules that must be respected in order to keep on playing the games instituted by these rules. For in the interim the child has become an adult; and this was possible only thanks to the (social) acquisition of language.

## Real and Unreal in Language

Vis-à-vis reality, language, too, has a particular status, real-unreal, because it must both *designate* real objects (to permit their manipulation) and *create* meanings, forms, and imaginary beings. Moreover, as the nexus of body and mind,[50] language is today viewed in its function as foundation—not philosophically, as the rational ground of things, but existentially and biologically, as the sine qua non for the development of individual human beings. Psychoanalysis and developmental psychology have extensively demonstrated how the acquisition of language is the foundation on which the ego is constituted and without which adult life, closed up in psychosis, is merely a form of death. As such, language functions more as the foundation of a structure (the self) than as the rational foundation of ostensible Truth (of the subject and the world). By making it possible to conceal[51] what psychoanalysts call the "truth of the subject," the acquisition of language permits the child to constitute itself as a being that is at once separate and connected, autonomous and social. Moreover, contrary to what one might believe under the influence of formalizing linguistic theories, what grounds language is not a priori rational truth—in that case its ideal form would be that of a formal, logico-mathematical language or grammar—but rather the practice of human development and experience, which organizes itself hand in hand with language itself.[52]

The attempts to formalize language[53] have taught us that what resists formalization is its semantic component, by which phrases have or acquire a meaning. Phonetics and syntax, on the other hand, can be easily represented by an artificial language, perhaps logico-mathematical, usable by a computer. The polysemic richness of natural languages, rooted in the pragmatic contexts of their use, which render formalization difficult if not indeed impossible, is often considered to be of recent date—as if the earliest forms of natural language must have been closer to formal languages, because we deem the latter to be simpler (to formalize), whereas polysemy is the result of progressive enrichment. Hence the literal sense would be primary and determined by our hypothetical innate language "organ," and the metaphorical meanings, although we use them all the time and quite "naturally" in everyday life, would be secondary, acquired through later experiences of life in society. This notion undoubtedly contradicts the fact that logico-mathematical language is acquired later, at the cost of greater or lesser effort, such that patent inequalities appear among adults with regard to mastering it. Some are open to it, learn it, understand it, and manipulate it; others, by their own testimony, "have never understood anything, or hardly anything, in mathematics." The use of natural language, however, does not lead to such disparities of learning. Today it is easier to conceive of an inversion of the process, such that undifferentiated polysemy and the metaphoric meaning come first, part of the child's use of natural language, and the unique and unambiguous literal sense appears only later, by elimination, culminating in the acquisition of the most univocal language there is, the logico-mathematical, from which all ambiguity and all polysemy have been purged. Here too we have *a reduction of possibles*, progressive elimination of all the initially possible meanings inhering in natural language before the attempt to use precise and univocal definitions, under the influence of education.[54]

In the general movement of individuation, this process is the reduction of possibilities characteristic of maturation and growing older. At the same time, as Fink has shown us, play as a cosmic (natural) activity effected through human beings can liberate us from this process of reduction by relinking us, even if in an "unreal" (artificial) manner, with possibilities whose exclusion would have otherwise been constrained by the necessities of practical life. This is why *Homo ludens* creates more or less artificial languages in which meanings are created by more or less artificial contexts, frames of reference about which a partial consensus can be obtained, whether this creation is effected conventionally and explicitly, as in the games of scientific knowledge, or implicitly, as in Wittgenstein's language games, with their self-constituted rules, played within various domains of social activity whose limits are circumscribed by the same movement. Thus we pass from the *game of language*, a game of possibilities whose counters are drawn from the undifferentiated polysemy of the child's language, of dreams and poetry, to the *language games* of adults in society, where the multiplicity of domains, each of which institutes its own rules of meaning, provides some sort of guarantee against an excessively univocal reduction of the field of possibilities.

It should be noted, moreover, that the ultimate perfection of this process of "reduction of possibles" is a formal logico-mathematical language in which all efforts are directed at obtaining a unique and unambiguous meaning that can be attributed to everything spoken or written; at the same time, this formal language is characterized by the total elimination of any effect of the particular meaning of symbols. All that remains are the meanings of relations, that is, the aggregate of syntactic rules for manipulating symbols and composing propositions.

A number or $x$ can designate anything and hence has no particular signification; it is ready to acquire any and all meanings we give it, in whatever particular use we make of it. Meaning inheres only in the relationships that make it possible to write the propositions that contain them, such as equalities, inequalities, assertions of existence or nonexistence, and the like. These relationships themselves are only rules for constructing these propositions on the basis of a number of initial propositions that, resting on the principles of identity and noncontradiction, constitute the axioms of the formal language in question. Thanks to this absence of particular a priori meanings, in the sense of particular referents of the symbols used, the mathematical formalism can be used, in the case of any theory, physical or otherwise, to "make it work" and endow it with the status of a mathematical model of one segment of reality. This segment is of course clearly differentiated and circumscribed (unlike the formalism) by definitions, referents, and operational identifications. As A. Lichnerowicz puts it: "The axioms of a new theory in fact spring from the pure imagination of a theorizing mind; only later do we make the theory work mathematically and compare it with experience, the axioms appearing only as 'the rules of the royal game' (to use an expression of Einstein's) played by the scientist."[55]

In other words, in the fabrication of logico-mathematical formal languages from which every ambiguity of meaning has been eliminated, the reduction to a unique and unambiguous meaning—that of the formalized proposition making it possible to apply thereafter, if appropriate, an unequivocal true/false decision criterion when it is projected on a given concrete situation—involves eliminating meanings from the world as part of the process of constructing formulas, as long as one remains at the abstract level of construction.

Thus it is as if the world of meanings exists *only* in polysemy and metaphor, as if every literal meaning is at the same time metaphorical;[56] such that the reduction to a single, literal, nonmetaphoric and unambiguous meaning is tantamount to the elimination of all meaning. This is another way of saying that the world of meanings of natural language is only pragmatic and concrete. It can escape the total arbitrariness of the infinitude of possibilities only by virtue of the spatially and temporally limited consensus of individuals who agree to cut out from within this infinity and circumscribe domains of application, frames of reference that spawn the rules of the particular language game that this domain institutes by being separated out. The rules of any particular language game are instituted by this dissection, along with its own circumscribed domain of application. Whether this institution, this definition of the rules of the game, explicitly goes all the way and is unambiguous—as in the extreme case of mathematical language—or whether it is only implicit and always susceptible to modification without a priori knowledge of this (games whose players change the rules)—as in the natural-language games—is merely a question of degree, within the same process of instituting rules for games by circumscribing the fields of possibility in which these rules can—by convention—be applied. Wittgenstein's general term "language games" is extremely apt, because it also takes in "one of those games by means of which children learn their native language," as well as "the whole, consisting of language and the actions into which it is woven,"[57] always manifesting "the fact that the *speaking* of language is part of an activity, or of a form of life."[58] Wittgenstein, enumerating the multiplicity of language games in a series of examples,[59] adds an ironic comparison of the many types of words and phrases, seen as tools used in language through different ways of using it, with what logicians have been able to say about the structure of language ("including the author of the *Tractatus Logico-Philosophicus*"[60]).

## A Review of the Possible and the Logical

L inking up with the end of the *Tractatus*, the "second" Wittgenstein observes that the order of logic is in fact the order of possibilities and at the same time the order of the most concrete world there is. But this observation that the order of logic is "the order of *possibilities*, which must be common to both world and thought,"[61] collides with our need as logicians ("including the author of the *Tractatus*") to search for "the crystalline purity of logic."[62] If this primordial logic must precede all experience, if its order must be "*utterly simple*...no empirical cloudiness or uncertainty can be allowed to affect it.—It must rather be of the purest crystal."[63] At the same time, however, it is not an abstraction, precisely the one we think we see when we observe the world through "the strict and clear rules of the logical structure of propositions."[64]

The illusion of the logician-philosopher consists of believing that this crystalline and unclouded purity was the "result of study" when it was in fact "necessity"; it is itself illusory, because "there must be perfect order even in the vaguest sentence."[65] This contradictory necessity, which is also that of the *Tractatus* (sections 2.012, 2.013, 2.014), is equivalent to a wish to identify the two types of possibility discussed previously: the logically possible (that is to say, the noncontradictory) and what is possible in material reality. Like every logician-philosopher concerned with the possible, or with "possible worlds"[66]—but still leaving the door open for what cannot be said but only "shown"[67]—the philosopher of the *Tractatus* posits this identification, necessary if one would have the order of logic able to describe the order of things. But he knows that there is no identity between the content of a logical description—the "picture" (2.1) within which natural laws appear, or again the "sufficiently fine square mesh" that constitutes the "description of the world" (6.341) by projecting it on and covering reality like a surface that can be seen only through this mesh—and the reality of the things thereby described: between natural laws and objects in the world.[68] "Laws like the principle of sufficient reason, etc., are about the net and not about what the net describes" (6.35).

> There is no compulsion making one thing happen because another has happened. The only necessity that exists is *logical* necessity.
>
> The whole modern conception of the world is founded on the illusion that the so-called laws of nature are the explanation of natural phenomena.
>
> Thus people today stop at the laws of nature, treating them

as something inviolable, just as God and Fate were treated in past ages.

And in fact both are right and both wrong: though the view of the ancients is clearer insofar as they have a clear and acknowledged terminus, while the modern system tries to make it look as if *everything* were explained. (6.37, 6.371, 6.372)

In fact, even while recognizing that "logic pervades the world: the limits of the world are also its limits" (5.61) and that one cannot escape it, one has merely to relativize logic in order to deprive this identification between logically possible and really possible of its inevitability. We need only realize that several "possible worlds" exist that are not inside logic and created by logical laws, just as there are several possible logics and perhaps no logic at all. It is *possible* for us to conceive (and even experience) a reality that is contradictory and thus logically impossible! We have this experience whenever we encounter phenomena for which we can give no rational explanation, because they seem to contradict what we know of reality (the idea we form of it for ourselves). The scientific process reposes on our faith in our ability to resolve these contradictions one day. But there is no guarantee of this. Nothing forces us to this act of faith, and a contradictory reality remains a possibility, even if it is not logically possible.[69] Nothing permits the affirmation that possible worlds, where the laws of logic would not be applicable—contradictory worlds[70]—do not "exist," even though it is precisely the mode of existence of the possible, as compared with that of the real, that is in question.[71]

This is what Wittgenstein is suggesting when he states: "The exploration of logic means the exploration of everything that is subject to law. And outside logic everything is accidental" (6.3).[72] And again, when he questions questions themselves: "Does it make any sense to ask what there must be in order that something can be the case?" (5.5542). This question, too, whose own meaning is being questioned by Wittgenstein, proceeds from the a priori identification of the two types of possibility. It implies the idea that something *can* be the case only if it is logically able to be the case, and thus that this something must have a certain type of being in order to be *logically* possible. Otherwise, this something *could not be* the something that is the case. But this type of being would not prevent it from possibly being the case, either really, if someone later experiences it, or in potential, before it is the case. If in potential, this something remains in the order of the possible, even if "what there must be" does not obey what it would have to be so that this something *could be* what is the case!

This is why, with the "second" Wittgenstein (whose negative image was of course already present in the "first," in the paradoxical character of the "nonsense" of the *Tractatus* resulting from what the *Tractatus* says [see 6.54]), and in opposition to our need for "crystalline purity," we must admit that the "perfect order" that exists in natural language, as evinced by the very fact that we understand it,[73] must exist "even in the vaguest sentence."[74] Here we find the same inversion of the process that we spoke of earlier. In Wittgenstein it is manifested by a reversal of his explicit attitude concerning natural language. He starts out from daily language as "part of the human organism...not less complicated than the latter" and consequently a travesty of thought, it being understood once and for all that we can think only logically[75] and that only a logically perfect language can express thought in a meaningful manner or can perfectly realize the function of language "to affirm or deny facts," as Russell states without discussion in his introduction to the *Tractatus*. Eventually Wittgenstein recognizes this same daily language as no less perfect than the ideal language constructed by the logician. In fact, this about-face has to do with the limits of logic. Because he initially designated it the ineffable, the mystic element, that which cannot be demonstrated, the transcendental character of logic, it is not astonishing that Wittgenstein, after his long silence, could begin to speak again only through the theory or dimension of language games. In effect, the search for logical perfection encountered its limits with regard to concepts or pseudo-concepts that have in common an uncertainty about the reality of what they designate: "the scaffolding of the world" described by logical propositions collides with *totality, negation,* and the order of *possibles* (6.124).

As compared with the reality that can be described by the projection of a logically perfect language upon the factual world, here we are dealing with pseudo-concepts that display an "unreal reality" that conditions this language without being speakable by it.[76]

## Games of Knowledge and Language; Domains of Legitimacy

On the other hand, recognition of the perfect character of daily language (even in its vaguest phrases), viewed as a series of games adapted to limited ends, consists of positing game-playing as the symbol, in Fink's sense, of *negation* and *possibility,* unreal-realities that make up the *totality* of the world. This represents a change of the perspective from which we perceive reality, or an inversion of the same type we encountered with regard to nature and the processes of this perception. It involves a transition from one form of intelligence to another, from the philosophy of Being and Identity to that of becoming and change, from certain knowledge to approximate and conjectural knowledge; from science that has a relationship with "an order conceived as already inaugurated and henceforth definitively fixed and stable,...[which] spells out the future as if it were already written,...[expressing] what will be as if it were what is"[77]—and in which, as "in logic[,] process and result are equivalent. (Hence the absence of surprise.)"[78]—to knowledge by crafty knowledge,[79] the cunning reason of the artisan,[80] the "wisdom of the left side."[81] This is the domain of Metis, in which the future is "seen from the point of view of its uncertainties: her pronouncements are hypothetical or problematical statements.... She tells of the future not as something already fixed but as holding possible good or evil fortunes and her crafty knowledge reveals the means of making things turn out for the better rather than for the worse."[82] This is the mode of knowledge by agile and subtle intelligence, resourceful and improvising, which defies preestablished rules if modifying them proves fruitful for achieving the goal in view; it is the mode of knowledge for those who allow no other field of action than that of "Becoming, of change and of that which never remains the same as itself."[83]

These latter, opponents of Socratic philosophy (which banishes them to the disparaged domain of opinion), include the sophist, the physician, and the politician, all of them champions of this practical, conjectural, and "stochastic" intelligence;[84] that is to say, ultimately, they include those for whom the initial paradigmatic and grounding experience is not geometry but life, the complexity of the human organism and its productions. Metaphorically, and not without irony, we can note the return of the image of the net, used by Wittgenstein to depict the relationship between logical laws and reality, in which the former "are about the net and not about what the net describes."[85] The image of being trapped in the net is one of the most persistent symbolic representations of the craft and cleverness of Metis, in which "the true and the false are closely linked"[86] and the bond serves simultaneously to circumscribe and to entangle.

It is this same about-face that Wittgenstein makes in his later works. Setting out from the "crystalline" idea that "a sentence must nevertheless have *a* definite sense. An indefinite sense...would really not be a sense *at all*,"[87] he subsequently recognizes that this idea stems from the same illusion, caused by our need for purity and the ideal, which makes us refuse to consider a game to be one if we find "some vagueness *in the rules*."[88] Here Wittgenstein is describing his own progress, because the *Tractatus*, too, begins from this illusion: "The general form of a proposition is: This is how things stand (*Tractatus* 4.5). —This is the type of proposition that one repeats to oneself all the time. One thinks that one is tracing the design of the nature of the thing, still and always, when one is simply in the process of sketching out the limits of the framework through which we see it."[89]

Having fallen silent because "what we cannot speak about we must pass over in silence,"[90] when Wittgenstein decides nevertheless to speak again of what "cannot" be spoken, it is only normal that he hit on the idea—the symbol—of the game as an interspace, real and unreal, which one speaks about in language as a game even though one "cannot" speak about it! Consequently, he assigns the philosopher a new task: to deal with the engine "at full speed," and not only when "idling," with what exists *before* logical-mathematical language has caused the contradictions to disappear.

> It is the business of philosophy, not to resolve a contradiction by means of a mathematical or logico-mathematical discovery, but to make it possible for us to get a clear view of the state of mathematics that troubles us: the state of affairs *before* the contradiction is resolved....
>
> *The fundamental fact here is that we lay down rules, a technique, for a game, and that then when we follow the rules, things do not turn out as we had assumed* [emphasis mine]. That we are therefore as it were entangled in our own rules.
>
> This entanglement in our rules is what we want to understand (i.e., get a clear view of).
>
> It throws light on our concept of *meaning* something. For in those cases things turn out otherwise than we had meant, foreseen. That is just what we say when, for example, a contradiction appears: "I didn't mean it like that."
>
> The civil status of a contradiction, or its status in civil life: there is the philosophical problem.[91]

In this original character, the object of philosophical study resembles the object of children's games as a primal activity—not only the games by which they learn their mother tongue, but every vaguely defined game, physical or otherwise, for which the *question of their rules crops up*. Take, for example, "a game played by children: they say that a chest, for example, is a house; and thereupon it is interpreted as a house in every detail."[92] This character of being simultaneously a (closed) game with rules and an (open and creative) game without rules—both game and play—is very important for what interests us here, namely, our games of knowledge, which are played by adults who once upon a time constituted themselves by means of children's game-playing. The entanglement in the rules of knowledge that we have postulated for ourselves becomes a creative activity when seen through this "analogy between language and games."

We can easily imagine people amusing themselves in a field by playing with a ball so as to start various existing games, but playing many without finishing them and in between throwing the ball aimlessly into the air, chasing one another with the ball and bombarding one another for a joke, and so on. And now someone says: The whole time they are playing a ball-game and following definite rules at every throw.

And is there not also the case where we play and—make up the rules as we go along? And there is even one where we alter them—as we go along.[93]

If we recognize, along with Wittgenstein, the "illuminating character of this analogy" and discard the illusion that underlies belief in the universality of a certain type of rule we happen to use in scientific and philosophical enterprises that aim at uncovering the Truth of things or the Ultimate Reality of the universe, what remains of this undertaking is a labor of dissecting out and limiting possibilities, by means of rules. These rules themselves define, inside each domain that *they*[94] institute, the "form of the particular representation" that permits that picture to have something in common with the reality of things. Other rules would institute a different form of representation, which would allow a different picture to have something—different—in common with reality.[95] Working this way, dissecting out restricting possibilities, is like dealing with this real unreality of play. When we note the role of language in this task, it strikes us as being, of all human activities, the arena where this cosmic game, this game of man as "symbol of the world," is played out most fully; it is both a means of our openness to the world of relation—of *knowledge*—and a power that organizes and structures ourselves and our reality.

In the game of language, too, this activity appears as a game of possibles, played with possibles, a back-and-forth game of reducing possibilities to reality, followed by the breakdown of reality into new possibilities.[96] Note that this conception is the most realist and least naively functionalist there is. For Russell and many philosophers, the role of language is to state what is. For psychologists and psychosociologists, the function of language is to permit communication within human societies. But why should people "say what is"? Why was human language necessary as a mode of communication, when animal and even vegetable languages do quite well? Rather than trying to provide an a posteriori justification of what exists through a demonstration that it could only be this way, or arbitrarily deciding that the "obvious" goal of an organism is "surviving," or "reproducing its genome," or what have you, we ought to consider that, for human organisms, the function of language, like that of the nervous system, the digestive system, the cardiovascular system, and so forth, is to further the auto-organization of an organism endowed with these faculties of digestion, information processing, circulation, and respiration, as well as speaking and writing.

Language games, like the world-symbol game, are what remain and are discovered if one pushes modern atheism to the end, that is, to the desanctification of the "so-called laws of nature."[97] Nevertheless, these language games, like all *adult* games, must be games with rules, even if the rules can change in mid-match. For adult play necessarily has a different character than the child's creative and indefinite play (what Winnicott calls "playing"). It is located somewhere between playing and games, between playing, in which *everything* is possible (because of the absence of rules or rules that change all the time) in the infinite and unformed original chaos, and rule-bound games (more or less inflexible, depending on the type of game and the relative importance it ascribes to luck, physical prowess and skill, cleverness, and inductive and deductive reason). The child's acquisition of language is also accompanied by a reduction of possibilities—on a metalevel this time: the metalevel of rules that are initially, when the child "plays alone (without speaking) under his mother's gaze," of infinite diversity and are then reduced to a few that are maintained in relative fixity when it becomes a matter of group play and communication, in which a relative stability is necessary, if only to continue the game.

As constituted and constitutive language, and in order to constitute itself, the acquired language of the child, and later of the adult, limits its own creative power. This acquired language, while remaining in principle infinite, is nevertheless limited by whatever restricts the field of possibilities within language itself. In effect, *everything* is no longer possible, for, a priori, nothing in particular has—or still has—a meaning. The institution of language already limits the field of possibilities within its own rules, those by which a proposition does or does not have or acquire a meaning.

Thus it is as if the acquisition of language and physiological and social maturation, the passage from childhood to adulthood, are accompanied by a transformation of what nevertheless remains, after the elementary needs of nourishment and reproduction have been satisfied, the principal activity of human beings (and also, apparently, of many animals, as far as it is possible to judge from the anthropomorphic meaning of their behavior): game-playing. This is a passage from playing (without rules) to games, (*with* rules), even if the latter are less stimulating and are indeed obstacles and impediments to development when they prematurely replace creative play for the child. For Winnicott, this transformation can have a protective role, because the unformed character of the child's creative playing, nourished by the original chaos, can be a source of anguish if the child does not feel protected, come what may, under its mother's watchful eye: it must be recognized that "playing is always liable to become frightening.... The precariousness of play belongs to the fact that it is always on the theoretical line between the subjective and that which is objectively perceived." Hence "games and their organization must be looked at as part of an attempt to forestall the frightening aspect of playing."[98]

In consequence one can understand that mature and (self-) creative adults have internalized the mother's protective and regulatory role, which is manifested by the rules of the different games (language and other) in which their culture makes them participate. But too great a need for stability and security, excessive fear of the unknown and of disorder, can cause the playful character of the game to be forgotten, its rules to be absolutized and frozen; everything—the game, its rules, and the society of players—is finally and cheerlessly "taken seriously." By the same token, of course, not all adult activities, especially not social activities, can take place in what we see as the nondifferentiation, lability, and instability of children's play. It is this transition in the *mode* of playing—and thus on a metalevel above the interspace already constituted by playing itself—that we practice, with greater or lesser success, our knowledge activities. This is why, in these activities, we must posit and respect systems of rules. Like the sphere of the sacred, but "in another fashion," ludic activity institutes "through the medium of 'unreality'...the all-working totality within itself,"[99] within which we can play "legitimately" (if the term be allowed), that is, in a way that is both creative and stable. There we oscillate between two dangers that threaten to put an end to the game. One danger is universalizing and absolutizing one of these systems of rules, to the exclusion of all others; this entails a definitive curtailment of the reality of our experiences to the single closed domain instituted by these rules.[100] The other peril is falling back into the original nondifferentiation—into the shelter of a recreated mother and a primordial All represented, for example, by a church—by confounding all systems of rules, passing deliberately and without transition from one game to another, and finally forgetting that these are games whose rules we are breaking (just as a small child does not *yet* know that playing *can* have rules).

If we want to protect ourselves from these two dangers, we must always consider *at the same time* what is common to all and what is specific to each of our knowledge activities. What they have in common is that they are all games, games of divination or games of reason (whether following rational rules, in orthodox usages, or systematically transgressing such rules in paradoxical usages that function only in relationship to some orthodox usage that is necessarily present in the background). What separates them are the different rules of each game, circumscribing their closed spaces, their own domains of legitimacy. All activity aimed at knowing is the same, insofar as it is ludic activity. Each type differs according to the objectives and rules given and the constructions produced, which have no meaning, of course, except in relation to these rules, within each of these domains. As François Jacob observes, in *The Possible and the Actual*, if "the scientific attitude has a well-defined role in the dialogue between the possible and the actual," there exist other kinds of dialogue between the possible and the real; in particular, when it is not a matter merely of describing nature, but of grounding hope. "It is hope that gives its meaning. And hope is based on the prospect of being able one day to turn the actual world into a possible one that looks better."[101] Moreover, the rules and objectives can evolve, change in midstream like Wittgenstein's ball games.

It certainly seems that twentieth-century science, that of the great research institutes and the institutions that finance them, relegates the description of nature to the background, while operational mastery is the main objective. In esthetic knowledge, each artist and, carried to the extreme, each work of art institutes its own rules; but once instituted, the constraints they produce are indispensable to the construction of a work of art. In divinatory and mystical knowledge, more or less elaborate rules of interpretation derived from simple recipes or from refined and rationalized formulizations make it possible to construct unified explanatory schemas where every event finds its place in a universal order that embraces nature and man, humanizing nature at least as much as it naturalizes human beings. There, too, nothing remains of the work of knowledge outside the scope of these rules. Similarly, scientific knowledge exists only by virtue of the rules that it imposes upon itself, those that must be obeyed by experimental protocols and logical-mathematical deductions in order to persuade the community of those devoted to this activity. In fact, there is no ready consensus except as to whether the rules have been respected, and such respect is the only thing that the community requires of each of its members, qua scientists. Everything else—ideas and theories—is second-degree games, games whose results are those of the empirical-deductive game. We have seen that there is a strong temptation to see these results as universal and definitive, independent of the context in which they were obtained, and to use scientific theories as the only means to interpret the events of our life, by giving them unifying explanations that are supposed to replace or complete (or compete with) the globalizing explanations of the mystical traditions. We have also seen how—just like the countervailing temptation to find gobbets of scientific knowledge in the teachings of mystical traditions—this involves deviating from one game to another, a deviation that has no legitimacy either from the scientific perspective or from the perspective of an adept of one of these traditions. The scientific method defines a field of application from which are excluded all nonreproducible phenomena, subjective and otherwise, and in which the truth of a theory is measured by its operational power more than by its explanatory and interpretative power. Every mystical tradition, on the other hand, incorporates a total explanatory and unifying approach whose a priori truth is in some sense posited by definition; it cannot be called into question if it is to be projected, in principle, as an interpretive grid on the totality of our lived experience. Even if this approach can be expressed rationally, it has no need for any sort of confirmation by what the sciences can teach, nurturing a false apologia for the teachings of these traditions and claiming that "even modern science *recognizes* their truths"!

Nevertheless, although these deviations and trespasses from one game to another can be in no way justified from the perspective of the conduct of the games themselves—imagine a chessplayer suddenly invoking the rules of checkers, or an athlete claiming points (a "home run") for knocking a football into the stands—there seems to be a certain irrepressible need to do just this, as much among practitioners of science as among mystics and even educated laypersons.

## The Need for a True Ethics versus the Jokes of Theory

It is important that we consider the nature of this need to transgress the rules of knowledge games so as to return to that infantile state of undifferentiated play where all is permitted, but having forgotten that that was a children's game and claiming that we thereby find the most precious gems of hidden truth. This need seems to be for a true ethics in a civilization (our own) where the traditional sources of ethics, religion and philosophy, have lost their credibility as sources of *true* doctrine in favor of the natural sciences, whereas the latter, necessarily reductionist (even if only "weakly") and reduced to themselves, are increasingly losing their relevance, as we have seen, with regard to their applicability to the problems of our daily nontechnological life.

I would like to demonstrate that this need for a true ethics as an *object* of knowledge (and not of practice) rests on the illusion that a formulated truth exists a priori and its discovery—revelation—would automatically lead to "applications" to all domains of reality; including, of course, all of our experiences as human beings in relation with ourselves, time, nature, and other human beings—experiences that are largely unpredictable and the possible site of creativity.

This illusion is tenacious because it is grounded on and reinforced by centuries of religious catechism in which education proceeded not only "from top to bottom" but also dogmatically, based on revealed articles of faith in which one had to believe a priori and which alone expressed the total and unique truth; thereafter one had only to refer to these tenets to deduce explanatory schemes applicable to all domains of our experience. Because of the polemic anticatechistic context in which Western science developed, the latter, triumphant, is frequently taken as having simply replaced the former. The game of explanatory, globalizing scientific theories of the universe is taken seriously. Admitting that scientific discourse at this level of generality is not *the truth* remains very difficult, not only for the general public, but for many scientists as well—despite the fact that for some decades now the critical reflections of the philosophy of science have not stinted in their efforts to persuade us of this. Curiously, though, these critiques are not taken seriously, so great is the aggregate power of catechistic prejudice and technological success, which reinforce each other. To cite one example among many, consider the fate of Popper's attempt to save the scientific method from a nihilist skepticism while taking into account the relativity of its theoretical accomplishments. All that most scientists have kept from this is that experimental falsifiability is an a priori criterion of the scientific character of an explanatory discourse.[102] Very few, however, have drawn the consequence, which seems quite evident; namely, that a *global* scientific theory deriving its degree of "verisimilitude" only from its high degree of "corroboration," *while waiting to be falsified*, must be considered to be quite probably false[103] (because it will probably be falsified, at least in part, and will then have to be modified) from the point of view of the absolute truth supposed to be disclosed by the theory and posited once and for all.

Another result is that the legitimate domains of application must remain separated. On the one hand stands the intellectual activity of scientific theorizing as it interacts with its technological applications. On the other hand is *our* experience of our world in the light of our subjectivity, our intersubjectivities, and our ethical needs. This does not mean, as we have seen, that dialogue is impossible, nor that attempts at (a different) rationalization are not legitimate in this second domain as well. This active (nonnihilist) skepticism is arduous because scientists are also people (and, moreover, the children of Western culture, marked by those centuries of catechism) and need to believe in the rational Truth of what they believe in! We should note that this dissociation of different domains of legitimacy does not seem to have posed major theoretical problems[104] in so-called primitive and mythological cultures, where the domain of the "symbolic," as the source of explanation and unification of the hidden and visible, is segregated from that of the immediate experiences of reality, even if the effect of ritual and social organization is to make these two domains coexist.[105]

In the Christian West, this attitude was formerly explained in the most striking manner as *credo quia absurdum*, which goes back to Tertullian, followed by St. Augustine and Pascal. But that formula has not had outstanding success—no more so than Buddhist *koans* or the "both [contradictory statements] are the words of living god(s)"[106] of Jewish tradition—except to justify unsophisticated antirationalism. The churches of the West have always wanted to prove the rationality, that is the noncontradiction, of their catechisms. To accept *credo quia absurdum* or the richness of the contradictions in nature one must be able to associate profound and rigorous thought with an authentic mystical experience—profound thought to dislodge the false explanations of pseudo-rationalisms, which lull us to sleep, and authentic mysticism to look the contradiction straight in the face without losing ourselves in it, while enriching ourselves with the pendular movement between this contemplation and the attempts to reduce it.

A good viaticum for the traveler on this road consists of always considering the global explanation, including the vulgarized scientific theory, as a good joke, played on us by the games of language and reason that would make us believe in it. In fact, we often sense this jocular character when scientific theories are used as universal explanations, as vulgarized—but exalting—descriptions that serve as Science's answers to the eternal questions about the origin of things, their ultimate how and hidden reasons. This ambiguous smile, which forestalls belief but does not prevent appreciating it, is consciously assumed by science fiction. Very often, however, the need to believe is stronger. The Big Bang can be taken as a theory of the origin of the universe only with a wink, as a sort of jest that pretends to consider time to be an a priori and immutable framework that preceded the universe and within which the latter is supposed to have appeared. Specialists know quite well that this is not the case and that such cosmological theories pose new problems concerning the proper time of these "origins," which can be extended to infinity in the past simply by a change of unit.[107] They also know that they contain conceptual difficulties of the same type as those we have analyzed with regard to certain problems of quantum physics, notably that of nonlocalization. Nevertheless, this does not prevent scientists from speaking with straight faces about the "first three minutes of the universe" and acting as if this discourse was the answer offered by modern science to the question of the origin of the universe, replacing those of traditional catechisms.

Similarly, the notion of the genetic program, originally a metaphor proposed by biologists to target new problems and define new research directions more than as an answer to the eternal questions about life, has become the constant refrain and crux of reflections about the innate and acquired, which are so many false problems derived from the fact that its metaphorical character has been so quickly forgotten; the "dogma" of molecular biology, so designated by molecular biologists in an attempt to be provocative and facetious, has indeed effectively become a dogma, in the vulgate of this discipline. The zenith of this line may have been reached by the theory of "selfish genes,"[108] abusively applied to extend sociobiology to political sociology. This theory, pushing to an extreme a useful working hypothesis, has repeated, by transposing from eggs to DNA, Samuel Butler's witticism that "a hen is only an egg's way of making another egg."[109] Originally it was just a way to avoid the extreme attitude, habitual among many molecular biologists, of systematically searching for a specific functional justification for every DNA sequence, whether as a functional gene or as a regulatory gene. The idea of selfish DNA entertains the possibility of DNA distributed at random in the genome, initially without functional utility for the organism—even if it could later acquire one—and analyzes the consequences of this hypothesis from the perspective of molecular mechanisms of evolution. What was only a joke, permitting a graphic representation of the separation of germ cells and somatic cells in neo-Darwinian evolutionary theory, where the selective value of a species (or of a mutant within a species) is measured by its capacity to reproduce its genes in a given environment, became a serious description of how life is supposed to be in reality, beyond the appearances of living beings, their behavior, and their functions, as we experience these. In all these cases, scientific discourses were taken as new dogmas to be handed down religiously after being dissected out from the context of the works and discoveries that motivated them.

Another example we have analyzed here is that of psychological functionalism.[110] Based on the analogy between the operation of the mind and a computer, it involves a group of psychological theories that make it possible to happily circumvent the difficulties of the classical mind-body problem and the holistic-reductionist conflict to which they relate. But this analogy was later extracted from the problematique where it was born; taken seriously, it leads to the situation in which only a computer—like those which state-of-the-art technology allows us to design—can be imagined as a model for the operation of the mind. Hence philosophers and essayists have had to harness themselves to present corrective reactions, such as those of Dreyfus,[111] Dennett,[112] and Hofstadter.[113]

Thus the character of allusive joke or metaphor or analogy quickly vanishes from scientific discourses when the latter are extracted from their original contexts, vulgarized and used as sources of definitive explanations in which every sensible person of the modern age is expected to believe. It is curious to observe how well this works and the degree of credence it receives, even from scientists who, despite possessing all the knowledge required to understand what lies behind the vulgarization, evidently have forgotten it and fallen into the trap of humorlessness and the closure of definitive explanations. They are evincing a deep need for security, a need for a belief that is a true guarantee, apparently indispensable for grounding ethics if one would have it emanate directly from knowledge of Truth.

## Notes

1. See the chapter on playing and seriousness in Gregory Bateson's "meta-logues," *Steps to an Ecology of Mind.*

2. See F. L. Mueller, *L'Irrationalisme contemporain* (Paris: Payot, 1970), who associates Schopenhauer, Nietzsche, Freud, Adler, Jung, and Sartre as having all located the exercise of reason within the framework of real human activities rather than above or outside them. In this way they institute a critique of these activities that does not spare the uses of reason, but also does not abandon rationality in their discourses.

3. Louis Dumont, in *Homo Hierarchicus: The Caste System and Its Implications*, trans. Mark Sainsbury, Louis Dumont, and Basia Gulati (Chicago: University of Chicago Press, 1980), and *Essays on Individualism: Modern Ideology in Anthropological Perspective* (Chicago: University of Chicago Press, 1986), has proposed such a change in sign (akin to the one I proposed for the role of noise in self-organizing systems, from negative at one level to positive at the other [*L'Organisation biologique*; "Self-Creation of Meaning"]). For Dumont, the change of sign is an anthropological law, according to which an inversion in the hierarchy of values characterizes the transition from one level to another in hierarchical societies. For us, only laughter and humor in the judgments we may make about our knowledge permit a similar inversion when we go from the level of the content of knowledge to that—which encompasses and conditions it—of cognitive activities in all their aspects, psychological, sociological, historical, institutional, political, etc.

4. Pierre Auger, *L'Homme microscopique* (Paris: Flammarion, 1966). This is the status also described by Popper, using another image, that of his third world (K. R. Popper and J. C. Eccles, *The Self and the Brain* [New York: Springer-Verlag, 1977]).

5. This is clearly shown by all the work of Judith Schlanger, from *Penser la bouche pleine* (Paris: Mouton, 1975) through the felicitously named *Le Comique des idées* (Paris: Gallimard, 1977) to *L'Enjeu et le Débat.* The unconscious role of the language of an age in the orientations of its thought and the role of the contingent and random stakes concealed behind the theoretical debates render the protagonists of those debates ridiculous when they pretend that there is an absolute necessity (logical or empirical) underpinning their truth.

6. D. W. Winnicott, *Playing and Reality* (London: Tavistock Publications, 1971), p. 110.

7. Ibid., p. 96.

8. Ibid., p. 107.

9. "The experience is one of a non-purposive state" (ibid., p. 55), and acceptance of chaos and the formless, of "the nonsense that belongs to the mental state of the individual at rest" (p. 56) "out of which a creative reaching-out can take place" (p. 55); even if, a posteriori, objects and gestures acquire the meaning of their signification within the world they have helped to construct. This is a fine example of complexity from noise and of a "meaning-making machine" (cf. Atlan, *Entre le cristal et la fumée*).

10. Winnicott, *Playing and Reality*, p. 53.

11. Ibid., p. 137.

12. Ibid., p. 146.

13. "It is assumed here that the task of reality-acceptance is never completed, that no human being is free from the strain of relating inner and outer reality, and that relief from this strain is provided by an intermediate area of experience...which is not challenged (arts, religion, etc.). This intermediate area is in direct continuity with the play area of the small child who is 'lost' in play.

"In infancy this intermediate area is necessary for the initiation of a relationship between the child and the world, and is made possible by good-enough mothering at the early critical phase. Essential to all this is continuity (in time) of the external emotional environment and of particular elements in the physical environment such as the transitional object or objects.

"The transitional phenomena are allowable to the infant because of the parents' intuitive recognition of the strain inherent in objective perception, and we do not challenge the infant in regard to subjectivity or objectivity just here where there is the transitional object.

"Should an adult make claims on us for our acceptance of the objectivity of his subjective phenomena we discern or diagnose madness. If, however, the adult can manage to enjoy the personal intermediate area without making claims, then we can acknowledge our own corresponding intermediate areas, and are please to find a degree of overlapping, that is to say common experience between members of a group in art or religion or philosophy" (ibid., p. 13f.).

Winnicott concludes his exposition of his theory of transitional objects and phenomena in the following words: "Transitional objects and transitional phenomena belong to the realm of illusion which is the basis of initiation of experience. This early stage in development is made possible by the mother's special capacity for making adaptation to the needs of her infant, thus allowing the infant the illusion that what the infant creates really exists.

"This intermediate area of experience, unchallenged in respect of its belonging to inner or external (shared) reality, constitutes the greater part of the infant's experience, and throughout life is retained in the intense experiencing that belongs to the arts and to religion and to imaginative living, and to creative scientific work.

"An infant's transitional object ordinarily becomes gradually decathected, especially as cultural interests develop.

"What emerges from these considerations is the further idea that paradox accepted can have positive value. The resolution of paradox leads to a defence organization which in the adult one can encounter as true and false self organization [i.e., organization of the true and false self]" (ibid., p. 14).

14. Eugen Fink, *Spiel als Weltzymbol* (Stuttgart: W. Kolhammer, 1960).

15. Winnicott, *Playing and Reality*, p. 99.

16. C. Geets, *Winnicott* (Paris: Editions universitaires J.-P. Delarge, 1981), p. 97.

17. Ibid., p. 54.

18. Winnicott, *Playing and Reality*, p. 65.

19. Ibid., p. 99; Winnicott continues: "Conversely, no one in the line of cultural contributors repeats except as a deliberate quotation, and the unforgivable sin in the cultural field is plagiarism. The interplay between originality and the acceptance of tradition as the basis for inventiveness seems to me to be just one more example, and a very exciting one, of the interplay between separateness and union."

20. Whether by "doctors of the law" or doctors of science.

21. Jacob, *The Possible and the Actual*.

22. Fink, *Spiel als Weltzymbol*, p. 9.

23. Ibid., p. 16.

24. "In human play, the totality of the world is reflected in itself, and allows lineaments of the infinite to glimmer to and in an inner world, a finitude.... Precisely to the extent that man is essentially determined by the possibility of play, he is determined by the unfathomable and indeterminate, by the impermanent and open, by the fluctuating possibility of the active world that is reflected in him" (ibid., pp. 230f.). As to the question of the finite or infinite character of the real world as the physical universe, physics offers no definite answer at present. On the other hand, it is easy to demonstrate that the world, including all possibles, is infinite. Limiting ourselves to those possibilities conceived (or created) by combinations of real objects, the number of combinations is indeed finite, if the number of objects is. But nothing keeps us from proceeding to combine the combinations, and combining the combined combinations, making as many jumps of level as one wishes (infinity, in the mathematical sense). In a work in progress, the mathematical physicist F. Bailly (personal communication) is trying to show how the mathematics of infinity (that of Cantorian transfinite numbers) can be applied in a human

science in a manner analogous to the use of finite numbers in physics. This study, if rigorously conducted, while guarding against the traps of spiritualism and of strong reductionism, can only push further the question of the reality of numbers.

Finally, we should note that the relations between the possible and the infinite seem to be reversed in the mathematical definition of infinity: recalling the inversion between mathematical and physical models (Chapter 2), here our intuition of the possible comes first and defines infinity as a potential (a "power") of the enumerable; whereas formerly it was infinity that seemed to characterize the possible.

25. Fink, *Spiel als Weltzymbol*, p. 36.

26. "Time (*aion*) is a child playing checkers: the reign of the child," which Heidegger translates and comments upon on the last page of *Satz vom Grund*: "The destiny of being (*Seinsgeschick*) is a child at play, playing a board game; to a child belongs the kingdom,...what founds, constitutes, and governs, being for what is. The destiny of being is a child at play" (Heidegger, *Satz vom Grund*, p. 188).

27. Fink, *Spiel als Weltzymbol*, p. 47.

28. "As large, as powerful, as strong, and as wise as one may imagine a person, one cannot, in the strict sense, imagine it omnipotent, powerful like the totality, because its relationship with itself distinguishes it from all other things. Omnipotence cannot be a person and no person can be omnipotent. The world is not a god and no god can be the totality of the world" (ibid., p. 240). "The god of metaphysics masquerades as the world and does so even better in proportion as he is postulated farther beyond any idol,...in proportion as he becomes by some sort of gradual elevation a *Deus absconditus*" (p. 46).

Fink's continuation here should not surprise us: "Properly understood, this is true only for the god of the philosophers and metaphysicians, and not for 'the God of Abraham, Isaac, and Jacob,' nor for Zeus and Apollo, nor for Odin, the all-father, nor for Isis and Osiris" (p. 46). Like the gods of Heraclitus and Nietzsche, the god of the Hebrew patriarchs, as well as the personal divinities of pagan myth, constituted a lesser obstacle, in a certain way, to this opening to the totality of the world than the mixture of personal god and *Deus absconditus* of Christian theology (and its recent so-called Judeo-Christian derivative). Closer to and more present in the world through the experience of the content of the myth and the cultic game, they could be perceived, gods in their own sphere, human beings in theirs, as the agents and vehicles in the world of the all-organizing power. One can profitably compare this idea with that of the twelfth-century Jewish philosopher Judah Halevi in the *Kuzari*, and, more recently, that of Rabbi A. I. Kook (see H. Atlan, "Etat et religion dans la pensée politique du R. Kook," in J. Halperin and G. Levitte, ed., *Israël, le Judaïsme, l'Europe* [Paris: Gallimard, 1984]; see also Atlan, "Ce peuple qu'on dit élu," *Le Genre humain*, no. 3–4 [1982], pp. 98–126).

29. Like playing for Winnicott, here the game has no plan or value in its content. But one can clearly object that in Fink's thought (as for Winnicott) it acquires a status that gives it utility, cause, and meaning, even if at another level and

in another manner. Perhaps this is what Fink was driving at when he remarks, a bit later in his text, that one cannot speak seriously of the lines by which playing appears as the reflection or symbol of the world. This suggests that one cannot speak of play except by playing, that is, in the strict sense, as we shall see, through "language games."

30. "But we must make it clear and distinct to ourselves that the world's lack of reason (*Grundlosigkeit*), its lack of goal, objective, value, and plan, cannot be thought on the model of some worldly valueless thing" (Fink, *Spiel als Weltzymbol*, p. 235). For even though the world is "without reason and without goal...it has within it all reasons for every being in the world, all of which are without exception grounded; it encompasses within its universal lack of goal the paths on which goal and objective were pursued.... [The world] keeps space and time open for the being of things, which has reason, goal, sense, and meaning" (ibid.).

31. Ibid., p. 237.

32. "The ambiguity of such a characterization rests on the inevitable entangling of real and unreal. Play frees us from freedom, but in an 'unreal manner.' And this 'unreality' of play is an essential relationship between man and the world. The symbolic representation of the universal totality of things cannot be something that is solidly real.... The world appears in the appearance of play; it is reflected in itself by the fact that a worldly behavior assumes, even if in an unreal form, the lineaments of the active All. The reflection of the world in itself, in a specific inner-world, in man who imitates this world: man who is as it were 'omnipotent,' as it were 'irresponsible,' as it were at the same time in all possibilities; seen from the cosmos, this reflection is the same thing as what we have called, from the perspective of man, the ecstasy toward the totality of the world" (ibid., pp. 231–232).

33. Ibid., p. 62.

34. "The more we acquire of determined reality in our active self-realization, the less numerous our possibilities become. The child is, potentially.... The old man has the history of his self-realization behind him; he has consumed a thousand possibilities in one fashion or another....

"Man's fate in general...cannot become 'real' except by continuing to lose possibilities. The child is, in indeterminate fashion, everything; the old man, very little, in a determinate fashion. One enters the world as a multiple being; one dies as a single being.... Play softens the inexorable law of the seriousness of life, the sadness that flows from the incessant curtailment of our possibilities that accompanies us throughout our life. In fact, in play we enjoy the possibility of recovering lost possibilities" (ibid., pp. 78–79).

My own theory of self-organization by reduction of redundancy and creation of complexity springs to mind here, even if it involves an objective angle on self-organizing systems observed from the outside and analyzed in the biological context of the postulate of objectivity. This is why, unlike what was just quoted about self-realization, self-organization cannot invoke our inner experience of meaning and liberty as determining factors. It is noise, random and gratuitous, without value and without plan, and not conscious and voluntary choice, that curtails possibilities by reducing the initial redundancy. Thus I find myself in agreement with Fink when, as he does, we leave the domain of introspection to consider man as in some fashion "self-organized from the outside," just like living beings in their totality, the loci and products of differentiation derived from their initial undifferentiated state (see Atlan, *Entre le cristal et la fumée* and "Self-Creation of Meaning").

35. Fink, *Spiel als Weltzymbol*, p. 205. [Fink himself uses the word *Chance* in his German text, playing on its multiple meanings in German, French, and English: prospect and outlook; occasion and opportunity; and luck and fortune.—LJS]

36. Ibid., p. 135.

37. Ibid., p. 24.

38. Ibid., p. 34.

39. Ibid., p. 25.

40. Ibid., pp. 205–206.

41. Ibid., p. 144.

42. Mathematical theories of games, in the wake of Morgenstern and von Neumann, have played an important role in the development of information science and artificial intelligence. Of this instance of science as game using the game as its object, we can observe: turnabout is fair play!

43. Bateson, *Men are Grass*.

44. Fink, *Spiel als Weltzymbol*, p. 114.

45. See Atlan, *L'Organisation biologique*, pp. 283–284.

46. Bateson (*Men Are Grass*) remarks that the faulty syllogism—"Grass dies. Men die. Men are grass"—if it breaks the rules of logic, remains nonetheless an illustration of metaphoric thought, which is often that of science, poets, and schizophrenics. As for imagining that nature prefers "correct" syllogisms of the type "Socrates is a man. Socrates is mortal," where the link is between subjects (Socrates, man) and not between verbs (die, die), we would have to suppose that nature, even before language and grammar made their appearance among the human species, had already determined the grammatical distinction between subject and verb!

47. See Chapter 2.

48. H. Simon, *The Science of the Artificial* (Cambridge, Mass.: MIT Press, 1969).

49. See Atlan, *Entre le cristal et la fumée*, Chapter 1.

50. See Chapter 2.

51. See Chapter 9.

52. T. John and A. Bennett, "Language as a Self-organizing System," *Cybernetics and Systems* 13 (1982), pp. 201–212.

53. T. Winograd and F. Flores, *Understanding Computers and Cognition: A New Foundation for Design* (Norwood, N.J.: Ablex Publishing, 1986).

54. See H. Atlan, "Noise Complexity and Meaning in Cognitive Systems."

55. A. Lichnerowicz, "Mathématique et espaces de vérité," *Le Genre humain,* no. 7–8 (1983), pp. 53–56.

56. B. Shanon, "Que disent les oiseaux? Réflexions sur une théorie de la communication," in *L'Auto-organisation*, pp. 407–411.

57. Wittgenstein, *Philosophical Investigations*, I.7, p. 5.

58. Ibid., I.23, p. 11.

59. Giving orders, and obeying them—
    Describing the appearance of an object, or giving its measurements—
    Constructing an object from a description (a drawing)—
    Reporting an event—
    Speculating about an event—
    Forming and testing a hypothesis—
    Presenting the results of an experiment in tables and diagrams—
    Making up a story; and reading it—
    Play-acting—
    Singing catches—
    Guessing riddles—
    Making a joke, telling it—
    Solving a problem in practical arithmetic—
    Translating from one language into another—
    Asking, thanking, cursing, greeting, praying (ibid. I.23, p. 11f.).

60. Ibid., I.23, p. 12.

61. Ibid., I.97, p. 44.

62. Ibid., I.107, p. 46.

63. Ibid., I.97, p. 44.

64. Ibid., I.102, p. 45.

65. Ibid., I.98, p. 45.

66. See, for example, Kripke, *Naming and Necessity*, and Hintikka, *Logic, Language-Games, and Information*.

67. One example of the reduction of the *Tractatus* by the Vienna Positivists (discussed by D. Lecourt in *L'Ordre et les jeux*) appears clearly in Carnap's "translation" of 2.0123, where the identification of possible in the world and possible in propositions is made explicit, so that no room is left for this opening (see the note on 2.0123 in P. Klossowki's French translation [Paris: Gallimard, 1961]).

68. "What a picture must have in common with reality" (*Tractatus* 2.17) is what Wittgenstein calls the "form of an object," "the possibility of its occurring in states of affairs" (2.0141), or "the possibility of structure" (2.033) or "pictorial form" (2.17), but this cannot be depicted, only displayed (2.172), even if "a picture...also includes the pictorial relationship, which makes it into a picture [and which] consists of the correlations of the picture's elements with things" (2.1513–2.1514).

69. See Chapter 4, on the undecidability of noncontradiction.

70. Unlike the postulate of the logician-philosopher's (science of) logic, one *can* not only believe in something contradictory, one can even *know* that observed facts are contradictory when we lack a theory that would alleviate the contradiction. Scientists, and the rationalists in general, hope that the contradiction is merely apparent, whereas mystics—at least some of them, particularly those of the Far East—see it as the door to "ultimate reality," which makes it possible to leave the contradiction behind (thereby making it disappear without resolving it).

71. The distinction made by Gilles Deleuze (*Différence et répétition* [Paris: Presses universitaires de France, 1972]) between logically possible and virtual concerns the existence of a process in which a reduction from a virtual multiplicity to an actualized unity can also be observed. This reduction is produced by the process of actualization and may bring invention and novelty in its wake. The virtual is not less real. On the contrary, the possible, which is sometimes considered to be merely logically possible, is opposed to the real by its "nonexistence," but resembles it conceptually. This distinction is important in that it endeavors to locate evolving dynamics in relationship to the real; but it is far from exhausting the problem, because the contradictory possibility—*logically* impossible—is not always accounted for. In addition, a possibility can be transformed into virtual, in Deleuze's sense (and thus be real), when we manage to discover and identify a physical substrate for its existence and process of actualization, even before this comes into being and without its having to be reduced to it. Subsequently, the reduction of this possibility transformed into virtual by an avatar of our knowledge can itself lead to invention and creation. In other words, once again the question of the creation of something new cannot be extricated from that of the state of our knowledge about what does and does not exist. It is always epistemic and not ontological. From this perspective, where the limits of the world are always confounded with those of logic, the position of the "first" Wittgen-

stein is more satisfactory, in that "reality" is constituted by both the existence and nonexistence of possible states of fact: the fact that a logically possible state of fact is proved false by empirical experience is part of—or is produced by—reality. But knowledge as games creates an opening through which the limits of the world—without which the latter is no longer posited as knowable—are no longer confused with those of logic.

72. Certainly the computation of probabilities and the law of large numbers seek to tap the accidental within logic. But the metaphor of the net or grid with a coarser or finer mesh (rather coarse in this case, as it lets much of this accidental escape) appears in full force here.

73. Wittgenstein, *Tractatus* 4.002.

74. Wittgenstein, *Philosophical Investigations*, I.98, p. 45. This vagueness of natural language is nevertheless not just anything. Attempts have been made to circumscribe it, notably by specifying its origin. On this subject, see the analysis by A. Margalit ("Vagueness in Vogue," *Synthese* 33 [1976], pp. 211–221), who attempts to answer whether this vagueness is found in the words (semantic origin) or in how we use them (pragmatic origin). This question is important for a logician, who needs to know whether or not the logic of natural language is that of the excluded middle, which leads us back to our question about noncontradiction in nature. Recognizing, with Quine, that the adaptability of natural language to any use, any possible intentional purpose, lies at the root of this phenomenon of vagueness (see Chapter 8, p. 371), he analyzes the nature of the operations (idealization and legislation) that make it possible to eliminate vagueness from speech; that is, to make logical inferences in natural language. A distinction between the vagueness of words and that of sentences (the former does not necessarily entail the latter) allows him to take an intermediary position where natural language, although not two-valued, nevertheless has the (empirical) property of being able to support a two-valued (true/false) logic; that is, to be reducible to a usage in which only precise and definite meanings are taken into account.

75. Wittgenstein, *Tractatus* 3.

76. With regard to *totality*, see Bertrand Russell's introduction to the *Tractatus Logico-Philosophicus* and his discussion of the difficulties left untouched by that volume with regard to generalization as an operation and logical denotation ("for every *x*," "whatever *x*," etc.), whereas the thought of the totality cannot be expressed in the *Tractatus* without nonsense ("'the feeling of the world as a bounded whole is the mystical'; hence the totality of the values of *x* is mystical [6.45]" [*Tractatus*, p. xxi]). See also, for example, 5.521, 5.5561, 5.6, and 5.61.

As for *negation*, we have already indicated (in Chapter 4) its fundamental role in logical structures. It clearly plays a founding and fundamental role in the *Tractatus* (see notably 5.5 ff.), one of whose great successes is to have reduced the symbolism of the propositional calculus by demonstrating that all propositions that have a meaning in a perfectly logical language can be constructed from "the general form of a truth-function," which is at the same time "the general form of a proposition" (6), whereby all possible propositions are immediately given (because "form is the possibility of structure" [2.033]). As Russell notes, this general form is obtained from an extension of a result known in the logic of binary functions, where the Sheffer bar function (not-$p$ and not-$q$) makes it possible to generate all other logical functions (for details, see Atlan, *L'Organisation biologique*, p. 134). This leads to an asymmetry in the affirmation-negation pair, which must not be confused with the symmetrical existence–non-existence pair: "The existence and non-existence of states of affairs is reality. (We also call the existence of states of affairs a positive fact, and their non-existence a negative fact.)" (2.06). "The sense of a proposition is its agreement and disagreement with possibilities of existence and non-existence of states of affairs" (4.2). "Truth-possibilities of elementary propositions mean possibilities of existence and non-existence of states of affairs" (4.3); i.e., according to 2.06, of reality. But what is the possibility of reality other than simply possibility? And because, as we are warned elsewhere, "the only impossibility that exists is *logical* impossibility" (6.375), it follows that, somewhere in the realm of the possible, logic and reality are a single identical "thing," although the whole task of the logician is to untangle their relations.

The fundamental role of negation, along with its nonmaterial, unreal (?) status, is clearly underscored: "Negation, logical addition, logical multiplication, etc. etc. are operations. (Negation reverses the sense of a proposition)" (5.2341). "Truth-functions are not material functions. For example, an affirmation can be produced by double negation: in such a case does it follow that in some sense negation is contained in affirmation? Does '$\sim\sim p$' negate $\sim p$, or does it affirm $p$—or both? The proposition '$\sim\sim p$' is not about negation, as if negation were an object: on the other hand, the possibility of negation is already written into affirmation. And if there were an object called '$\sim$', it would follow that '$\sim\sim p$' said something different from what '$p$' said, just because the one proposition would then be about $\sim$ and the other would not" (5.44).

Nevertheless, this "clearly" nonmaterial character of logical functions *seems* to be contradicted by the construction of electronic components that perform them, as well as by the discovery of neuron structures in which these functions are materially realized in nature—and not only by human thought and knowledge—in the form of inhibitory synapses. In fact, though, these observations actually reinforce the "unreal" character of *logical* negation. In effect, in these material realizations it is only abstractly and ideally that a double negation can be considered to generate an affirmation, by abstracting from the physical process through which the result is obtained. But the material nature of this process, with its (thermodynamically) irreversible character and the always present possibility of amplified fluctuations, such that double negation is not finally equivalent, even approximately, to affirmation, cannot itself vanish. And, in another domain, the psychoanalyst M. Neyraut (*Les Logiques de l'inconscient*), observing this extremum of the complexity of natural organizations constituted by the human mind, correctly notes that it presents a "logic" where two negations do not equal an affirmation.

Finally, with regard to the order of *possibles*, we have already underlined the special status in the *Tractatus* of the *possibility of occurrence* of objects as the "pictorial form," i.e., that which what the picture and what it represents have in common and which therefore cannot be depicted, but only displayed, in relation to the *totality* of objects. We have already noted the problematic and paradoxical nature of the latter, from a perspective inside Wittgenstein's logical structure, where propositions like 2.0124 ("If all objects are given, then at the same time all *possible* states of affairs are also given"), 2.0141 ("The possibility of its occurring in states of affairs is the form of an object"), and 2.033 ("Form is the possibility of structure"; cf. 2.15)—propositions that point up and explain the unease that Russell cannot overcome in his introduction—coexist with 6.45 ("Feeling the world as a limited whole...is mystical") and 4.1272 ("Wherever the word 'object'...is correctly used, it is expressed in conceptual notation by a variable name.... So one cannot say...'There are objects,' as one might say, 'There are books.'"). See also 6.375 ("Just as the only necessity that exists is *logical* necessity, so too the only impossibility that exists is *logical* impossibility"). Or again, with regard to the possibility of representing reality by signs—a second-order, possibility of possibility, in a manner of speaking—"The possibility of propositions is based on the principle that objects have signs as their representatives. My fundamental idea is that the 'logical constants' are not representatives; that there can be no representatives of the *logic* of facts" (4.0312). And finally: "Propositions can represent the whole of reality, but they cannot represent what they must have in common with reality in order to be able to represent it—logical form. In order to be able to represent logical form, we should have to be able to station ourselves with propositions somewhere outside logic, that is to say outside the world. Propositions cannot represent logical form: it is mirrored in them. What finds its reflection in language, language cannot represent. What expresses *itself* in language, *we* cannot express by means of language. Propositions *show* the logical form of reality. They display it.... What *can* be shown, *cannot* be said" (4.12, 4.121, 4.1212)

What sort of impossibility ("cannot") is involved here? Given that there is only logical impossibility, it seems that it could only be a contradiction, because "the certainty, possibility, or impossibility of a situation is not expressed by a proposition, but by an expression's being a tautology, a proposition with sense, or a contradiction" (5.525). But are states of affairs at issue here? Whatever the case, it rather seems to be an a priori impossibility, antecedent to logic (thus concerning "how?," according to 5.552), because it concerns the representation of the logical form itself. In this context we should also note the difficulties of the theory of probability in the *Tractatus* (5.15–5.156), discussed previously (n. 72).

77. Detienne and Vernant, *Cunning Intelligence*, p. 107.

78. Wittgenstein, *Tractatus* 6.1261

79. Detienne and Vernant, *Cunning Intelligence*, p. 107.

80. Elkana, "A Programmatic Attempt."

81. Zohar Exodus 34b. See Chapter 3, pp. 125–127.

82. Detienne and Vernant, *Cunning Intelligence*, pp. 107f.

83. Ibid., p. 307.

84. Ibid., pp. 314f.

85. Wittgenstein, *Tractatus* 6.35.

86. Detienne and Vernant, *Cunning Intelligence*, p. 304.

87. Wittgenstein, *Philosophical Investigations*, I.99, p. 45.

88. Ibid., I.100, p. 45.

89. Ibid., pp. 50–51; and cf. I.125–133.

90. Wittgenstein, *Tractatus* 7.

91. Wittgenstein, *Philosophical Investigations*, I.125, p. 50.

92. Ibid., II.ix, p. 206.

93. Ibid., I.83, p. 39.

94. In particular, the relation between knowledge and truth, too, is determined by the rules that circumscribe and define its domain of legitimacy: "To say that a proposition is whatever can be true or false amounts to saying: we call something a proposition when *in our language* we apply the calculus of truth functions to it" (ibid., I.136, p. 52; see also I.499–500, pp. 138f.).

95. A propos here is a line from one of the "bouteilles" of the French essayist Marc Beigbeder: "Reality is a 'good' girl willing to accept all offers."

96. A reloading with redundancy, with indifferentiation, seems to be a necessary condition for the pursuit of processes of nondirected learning seen as processes of self-organization. This is what allowed me to formulate a hypothesis assigning this function to dreams (Atlan, *Entre le cristal et la fumée*, p. 145) and to metaphoric activities of natural language and poetic language (Atlan, "Noise, Complexity and Meaning in Cognitive Systems").

97. *Tractatus* 6.371; see also p. 304.

98. Winnicott, *Playing and Reality*, p. 50.

99. Fink, *Spiel als Weltzymbol*, p. 231.

100. A particularly suggestive example returns us once again to the mind-body problem. Jean-Pierre Changeux's idea that there is no more room for Mind (*Neuronal Man*) must be put back in the reductionist context in which it is conceived. For one cannot say that there is no more room for Mind *in general*. We say that there is no room (and has not been for at least three centuries, since Descartes) for Mind as the explanatory principle in the praxis of the natural sciences. Spirit is not "congruent," unlike the affirmations of Henry Moore and Renaissance philoso-

phers, with the concepts that have proven themselves effective in scientific praxis: forces, trajectories, energy—or, more recently, information, code, and program. Once these concepts have acquired a logico-mathematical content they can be manipulated and in turn permit the manipulation of natural objects and spectacular constructions of artificial objects. But one cannot *not* speak of Mind, or of spirits, when one delves into interpretive systems in which the grounding experience is that of the subjectivity of inner life, of personal responsibility, of mystical illumination, or even that of idealist philosophies of the Mind. These interpretive systems sometimes rest on pedagogical traditions and discourses or language games that are no less rational than those of the scientific tradition; in them, Mind, spirits, and demons, Soul and souls, the sephirot of the Kabbala, the images of Muslim mystics, the spheres and stages of illumination of the Hindus, all play the role of irreplaceable categories of discourse, through which reality, extended and projected from the inside toward the outside, is interpreted.

Recognizing how scientific praxis has instituted a domain of legitimacy where it is illegitimate to speak of Mind, and, at the same time, how mystical and philosophic traditions have instituted other domains where, on the contrary, it is legitimate and indispensable to do so, is also recognizing that we are no longer speaking of the same thing. The Mind invoked by spiritualist physicists and biologists in the confusion we are trying to dispel in this volume is not the same one dealt with by mystical traditions and philosophers of Mind. The former is daubed on as an explanatory principle in place of "matter," when it becomes apparent that the latter, as we conceive of it through the natural sciences, is no longer as immediately concrete as might have been thought. The latter, mystico-philosophical Mind, has always played the role of fundamental explanatory principle based on initial experiences stressed by mystics and philosophers and taken by them as the starting point and terminus of their speculation. In this, moreover, it has played the same role as matter for scientists, except for the fact that the underlying experiences are different: mystical experience and illumination, that of ethics or philosophical reflection, in one case; immediate sense data and their perception, in the other.

101. Jacob, *The Possible and the Actual*, p. 68.

102. Here I do no not want to discuss the truly universal character of this criterion, for which scientific praxis offers many counterexamples. Nevertheless its value is indisputable as self-discipline and a game rule that should usually be observed—except when everyone seems to have agreed not to do so (which clearly poses new problems that post-Popperian philosophers such as Lakatos, Agassi, and Feyerabend have had to address).

103. Popper sees science, he says, "as the result of human endeavor, of human dreams, hopes, passions, and most of all, as the result of the most admirable union of creative imagination and rational critical thought" engaged in the human adventure of the Enlightenment, aiming at self-liberation by intelligence. "As to its authority, or confirmation, or probability, I believe that it is nil; it is all guesswork, *doxa* rather than *episteme*. And probability theory even 'confirms' me in this, by

attributing zero probability to universal theories" (K. R. Popper, *Realism and the Aim of Science* [Totowa, N.J.: Rowman and Littlefield, 1983], p. 259).

104. *Practical* problems of adapting to the dominant Western world are not to be ignored, but this is not what concerns us here.

105. See, for example, Dan Sperber, *Rethinking Symbolism*. See also the jux-taposition of different domains with different value systems and Dumontian hierar-chical inversion, in C. Barraud, D. de Coppet, R. Iteanu, and R. Jamons, "Des rela-tions et des morts. Quatre sociétés vues sous l'angle des échanges," *Différences, Valeurs, Hiérarchie* (Paris: Editions de l'Ecole des hautes études en sciences sociales, 1984), pp. 421–520.

106. This talmudic statement concludes the discussion of two irreconcilable theses that are both considered to be authoritative and thus in some manner simul-taneously "true." [The Hebrew word *elohim*, normally construed as a singular, is plural in form. Although Prof. Atlan prefers to emphasize the latter and renders it in French as "dieux," here and elsewhere I have written "god(s)" in an attempt to con-vey its underlying duality(!) of meaning.—LJS]

107. One need only count time on a logarithmic scale for zero to disappear and the first instants to be transformed into a duration extending infinitely into the past. But it is simpler and more convenient to represent things by imagining the Big Bang as a singularity in linear time that is traced back causally into the past. This means that the question of origins is not raised. Instead, one attempts to give the simplest possible causal explanation for astrophysical observations by applying the game rule that allows us to use, to this end, only theories provided by physics (excluding, for example, animist and mythological explanations that would have the universe born, like a living creature, delivered of its mother in some extraordi-nary fashion).

108. R. Dawkins, *The Selfish Gene* (Oxford: Oxford University Press, 1976). See also W. Ford Doolittle and C. Sapienza, "Selfish Genes, the Phenotype Paradigm and Genome Evolution," *Nature* 284 (1984), pp. 601–603; and L. E. Orgel and F. H. C. Crick, "Selfish DNA: The Ultimate Parasite," ibid., pp. 604–607.

109. Samuel Butler, *Life and Habit* (London: Jonathan Cape, 1978), p. 134 (cited by C. S. Pittendrigh, "Adaptation, Natural Selection and Behavior," in *Behav-ior and Evolution*, pp. 390–416).

110. See Chapter 2.

111. Dreyfus, *What Computers Can't Do*.

112. Dennett, *Brainstorms* (see esp. Chapter 11, "Why You Can't Make a Computer That Feels Pain").

113. Hofstadter, *Gödel, Escher, Bach*; D. R. Hofstadter and D. C. Dennett, *The Mind's I: Fantasies and Reflections on Self and Soul* (New York: Basic Books, 1981).

*Chapter 8*

# An Ethics
# That Falls from Heaven;
# or, A Plea for Wishful Thinking[1]

## *The Impulse to Knowledge and the Question of Ethics*

We have seen that different brands of rationality, the scientific and the mythic, can resemble each other (both are rational) even while differing profoundly with regard to the domains of legitimacy of the underpinnings of their truths and with regard to the interests of reason brought into *play* in their exercise. We have compared them to different systems of reference, such as those we experience in different games, each of which exists only by virtue of the specificity of the rules that define it. Nevertheless, it remains difficult to accept that the conventional and apparently arbitrary character of the rules of a game can be applied to our cognitive activities. As Judith Schlanger put it: "A game rule that succeeds is not arbitrary."[2]

It is very hard for us to abandon our confidence (or faith?) in our cognitive activities as a means of uncovering the Truth about the world, what is hidden behind the illusions of our senses and of our desires, which, clearly, we also experience. Why is this so difficult for us? Why are we repeatedly tempted to believe in the Truth supposed to be uncovered this way or about to be uncovered? The attempts at a unified discourse about an Ultimate and Absolute One, of which the Cordoba colloquium will perhaps remain a prototype (if not an archetype!), unabashedly yield to this temptation. But many scientists, philosophers, and moralists of all sorts, materialists as well as spiritualists, classical rationalists and neorationalists, give in to this same temptation, albeit with slightly more finesse. Here the Absolute that would be disclosed in this way returns in its multiple avatars: Nature, Matter, Spirit, World Soul, and so on. Only logical positivism seems to escape this unifying temptation, positing instead criteria of demarcation between scientific and nonscientific speech, between meaningful and meaningless propositions. But this enterprise itself is not immune to misunderstandings, once the inevitable question recurs of the relations between formal language and lived reality, between objects in the world and the logic of words. Evidence of this is provided by the careers of Wittgenstein and Popper who, for all their divergences, foreshadow the post–logical positivist reaction that followed.[3]

Our cognitive activities, even the most abstract and most formal among them, do not take place in a vacuum; they are part of the totality of our individual and social behavior, even if ideas have a life of their own and a history that seems to transpire independently, parallel to that of the brain that they inhabit like symbionts (to borrow Pierre Auger's metaphor).[4] From a behaviorist point of view, our cognitive activity can be seen as animated by a need of the same nature as our individual and specific physiological needs. Psychoanalysts, following Freud and Melanie Klein, speak of the "epistemophilic impulse," whose earliest manifestations are the nursing child's exploration of the mother's body and breast. This need is found later, in the adult, as the need for explanation. We have seen that these explanations function as ordering devices produced by various methods of interpretation. What is common to all these methods is that they adumbrate relations (causal or other) among the otherwise disjointed and disordered data of our senses,[5] thanks to various interpretive schemes. These schemes characterize the different kinds of order produced by the various types of explanations that we use (or reject): scientific, intentional, magical, religious, metaphysical, mythical, mystical, and so forth. But whatever the type of explanation, it seems clear that a need for explanation is always present as the initial motivation or determinant of our cognitive activities. Hence any explanation, however imperfect, is often preferred to the absence of explanation and the acceptance of disorder. Hence, too, one can pass from one type of explanation to another if the former does not succeed, even if the interpretive schemes—the rules of the game—are mutually exclusive. This is particularly evident when scientists who are strong reductionists in their laboratories and papers use personalized and intentionalized explanations to interpret their own behavior or that of other individuals (colleagues, friends, rivals) with whom they are in contact.

Here I too am succumbing to this need for explanation, to the need to explain our explanatory activity—to explain the need to explain. We must be aware of this so as not to be seduced into believing in the ultimate truth of this or that explanation—in the present instance, that of the "epistemophilic impulse." Here too, "everything happens as if" is a good methodological handrail, employing the hypothetical conditional. Everything happens as if our cognitive activities, responding to this need for an ordering explanation, were inscribed in a larger frame, that of our behavior conditioned by our biological and social determinants. Piaget[6] rightly attempted to study human cognitive activity in continuity with the assimilatory activity of living beings in general, whereby plants and animals use their environment and assimilate it in order to nourish their own organization, which in turn permits just this assimilatory activity. Through our mental activity we assimilate our environment, by knowing it, thus contributing, here too, to nourishing our mental organization, which in turn permits just this cognitive assimilation.

If our cognitive activities are written inside the frame of our impulsive or instinctive behavior, they are also subject to the law of reinforcement, in that the success of a certain behavior (as judged by a particular criterion of satisfying a need or a desire) reinforces our predispositions to behave in this way. Moreover, the question of good and evil—that is, of ethical judgment applied to all our behavior (whatever its origin, as we shall see later)—is applied then to our cognitive activities as well. They too are subject to ethical judgment: knowledge as a source of good or evil, of happiness or unhappiness, of construction or destruction. As a result, quite naturally, the need for ordering that determines it cannot pull up short before ethical judgment itself. In an almost inevitable inversion, knowledge wants itself to be *of* good and *of* evil.[7] Our need for explanation and unifying order can be truly satisfied only when it includes not only our sensory perceptions of our environment, but also our perceptions of ourselves in our conduct, with the full gamut of physical, biological, social, and ethical traits. This seems to be why the stakes of our cognitive activities are always impregnated to some extent by ethical motives, even when, as in the case of science, these activities are posited a priori as occupying a domain of objectivity where the question of ethics is set aside. As for this unifying temptation—which desires at all costs to unify objective scientific knowledge (said to produce "true" knowledge) with other modes of knowledge, themselves to some degree objective even though traditionally associated with the question of ethics, and that produce knowledge about *ourselves*, knowledge from which our perhaps subjective experience of our own behavior is not excluded—we must seek its origins not only in a superficial credulity, but also in a need that is deeply rooted in our condition as human beings.

In particular, the mind-body or mind-brain[8] problem, which we have already encountered, and which is generally treated as a problem of metaphysics or epistemology, has in fact always had an ethical ground bass. More or less overt and analyzed ethical motives, quite as much as an interest in pure and disinterested knowledge, lie at the origin of different ways of "resolving" this problem, provisionally or definitively, from Descartes and Kant to contemporary philosophers, whether reductionists or idealists. In broadly schematic terms, these motives seek to found, or eliminate, or circumscribe and relativize our immediate experience as a subject responsible for its actions[9] (even if only in a court of law, where accounts must be rendered), taking into account external (impersonal) determinisms that have proliferated with the advance of the sciences of the body and those of the "spirit."

We have already seen that the objective knowledge inaugurated by ancient philosophy and science and which reached its zenith in modern science leads ineluctably to a separation of subject and object already contained in its methodological presuppositions. The result is a recognition and analysis of physicochemical determining mechanisms with regard to the body and the mind studied as objects, and of unconscious determining mechanisms with regard to the mental life of the subject. We have also seen that we can try to bridge the conceptual gap between the disciplines that study these two types of determinisms, notably by studying languages and their (self-) organizing power, but can never reduce one to the other or include them in a unified metatheory that still respects the rules of the scientific game. Hence this objective knowledge causes the person to disappear by splitting him into incommensurable constituents and showing the objective (i.e., impersonal) determinations of each of these constituents. Nevertheless, our subjective and intersubjective experiences are sufficiently significant that our existence, as individuals and as societies, remains largely conditioned by law and by the notion of personal responsibility implied by it. Questions of ethics will not go away. This is an eminently uncomfortable and frustrating situation for someone who is searching for an assurance of Truth that is single, objective, and universal (which knowledge of Reality would provide) as the underpinning of a law deciding what is desirable and permitted and what is forbidden; of univocal and objective knowledge that would coincide with knowledge of good and evil. This leads to the temptation to scramble the rules of the game (for no one forces us to observe them), even at the risk of killing the game itself, so as to unify, in a Grand Holism, the fruits of objective and scientific knowledge with the teachings of other great traditions, because, in the latter, the question of the subject and of our most unutterable interior experiences is the crux and point of departure of every attempt at theory, rational or not.

This is why, even if we would resist this temptation, we cannot avoid the question of ethics. Of course, its relations with the various forms of objective knowledge cannot be those of being grounded on or deduced from them, but rather those of dialogues, and frequently debates, based on differences rather than on similarities. If there is unity, it can be found only in the existence of this dialogue and not in what can be said in it; that is, once again, in the silences and the unsaid of speech, in the "white space on the page."[10]

## The Ethics of Life Dissociated from Objective Knowledge

This is where critical reflection joins up with observation. The de jure dissociation of ethics and objective knowledge is carried through by their dissociation de facto. Ethics as an imperative that orients, directs, and regulates behavior in the lived reality of existing societies does not derive from rational knowledge of the philosophical and scientific type that characterizes our modern Western societies. Despite the efforts of numerous philosophers, it could not have been founded on such knowledge. The edifices reared by these philosophers, from Plato's *Republic* through the utopias of the sixteenth century, have remained utopias. As for revolutionary political philosophies, from Locke to modern humanist ideologies (including Marxism), these have proven unable to rid themselves of an implicit morality that remains Christian morality (or sometimes its mirror-image inversion, as in the case of Nazi or neo-Nazi neopagan ideologies).

We have already been led to observe that, vis-à-vis the operation of objective and rational knowledge, ethics must come from somewhere else. And it does indeed do so. This somewhere else can hardly be found outside the past of existing societies, in particular their religious traditions. This dissociation is evident in the case of Western societies nurtured by Christian morality and scientific knowledge. But it seems possible to generalize to other societies, even if this dissociation dons a different garb where scientific tradition is not yet segregated from religious tradition: there too, the law of behavior does not seem to be grounded on (in the sense of deduced from) the rationality of knowledge, which may nevertheless appear behind the symbolism of myths and rites. Something more than a rationalized empiricism, even extended to a rationality of magic and myth or to some form of reason that recognizes other "interests" than those of our philosophical and scientific reason, is still there: something that belongs to the order of the mythical, if not the mystical; even if, sometimes, something more can subsequently be rationalized. Its empirical foundation, too, is other: lived or reported experiences belong to another reality. Clearly this does not prevent a society's mode of knowledge, scientific or mythological, from serving to nurture interpretations of the law that make it possible, after the fact, to "justify" it (or attack it) with the greatest rationality in the world and to internalize it (positively or negatively).

Despite the efforts of philosophers from Plato through Fichte, passing by way of Thomas More, Spinoza, Hobbes, Rousseau, and others, the ethics of any society always appears to have already been there before philosophical reflection was cognizant of it; it is never the conscious and planned result of such reflection, which has never been incarnated in any society. As for Kant's project of a universal religion based on morality, it has met the same fate as the Cult of Reason of the French revolutionaries of the Year II. In fact, as with Voltaire before Kant, and with Marx, Bergson, and many others after him, this morality, which asserts its universality by virtue of its being grounded on reason, just "happens" to take over value judgments derived from Christian morality and then more or less secularized. It is not that the latter is intrinsically universal, just that the philosophers of the Universal sprang from Christian civilization; and their philosophical vocation does not always shelter them from the particularisms of that tradition, in particular those expressed in deprecatory value judgments, if not indeed racist prejudices, concerning other civilizations and their morals. But this also applies to non-Western societies where traditions of knowledge have followed other paths: to the extent that a rationality appears there, with different interests and through different language games, ethics cannot be deduced from it. Ethics is there, instituting its own values, which rational knowledge, philosophical or mythical, can take into account but cannot found. The recourse to revelation, to the divine origin of these values—whether the gods are great ancestors, members of a mythical pantheon, the one God of monotheist theologies, or the divinities of the mystical experiences of shamans or prophets—makes it possible to posit these values per se alongside, and perhaps in more or less contradictory dialogue with, what the exercise of the faculties of knowing and explaining makes us see and understand behind what the eyes behold and the ears hear. Modern Western societies represent an extreme case,[11] in that knowledge has developed in a dialogue divorced from any interest in value, but it is only a question of degree. Ethics is everywhere a collective reality not grounded in knowledge, which Cornelius Castoriadis attributes to the sociocultural reality, largely unconscious but the generator of historical creations, that he calls the "social imaginary." He observes that in the past these creations have always had a religious character implying a heteronomic consciousness; that is, an origin outside the members of the society and alienating their autonomy. For him, our modern societies are wagering a possible autonomy that preserves the creative character of the social imaginary.[12]

Whatever may lie in the future of our societies, the current state of affairs invites us to what J. Beaufret calls "a genealogical reflection," which would trace back "to the source, starting from what emanates from the source, but where the presence of the source has been allowed to sink into oblivion."[13]

## A Genealogy of Ethics

L et us accept Beaufret's challenge and try to trace back to the source of ethics, starting from what emanates from the source, through ritual, where the presence of the source has been allowed to sink into oblivion. For any society, the question of the source of its ethics cannot be dissociated from that of ritual, from the set of rules that regulate the individual's relations with the gods and nature, with other members of society, and with outsiders. This set of rules assimilates into a unity what modern societies segregate into religious rules and ethical rules. The latter, however, always have their origin in ritual, whether they remain an integral part thereof or whether they are separated from it at some relatively late historical epoch, as a result of the secularization process characteristic of modern societies. Castoriadis rightly observes that the initial expression of what he calls the "social imaginary," which grounds the social structures and values of each society in the irreducible movement of historical creation through which societies create themselves, has always been in religious forms. The difference, undoubtedly fundamental but not relevant for our purposes here, is that traditional ritual has almost completely disappeared from modern societies, which, after passing through a theological phase, it too peculiar to the civilizations of the Mediterranean Basin, have adopted a philosophical and secular ethics. In other civilizations, by contrast (as well as among the small groups that segregate themselves from the modern world and continue to live the Jewish, Christian, or Muslim tradition), ritual is still present in the ethics that regulate behavior. Thus the question of the origin and foundations of ethics, along with the different forms in which it is lived in different civilizations and social systems, is shifted to the question of the origin and source of ritual.

I would like to propose elements of a response to this question, a response that excludes nothing and supplements all that we have learned from the many anthropological theories about the social functions of ritual: functions of cohesion, structure, and spatial, temporal, and kinship organization, in strict relationship with the founding and organizing myths of the societies where they are practiced. Similarly, we shall locate ourselves at a different level than that at which psychoanalysis accounts for the more or less successful internalization of paternal law in the superego, through a process of sublimation whose mechanisms are still poorly understood, when we consider its interactions with the institution of particular social values that give a specific collective content to the injunctions of the law.[14]

I propose that to this we add elements of an answer that strikes me as appropriate for an account of precisely this extraordinary possibility of the internalization of ancient rituals by the members of primitive societies: internalization by which the individual and the social can link up with each other and without which ritual could never have been effective in any of its supposed social functions. These elements of an answer are made possible by the rediscovery, in the twentieth-century West, of the positive aspect of the world of dreams and hallucinations, which some traditional societies had never forgotten. It is through psychochemistry, literary analysis of mythical figures, ethnobotany, and psychoanalysis that the West (specifically the West Coast of the United States) rediscovered this positive aspect underlying the hallucinatory experience of LSD in the psychedelic revolution of the 1960s.

Somewhat in the line of Julian Jaynes,[15] but without accepting all the details of his sometimes risky hypothesis, we can imagine today a plausible scenario of the "supernatural," "fallen-from-heaven" origin of ritual injunctions, from an external point of view (that of an "objective" observer) that yet does not deny the internal perspective (that of the participant, at the same time subject and object of these experiences). Alongside this scenario, however, it is mainly the sociocultural fallout of psychopharmacology and ethnobotany that will guide our path.

## The Voices of the Right Brain

For Julian Jaynes, the universal character of the mythical narratives of antiquity attest to a psychic reality peculiar to the people of that epoch, different from our own, and characterized by the lack of self-consciousness capable of conducting an interior dialogue with itself. In place of this consciousness, they had a doubled mind, split in two like the brain itself, which produced hallucinogenic experiences lived as if they were dialogues with external voices and visions: the gods, demons, and other oracles that people their mythologies. The internalization of these voices, making possible a self-consciousness capable of internal speech and dialogue with itself (or more precisely, interior monologue), developed only progressively,[16] at a relatively recent date that signals the end of the mythological epoch, by a mechanism of natural selection occasioned by the social upheaval that accompanied the rise of cities and the distancing of sources of power. These conditions favored those individuals best able to internalize the injunctions of the royal-divine power once and for all and to develop the psychic autonomy that this distancing permitted and encouraged. In these societies, those individuals—fewer and fewer in each successive generation—who continued to live comfortably in the previous hallucinatory reality enjoyed the special status of seers and prophets, until this status itself disappeared, at least in our societies, to be replaced by that of the mental patient or the victim of demonic possession.[17]

Jaynes, after analyzing ancient Greek and Hebrew texts, locates the date of this psychic transformation between the Iliad and Odyssey, or between the earliest and latest biblical narratives. Only in the more recent texts do individuals with a psychological depth appear. Previously we encounter only characters manipulated by the gods, executing orders immediately and without distance, possessed by whatever god makes them act, speak, suffer, or rejoice; the very question of their autonomous psychological reality never seems to be asked. In all cases, the neurophysiological foundation of the phenomenon is the dialogue-transmission of signals from the right cerebral hemisphere to the left, experienced and interpreted in the hallucinations of antiquity as separate and of external origin. Certain manifestations of such separation, observed in syndromes of faulty interhemispheric communication and today considered to be pathological, are the constitutional or accidental vestiges thereof and make it possible to reconstruct the conditions of these states.

## Modified States of Consciousness as Sources of Ritual

Another approach, this one based on psychopharmacology and ethnobotany, leads to similar conclusions with regard to the reality of the world of dreams and hallucinations and the fundamental role that the perception of this reality played in the myths and rites of ancient societies. In a profusely documented book, utterly persuasive for anyone who does not reject such arguments a priori—due to a lack of personal experience and for quite ethnocentric "moral" reasons?—Peter Furst[18] provides clear evidence of the central role of hallucinogenic plants in the prehistory and then in the cultural (and cultic) history of human societies. In the wake of the work of ethnobotanists such as Weston La Barre[19] and especially Gordon Wasson,[20] one can with difficulty reject the hypothesis that

the magicoreligious use of hallucinogenic plants by American Indians represents a survival from a very ancient Paleolithic

and Mesolithic shamanistic stratum...; while profound socio-
economic and religious transformations brought about the
eradication of ecstatic shamanism and knowledge of intoxicat-
ing mushrooms and other plants over most of Eurasia, a very
different set of historical and cultural circumstances favored
their survival and elaboration in the New World.[21]

Wasson's discoveries as to the nature of the mysterious *soma* of the
Vedic scriptures and its identification with the fly-agaric mushroom (*Amanita muscaria*) reinforce the verisimilitude of this hypothesis by demonstrating the
role of these plants in one of the most important civilizations in human cul-
tural history, carried down to our own time by a still-living tradition, that of
the Vedas and the Upanishads. The fact that this hallucinogenic mushroom
does not seem to play a central role in the life of Hindus *today* merely
demonstrates how the theoretical and practical elaboration of the myths
and rites of this tradition over the course of the centuries has led to its
replacement by images (of gods and worlds) and ritual techniques (of meditation and illumination). The source has been allowed to "sink into oblivion" in what emanates from it. We may suppose that a similar process could
have occurred in the history of other traditions, especially since the history
of religion reveals striking similarities in esoteric teachings with cosmological and psychological scope, beyond the differences in daily exoteric practices, where historical and geographic factors predominate. The case of
American Indians, among whom the ritual usage of illumination and divination by hallucinogenic plants have continued up to our own time, completes this picture. We could never have observed it in the West, because
these customs have been totally eradicated in our own traditions, replaced
at a very early date by the theological and cultural elaboration of the
monotheistic religions.[22] The use of reason, initially theological and then
scientific, led to the repression of the entire world of dreams, myths, sorcerers, and demons; one illumination fought against another, pitting Enlightenment against mystical ecstasy.

The discovery of LSD, along with the subsequent period during
which tens of thousands of individuals in Europe and the United States
experienced the "reality" of modified states of consciousness, can be
viewed as the discovery of the psychologically objective character of the
reality of these states, which then permitted recognition of their fundamental role in the cultural history of societies. This discovery was crucial for
the history of knowledge in the West (and hence in the world) because it
was effected thanks to neurochemistry; that is, in the context of the scientific praxis and discourse that typify our societies. In these societies, the
search for such states was initially rejected and condemned by the churches

as idolatry and the work of Satan; next, their reality was utterly denied and relegated to the pathology of the unreal and illusory; finally, unreality and illusion came to be the hallmark not only of these states, but of the religious and theological that had fought against them. Henceforth the only reality worthy of interest and knowledge was that accessible by "normal" sensory experience, informed and fertilized by a reason[23] that use of the critical and scientific method had progressively fashioned and modeled, totally divorced from everything that might recall its troubled origins, still present in the rational theology of the Middle Age and in alchemy.

None of this is intended to cheapen or deprecate the ancient revelations, but, on the contrary, to demonstrate the importance and the mental and sociocultural reality of those experiences known as "modified states of consciousness," which have led to the notion, more or less fabulous, of a "separate reality."[24] Certainly this notion is eminently debatable; one can just as well conclude, along with Weston La Barre, that "in hallucinosis, cultural or chemical, we do not need to postulate some mad 'separate reality' because it is always a case of our self-same selves in different psychic states."[25] Nevertheless, one can no longer deny the reality of the phenomenon of different psychic states in a dimension that is no longer pathological but extends to the very sources of humanity and the birth of civilization. In addition, the discovery of the neurophysiological and neuropharmacological basis of these states, far from devaluing the content of the "inspired" and "revealed" teachings of yore, helps show us—and perhaps makes us experience—this "elsewhere" that is the probable origin of rite and of the internalization of ritual injunctions, and subsequently of ethical ones, when they replaced the former.

Furst seems to be right on target in the conclusion to his narrative of the discovery of LSD by A. Hofman in the Sandoz Laboratories in Basel:

> Thus began the saga of LSD-25, the most potent psychoactive or "psychedelic" compound known up to that time, whose discovery ushered in a whole new era of exploration into the nature of the unconscious and the historical role of hallucinogens in the evolution and maintenance of metaphysical and even social systems. And inasmuch as it opened new vistas for the cross-cultural and multidisciplinary investigation of what has been called "inner space," one cannot but agree with psychologist Duncan B. Blewett (1969) that the discovery of LSD marked, together with the splitting of the atom and the discovery of the biochemical role of DNA, the basic genetic material of inheritance, one of the three major scientific breakthroughs of the twentieth century.[26]

To the discovery of LSD one could add that of the unconscious, but in fact the former leads back to the latter: whereas the discovery of the effects of hallucinogens made it possible to objectify the reality of mystical experiences, and their role in the origin and development of the cultures that nurtured us seems extremely likely, the world of dreams has been individualized, in its specific psychic reality, as the privileged mirror of the unconscious. This, inter alia, is how Freud and his disciples rediscovered the unconscious, in Western civilization from which Reason and Enlightenment had banished it, using the very tools of the scientific and critical method that reason and enlightenment had forged.

As a result, we can now describe a continuum of excited states of the central nervous system, characterized by quite different states of alertness, perception, and, more generally, presence in the world, from paradoxical sleep with dreams through hallucinatory states, whether apparently spontaneous, as in schizophrenic states, or culturally triggered and controlled by ecstatic techniques, or chemically induced, externally, by psychomimetic substances. A neurophysiological theory of the continuum of these states, characterized by a greater or lesser degree of depolarization of the neuronal membranes, itself produced by various sorts of inhibition of neuronal metabolism, naturally leads to the hypothesis of endogenous psychomimetic substances that would be the products of "abnormal" metabolic paths starting from the normal neurotransmitters of cerebral functioning, metabolic paths that have actually been identified and provide a basis for this hypothesis.[27]

Once this continuum is recognized, whatever may happen to the precise biochemical hypotheses that attempt to give an account of it, the result is a particular situation with regard to our judgments concerning the nature of reality. On the one hand, reality as it appears to us through these states is multiple and diverse. On the other hand, the experience we can have of this continuum, that is, of the self-identical self that traverses all of these states, permits us, despite everything, to have a glimpse of a unified reality—precisely to the extent that our self can remain unified and does not fragment into the diversity of these states. This particular and unaccustomed situation, of which we can speak in the language of our culture on the basis of extreme experiences rediscovered and decoded in the language of neurophysiology, was known and described by all so-called primitive societies in *their own* languages. The history of religions and of Reason in the West caused us to forget it, until we rediscovered it thanks to LSD and psychoanalysis. It was this experience of multiple states of consciousness that was expressed in the multiplicity of worlds described by the ancient traditions and especially in the distinction, which anthropologists have accustomed us to describe and find everywhere, between the sacred and the profane, with their different levels or concentric circles.[28]

It is the ritual object that unifies these worlds, that presentifies the world of dreams and hallucinations in the waking world of effective action, without, however, erasing the distinctions and evaporating the divisions. Once the individual perceives itself as subject, simultaneously dispersed and unified, the ritualization of language, the sexual, the alimentary, work, and passion institutes its relations to space-time and to the Other as privileged vehicles of the revelation of the sacred. Whether these revelations are the occasion of an opening onto the infinite or, on the contrary, of a closure even more effective in that it closes on a grandiose palace, it is clearly the ambiguity of the forbidden tree, "good-evil," of the Garden of Eden; that which the prophets of Israel denounced as occlusive idolatry, in which what is revealed threatens to replace and shatter revelation. D. H. Ingalls discovered in the Rig Veda two sorts of rituals, chanted in two sorts of hymns, which he described and differentiated as follows:

> The typical Agni hymn juxtaposes a given ritual with a mythical prototype, with the *"prathamani dharmani."* The ritual is intended to reactivate the prototype and to give to the participants the strength of their semi-divine ancestors. The Soma hymns, on the other hand, employ their imagery quite differently. The ascent of Soma to the river of heaven is not an act in the mythical past. It is happening right now, as the Soma juice cascades through the trough.... I am speaking of two sorts of religious expression and religious feeling, one built about the hearth fire, with a daily ritual: calm, reflective, almost rational; the other built around the Soma experience which was never regularized into the calendar, which was always an extraordinary event, exciting, immediate, transcending the logic of space and time.[29]

Although Ingalls criticizes Wasson's thesis about the nature of soma, and whatever the difference between these two types of rituals may be, we are still dealing with "the two great roads between this world and the other world...; they are the great channels of communication between the human and the divine."[30] This brings to mind the kabbalistic formula that precedes and introduces the performance of each precept in Jewish ritual: "In the name of the unification of the Separate–Increased–Who-is and of his presence."

## Transcendentalities of Ethics and Logic

Wasson traces this first function of ritual back to the earliest cultural creations of mankind. "Its role in human culture may go back far, to the time when our ancestors first lived with the birch[31] and the fly-agaric, back perhaps through the Mesolithic and into the Paleolithic."[32] It is normal that little by little it became incomprehensible, as the world of dreams and hallucinations disappeared from our cognitive universe, ultimately to be locked away in psychiatric hospitals. Its only remaining permissible manifestation was artistic expression, licit only on condition, however, that it not try to interfere with "true" knowledge. It is also normal that the problems of the foundations of ethics and esthetics have remained mysterious and insoluble in such a world, where the multiplicity of cognitive experiences is reduced to the single reality of our so-called normal waking state. We might well take as our own Wittgenstein's remark that "ethics is transcendental."[33] This is indeed the case, if immanence concerns only the world of our objectifiable sensations, which constitutes the totality of the real for the normal mind in the West: the world that can be known precisely through the methods of logical positivism.

For the very same Wittgenstein, however, following Kant, logic too is transcendental[34] (and in relation to this same world), but in a different way. We are not dealing with the discovery of a single and unique transcendence, in the manner of theology, but with two transcendentalities, known through two separate cognitive experiences, differing from each other and from sensory data.[35] The transcendental character of logic derives from a cognitive experience diversely described: that of logical *necessity*, or of the conditions of the a priori possibility of rational knowledge of reality, for Kant;[36] or more simply, as for Descartes,[37] the ordering of our sensations by our reason, and the consequent construction of a coherence that guarantees for us the reality of a world that God, a perfect being who does not wish to deceive us, wanted to be accessible to our understanding; or again, the ludic experience of infinite, although ordered and defined, multiplicity, of different "rationally possible worlds" described in Hintikka's manner[38] by formal languages, and tested for their "immanence" (i.e., their "real" existence) by algorithmic games of hide and seek.

Starting from this world of objective knowledge one encounters, instead of one transcendence, at least two transcendentalities, deriving from two of our fundamental cognitive experiences: dreams and logic. Both differ from that furnished by our "normal" perceptions, ordered and socialized by our natural languages.[39] From this perspective, too, the object of ritual is to unify all these worlds.

The unification of the world of logic with that of sensations has always been the goal of philosophy and science in their explanatory praxis, in addition to their goal of mastery and transformation, accomplished through technique; that is to say, in their practical aspect through which they most closely resemble the mystical and mythical traditions from which they have taken the baton. Moreover, the explanatory goal often

seems to be attained, and this appearance leads to the petrification of dogmas in which unification assumes an air of success and completion (unless
this too is a case of wishful thinking, in which we wish it were so, perhaps
to reassure ourselves against the disquieting strangeness produced by the
experience of the separation of the two worlds and the transcendentality of
one vis-à-vis the other). This dogmatic fixation is at the source of the confusion between the rational and the habitual: when a delimited field of our
experiences becomes habitual for us and we have also successfully rationalized it (in the positive sense of the term, i.e., explaining and mastering it
through reason), then everything that diverges from this domain of experience strikes us not only as abnormal, but even as irrational.

Moreover, each culture plays a fundamental role in this confusion. In
our societies, under the influence of a certain use of the *sciences humaines*
and of what M. de Dieguez has called the "rational myth of the West,"[40]
this confusion often winds up by seeing rationality only in the habitual repetition of predictable behavior, common to all or to the majority that constitutes the norm. This norm is then imposed, not as an external heaven-
fallen rule, but as the ineluctable result of the rationality of our knowledge;
to deviate from it constitutes a transgression not only of moral or social law
but also "insanity," the transgression of the laws of reason. For this unifying
myth that has invented its own rituals, scientific method is the only source
of "objective" truth; that is, truth that can be accepted by everyone and is
therefore compulsory. As we have seen, technical effectiveness serves as the
foundation for the belief in the truth of the results of the same method
when applied to human phenomena.

Unfortunately, the application of this method requires that its
object—in the present instance, the reality of the life of human beings as
individuals and in society—also be made as controllable and reproducible
as possible. To use the expression of H. van Foerster and J.-P. Dupuy,[41] individuals must be "trivialized." But this renders them less and less human
and increasingly distances the object of these sciences from the lived reality
that was their point of departure. As we saw previously, the so-called soft
sciences involve us more in proportion as they are less "true"—less true
than this scientific truth, whose criteria are instituted by the game of the
natural sciences when applied to idealized and cut-to-order human affairs,
for the needs of the "cause"; and less true than the "truth that does not concern us" of which Nietzsche speaks. On the contrary, the more that a scientific discipline concerns us, the less chance it has of being true, of tying
together, because it has no choice, "convictions and lies."[42] The preachers
of antiquity, knowing that it could not be otherwise, posited as the origin of
the convictions that regulate social behavior not science or Reason, but
something beyond Reason, which they called a "god."[43] Closer to us, the

example of psychoanalysis, which we have discussed at length in the context of the controversy between Jung and Freud over the scientific character of their respective approaches, is also particularly vivid. It is the profound implication of the practitioner's life in his practice, interacting with the life of the subject-object of study, that allows Lacan[44] to situate psychoanalysis somewhere between magic, religion, and science, that allows Michel Foucault to characterize it as an "antiscience,"[45] and that allows Castoriadis to see in it a project of change more than a project of knowledge,[46] all of them following Wittgenstein, who saw it, quite simply, as a mythology (although endowed with "a great power"[47]).

Thus the transcendentalities of ethics and logic began by being transcendent. Initially the former could not function by being internalized, except thanks to the experience[48] of this transcendence in dream states and all sorts of hallucinations. As for the transcendentality of logic, it was at first that of the ancient revealed texts of the mystical traditions, continuing through alchemical knowledge founded on *prisca sapientia*, the primordial knowledge from which Newton still drew inspiration. It was replaced, thanks to Kepler and the same Newton,[49] among others, by that of the calculus, leading to the mathematization of science, as represented by contemporary physics. It is also what produced, despite all the ruptures, denials, and alerts, the mystical temptation of science, whose most refined form was perhaps that of Jung and his disciples. That is how this temptation rejoins the need to unify ethics and knowledge, no longer in ritual, but in a unifying theory or lore.

Far from this temptation, however, the transcendentality of ethics continues to pose its own problems: it is confounded with the experience of our own life, which is both passionate and cognitive, hallucinatory and rational, individual and collective, the permanence of the I and the constant renewal of the Me.[50] Thus this transcendentality,[51] like that of logic,[52] appears to be very different from transcendence. It is not that of meaning and the origin of meaning, posited as outside the world. Quite the contrary: what is transcendental in life is the absence of all possible meaning concerning our experience of meaning, when we realize that every meaning is *in* the world because every meaning is interpretation, construction, self-creation.

## Symbols and Rituals

There remains the question, need, or desire to make the sacred present in the profane, to project the "black and opaque light" of dreams and prophecy in the light of day. This need permits internalization of and participation in the rituals, magical and religious, from which are derived—

sometimes by breaching them—social codes and morals. Such unification by ritual, unlike mystical ecstasy itself, corresponds to a need or desire for union without fusion, for establishing a relationship among the different worlds of our experience. Each civilization has evolved in its own unique character through the different modalities of such relations. Magic, in which ritual establishes a direct one-for-one correspondence between the elements of the diurnal world and those of the nocturnal world, was followed by theistic religions, in which ritual achieves this unification through the mediation of personal gods, whose intention and will are expressed by this ritual. Humanist morality can be seen as another such modality, subsequent to the latter, in which the god of monotheism is replaced by a humanity that is abstract even though (and because) it is illuminated by Reason. Without delving here into anthropology or the history of religion, we can imagine how the variations in rites and morals[53] that characterize these civilizations resulted from geographical and historical determinants that differentially modulated this ritual and ethical function or need. Furthermore, the theorization of ritual by traditional teachings, its depiction as rational or irrational, depending on the situation, follows its own course in each tradition, where the "worlds" are depicted in relation to the historical and cultural experiences of that society. In particular, the degree of rationalization may be different. The question of the tripartite relations—the relations with each of the two transcendentalities, the transcendentality of dream and that of reason, of "worlds above" and "possible worlds," as well as the relations between them—is always posed in one fashion or another.

In certain currents of Jewish mysticism,[54] still marked by the talmudic tradition, the concern for rationalization remains; the use of different kinds of reasoning serves as an authentic intermediary between the initiatory experiences of revelation, to which the readers are not necessarily supposed to have had access, and those of the daily world of "action," where the content of these experiences must be made present and known to them. A narrow but critical collaboration evolved between the enlightened sage and the illuminated prophet, with no fusion between them,[55] in which the sage had the last word. A remark attributed to the hasidic master Rabbi Nahman of Bratslav (1772–1811), mystic, poet, and also leader of a community, underlines this orientation. H. Weiner, writing of the universal and ultimately identical character of the content of the illumination that all mystics attain, and also of the originality of the Jewish mystical tradition in the context of the psychedelic discoveries of the 1960s, reports that Rabbi Nahman said one day: "For us the true problem is not going, but coming back."[56] This is an allusion to the incessant back-and-forth movement of the angels in Ezekiel's vision, a metaphor for the paths of illumination. It almost amounts to saying: "The whole world ascends the same steps in illumination, but we have specialized in the descent." The ultimate goal is not illumination-that-unifies, but the return to dispersion. The goal is never ultimate, because it is a back-and-forth movement from one world to the other, whose reality we accept even though our experiences of them are mutually exclusive.

## The Rationalities of Magic and of Science

This need for unification through ritual, or rather of passage without fusion from the world of night (and dreamlight) to that of day, does not correspond only to some need for reconciliation felt by our "I," which perceives itself as sundered by the fundamental experiences of its own reality. Bringing these two worlds together is necessary, not only for the convenience of our life as social individuals, but also to *guarantee the growth of analytic knowledge itself*, knowledge of the world of the waking state and rationality. The world of hallucination and dreams is a world without negation, and thus without a principle of noncontradiction, in which everything is unified, interwoven, and confounded—but, curiously, in which differences are not abolished. There is no opposition between affirmation and negation in a dream, as Freud understood immediately. This can be an advantage for processes of discovery, scientific and other, because new syntheses can be undertaken in a world without contradictions. It is subsequently a matter of passing them through the matrix of analytic and critical formulation, which either rejects them or gives them, if "possible," a rational, that is, noncontradictory, form, in accordance with the criteria of the waking world in which the principles of identity and noncontradiction reign supreme. This is equally relevant for nonscientific rationalities, such as magic, which are just as sensitive to the constraining character of these principles in daily life, which we are tempted to call nonsymbolic or profane.

There is one difference, however: in ritual and magic[57] one encounters, in addition to their symbolic character—also to be found in the abstractions of scientific discourse, notably mathematics—an *a priori value* on which the symbol rests. Unlike the symbolic expressions of scientific formulas, here the symbols are always of *something with value*.[58] The power or efficacy attributed to these expressions derives from this value. We may wonder about the origin of this value, about what allows people to believe a priori in the power of the deities or forces of which the expressions are symbols. It cannot be a case of empirical observation only, of lived or recounted experiences. Unless we hold that individuals or civilizations who accept and transmit these beliefs are rationally deficient, by comparison with us Westerners, we cannot imagine that the experience involved is the same as we all have in our own so-called normal waking state. For that would mean that the causal relations we have discovered in or projected on that state are constitutionally beyond the mental capacities of these individuals and civilizations. We know that this is false: magical systems of explanation frequently coexist with technical scientific systems, because magician and adept can perfectly distinguish a ritual from a nonritual act, just as they are aware of the symbolic character of a symbol, which they do not confuse with a thing of which it may or may not be the symbol. Hence it is not absurd to hold that these fundamental experiences are indeed those of "the other reality," taken seriously in these civilizations, whereas ours has rejected them.

Once again, it is not a question of rejecting the functional explanations, which assert that magical practices stabilize society by virtue of associating the more or less unconscious needs of individuals with their manipulation by the wielders of power, preachers and sorcerers, humbugs or not. It is to this function of social stabilization that the classical explanations assign the origin of mythico-ritual systems, which religious and later ethical systems have replaced in our latitudes. But these explanations are insufficient if they leave aside the conscious internalization of these practices, or the belief in their effectiveness held by those who live them, or again the rationality of their behavior when this is defined as an "adequacy of means to the ends pursued." As Tom Settle wrote in "The Rationality of Science versus the Rationality of Magic": "Functionalist analysis insults those who practise magic by explaining their magic without recourse to the assumption of their rationality (in any normal sense)."[59]

Thus we must admit the existence of a powerful process of internalization by which these sociocultural systems, whether or not imposed by mystifying powers, have been developed and taken over in their turn by individuals endowed with reason, critical sense, and creative capacities. We can even admit, with Settle, that the critical tradition, as a sociocultural phenomenon, is peculiar to the Western—and quite recent—practice of science, in which explanatory incompleteness, the correlative of unbounded openness and questioning, has been most highly valued; whereas the magical mode of thought is traditionally uncritical, because it seeks a final explanatory completeness. This fundamental difference, even if one admits its generality and absolute dichotomous character,[60] does not imply that individual participants in this noncritical tradition are themselves devoid of critical sense and rationality.

Once again, we can identify this process of internalization with the experience of the "other worlds" of hallucinations and dreams, thanks to which we have (or can have) immediate access to this "other reality," a source of value even if only by the enjoyment of these experiences, that is, their character of ecstasy, of going beyond, which posits them ipso facto as objects of desire, goals to be obtained, encounters to renew, lost paradises to be regained.

Even in our civilization, despite the repression of the content of these experiences and their transformation into theological pseudo-rationalizations or incomprehensible acts of faith—valued all the more because they are incomprehensible, irrational, and absurd—we have been able or compelled to preserve at least a possible access to these worlds. This access still assumes an institutionalized and codified, controlled and ritualized form, in which we encounter this presence in the individual of more-than-the-individual, thanks to which something that is other and outside can be internalized and given a value. The most "common" (even if contradictory) access route to these worlds of ecstasy and enjoyment, one that seems in principle to be available to all, is clearly love, with the multiple forms that "love stories"[61] can assume in various civilizations, from the sacred prostitutes of antiquity through today's 'desire', by way of the courtly love of medieval chivalry and other more or less explicit, more or less sublimated, more or less desexualized eroticisms, depending on time and place.

Here, however, the manifest physical roots of the body, sex, and reproduction, and the fact that this physical presence is, from the outside, common to the human race and to animals (at least to mammals), have permitted scientific rationalism to attempt to acquire "objective" knowledge of it. This is what allows us to speak of it in terms of impulses, of "machines of desire,"[62] or of "machines to fabricate meaning,"[63] in succession to Freud's sexual energy. Today this last is somewhat out of fashion[64] in many psychoanalytic schools, which see the libido in a broader fashion than as an energy or fluid obeying a principle of conservation and the law of communicating vessels—to the point that Lacan can affirm, just as legitimately in a context of transference or of "pleasure," in his sense of the term, that there is no sexual relation; whereas Julia Kristeva, observing that the only remnant in contemporary society of the ecstasy and access to higher worlds of antiquity is Art and amorous states, notes that "the only ones who are alive are lovers, those undergoing analysis, or those captivated by literature."[65]

## Modern Unifying Temptations: Jung and Complementarity

The games of love, ritual, and knowledge are all that remain of game-playing as the symbol of the world. Only on condition that we live them as games can we also tackle the question of ethics and not be swept away by the impossible alternative between unsmiling belief in dogma and an authentic nihilist skepticism that generally leads to schizophrenia and/or suicide.

Before we reach there, however, a number of pitfalls lie in wait on our path, all the more effective because they satisfy, with subtlety and finesse, what we have seen to be a fundamental human need, such that we are fooling ourselves if we pretend to eliminate, ignore, or bypass it. Certain crude and occult forms exploit the success of science fiction—which, as we shall see, constitutes an important vista on this universe of the games of knowledge—by making it drift insensibly toward pseudo-science. This is not the place to analyze in detail these forms, which can easily be demystified,[66] precisely because of their excesses, even if they do not cease to be dangerous by abusing the credulity of nonspecialists.

It seems more important to return to a vein we have already encountered, sufficiently rich to inspire profound thinkers, scientists and philosophers, one that runs through our century—sometimes underground and untoward, sometimes bursting forth and triumphant. I am referring to the work of Carl Gustav Jung and its various extensions.

Jung endeavored to rehabilitate alchemy by demonstrating its foundations in the archetypical structures of a universal and objective unconscious, at work in the productions of the human psyche, in all their forms—mythic and scientific—and also in the very structure of the universe that this psyche strives to uncover. This amounts to creating a neoalchemy, precisely that of the Jungian schools, where the vocabulary has changed slightly but the method is the same. Instead of speaking of the philosophers' stone and liberation, we are now dealing with individuation and cure; instead of grounding the initiatory path on the labor of the forge, the transmutation of metals, and the search for the philosophers' stone, it is based on the practice—whether as collective knowledge or mediated by physicists—of particle and high-energy physics searching for the ultimate secrets of matter. As in the case of the ancient traditions, including alchemy, the concern of this enterprise—quite legitimate in this context and on condition that we know and state it—is still to ground ethics, with the aim of liberating neurotic alienations, on the basis of psychoanalysis. Jung formulates it quite well in his theories of individuation and the self as a process of unifying light and shadow; whereas Freud, surrendering himself to the scientist's illusion, sees it as a chase after an illusion and will-o'-the-wisp, later taken up by his more or less dissident Lacanian disciples as an attempt to "unmask reality" or to make the "truth of the subject" appear. There too the necessary guard-rail that the Jungians were unable to erect consists of cautiously distinguishing between the enterprise as a project of transformation (liberation, individuation of the subject) and as a project of knowledge, to borrow Castoriadis's terms. The Freudians have been, relatively speaking, better endowed from this point of view, and in any case Freud himself displayed an exemplary rigor on this point: through his attachment to analysis in the strict sense, as a process of separation and diversification, he reserved for synthesis and unification a status that is always provisional and ultimately secondary to criticism that never flags, in the "interest" of a reason that is socially identified with that of the scientific community he wanted to persuade.

As a project of transformation, in a direct line of descent from mythical traditions, and on condition that we not see it as a science of reality (veiled reality and unconscious being taken for indistinguishable synonyms), the Jungian enterprise is not lacking in majesty. It makes it possible to link up, through one language of our age, with the founding experience of ethics—the experience of the worlds of hallucination and dreams, where the archetypes have their place, rather than in mathematical physics. We may nevertheless wonder whether, as a means of retrieving this experience, the paths offered directly by the teachings of the various mystical traditions themselves, in their original languages, might not be at least as effective, perhaps aided by the exploration of modified states of consciousness induced in some fashion.[67] Probably, though, these teachings are insufficiently "scientific" and are thereby disqualified in the eyes of those who do not wish to accept such a distinction between objective science and mystical knowledge. It is as if the latter needs a scientific robe and label to stand upright as Truth.

Let us stop, nevertheless, at a more refined manner of invoking the Unity of the Whole, toward which science and mysticism converge (or from which they proceed): that which speaks of complementarity. Once again, quantum physics has clearly made its contribution, this time in the form of the Bohr complementarity principle. This originally consisted of noting the duality with which we can represent a photon or electron or any elementary particle—as a wave or as a particle—depending on the type of experience to be accounted for; for example, interference as a wave phenomenon, the photoelectric effect as a particle phenomenon. Lévy-Leblond's metaphor of the cylinder[68] has shown us how physicists' greater familiarity with quantum mechanics' computational tools and reasoning reduces this principle to two different perspectives on the same phenomenon, which is described and represented, even if abstractly, as a quantum object that is just as well defined as instantaneous velocity or inertia, objects of classical physics that are equally as abstract but have become thoroughly familiar after centuries of use. In the early years of quantum physics, however, Bohr posited the complementarity principle and tried to provide it with an epistemological or even metaphysical justification. Similarly, the writings of Pauli, von Neumann, and Wigner always contained material for extrapolations and extensions that could be seen as physical justifications of metaphysical or mystical concepts, as in Jung's article on synchronicity, published along with Pauli.[69] This is the current situation among Jung's disciples,[70] for whom complementarity has been extended to mediate "between science and mysticism": the two are no longer unified, as certain naive physicists would believe, but rather complementary, in the sense that they represent two different points of view on the same hidden reality. This reality peeps out through them, and especially through the "unknowing knowledge" offered by Jung's theory of archetypes and the collective unconscious. Despite the many passages about the inconscient or unknowing character that overlays this unveiling of the unconscious in the psychology of depths (i.e., Jungian psychoanalysis), the number and volume of the writings that deal with it, by the master and his disciples, more closely resemble a corpus of knowledge than of ignorance!

Hence, although this complementarity explicitly rejects a fusion of scientific and mystical discourse, it is nevertheless expressed in a metadiscourse, the Jungian discourse where this fusion is said and written through many long pages and books. We can understand the interest expressed by these authors in the theory of implicate (and implicit) order of D. Bohm,[71] who endeavored, *explicitly*, to produce a theory of this fusion, once again as a metadiscourse inspired by physics, whereas Jung's is clearly of psychological inspiration.

At a certain level, the complementarity of science and mysticism is trivial, in the sense that the same humanity collectively produced both methods; and in the sense that, individually, it is possible to borrow from both of them, playing the rules of each game. But the rules make these two methods mutually exclusive, for each claims exclusivity as a matter of principle. Each posits, as its point of departure, that its horizon of relevance is unbounded and that it is capable, in principle, of accounting for all that exists. Thus there cannot be any logical or cognitive or even simply discursive complementarity of science and mysticism. The complementarity of fact, which is trivial, implies nothing else that can be said other than the side-by-side existence of these two mutually exclusive methods.

But this is not nothing: they can still conduct a dialogue. And this dialogue can be fruitful for both of them, on condition, again, that it is not really a quest for a metadiscourse that would swallow them both up.

This mutual fertilization can be decisive in the *genesis*[72] of scientific discoveries or of mystical illuminations, but it quickly becomes sterile when it goes beyond the instant of discovery and claims to establish theories, metatheories, or even philosophical meditations that are to be taken seriously as objects of belief.

## The New Myths of Science Fiction

"An epochal scientific theory may regenerate in contemporaneous poetry into an elemental myth."[73] A single path still appears possible, if one does not want or cannot remain silent; namely, science fiction as a source of new unifying myths, *on condition that they are presented as such.* Science fiction plugs us back in, in a way, to the experience of multiple worlds, of a "separate reality," but as literature allows us to maintain a certain distance. Thus, and by a different road, it satisfies the demand for distinction and differentiation; the demand that made Freud—who was plugged into the other reality, too, by the discovery of the unconscious— resist, perhaps without knowing why, the Jungian temptations of the black mud of occultism.

Science fiction, and myth that presents itself as such, clearly raise the ambiguity of the ineffable that is nevertheless spoken, of the merely implicit that is nevertheless made abundantly explicit, because the character of truth of what they say is eliminated straight away, with no danger of being taken seriously, in the sense of becoming a creed. This complementarity can be expressed *only in such a fashion that one cannot believe in it*: this is precisely the function of science fiction.

Steven Weinberg's *The First Three Minutes* must be read as science fiction, as must Carl Sagan's *Cosmos*; so too the work of Jung and his disciples on the principle of synchronicity. As such, these theories or descriptions can be useful by answering the need for new unifying myths, to the extent that the ancient myths can no longer be understood directly.

The question of ethics and its ancient mythic origin remains, even if the latter has been forgotten and repressed by the Indo-European religions and by philosophy. We cannot rid ourselves of the conviction that "man as man is summoned to know what is right and what is wrong, for emptied of such knowledge he is unable to decide what is better or what is worse."[74] At the same time, science, which is supposed to tell us what is true and what is false, can do this only by renouncing the role of helping us decide what is better and what is worse, because its successes have been obtained only by a surrender of the right to ask about moral values. Certainly this renunciation is, in principle, provisional; we know that the reductionist program of the scientific method, even in the weak sense, implies the hope that one day it will be possible to give an account of behavior in terms of psychosocial states, themselves described in terms of neuronal states of brains interacting among themselves and with their environment. But "man as man is summoned" to make a decision here and now; we do not have time to wait for the success of the reductionist program, even if we seriously believe in it.

Nor can we base our decisions on the injunctions of ancient traditions, which are often incomprehensible and inadequate, because of the changes that have taken place in our physical and social environment and in the types of interaction that are possible with that environment. Moreover, the responsibility of science, and of the technology that it has produced, for the occurrence of these changes is evident. This reinforces the idea and the demand—albeit contradicted by the scientific method itself—that the true and false that make it possible to decide about good and evil be enunciated by science; and the circle is closed on itself.

To escape from it, only a new myth supported by science, but not scientific, can pick up the torch of the ancient myths, which have themselves handed on the experiences of ecstasy, hallucination, and dream—whatever their origin, induced by soma or by the Tree of Knowledge, produced by Jaynes's bicameral mind, or something else. This role of new myth is played by science fiction. But at least science fiction knows that it is a myth; whereas the grand unifying theories that present themselves as science, true because rational (truth without fiction), deny their mythic function even while nevertheless playing their role of myth, as in a variation of the "return of the repressed." The ancient origins of ethics in the experience of different worlds that transcended each other (but were also immanent, in that the same individuals experienced them) and in the need to unify these worlds in a life wherein night is not totally severed from day, dream from the waking state, the sacred from the profane, have been denied and repressed: first by the monotheist religions, in which unification eventually killed the experience of the plurality of worlds, and later by unifying science and the philosophy of universal reason, which did an even better job of denying and repressing original experiences. It is this repressed need that returns, in the twin forms of what is called the "return of the irrational" and the need to nevertheless ground this irrationality in scientific truth. Now, however, the need is for more complete unification, encompassing the experience of other worlds, which makes possible a return of transcendence able to ground ethics, as in the past, along with the experience of scientific truth as universal Truth, uncovering the hidden but One reality of things.

## Severing Science from Its Origins

This need for unification spawns these attempts—fascinating when expressed with talent, as in certain works by Jung and philosophers who followed him—to relink science to its mythical and alchemical origins. These origins are unmasked both in history, where the rifts between

Greek philosophy and myth, between modern science and alchemy, are described with an emphasis on the continuity of the terrain on which they occurred, and in modern scientific creation, from Newton the kabbalist(?)[75] and alchemist through the fathers of quantum physics, with the focus on the role, still alchemical albeit repressed, that mathematical abstractions, as revelations of archetypes, played in the genesis of these theories. From this bifold origin, in history and in the mental mechanisms of contemporary scientific creation, we are led to "wonder whether the myth of pure science, the historical rationalism that we have seen develop since the last century, and the materialist theses that accompany it, are not frequently at first the products of a discourse that is cut off from its deepest sources."[76] Science has indeed been severed from its origins. But what these authors do not want to see is that it cannot be what it is *without* remaining severed from its deepest sources and that any attempt to reestablish the continuity, even in some grand cosmic and archetypal complementarity, extrapolated from the small and provisional wave-particle complementarity, leads only to the sterilization of scientific research, to its speedy and dogmatic closure within a metatheory where everything is definitively explained in the context of a single interpretive system, necessarily limited in content but asserting universal pretensions.

Like the metaphysics of the cosmic soul nourished by mystical traditions,[77] this metatheory can certainly nurture religious élan and authentic mystical communions; but as epistemology it leads to the closure on themselves of the still-open fronts of the various domains of scientific exploration. For Jung, at "the moment when physics touches on the 'untrodden, untreadable regions,' and when psychology has at the same time to admit that there are other forms of psychic life besides the acquisitions of personal consciousness—in other words, when psychology too touches on an impenetrable darkness," then, instead of exploring beyond these new enigmas and what is specific to them, "the intermediate realm of subtle bodies comes to life again"—the "intermediate realm," which characterized alchemy, "between mind and matter, i.e., a psychic realm of subtle bodies whose characteristic it is to manifest themselves in a mental as well as a material form," and where "the physical and the psychic are once more blended in an indissoluble unity."[78] The result is a mystical fusion, once again with authentic accents, into the indissociable unity of their own psyche and physique, of those who allow themselves to be carried away by the current. At the same time, however, there is a violent halt to the exploration of the unknown, posited initially as unknown and not as *anima mundi*; even if today (unlike the prescientific epoch of medieval alchemy, and because of the nevertheless unavoidable character of contemporary science) [the *anima mundi*] is no longer the magic motor, the imaginary force that moves the universe, but rather the unconscious that is revealed and takes shape in the reversion of the conscious..., an objective psyche that man can see, that can be lived and thought, and is established in the soul.[79]

Instead of holes in knowledge that must be filled in, step by step, in an asymptotic progression, the unifying and recovering blanket of the world soul and of Being is posited a priori. This inversion of the scientific process is characteristic of mystical fusion, which thereby denies its pretensions to unify science and mysticism: ultimately these remain apart, because despite everything one of them is denied in its practice, denied by the fact that the other is affirmed.

This neoalchemical metatheory inaugurated by Jung and his disciples, *which presents itself not as a unifying myth but as Ultimate Scientific Truth*, is supposed to derive its "ultimate" character from its openness to the transcendent origins, and its truth from its dependence on the sciences. As such, it can only sterilize the multiple courses of the various sciences toward their ever-open future and never-realized unity, because it seeks to forcibly return them to their origins, with which they must break. It emasculates the scientific method even if one takes into account those of its original aspects that continue to mark it, on the level of the creation of new theories and hypotheses, in the brains and with the unconscious of those in whom they germinate, anarchically or not, before being tested—if the consensus of specialists accepts them as susceptible to testing. This is the twin trap to which Popper did *not* fall victim:[80] on the one hand, he located the formation of hypotheses and theories outside the scientific method, in a domain he called "metaphysical" and which did not seem to be his main object of concern; on the other hand, he recognized the reality of this process and its function at the origin of scientific discoveries. That his thesis concerning the falsifiability of theories completely ignored the problem of the acceptance or rejection of a theory as even susceptible of testing— evidently a psychosocial problem in which unconscious interactions continue to play a role—detracts not a whit from the *importance of the unlinking* of the repressed although active origins of science from its conscious method, no longer curious about its origins; a method that characterizes it, for better and for worse, and without which it would not exist.

## Scientistic Temptations

The explicitly idealistic unifying metatheories, such as those of the Jungians, are not the only peril. Others play an even more pernicious role, for they seem to rest exclusively on a genuine materialism, anticipating only slightly the definitive successes of the reductionist program. These include theories such as that of Skinner[81] or those of sociobiology as abusively extended to human societies.[82] Here the question of ethics is "resolved" by being eliminated; but this solution is clearly none at all, because it does not *suppress* the question, which persists despite its theoretical elimination, because, as Heidegger puts it, "materialism has absolutely nothing to do with material. It is itself a form of spirit."[83] One of the simplest yet most profound critiques of these theories is that of W. I. Thompson,[84] attacking Skinner (as well as Delgado, of the Harvard-IBM seminar on technology and society, and the adepts of sociobiology who have gone beyond its legitimate domain by presenting it as a universal sociological theory). To Skinnerian theories of conditioned human behavior as a means of regulating social problems by making the notions of liberty and dignity outmoded and illusory, because relative to this conditioning, Thompson opposes the dualistic and contradictory character of the process of information processing by our (perverse) mind:

> The structural processing of information in the human mind is dualistic: light and dark, good and evil, yes and no, this or that, 1 or 0. *It follows, then, that any social rule, implicit or explicit, is set in consciousness so that its negative inversion automatically comes into existence with its positive formulation.* If you say, "Love Big Brother," you are setting up the syntax to say, preconsciously, "Do not love Big Brother." If you say, "Behave nicely," you are bringing into consciousness the possibility of its opposite. All human thoughts come into the mirror as they become reflected in consciousness; the subconscious is, therefore, not so much Freud's jungle of repressed desires as it is the mirror-image of a particular culture. Any society, behavioral or Baptist, is therefore going to contain the negation of itself *if the people are conscious....* Only by altering the very structure of consciousness can conflict be eliminated, but to effect that alteration, we would have to eliminate the mind.... Thus in order to perfect man, science would have to create a society in which no science was possible.[85]

We encounter this same vicious circle, of science that cannot be used for ethics but is the indispensable reference for a modern mythology that seeks to ground ethics, in the counterproductive phenomena analyzed by Ivan Illich and echoed by Thompson in his description of the processes by which "we become what we hate."[86]

## Science Fiction and Prestidigitation: Effective Nonbeliefs

Finally, to escape this vicious circle, we can fall back only on the grand syntheses that recognize themselves as science fiction. One example among many is that by John Lilly, author of a book on the intelligence of dolphins which is full of digressions, notably anthropological and sociological. He justifies them by presenting himself as a scientist of a particular sort, what he calls a "generalist."

> This term "generalist" means that I do not any longer recognize the walls that have been arbitrarily set up between the sciences. The science of man is to me as important as the science of nuclear physics, or of biology, or of chemistry. In my opinion, the sciences are a continuum of knowledge, broken only by the holes of the unknown.... For example, I need Christ's teachings, the works of Shakespeare, the writings of Aldous Huxley, Prokofieff's and Beethoven's concertos and symphonies, the paintings of Da Vinci, La Tour Eiffel, and the Empire State Building.[87]

In other words, his grandiose synthesis with extrapolations in all directions, based on observations of dolphins, led Lilly, as W. R. Thompson puts it, to be

> the paradox of a man who celebrates the very sciences against whose traditions he seems so bizarre. But paradoxes are appropriate, for what we learn from Dr. Lilly's dolphins is not zoology but anthropology. For a society strangling in its own technology, the dolphins express the ultimate in cultural design: no industrial class stratification, no polluting machines, no civilization with its repression-generated neurosis, but simply a medium through which the sensuous body moves beeping five-dimensional musical metamathematics to its companions and playing space-time chess with the stars.[88]

The result is a process that only seems to be ambiguous, in that Lilly continues to call himself a scientist in his syncretic work of fiction. But his method clearly cannot be accepted as scientific anthropology (since it is in fact delphinology), even while it plays perfectly its role of grounding values that may be active in a human society.

Only the mythic form—and in this regard the ancient myths are just as effective as modern ones, if not more so, when received and understood in a new fashion—permits the indispensable dialogue and cross-fertilization of scientific disjunction and illuminated synthesis. But this is fertilization, once again, and not fusion, neither in a new "materialist" synthesis nor in some alchemical complementarity. Only the mythic form, like art, can function and act without having to be "believed in"—precisely because one need not believe in it—thanks to the distance it establishes from the outset with the operational reality that the search for scientific truth has instituted around us.

It is this that makes science fiction—science viewed as the source of fiction—superior to scientific dogma, games superior to creeds, prestidigitation superior to parapsychology. It is not to scientists that we should appeal to unmask the fakeries of paranormal con artists. Far more effective are the prestidigitators, whose tricks are just as spectacular and just as mysterious, so long as their secrets are not revealed. Science fiction is to the scientific unveiling of ultimate reality what prestidigitation is to parapsychology: both are cases of a partial unveiling of the hidden, with a promise of total disclosure. But unlike the mystics of science and scientific parapsychologies, science fiction and sleight of hand are effective through *nonbelief*.

For a belief is not effective in *practice* (as a source of values) except insofar as it leads to the destruction, in *theory*, of the foundations on which it rests as belief. These foundations can only transform it into dogma and thereby kill any creative effectiveness it might have.

Hence we remain with the conclusion of Ecclesiastes, after its author has noted the dual character of our experiences[89] and warned against the illusions of wisdom taken as the ground for behavior, even while he celebrates its incommensurable superiority over foolishness: "The sum of the matter, when all is said and done: Revere the god(s) and observe his commandments! For the whole of man is made of it."[90] In other words, and in the final analysis, accept that the law comes from somewhere else and is not the object of a theoretical belief "grounded" on or deduced from objective knowledge of reality, but is rather the object of practical behavior, aiming *perhaps* at creating a reality. This attitude, natural in traditional societies, is extremely difficult to maintain in our modern societies, where the intrinsically irrational need for a rational foundation for ethics and behavior leads to the impasses and contradictions we have tried to analyze.

This attitude does not necessarily lead to a sociocultural ethical relativism where anything goes: where human sacrifice, cannibalism, slavery, and torture are justified once codified in the culture of a particular society. On the contrary, the relativism of knowledge that permits a true dialogue of cultures permits the erection of a platform from which the law itself can be judged, not on the basis of an a priori ethics that imposes its universality along with that of Reason, but on the basis of the irreducible character of the individual, which is ineluctably discovered when we cross frontiers and learn to live as members of more than one culture. Then, fulfilling the law, like the actor's role playing, preserves the distance between individual behavior, which flows from the role that must be played in the transforming function of the law, and the *I*, which, even while playing this role, can observe, know, and judge: not from the perspective of an Absolute Being to which knowledge provides access and which must be incarnated in some fashion or other, but from the immediate perspective of the quality of the game; that is, of the effects that playing it has on individuals and on the society in which it is played.

If there exists a universality of ethics, it would be the result of a structure growing progressively out of the uniqueness of cultures and not the result of deduction, of a priori submission to a cultural empire—even that of reason—that would abolish all frontiers under the one-dimensional juggernaut of its uniform law. To renounce judging the multiple variety of ethics and laws on the basis of deduction or a priori principles does not mean to renounce judging their effects and consequences, as the fulfillments of transformational purposes, and certainly not to forget the purposes of knowledge. Judgments of consequences certainly differ according to whether they are rendered by wise men or fools (even though the former cannot be more confident than the latter of the success of their plans).

## From Relativism to Social Theories of Knowledge: The Last Temptation?

Finally, we must guard against falling back, as a last recourse, on another form of metatheoretical unification, this time with the opposing orientation, found in a particular sociology of science.[91] I am referring to another metadiscourse, it too motivated by a concern for ethics, which spawns equally pernicious metatheories in which the question of the specificity of different methods of knowledge is drowned in the unique explanatory system provided by the sociology of knowledge.

Here we must demonstrate that the interests that shape scientific knowledge are not only those of reason, but also those of pressure groups close enough to the structures of political power, decision making, and finance to be effective. These view and judge scientific praxis exclusively as a social practice, measured against ideologies or, at best, sociological theories, from which ethical and/or political considerations cannot be absent. That is how—demystifying the naive image of a pure and disincarnate science constantly advancing toward the disinterested discovery of the Truth about the universe and obeying a transparent internal rationality, the very one reconstructed in a process of a posteriori rationalization by the history of science, which fabricates this image—these ideologies or theories reduce the production of scientific knowledge to the outcomes of battles for influence and the balance of social forces. The stakes are political, in every sense, concerning power and domination on the national and international scale as well as power within research and teaching institutions, with the two interacting through research orientations and budgeting priorities.

I do not mean to disregard these stakes and deny their importance; but the idea that a sociological science can serve as a science of science, that it can help us illuminate these determinants and understand the hidden rationality of science so that we can master it and not be manipulated by occult and demoniacal social forces, proceeds from the same temptation to unify knowledge and ethics, now transformed into a desire to ground knowledge on ethics. Starting from ethical and political judgments (clearly formed or not) about war, oppression, lies, hypocrisy, mystification, and so on, the products of science are assessed against the same unifying presupposition that has ethics and knowledge go hand in hand. This presupposition leads to doubt concerning the knowledge value of the results of science, when the practice of these results no longer has the moral disinterestedness and purity of which the naive image would convince us. It is difficult to navigate between these shoals, between the Charybdis of naive scientific realism where Truth, one and ineluctable, is unveiled, and the Scylla of nihilist skepticism, where anything goes and Truth is merely that of those who rule the roost today. This naive sociology of science proposes an end run around the dilemma, but forgets to ask, in an infinite recursion, about its own hidden motives. Nevertheless, certain more elegant versions offer a middle course that allows radical relativism to coexist with a realism of knowledge viewed as an interpreting construction and a (relatively) effective ordering scheme.

Sociological tradition since Durkheim has always avoided applying to science the methods of critical analysis it applies to other forms of knowledge. The products of magical, mythical, or religious thought as social constructions were analyzed in the shelter of the evidence of the unique and absolute character of scientific rationality. The social science that produced these analyses benefited from what Yehuda Elkana calls "the great divide."[92]

This great divide, distinguishing scientific rationality from all other forms of knowledge, grants the former a privileged relationship with Truth, which protects it from the ravages of its own critical method. Once the evidence of this great divide was weakened by the onslaught of the crisis of positivism, science too was seen as the result of a particular culture, produced by Western societies. Continuing in this vein, the same sociological tradition could apply itself to science and arrive at a radical relativism in which even logic and mathematics lose their character of necessary truth. Like the natural sciences developed in the West, they too become no more than the products of the particular society in which they evolved. The social anthropology of Mary Douglas,[93] following the Durkheimian tradition in the present-day post–logical-positivist context, nurtured by the students of Popper and Wittgenstein, leads naturally to such a relativist radicalism.

But from this starting point there are several possible paths. One of them would shift the great divide and relocate it between sociology and everything else. No longer does science, in general, provide the universal context where Truth is uncovered, while other forms of knowledge are only stammering and illusory approximations thereof, because science is itself analyzed as a theory of knowledge. Instead, the role of metascience sheltered from the critical method that it applies to other forms of knowledge—this time scientific or otherwise—is assigned to social anthropology. Here too we encounter the habitual impasse of the closure of a critical method that recoils from criticizing itself. Another path relativizes the social theory of knowledge itself, as itself produced by one of the scientific disciplines developed in the West; hence it has no cachet enabling it to escape the common lot of these disciplines. It is then only too easy to transform this radical relativism into the nihilist skepticism where anything goes, leading most often to the most threadbare obscurantisms under the cover of "counterculture," spontaneity, and rehabilitation of individual experience that claims to be irreducible (artistic, religious, mystical, or simply that of life in the here and now).

We have abundant examples of the first type of impasse, encountered by social philosophies blind about themselves, in the social theories of (scientific) knowledge that have emerged in recent years. Quite schematically, the extreme form of these theories holds that science can assert no pretensions to universal truth because, like every other form of knowledge, it is a product of the society where it evolved. As such, it expresses only the outcome of conflicts of interest and balances of power that characterize this society. Of course, the critique of the foundations of the scientific method, following Popper and leading to the epistemological relativism of Lakatos and Feyerabend, paved the way to this social relativism. Popper himself, though, did not renounce a relatively autonomous sphere of truth, even if it could manifest itself only negatively (by demonstrating that a theory or proposition is false) and by reaching to infinity: truth as the object of an aspiration and quest necessarily pursued infinitely. Similarly, we should note how the paternity of the "second" Wittgenstein was invoked here—a claim even more out of line than that which calls the "first" Wittgenstein the father of logical positivism. His relativism of language games, in which the possibility of changing games allows changing the meaning of words, for which only usage and the needs of usage can be held responsible (in the absence of any metarule governing change), is transmuted and reduced to social relativism, susceptible of becoming in its turn the object of science or social philosophy. This is how D. Bloor,[94] for example, uses the deconstructions of Wittgenstein, those in which he tore down every structure that rests on necessary a priori absolute meanings, whose origin is either some internal and subjective sense perception[95] that precedes any social institution of language, or some "natural" objective universal language, like that of mathematics.[96] Bloor wonders about what remains as the source of the multiple and multiform meanings that appear in the mobility and multiplicity of language games, namely, in the only *use* of words practiced by the individual members of a linguistic community (including a scientific or mathematical community), and about the *needs* for change that derive from this usage itself. Wittgenstein went no further than to point to these "needs," created by use, by which and for which the rules of the game modify themselves, but he did not specify their nature. Some see this as a matter of incapacity on his part, whereas others view it as the wisdom of not letting himself get trapped or fall into a new metasystem of reference, in which the theory of these needs would be formulated. Bloor, for his part, would palliate this "incapacity" by interpreting such needs as none other than "social interests," objects of sociological research. This is how he, and others, move down the path that leads from Wittgenstein, quite wrongly, to a "social theory of knowledge."[97]

## *Taking One's Desires for Reality: The Scope and Limits of Wishful Thinking*

To make epistemological relativism lead to a social theory amounts to forgetting to apply to the latter the premises of the former, as we have already indicated on several occasions. What is more, the result is a certain attitude or even ideology concerning the social and ethical implications of knowledge, which, taken to the extreme, can be an apology for wishful thinking. This apology, which is of course never formulated but which flows naturally from the implicit assumptions of this attitude, demonstrates *ad absurdum*[98] the dead end that these theories constitute.

These theories frequently outline our ignorance, both as scientists and as consumers, of the more or less demoniacal social forces that orient research. These (meta)theories explain how such forces, moved by those well-known social interests, permit some scientific theory (not only psychosociological or economic, but also physical, biological, or other) or paradigm (used to winnow scientific from nonscientific questions) to reunite the consensuses that make them exist. Thus scientific research becomes, at least with regard to its means of operation and recognition, the prize of the battle of social forces (the class struggle, for example) or of attempts by pressure groups and ideologies to gain ascendancy and eliminate all rivals. Of course the role of the lucid and moral researcher is to shed light on these motives and reveal how a theory, a fashion in the scientific community, an infatuation with one subject rather than another, are explained by the social and political stakes of the time and place where these phenomena occur. In this role one can still find the means to satisfy the simultaneous need for Truth and Rectitude, as well as what seems to be the even more imperious need to unite the two. But taking such explanations seriously ought normally to lead us to want—this time consciously—to steer research and the establishment of scientific theories in the direction of those noble and lofty interests that we judge worthy of being defended, such as world peace, solidarity, liberty, equality, fraternity, and brotherly love.

If the acceptance of a scientific theory depends to such an extent on unscientific social forces, the question of the scientist's moral responsibility arises not only with regard to applied science, but also in the elaboration, refutation, and establishment of a theory until it is accepted by the research community. As a result, pushing this attitude and these beliefs to the limit, scientists who would assume this responsibility must consciously seek to deflect the results of their research in one direction or another, perhaps favoring superior social interests in the service of the lofty moral values that their sense of social responsibility enjoins them to respect. In other words, after having learned about the true social mechanisms that spawn and establish scientific theories—from the sociology of science, of course— scientists who would display moral responsibility must practice wishful thinking as the method of choice in their research!

Of course no one goes so far,[99] not even among the most ardent defenders of the sociology of science. Nevertheless, this is what is going on, if we take seriously these sociological explanations of how science is practiced and locate them in the search for a unified and reconciled context in which scientific truth (and the science of science) can "ground," in perfect harmony, "good" ethics. In other words, here too, as in other scientific disciplines, a good way to avoid these traps is to not forget that we are dealing with the game of research, a knowledge game like the others, even if this time it involves knowledge about knowledge. On this condition, incidentally, an inverted wishful thinking may become a virtue: we can maintain its advantages without renouncing scientific objectivity by choosing, from among different scientific theories or rather from among the different implicit modes of thought behind these theories—for example, those that lean toward static descriptions of states or, on the contrary, toward dynamic processes—those that are most appropriate; not to ground ethics on Truth, but to develop, deepen, and enrich reflection on certain traditional teachings aimed at regulating behavior, that is to say, that have ethical import. The dialogue between science and tradition can then take the form of a selection, made by a religious tradition, of what science can teach in order to deepen, or at least understand in another way or from a novel perspective, the teachings of that tradition. But this selection is dictated by considerations that are properly of an ethical or religious order; hence it is by no means grounded on or justified by any particular scientific truth. Inversely, a desire for change, or at least the more or less conscious purpose of transformation that characterizes every ethical system and every traditional structure of social organization, finds something in scientific discourse that allows it to dress itself up in a language that is not alien to natural reality, as this is constructed by the natural sciences. Any tradition can profit from this process. For there is a certain utility in promoting dialogue and tolerance, or even understanding, of different ethics and traditions of behavior by providing them with a common language, even if this language serves to express their differences more than their similarities.

## Knowledge Games about Knowledge

There are several ways to assess this game of knowledge about knowledge; that of Mary Douglas is a good example, although it may spawn interpretations that themselves contain the snare of "sociology unveiling the truth about the sciences." From her point of departure as an anthropologist in the field, restricted to a very limited domain (a tribe, a people, a culture), rather than as an epistemologist, she seems to be well aware of these traps; she is ready to relinquish her own explanatory concepts and to modify them rapidly, as a result, for example, of criticisms by other anthropologists.[100] In this she is simply applying the rules of the scientific game to her own discipline and work. What makes her approach especially interesting, however, is her use of an epistemological radicalism that, although based on the study of so-called primitive cultures, she extends to our culture, including its mathematical aspects. She sees this, too, as a particular social practice, thereby allying herself with Wittgenstein's approach in his remarks on the foundations of mathematics.

Nevertheless, her evaluation of these foundations, which she attempts to relate not to needs, but to particular social structures in which the practice of abstraction and formalization, which makes proof and refutation possible, could develop, does not lead her to a sterile skepticism. Neither does she fall into the trap of explaining mathematics—no more than other sciences—by means of anthropology. In fact, she never speaks of explanation in the sense of causal explanation and even less of the grounding of one science on another. So long as she adheres to this, she is guarded against closure within a self-refuting metatheory. She speaks only of the encoding or translation of the systems of classification, taxonomic and other (by which every society, mythological or scientific, perceives and thinks the world), in the structures of that society, as embodied in its customs and laws, kinship structures, marriage regulations, exchange of women and inheritance, dietary laws, rituals and ceremonies, and so forth. Classifying the raw experience of the world makes it possible to separate and define different objects by naming them and distinguishing them, along the lines of the taxonomic classifications of plants and animals. This activity of classification permits us to assign an *identity* to things and beings. This is also the form that our logical activity must take when it is based on a principle of *identity* and noncontradiction. It is a matter of "understanding the relation of individual mind to socially generated intellectual processes."[101] For it is necessary

> to insert between the psychology of the individual and the public use of language, a dimension of social behaviour. In this dimension logical relations also apply. This is the nub of my contribution to how intuitions of self-evidence are formed. Persons are included in or excluded from a given class, classes are ranked, parts are related to wholes. It is argued here that the intuition of the logic of these social experiences is the basis for finding the a priori in nature.... Apprehending a general pattern of what is right and necessary in social relations is the basis of society: this apprehension generates whatever a priori or set of necessary causes is going to be found in nature.[102]

Douglas weaves this relationship between the logical and the social as the connecting thread of her anthropological analyses, relying mainly on exceptions to rules, on what defies classification—monsters or taboos: their place in the myths and rites of a society expresses the logic of what is considered to be evident a priori or, on the contrary, as a source of bewilderment and rejection for the members of that society. Once again, however, it is only a question of the translation and encoding of a classification implied by the theory or the myth into another classification implied by the social regulations that characterize a particular society. Nor can we say that one explains the other: the two coexist and influence each other, as two different expressions of a single sociocultural reality, seen sometimes in the mirror of its conscious and even theorized rationality, and sometimes in that of its daily practices, repeated in the more or less unconscious consensus of life in society. In fact, though Douglas does not say so, this is the irreducible core of Castoriadis' social imaginary.

In addition, however—and unlike Durkheim, from whom Douglas claims descent although deploring that he did not take his social relativism as far as possible—she sees that these attempts at decoding and translation have implications for our own society. They lead to a classification of mental attitudes concerning scientific discovery, correlated with the various types of relations between the individual and society that have emerged in the West, and favoring the attempts characteristic of our society to demystify all cosmologies and to see ourselves "in the nature of things."[103] Quite naturally, Douglas does not resist the temptation of proposing theoretical syntheses in which everything is encompassed in an anthropological metatheory that employs a number of causally explanatory metaconcepts. But these in their turn cannot avoid being influenced by the theoretician's own sociocultural context.[104]

Believing in the truth of these syntheses leads to the arbitrary erection of a barrier just short of the sociology of knowledge, beyond which the critical method on which this discipline rests cannot be applied, to an arbitrary cutoff of the infinite regression of critique of critique or of sociological explanations of the sociological explanation that normally implies that all knowledge is socially constructed.

## Cunning Reason: "Two-Tier Thinking"

Not believing in the truth of these syntheses, but instead accepting this infinite regression, does not necessarily lead to nihilist skepticism, provided one can walk the liberating tightrope of what Yehuda Elkana calls "two-tier thinking."[105]

In a specific context of discoveries, that is, a specific discipline at a particular moment in its history, a consensus exists among the members of a group or community concerning problem-selection and the means of employing reason that are most relevant in this context and for these problems. This consensus in fact embodies a priori images (such as the quest for harmony in nature, the liberation of mankind by the power conferred by knowledge, the primacy of reproducible experiment over speculation, or the significance of the esthetics of mathematical forms and their explanatory simplicity) of what our knowledge—its form, its use, its methods, and the institutions in which all of these are elaborated—should be. These "images of knowledge," as Elkana calls them, provide criteria for distinguishing a good theory from a bad theory, for defining what can and cannot be accepted as scientific fact. Ultimately, in interaction with a particular content of knowledge in a particular context and for each particular case, "a consensus is possible on the ordering of theories according to proximity to truth or degree of rationality."[106] The fact that these images of knowledge are themselves socially determined, that "facts are facts with respect to a chosen conceptual framework, that problem-choice, criteria of validity, definition of relevance, are all social constructions of reality,"[107] does not imply that such criteria, in each particular case where the "body of knowledge" is modified, have no value. It entails only that there is no criterion of absolute truth or rationality, valid in all times and places, and for all forms of knowledge: "There is no cross-contextual reasonability."[108]

To engage in such two-tier thinking, one must again take seriously the games of cunning reason along the tortuous paths by which discoveries are made. Because of the multiplicity of its repertoire, the body of knowledge—the content of knowledge at a given moment—offers *many more possibilities than are acceptable*, taking into account the images of knowledge that condition the context of possible discoveries. In addition, the role of these socially constructed images—in association with classically invoked sociopersonal factors such as ideology, economic forces, career concerns, gratification, and institutional competition, which are not to be denied but are insufficient by themselves—is not so much to create or produce contents of knowledge as to draw and select from a surfeit of possibilities. To conceive of this multiplicity of possible rational bodies of knowledge, in which *local* criteria may establish a greater or lesser degree of verisimilitude, if not of truth, leads to an "epic" vision of science. Elkana, aware of his own molding by Greek culture, opposes to it the theatrical metaphor of the tragic vision, the perspective of those for whom reality per se, with its discourse and its formulas, is already there, but hidden, waiting to be unveiled through a process that can be accelerated or retarded but is always inevitable.

These holders of the tragic view "believe that there is only our science to be discovered, that the great truths of nature, had they not been discovered by a Newton or an Einstein, would sooner or later have been discovered by someone else; that, unlike religion or art, or music, or political ideology, there is no such thing as 'comparative science' among different cultures."[109] But in epic, on the contrary, one can study the necessary but not sufficient conditions such that what happened could happen and did, cognizant all the while that things *could* have turned out differently. "All idealistic attitudes, whether reductionism, positivism, or behaviourism, share the Greek drama view of science." On the contrary, according to the epic concept, "science could have been developed differently, other discoveries could have discovered different laws of nature; there is nothing inevitable in the uniqueness of Western science; a 'comparative science' between different cultures is meaningful."[110] Thus an anthropology of knowledge remains possible; but instead of being an explanatory and unifying metatheory, it becomes the locus of a dialogue between contradictory conceptual frameworks that determine different modes of defining what makes a fact a fact, different theories and different criteria of relevance. Even though criteria of truth can function in each of these frameworks, no single criterion traverses all of them. In the terms of our own discussion, even though each game has its rules, there is no unique rule for playing with the games.

Nevertheless dialogue is possible, this game of games can be played, as in the imaginary Castalia of Hermann Hesse's *The Glass Bead Game*.

This is because reality, though not irrational, overflows the rational, thereby spawning the vagueness and indeterminacy that characterize our use of words in daily language. This vagueness, far from being a failing or absence of rigor, as is often thought, when formal or mathematical language is taken as the model, is in this case a source of richness—the same richness that characterizes our linguistic faculties, which never let us stop creating new meanings, thanks to the play (in both senses) allowed by a certain vagueness and dose of indeterminacy in the metaphoric use of words. Our capacity to tolerate or rather to use this vagueness and indeterminacy in the meanings of speech allows us to constantly renew our mode of using language when we are confronted by new situations and new frames of reference. This is what distinguishes our natural language from the artificial formal languages that we produce with logic so that *programmed* machines can use them. (Perhaps we will also be able to build machines that can invent new meanings: as we have seen, they would probably reach that point by being themselves able to use the vagueness and indeterminacy in the meanings initially input to them.[111])

This use of vagueness is what Wittgenstein referred to when he wrote of the "bizarre fashion"[112] in which we understand the meaning of a word, with its infinitude of potential uses, when we grasp it in a flash. Saul

Kripke, in his analysis of the *Philosophical Investigations*, rightly underlines the relationship between the capacity for understanding the meaning of a potentially infinite procedure from a finite number of examples and the sort of vagueness or indeterminacy of the method whereby this infinite expansion is produced.[113] This is the "bizarre fashion" of which Wittgenstein speaks, bizarre, of course, to a logician, for whom the meanings of language can be conceived only in the form of a necessarily finite number of representations, by mental states.[114] Thus this sort of vagueness and indeterminacy is not an absence of rigor, but the fluid cement that enables us to live while drawing our sustenance from various fields that do not overlap and whose criteria of truth (and of the good and the beautiful) are sometimes contradictory. It is our capacity to deal with vagueness that allows us to coexist with the ambiguity of metaphor and the multiplicity of meanings. And it is this coexistence, which is in fact a permanent oscillation between one frame of reference and another, that permits learning and discovery of something new. As Elkana notes:

> Logic is expected to hold only in a totally static situation, when we make an attempt to check a theoretical network for internal coherence and we introduce only concepts and theories of the given theoretical domain. When we do that, we can eliminate vagueness and inconsistencies, *but* we have then to limit our domain to a subsystem of the whole theoretical network and to cut out all the open problems even from that subsystem.[115]

## Norm and Experience

This vagueness and these logical inconsistencies render possible esthetics and ethical choices that go beyond objective knowledge and logic— not so much conscious choices by individuals as unconscious choices of a "heaven-fallen" ethics of the imaginary of a given society, incarnated in its norms and specific social practices. Here the vagueness and ambiguity of spoken meanings do not rule out rigor. Quite the contrary: logical rigor is possible only in each domain of legitimate application of the rules of a game; whereas in this game of games, a contradictory dialogue between one domain and another, the same rigor rules out unification at any price. The imperative is no longer that of the logic of a unifying objective knowledge, rooted in identity and noncontradiction, but that of the moral norm, which comes from somewhere else, and of the esthetic norm, which also comes from elsewhere. This, as we have seen,[116] is what confers on norms their capacity for liberty. Mary Douglas reaches the same conclusion: "The problem of freedom is the problem of how to divest our categories of their halo of eternal truth."[117] These are the categories that permit us to dissect reality and classify our sensory experiences and transform them into identities–objects-of-knowledge. "Mercifully, the system of classification never fits," because dynamic lived reality overflows the domains of applicability of the rules that make it possible to play with these identities. "When there is non-fit, there is choice."[118] Liberty is not derived from our ability to dispense with rules once we have demystified their sacred origins, but from the fact that we can play with the rules, because they can never be fully adequate. Playing with the tension between norm and experience is more liberating than throwing aside the norm and being guided only by the totalistic truth of what claims to be an objective description of what is.

## The Barrier of Responsibility

In our society, where an ethic of individual responsibility and respect for the individual has developed alongside a science grounded on a necessarily reductionist (at least in the weak sense) physical causalism, an example of such a necessary logical inconsistency appears whenever one tries to conduct a dialogue between biology and our experience of intentionality (see Chapter 2). But it is hard for us to avoid such a dialogue, because our experience of subjects oriented by intentions like our own is so vital, beyond any theoretical denial, that it largely grounds the law that governs all of us, including physicists, biologists, and the most reductionist philosophers.

When we speak or act in an intentional manner with the goal of saying or doing something, no theory or science that could persuade us of the illusory character of this experience can suppress our experience of it. Furthermore, we are in the habit of attributing a meaning to the speech and behavior of others whenever, projecting this experience of our own intentionality, we see behind it a finality of saying or doing something: what they say means something because it intends to say something; what they do is not absurd because it is adapted to a goal that they seem to be pursuing and that we perceive. Going beyond other people whose language we understand and with whom we communicate, we extend this projection to all people and to animals. We are even frequently tempted to project the experience of intentionality onto machines, when they are activated by computer programs that reproduce purposeful and intentional behavior. This is especially true with regard to certain artificial-intelligence programs[119] that go beyond the faithful realization of a task predefined by the programmer and can mimic behavior in which meaning seems to be created (but is in fact projected by naive observation) as they are executed, such that we might suppose them to have hidden intentions—or illusory and nonexistent ones—just as in the speech and behavior of an animal or human being. Or again, as we have seen, certain relatively simple computer programs that simulate the behavior of self-organizing networks thanks, inter alia, to the systematic use of some amount of randomness and to taking the observer's perspective into account, seem to reproduce the intentionalized behavior that creates meaning of the sort habitually observed in living beings endowed with cognitive faculties. We analyzed the circumstances under which, in an apparently arbitrary fashion, we do or do not ascribe intentions to living beings and machines when we observe purposeful behavior whose meaning was not created by a programmer. We ascribe it spontaneously to a dog and to a particular species of bat with diversified and adaptive behavior, but not to an isolated cell or to an automata network with self-organizing properties. We proposed accepting an arbitrary (from the perspective of objective knowledge) location for the barrier of intentionality, because of its psychosocial and ethical implications: because this recognition or nonrecognition of intentionality necessarily entails recognition or nonrecognition of a subject who is responsible, judicially and morally (wholly or in part), for the behavior we observe.

This is why I believe that the improper extension of logical coherence to a unifying metaphysics is at the origin of two opposing and in some measure symmetrical traps: the spiritualist trap, which sees intentionality in nature, a cosmic consciousness everywhere at work; and the reductionist trap, for which human intentionality and consciousness are at best indeterminacies if not indeed illusions. Note, moreover, that there is a certain lack of symmetry between these two. The former is a snare only if the spiritualist attitude claims to be founded on or derived from the natural sciences. If not, as in the case of mystical traditions accepted in their autonomy and specificity, it at least has the advantage of being a vision of the universe in which knowledge of nature and ethical concerns reinforce each other, albeit at the price of a knowledge that is less effective than science when it comes to mastering nature. In other words, if it is quite illegitimate to base ethics on scientific knowledge, this seems a posteriori less evident with regard to traditional lores. Even if, in their rationalized form, they frequently appear to be a posteriori rationalizations (not necessarily in the pejorative sense of the term) based on the law, rites, and myths that preceded them, their starting point is the experience of the subject and of our interior life in relation with nature and other people.[120] Thus it is normal, or at least not contradictory, that one (or several) ethics can be discovered in their teachings.[121] By contrast, a vision of the world in which science provides our knowledge of nature forces us into the logical inconsistency of erecting a barrier, somewhere, between beings endowed with the attributes of intentional and responsible subjects and those that we see as only causalist physicochemical systems that biology allows us to know and manipulate. But this logical inconsistency flows normally from the incompleteness and openness of science, which create its power and effectiveness.

We suggested locating this barrier at a spot that forces itself on our projecting activity, *before any theorizing*, as soon as we perceive the visible and audible (as well as the tactile, odoriferous, and savory), before reflexive knowledge comes to tell us about what is invisible but also real, perhaps even more real, despite its concealment, than what we do see. This spot is just short of the *human form* endowed with articulate language; only the form, the exterior aspect that has the capacity to produce an articulate shadow that I can recognize as such, without my having to require of it a specific content of meaning, that is, a theoretical definition of the subject that would always be too exclusive, or insufficiently so. The fact that this criterion of distinction poses problems of borderline cases and the fluid frontiers between these cases (the almost human form of the ape, comatose human beings in a vegetative state, reduced only to their form, a human embryo before it has acquired this form, etc.) need not trouble us excessively, because every *explicit* criterion of distinction generates such dilemmas, exceptions where the criterion is not applicable in any simple way.

## "Otherwise than Knowing, Otherwise than Being"?

Thus, having detoured by way of ethics, we return to the necessity of separating the playing fields—objective knowledge molded by scientific theory, and traditional lores of the subject—so that we can observe their respective rules. The metaphor of the game means that, beyond their domain of activity, ideas do not have to be serious. They are so made that we can play with them without taking them too seriously; it is only on this condition that they do not confine and can play their role of vital sources in the symbiosis of ideas and brain that, to borrow Pierre Auger's fine image, we all are. In scientific practice, an experimental protocol or a logico-mathematical deduction must obey certain rules. This is all that one has the right to ask of a scientist. Beyond that, the scientist's ideas and theories are games with the results of this game: it is only on this condition that science is serious, in the sense of being something that can maintain a relationship of responsibility to daily life.

But can the game metaphor be extended to the sphere of ethics itself? The break between objective knowledge and ethics can be even more radical. For Emmanuel Levinas, the similarity of corporeal envelopes, which enables me to project my subjective experience onto other person, is still insufficient. In this "analogy between animate bodies,"[122] which is the foundation of intersubjectivity for Husserl, Levinas recognizes the virtue of "passage from one knowledge to a better knowledge," of an awakening to a life "where the I is liberated from itself and awakens from the dogmatic slumber" of a naive knowledge, produced by the science of mastery, to a living apprehension that permits critical awareness of this knowledge.

But this analogy remains of the order of similarity, presence, and apprehension; that is, of knowledge as mastery: the other is recognized and known only to be itself mastered, like every object of knowledge. Levinas, by contrast, sees in the face of the other an intimation of the radically other, the transcendent, which cannot be *known*. Ethics that trace their source to this intimation certainly come from elsewhere, which Levinas calls "God," but which can be only absence and cannot be an object of knowledge. All his work[123] tends to demonstrate the possibility of another phenomenology, the phenomenology of the Other, of transcendence, even while being part of the philosophical tradition that, with Husserl and Heidegger, reaches the end of metaphysics. It is not knowledge that is the pioneer and founder, nor the totality of being, but rather the "idea of the infinite in us," or, better yet, "God who comes to one's mind"[124] ("who falls under sense"[125]), whose intelligibility is quite other than that of knowledge. Levinas sets out to follow its manifestations in modern philosophy, as a "new plot" starting with Descartes and his idea of the infinite, through the primacy of practical reason for Kant, and on to duration as pure change and source of novelty in Bergson. But in Western philosophy this plot has not yet succeeded in detaching itself from the dominion of knowledge as object and regularly falls back into the immanence of experience. For Levinas, by contrast, the transcendence of the face of the other and the ethical relationship founded on injunctions replace experience itself, to the extent that the latter can be only an extension of the I, without a true opening, because it aims at incorporating what was external to it.[126] This foreshortening of the infinite permits it to penetrate into the finite when summoned by the face of the other: this, for Levinas, is the origin of ethics.

## A Game of Games

We have seen how, starting from the experience of objective knowledge as the coexperience of various games of knowledge, ethics (and esthetics) that come from somewhere else can gain a foothold in the openness of a game of games—the openness of rules beyond the finite totality constituted by each domain of legitimacy of specific criteria of relevance and truth, precisely the openness produced by the game of games, in the absence of predictive cognitive rules and in the tension engendered by behavioral norms. Moreover, the game of games is not devoid of all rules. In particular, it includes negative rules such as: do not mix up the rules of the different games; be careful with analogies and use them only to make differences stand out more clearly; steer clear of the temptations of all-embracing fusions; do not give in to the fascination of grand cosmological syntheses or make them operate in the mode of legend and (science) fiction; finally, and above all, do not pretend to ground ethics (and even less, politics) on some objective knowledge, established scientifically (or otherwise), that is supposed to disclose the Truth of Nature. For what distinguishes game from ideology is that the latter is *believed*, while the former is played. Also, the rule of rules: *do not believe in* a content of knowledge without at the same time excluding optimistic confidence in its practical effectiveness.

But can one speak of this game of games with regard to ethics, even if we are dealing with the game of games that Eugen Fink calls a "reflection of the infinite in the finite"? For Levinas, also a post-Heideggerian philosopher, can this *role* of reflection and "trace" of the infinite, *summoned* by the face of the other, be considered to be *played*? In other words, does this place, where being and knowledge come to an end (because given, or rather taken, as presences) and where the ethics that asks us to give begins, also belong to the sphere of the game? The other-than-being, the nonpresence of transcendence—can they be lived as the unreal reality of the game? In this form the question does not have much meaning, or the answer seems to be already comprehended in the question. For how can one compare, with words, two experiences (or nonexperiences) that are described as at the limit of the sayable? Is transcendental phenomenology *sayable* other than in what it leaves unsaid, *doable* except by a practice in which speech serves only to underline and show without being able to demonstrate? This, incidentally, is what Levinas does against the backdrop of talmudic discourse, which is itself of this type. The fact that he begins from traditional philosophy and continues to situate his work as a continuation of Western philosophy is perhaps the sign that the latter always carried on this quest, what he calls this "spiritual intrigue."[127] If so, scientific practice was separated from it precisely on this point, at a certain moment in its history, when it resolutely chose the course of the search for objective knowledge.

In daily life, nevertheless, and in our societies that rest on a relatively large measure of individual responsibility, it seems out of place to speak of ethics as a game. Hence the question is asked in awareness of the roots of ethics in the sphere of the sacred and of ritual, even though, for Levinas, it is a matter of the transformation that this sphere undergoes in the talmudic tradition, where it is shifted from the "hallowed to the holy."[128]

Perhaps the Talmud, in the passage cited at the beginning of Chapter 7 (and, more generally, the experience of the particular brand of humor that can be discovered in its pages), makes it possible to answer this question, while distinguishing, yet again, the aspect of practice and behavior from that of intelligence and speech: the more the first of these aspects is "serious," especially by virtue of the obligations it includes, the more the second (which conditions the first through the discursive and argumentative quest that characterizes talmudic logic) is marked by humor and joy, as necessary conditions for an "open heart."[129] Yet the game is still present in ethical conduct through the tragic consciousness—the "awe"[130]—that accompanies at least the *enunciation* of normative law, or in the form of the theatrical game of ritual practices, or perhaps as the joy of performing a religious precept, which is supposed to accompany this practice in its most perfect form. One can hardly deny that the dramatic experience, with all its nuances, from comedy to tragedy and epic, thoroughly imbues practices such as those of the Purim festival, the Passover seder, or the Yom Kippur ritual. Finally, the Hebrew root (*s.h.q*) that designates both game and laughter in the Bible is read by the Midrash as designating sexual intercourse, which, in certain conditions, can be lived as openness to the call of the other, through and beyond the openness and ecstasy of union. In a similar vein, perhaps we can find an answer to our question in the fact that the Talmud[131] classifies gamesters (those who bet on races and play games of chance) with thieves as ineligible to testify in a court of law.

Like the latter, they are disqualified—expelled from the game, as it were—in the situation par excellence, legal testimony, where one person's existence depends on a solidarity based on the scruples and responsibility of another. But it may be that what is condemned here is not so much the ludic character of these activities as the fact that these games are taken seriously as forms for replacing the great game of life (social life, inter alia). Certainly, as Levinas notes, commenting on another passage in the Talmud,

> the café, house of games, is the point through which game penetrates life and dissolves it. Society without yesterday or tomorrow, without responsibility, without seriousness—distraction, dissolution....The world as a game from which everyone can pull out and exist only for himself, a place of forgetfulness—of the forgetfulness of the other—that is the café.[132]

But if life allows itself to be penetrated by these games, is it not that it too participates, that these games cannot dissolve it because they resemble it like a caricature resembles a face—just as, for the Kabbala, the "other face" (the other stage?) is the caricature, the ape, of the world that is to be constructed and made holy? In the same text, moreover, does not Levinas himself oppose these games of the café and gaming house to the those of the cinema and theater, where a common theme is proposed on the screen and stage?

Thus we learn to distinguish (yet another distinction!) between formalized games of chance and games of life, including those of knowledge, not only scientific and philosophical but also "biblical"; that is, sexual, the experience of which culminates in openness to another. The more the latter is the locus of epiphany, of the unveiling of the hallowed (or of the holy, to stick to Levinas's terminology), the more the former are ersatz, caricatures in which the rich abundance of lived experience is replaced by rules and stakes that seem to mimic those of the "game of the world": not only the game of the Heraclitean child described by Eugen Fink,[133] or the creator's game with wisdom,[134] but also that to which Moses issued an invitation, with heaven and earth as the referees and arbiters: "See, I set before you this day life and good and death and evil.... I call heaven and earth to witness against you this day.... Choose life—if you and your offspring would live."[135]

## Notes

1. Wishful thinking, or taking one's desires for reality, is clearly the property of bad science—bad in quality but also, sometimes, perverted by ideology. On the other hand, it should not be forgotten that this, along with "all power to the imagination," was one of the slogans that flourished during the student demonstrations of May, 1968, in Paris, while, an ocean and a continent away, the flower children of San Francisco were under the influence of chemical hallucinogens.

2. J. Schlanger, L'Invention intellectuelle (Paris: Fayard, 1983), p. 37. As we have seen, we are in fact returned to the question of the criterion for success, which need not be arbitrary, but rather the result of the consensus of a social group guided by particular "interests of reason." This consensus need not be fully conscious, nor these interests clearly explicit, for all members of the group. The group (the scientific community or one of its subgroups, the adepts of a tradition, etc.) functions in part as a self-organizing system with several levels of meaning. Schlanger cites Lakatos to the effect that many scientists understand no more of science than fish do of hydrodynamics (ibid., p. 45).

3. See, for example, Lecourt, L'Ordre et les jeux; P. Jacob, De Vienne à Cambridge; and the collection of articles about Popper, The Critical Approach to Science and Philosophy.

4. Pierre Auger, L'Homme microscopique.

5. By discovering in them or projecting on them (thinking to have discovered in them) the order in question.

6. Jean Piaget, *The Origins of Intelligence in Children*, trans. Margaret Cook (New York: W. W. Norton, 1963); *Adaptation and Intelligence: Organic Selection and Phenocopy*, trans. Stewart Eames (Chicago: University of Chicago Press, 1980); and Atlan, *L'Organisation biologique*, Chapter 10.

7. The Hebrew text of Genesis maintains the ambiguity of "good and bad knowledge" (knowledge judged by ethics) versus "knowledge of good and evil" (knowledge as the ground of ethics).

8. See Chapters 2 and 7 (n. 100). A profound and different treatment of the mind-body problem can be found in D. Hofstadter and D. C. Dennett, *The Mind's I*.

9. A talmudic version of the parable of the blind man and the cripple reviews the terms of the problem in the context of individual legal responsibility (BT *Sanhedrin* 91a–b). A Roman emperor asked R. Judah the Prince whether body and soul could not escape divine judgment by throwing the responsibility for their conjoint sins on the other. To which the sage replied with a parable: like a cripple who climbs on the back of a blind man to steal the fruit from an orchard, body and soul, separately impotent and not responsible (for "the body without the soul lies in the grave, immobile as a rock," and "the soul without the body merely flutters in the air like a bird"), can, together, be judged as an active and responsible unit.

10. See Chapter 2.

11. See, for example, Louis Dumont, "La Valeur chez les modernes et chez les autres," *Esprit*, no. 7 (1983), pp. 3–29.

12. In addition to Castoriadis' major works, already cited (*The Imaginary Institution of Society* and *Crossroads in the Labyrinth*), see "Institution de la société et religion," in *Mélanges*, ed. J. Ellul (Paris: Presses universitaires de France, 1983).

13. J. Beaufret, in his introduction to the French translation of Heidegger's *Der Satz vom Grund* (*Le Principe de Raison* [Paris: Gallimard, 1962]). This method "may appear to be one without scientific rigor. It does not tend any the less, perhaps, to become around us the correspondingly more rigorous, because more meditative, method of philosophy. The fetishism of scientific rigor is at base no more than a rather gross confusion of rigor with the objectivity of the 'exact sciences'" (pp. 11–12). Beaufret sees the genealogical method as already at work in Plato, constant in Nietzsche, passing by way of Bergson and Alain, resurfacing finally in the later Husserl, following Hobbes and Hume, and finally in Heidegger.

14. Castoriadis, *Crossroads in the Labyrinth*, pp. 42–45.

15. Julian Jaynes, *The Origin of Consciousness in the Breakdown of the Bicameral Mind* (Boston: Houghton Mifflin, 1976).

16. Jaynes proposes a realistic response, based on biological evolution, to a classic question of literary criticism concerning the analysis of Homer's characters. There seems to be a radical change in the nature of Greek man over the course of only a few centuries, when one compares the characters of the *Iliad* and *Odyssey* with those of the Dialogues of Plato. Classicists have analyzed this phenomenon in detail. See, for example, J. Redfield, "Le Sentiment homérique du moi," *Le Genre humain* 12 (1985), pp. 93–111. The Homeric "I" has no psychological or ethical depth, in the sense we understand today, and does not reflect about itself in terms of duty, sin, temptation, will, virtue, conscience, soul, or thought. In Homer's language these terms either do not exist or lack the abstract sense they acquired in later Greek, and refer only to concrete organic and impersonal realities such as the heart, breath, diaphragm, or bile, or the phantom-body in the Underworld (*psyche*), inner fire (*menos*), etc. Even the *noos*, the faculty of perception, reason, and awareness of something, cannot be confused with the mind of an individual person, because it is not itself "an object of which one can be aware. There is no *noos* of the *noos*.... This is why, even though it is a mental faculty, the *noos* cannot be assimilated to the mind" (ibid.). This organic perception of what happens within him means that the hero's conduct is determined by forces that he does not control; his capacity to act bravely, virtuously, or wisely, depends *always and for each detail of his daily life*, not on his personal qualities, but on external circumstances that the hero himself perceives as the incessant intervention of the gods. What is more, they intervene not only in his environment, but also inside or alongside him and other individuals with whom he comes into contact. There is no true inner discourse. Rather, it is split into a dialogue with a particular bodily organ or god.

It may be imagined that the disappearance of the person, to which reductionist biologizing metaphysics is leading today (see Chapter 2), could return us to a sense of the "I" not vastly different from that of Homer's characters. However, the gods to which human qualities were attributed (or delegated), so that it was possible to carry on a dialogue with them, would have to be replaced today by anonymous and interchangeable molecular reactions, unless we go so far as to create a mythology of these reactions, giving them names and transforming them into the divinities of a new pantheon.

17. The biblical and talmudic idea of prophecy does not contradict this vision of things. The prophetic status does not necessarily imply a special relationship with the God of theology and with His Truth, but rather a special faculty of perception that could be cultivated in prophetic schools, until the "objective" disappearance of prophecy or, as the Talmud has it, "since the destruction of the Temple prophecy has been given over to madmen and children" (BT *Baba Batra* 12b). The distinction between true and false prophets had nothing to do with the reality of these perceptions, but rather with the suitability or unsuitability of the interpretive discourses based on these perceptions to a practical truth applicable to the rest of society. The criteria for judging this suitability were external to prophecy per se and were given to the Sages: "The Sage is superior to the prophet" (BT *Baba Batra* 12a).

This attitude reappears much later, in the middle of the eighteenth century, in the harsh clash between the "mystical" streams of Eastern European hasidism and its *mitnaggedic* opponents (the meaning of the Hebrew term), led by the celebrated R. Eliyahu, the Gaon of Vilna. The latter's disciples attested to his having had mystical experiences quite as intense as those of the hasidic rabbis whom he opposed (hearing the voice of the Torah, visits from angels who revealed to them the secrets of the Law, especially the construction of the Golem, etc.). But unlike those whom he condemned, the Vilna Gaon refused to accept the truth of these revelations just as they were, as if they were sufficiently guaranteed by their "supernatural" origins. He forced himself to pass them through the crucible of reason and accept only what he could ground independently of the manner in which they were received.

Finally, we can find some support for our thesis in Maimonides' theory of prophecy (*Guide for the Perplexed*, part 2, Chapter 37). Prophecy, as a phenomenon unique to the prophets of Israel, as reported in the Bible, was a particular development of the imaginative faculties of certain individuals during a certain period of history. As such it might or might not be associated with a proportional development of the rational faculties. Only the association of both faculties could produce true prophets, because, ultimately, verification always had to come from reason, in accordance with the talmudic dictum cited earlier: "The Sage is superior to the prophet." Without this association, the development of the rational faculties alone characterizes the scientists and philosophers who have originated speculative truths, whereas the imaginative faculties by themselves produce the political leaders and statesmen who originate laws and rules of conduct!

18. Peter T. Furst, *Hallucinogens and Culture* (San Francisco: Chandler and Sharp, 1976).

19. Weston La Barre, "Old and New World Narcotics: A Statistical Question and an Ethnological Reply," *Economic Botany* 24 (1970), pp. 368–373; "Psychedelic Plants and the Shamanic Origins of Religion," in *Flesh of the Gods: The Ritual Use of Hallucinogens*, ed. P. T. Furst (New York: Praeger, 1972), Chapter 8.

20. R. Gordon Wasson, *Soma, Divine Mushroom of Immortality* (New York: Harcourt, Brace and Jovanovich, 1968); "The Divine Mushrooms of Immortality," and "What Was the Soma of the Aryans?" in *Flesh of the Gods*, pp. 185–200 and 201–213.

21. Furst, *Hallucinogens and Culture*, p. 2f.

22. Traces of it can nevertheless be found in ancient biblical rites reserved for the priests in the Temple of Jerusalem, such as, perhaps, divination by the Urim and Thummim (Exodus 28:30; Numbers 27:21) or by the incense (Hebrew *qetoret sammim* is literally "vapor of drugs"; see Exodus 30:7 and 34–38); or the use of the mandrake (Genesis 30:14–16); or finally, the narrative in Genesis concerning the Tree of Knowledge of Good and Evil, thanks to which the eyes are opened, and the True of Life, whose fruit held out the promise of immortality.

23. We should recall that Descartes begins his *Meditations* by doubting the reality of our sense perceptions, evoking the possibility that our normal waking world is no different from our dream world and that we are asleep without knowing

it (First Meditation, in *The Philosophical Works of Descartes*, trans. Elizabeth S. Haldane and G. R. T. Ross [Cambridge: Cambridge University Press, 1911], pp. 145f.). He subsequently qualifies these doubts as exaggerated and ridiculous, because of the coherence, in memory and understanding, of the sensations of the waking state; whereas the ease with sleep is quite different: "I find a very notable difference between [sleep and the waking state], inasmuch as our memory can never connect our dreams one with the other, or with the whole course of our lives, as it unites events which happen to us while we are awake" (Sixth Meditation, p. 199). Nevertheless, this criterion is no more persuasive than others reviewed by C. Wade Savage, "The Continuity of Perceptual and Cognitive Experiences," in R. K. Siegel and L. J. West, ed. *Hallucinations, Behavior, Experience and Theory* (New York: John Wiley and Sons, 1975), pp. 257–286: internal coherence and continuity are also to be found in some dreams and hallucinations; whereas external coherence, between dreaming and waking, can also exist but, even when it does not, offers no better argument against the reality of the dream rather than against that of the waking state. It is, finally, the argument that "God is no deceiver" (Sixth Meditation, *Philosophical Works*, p. 191) to which Descartes has recourse to convince himself that he is not deceived when he trusts in his reason to remove his doubts and guarantee the reality of the waking state against the illusion of dreams. Hence the capital importance for his method of the prior conclusions of the Third and Fifth Meditations; namely, "Of God: that He Exists" and "Of the Essence of Material Things; and, again, of God, that He exists."

Similarly, and closer to us, for Bergson (*The Two Sources of Morality and Religion*, trans. R. Ashley Audra and Cloudesley Brereton [New York: Henry Holt, 1935]), religion is primary, universal, biological in the broad sense, because "humanity has never subsisted without religion" (p. 98). But religion, rather than being the product of reason and intelligence, on the contrary manifests a particular function of the imagination, that of myth making or fiction, of which it is effect rather than cause. This myth-making function, "when it has the power to move us, resembles an incipient hallucination" (p. 99). It is produced by nature, at the same time as intelligence, whose effects it can thwart. These effects can be dangerous for society, by pushing the individual to selfishness, and for the individual, by making one aware of the inevitability of death. Moreover, religion, which "accounts for the myth-making function" (p. 98), is, like intelligence, one of the great manifestations of life, a product of the "elan vital" in its culmination in man, "a defensive reaction of nature against the dissolvent power of intelligence" (p. 112), "against the representation, by intelligence, of the inevitability of death" (p. 121), "against the representation by the intelligence, of a depressing margin of the unexpected between the initiative taken and the effect desired" (p. 130).

I do not subscribe here to a similar philosophy of "Life" as the foundation of ethics, which also leads to a grand synthesis in which everything can be justified, from Bergson's own apology for Christianity to Nietzsche's Antichrist. Rather, I want to highlight the founding role, in the prehistory of religions and civilizations, of hallucination and of what, to our eyes, illuminated by the lights of reason, is only illusion and fable.

24. Carlos Castaneda, *A Separate Reality* (New York: Simon and Schuster, 1971).

25. Weston La Barre, "Anthropological Perspectives on Hallucination and Hallucinogens," in *Hallucinations, Behavior, Experience and Theory*, p. 42.

26. Furst, *Hallucinogens and Culture*, p. 59. One can go still further (if one is not allergic to the kind of plays on words that Lacan has popularized in a certain milieu) and remark that LSD are also the initials used to designate, in quite a few articles and books on the philosophy of science, one of the seminal works of modern epistemological thought: Popper's *Logic of Scientific Discovery*!

27. Wallace D. Winters, "The Continuum of CNS Excitatory States and Hallucinosis, in *Hallucinations, Behavior, Experience and Theory*, pp. 53–70.

28. Mircea Eliade, *Patterns in Comparative Religion*, and *Shamanism: Archaic Techniques of Ecstacy*, trans. Willard R. Trask (Princeton, N.J.: Princeton University Press, 1972).

29. D. H. Ingalls, "Remarks on Mr. Wasson's Soma," *Journal of the American Oriental Society* 91, no. 1 (1971), pp. 188–191, cited by Furst, *Hallucinogens and Culture*, p. 102.

30. *Flesh of the Gods,* p. 213; cited by Furst, *Hallucinogens and Culture*, p. 103.

31. In this interpretation, the sacred trees of various mythologies, especially the birch revered by the shamans of Siberia (and also, perhaps, in derived fashion, the Tree of Life and Tree of Knowledge of Genesis), derive their property from their relationship with the sacred mushroom that grows around their base (or with hallucinogenic properties of the same order).

32. G. R. Wasson, "What Was the Soma of the Aryans?" cited by Furst, *Hallucinogens and Culture*, p. 103.

33. Wittgenstein, *Tractatus Logico-Philosophicus* 6.421.

34. Ibid., 6.13.

35. M. Blanchot, *L'Entretien infini* (Paris: Gallimard, 1969), p. 495

36. Immanuel Kant, *Critique of Pure Reason*.

37. René Descartes, *Meditations*.

38. Hintikka, *Logic, Language Games and Information*. See especially Chapter 5, "Quantities, Language Games, and Transcendental Arguments."

39. Natural languages are opposed to formal languages and overflow them just as the reality of our sensations overflows logic, which is itself "transcendental"!

40. De Dieguez, *Le Mythe rationnel de l'Occident*.

41. On the so-called von Foerster hypothesis, see J.-P. Dupuy and J. Robert, *La Trahison de l'opulence* (Paris: Presses universitaires de France, 1976); J.-P. Dupuy, *Ordres et désordres*; and the demonstration of this hypothesis in a computer model in M. Koppel, H. Atlan, and J.-P. Dupuy, "Complexité et aliénation, formalisation de la conjecture de von Foerster," in *Les Théories de la complexité*; also "Von Foerster's Conjecture: Trivial Machines and Alienation in Systems," *International Journal of General Systems* 13 (1987), pp. 257–264.

42. Friedrich Nietzsche, *The Antichrist*, trans. H. L. Mencken (New York: Knopf, 1918). See, in particular, §55, where, with regard to "the psychology of conviction, of 'faith,'" he proposes to consider "whether convictions are not even more dangerous enemies to truth than lies." In the context of this chapter, it is noteworthy that he defines lies as a variety of wishful thinking ("of which the most common is that with which we dupe ourselves"): "to refuse to see what one sees, or to refuse to see it *as* it is." Analyzing the function of this desire in the foundations of ethics is certainly one of the most radical ways of demonstrating the opposition between a project of knowledge and one of ethics; for we know that wishful thinking is viewed correctly by critical thinking as a caricature of thought that disqualifies all scientific practice.

43. The value to be attributed to these laws, all of them necessarily of "divine" origin for Nietzsche, but different in accordance with whether they are those that institute the power of modern priests or of ancient pagan priests, does not derive from their rational or irrational character; but from the nature of the god involved ("Pagans are all those who say yes to life, and to whom 'God' is a word signifiying acquiescence in all things" [ibid.]).

44. Lacan, "La Science et la vérité," *Ecrits*, pp. 855–877.

45. Michel Foucault, *The Order of Things: An Archaeology of the Human Sciences* (New York: Pantheon Books, 1971).

46. Castoriadis, *Crossroads in the Labyrinth*, pp. 60f.

47. Wittgenstein, "Conversations on Freud," *Lectures and Conversations*, pp. 51–52.

48. The paradox of a transcendance that can be experienced is only apparent: the transcendance in question is relative. It is that of one type of experience vis-à-vis another, of one "world" vis-à-vis another, that of dream and hallucinosis vis-à-vis that of our active waking life. Once again, "the unutterable is such relative to a particular system of utterance" (Blanchot, *L'Entretien infini*).

49. Dobbs, *Foundations of Newton's Alchemy*; see also Pauli on Kepler (Chapter 5).

50. R. Levi bar Hama reported the counsel of R. Simon ben Lakish (BT *Berakhot* 5a) that in the struggle of good against evil one should try in succession, if

ascesis proves inadequate, studying the revealed Law and then meditation on the Oneness. Finally, if this too fails, "let him remember the day of death." This can be understood, in a doctrinaire reading, as invoking the fear of death as the motive for what then seems to be taking refuge in morality and religion. But a mature reading of these texts, as propounded by kabbalistic exegeses, can see them as placing the ultimate source of the law in that realm, outside the world and outside meaning, which is death.

51. For Wittgenstein, it is also the transcendentality of the "metaphysical subject, the limit of the world—not part of it," which he carefully distinguished from the psychological subject (*Tractatus* 5.632 and 5.641). And, with regard to the transcendental nature of ethics, because it "cannot be put into words," echoing the previous note: "If the good or bad exercise of the will does alter the world, it can alter only the limits of the world, not the facts—not what can be expressed by means of language. In short the effect must be that it becomes an altogether different world. It must, so to speak, wax and wane as a whole. The world of the happy man is a different one from that of the unhappy man."

"So too at death the world does not alter, but comes to an end."

"Death is not an event in life: we do not live to experience death" (ibid., 6.43, 6.431, 6.4311).

52. See *Tractatus* 6.35 to 6.37, on logic; these sections precede 6.41 ("the sense of the world must lie outside the world") and 6.42, which deals with ethics.

53. Jewish tradition, both talmudic and kabbalistic, can be disconcerting for a Western mind and can consequently be instructive in this comparative process, because it seems to have preserved, juxtaposed, and sometimes fought against elements corresponding to all these modalities, while claiming to adhere to strict rationality. On this point, the classic opposition of the two possible attitudes concerning the conscious meaning (*qavvanah* or "intention") of ritual precepts is most revealing. One, with a modern religious connotation, holds for not attending to the particular meaning of each commandment but rather to obey them as if they were "royal edicts," not to be understood or discussed, but carried out "from fear and love, from love and fear." The rationality here is, of course, that of Scholastic theology, hard to accept today. The other attitude, which informs all kabbalistic tracts, and whose abstract and formal rationality can be better appreciated today, also seems to be much more magical in that it prescribes, for every ritual gesture and word, a precise and detailed awareness of its meaning and scope, from the angle of what is built or destroyed in the "higher worlds" (see, for example, R. Hayyim of Volozhin, *Nefesh Hahayyim* [Vilna, 1824]). Finally, modern exegesis has produced possible humanist readings of ancient Jewish texts. I am thinking particularly of Emmanuel Levinas's *L'Humanisme de l'autre homme* and *Nine Talmudic Readings*, trans. Annette Aronowicz (Bloomington: Indiana University Press, 1990).

54. Scholem, *Major Trends* and *The Kabbala and Its Symbolism*.

55. With the unique exception of the mythical figure of Moses, both sage

and prophet. See A. I. Kook on the talmudic dictum that "the sage is superior to the prophet" (BT *Baba Batra* 12a): in the latter days there will be an inextinguishable thirst for the prophetic, after centuries of domination by practical wisdom; the light of prophecy will emerge and the spirit of Moses, uniting the two, will again appear in the world (after *Orot* [Jerusalem: Mossad Harav Kook, 1985], p. 121).

56. Cited by H. Weiner, *9½ Mystics: The Kabbala Today* (New York: Macmillan, 1969), pp. 197 and 330.

57. Beathie, "On Understanding Ritual," in *Rationality*, pp. 240–268.

58. For his part, Louis Dumont ("La valeur chez les modernes et chez les autres" [*Esprit*] and *Essays on Individualism*) has analyzed this essential difference with the discourses of our Western civilization, which assert their objectivity and in which the value of truth is separated from social, moral, or other "values."

59. Settle, "The Rationality of Science," p. 188.

60. Some, like Yehuda Elkana, "A Programmatic Attempt at an Anthropology of Knowledge," in *Sciences and Cultures,* ed. Everett Mendelsohn and Yehuda Elkana (Dordrecht: D. Reidel, 1981), dispute, on sound basis, the very idea of such a "great divide": "The basic difference between Western scientific thought and modes of thought which have developed in other civilizations without science is not a 'great divide', but rather a continuum....That there are genuine differences there can be no doubt. The question has been whether scientific knowledge is absolutely unique in contrast with other types of knowledge, not only in the differentiatedness of the content but in its logical structure and its postulates" (ibid., p. 41). The negative response to this question offered by Elkana, who also does not accept that "method" can serve as an absolute dichotomous criterion of this "great divide," still does not imply confusion and total nondifferentiation. Scientific knowledge derives its differences from "images of knowledge" and "bodies of knowledge" that constitute "a chosen conceptual framework" and lie at the source of "problem-choice, criteria of validity, definition of relevance,... all social constructions of reality" (ibid., p. 50). We shall see that this is not, all the same, a naive and reductive sociology of science. Moreover, beyond the content of scientific knowledge, it would be the existence of "the idea of a scientific text which is self-contained," in which "meaning is in the text," and with no effect of context—an unattainable ideal always striven for and aspired to—that constitutes a "major feature of modern Western scientific thought in contrast with that of other nonscientific cultures" (ibid., p. 37).

61. It is hardly astonishing that among the great-grandchildren of Freud, two psychoanalysts have felt the need to take up again, in their own ways, the experience of these experiences: Julia Kristeva, *Tales of Love*, trans. Leon S. Roudiez (New York: Columbia University Press, 1987) and D. Sibony, *L'Amour inconscient* (Paris: Grasset, 1983).

62. Gilles Deleuze and Félix Guattari, *Anti-Oedipus: Capitalism and Schizophrenia*, trans. Robert Hurley, Mark Seem, and Helen R. Lane (New York: Viking Press, 1977).

63. Atlan, *Entre le cristal et la fumée*.

64. See Chapter 5, p. 214.

65. Kristeva, *Tales of Love*. For her, psychoanalysis seems to be essentially a relationship of transference, that is, ultimately yet another love story, although she does not ignore an objectifying scientific approach, this time in terms of self-organization from noise and of consciousness as memory (see Atlan, *Entre le cristal et la fumée*, Chapter 5). I should be the last to criticize her for this!

66. See, for example, in this vein, J.-C. Pecker, "Entre l'âge d'or et l'Apocalypse."

67. Dobbs, in his critical and well-documented *Foundations of Newton's Alchemy*, finds the sketch of an explanatory theory of the alchemical symbols (mythical animals, figures, etc.) as structural archetypes of the collective unconscious only with Jung. Hallucinatory experiences provide another explanatory theory, just as persuasive, of the symbols, which, moreover, does not contradict it, on condition that we see in it only structures of the human psyche and not those of some "objective" cosmic consciousness and the object of the investigations of the physical sciences.

68. See Chapters 5 and 6.

69. See Chapter 5.

70. M. Cazenave, *La Science et l'Ame du monde* (Paris: Imago, 1983); and *Science and Consciousness* (proceedings of the Cordoba colloquium).

71. D. Bohm, *Wholeness and Implicate Order* (London: Routledge and Kegan Paul, 1979)

72. Karl Popper signals as much, in passing, in the few pages on metaphysics at the beginning of his *Logic of Scientific Discovery*. This has been taken up and abundantly developed by his students, with regard to the nature of scientific problems and their roots in metaphysics (J. Agassi, "The Nature of Scientific Problems and their Roots in Metaphysics," *The Critical Approach to Philosophy and Sciences*, pp. 189–211; "The Ground of Reason," *Philosophy* 45 [1970], pp. 43–49), with regard to the rational foundations of modern rationalism (W. W. Bartley, "Rationality versus the Theory of Rationality," *The Critical Approach to Philosophy and Sciences*, pp. 3–31), and with regard to reflections on the rationality of those who belong to and are nourished by non-Western cultures that we have been led by philosophico-scientific rationalism to reject (Settle, "The Rationality of Science versus the Rationality of Magic").

73. Roman Jakobson, "Einstein and the Science of Language," in Holton and Elkana, *Einstein*, p. 149.

74. Ruth Nanda Anshen, "World Perspectives," introduction to W. I. Thompson, *Evil and World Order* (New York: Harper and Row, 1976), p. xviii.

75. See Cazenave, *La Science et l'Ame du monde*, p. 42.

76. Ibid., pp. 109–110.

77. The meditations on the "image world" by Henry Corbin, a philosopher deeply influenced by Islamic mysticism, nourish the thought of many of the Jungian participants in the Cordoba colloquium. A lucid presentation of this can be found in C. Jambet, *La Logique des Orientaux*.

78. Carl Gustav Jung, *Psychology and Alchemy*, 2d ed., trans. R. F. C. Hull (Princeton, N.J.: Princeton University Press, 1968), pp. 278f.

79. Cazenave, *La Science et l'Ame du monde*, p. 116.

80. Popper, *The Logic of Scientific Discovery*, Chapter 1.

81. B. F. Skinner, *Beyond Freedom and Dignity* (New York: Alfred A. Knopf, 1971).

82. E. D. Wilson's *Social Behavior in Animals*, published in 1929, led to *Sociobiology: The New Synthesis*, in 1975, and then to *Sociobiology: The Abridged Edition*, which, in 1980, reproduced in full the last chapter of the 1975 volume, dealing with *human* social behavior.

83. Heidegger, *Satz vom Grund*, p. 199.

84. Thompson, *Evil and World Order*.

85. Ibid., pp. 24–25

86. Ibid., the title of Chapter 2.

87. John C. Lilly, *The Mind of the Dolphin: A Non-Human Intelligence* (New York: Avon, 1969), p. 35 (cited by Thompson, ibid., p. 41).

88. Thompson, *Evil and World Order*, p. 41.

89. "A season is set for everything, a time for every experience [and its contrary] under heaven" (Ecclesiastes 3:1).

90. Ecclesiastes 12:13. One of the implications of this nonstandard rendering of the verse comes across more clearly in French, where *ça* 'this, it' also means 'id' in the Freudian sense. The idea of interpreting the verse in this way was suggested by many Jewish exegetical texts in which the word *zeh* ("this, it") bears the sense of a structure representing the more or less conscious affectivity of the individual, quite apart from the intellect.

91. It is not a question here of undertaking a critique of the sociology of knowledge in the broad sense, as founded by Durkheim and Weber, and which spawned the sociology of science (see Max Weber, "Wissenschaft als beruf," in Gesammelte Aufsätze zur Wissenschaftslehre, 2d ed. [Tübingen: Mohr, 1951], pp. 566–597; and "Politik als beruf," in Gesammelte politische Schriften, 2d ed. [Tübingen: Mohr, 1958], pp. 493-548). Certainly much is to be done to renew this process and apply it to contemporary science. J.-M. Lévy-Leblond (L'Esprit de sel [Paris: Fayard, 1981]) provides some glimpses of what this could and perhaps should be. For his part, Edgar Morin (La Méthode I, II [Paris: Le Seuil, 1977 and 1980]) has been trying for a number of years to extract all the consequences of the sociology of sociology, which necessarily calls any sociology of knowledge into a "fundamental aporia...that it does its best to conceal" (Edgar Morin, Sociologie [Paris: Fayard, 1984], p. 31; see also E. Morin, "La méthode en question," a critical discussion with J. Choay, J. Robin, J. de Rosnay, and M. Serres, Prospective et Santé, no. 3 [Autumn 1977], pp. 91–116). Finally, starting from the history of science, P. Thuillier was led to a critical reflection that moves in the same direction, with which we clearly feel a community of interests (see especially Les Savoirs ventriloques [Paris: Le Seuil, 1983]). My purpose here is merely to highlight some of the consequences of a certain sociologizing ideology so as to compare them, a contrario, with the relativism I am defending here.

92. See above, p. 348; Elkana, "A Programmatic Attempt."

93. Mary Douglas, Implicit Meanings (London: Routledge and Kegan Paul, 1975)

94. D. Bloor, Wittgenstein: A Social Theory of Knowledge (New York: Columbia University Press, 1983).

95. Ludwig Wittgenstein, "Notes for Lectures on 'Private Experience' and 'Sense Data'," Philosophical Review 77 (1968), pp. 271–320, ed. with notes by Rush Rhees; reprinted in Introduction to the Philosophy of Mind, ed. Harold Morick (Glenview, Ill.: Scott, Foresman, 1970), pp. 155–194.

96. Ludwig Wittgenstein, Remarks on the Foundations of Mathematics, ed. G. H. von Wright, R. Rhees, and G. E. M. Anscombe, trans. G. E. M. Anscombe (Oxford: Basil Blackwell, 1956).

97. Bloor, Wittgenstein.

98. A relatively reasonable place can be found for wishful thinking if one accepts Quine's thesis about the underdetermination of theories by experience (Word and Object): we cannot have enough experiences to decide among different theories, nor does the criterion of simplicity—not all that simple in itself—allow us to decide. Thus, several theories may coexist, and none of them is any closer than the others to an ideal of truth or an optimum of verification. This conception, in which the history of science is no longer an asymptotic progress toward Truth, even projected to infinity, allows one to make a conscious choice among theories on the

basis of extrascientific criteria, if one admits that researchers in any case make such choices, unconsciously and unknowingly. Such a vision, pushed to the extreme, can lead to a caricature of research and the end of any scientific activity worthy of the name. A reading of grand syntheses shows that this is indeed the case—not at the level of theories per se, operational because limited to a relatively narrow field of experience, but at that of metatheories and grand synthetic expositions whose purpose is educational more than research oriented, in which the role of extrapolation and generalization is large as compared with that of experimental data. Here interpretation—the translation of specialized technical jargon, mathematical or otherwise, into natural language—plays a decisive part.

99. Except, perhaps, H. von Foerster, in one of his characteristically humorous papers, where he poses the question of the social responsibility of the scientist in a relativist epistemological context, under the sign of Gregory Bateson and his story of the little girl who was told that "instinct" and "gravitation" had no other reality than that of "explanatory principles" (see Bateson, *Steps to an Ecology of the Mind*, pp. 56–73); H. von Foerster, "Discovery or Invention?" in *Disorder and Order,* ed. Paisley Livingston (Stanford, Calif.: Anma Libri, 1984), pp. 177–189.

100. See Douglas, *Implicit Meanings*, especially Chapter 17, where she calls into question, in an attempt to enlarge them by means of new hypotheses, explanatory schemas she had previously proposed. She accepts with good grace the criticisms that had shown their restrictive and insufficient, and thus inadequate, nature.

101. Ibid., p. 192.

102. Ibid., pp. 280–281.

103. Ibid., Chapter 14. See also Kenneth L. Caneva, "What Should We Do with the Monster? Electromagnetism and the Psychosociology of Knowledge," *Sciences and Cultures*, pp. 101–131.

104. Examples of this are to be found in her successive theories concerning the dietary rituals of the Hebrews, the role of the pangolin in the rites and myths of the Lele, and that of the cassowary in those of the Karam (Douglas, *Implicit Meanings*). In response to criticisms that she accepts willingly, she reworks her previous explanations and incorporates them into a new theory that is clearly broader and more profound. But the new theory, too, remains marked by the Western Christian sociological context of its author, manifested in at least two points. One is the a priori assumption that a contradictory logic (similar to that of the unconscious for psychoanalysts, in which the negative can mean the positive and vice versa) cannot be active in the underlying structures of these myths and rites, even though their (non-Western) cultural milieus can indeed accept that the principles of identity and noncontradiction are respected only in certain contexts (those oriented toward effective action, for example) and not in others (especially those of the symbolic theorizing of myth and ritual). It is not even necessary to go so far as such exotic cultures as those of the Lele and Karam to observe such uses of contradiction. They are also found, as was shown by Louis Dumont (whom Douglas nevertheless warmly esteems in her

book), in Hindu society, with its principle of hierarchical inversion, whereby the inferior in one domain is the superior in another (Dumont, *Homo Hierarchicus*). Another example is provided by biblical Hebrew society, where this principle is found with regard to men and women, the priestly tribe and the other tribes, and the role of the serpent: sometimes negative (Genesis 2) and sometimes positive and saving (Numbers 21:9). The second point involves the (meta)concept used to account simultaneously for the Hebrews' social structures and dietary rites: here we encounter all too clearly the stereotyped Western judgment that modern Jewish communities and their religion are "abnormally" closed. Elsewhere I have endeavored to trace the origin of this stereotype to modern missionary universalism, which is essentially Christian (Atlan, "Ce Peuple qu'on dit élu," *Le Genre Humain*, nos. 3–4 [1982], pp. 98–126). This stereotype underlies the common prejudice according to which the social behavior uniquely characteristic of the ancient Hebrews was to rigorously distinguish between "two classes of human beings, the Israelites and the rest" (Douglas, *Implicit Meanings*, p. 283), as if such a distinction was not rather the rule than the exception among all non-Christian civilizations. The power of this prejudice is so great that it leads Douglas to blatant mistranslations of biblical texts (Leviticus 21:14–15; Numbers 36:7–9), according to which tribal endogamy was prescribed, especially for the High Priest—which is of course false, even for the latter. To buttress her theory she also relies on assertions that are, at the very least, contestable, concerning the rarity if not absence of intertribal exchanges of women, not to speak of marriages with non-Hebrews. See, for example, Deuteronomy 21:10–14, and the report in the Talmud (BT *Horayot* 13a) about the ancient Hebrews' enthusiasm for marrying foreign women.

105. Elkana, "A Programmatic Attempt."

106. Ibid., p. 46.

107. Ibid., p. 50.

108. Ibid., p. 45.

109. Ibid., p. 67.

110. Ibid., p. 69.

111. See Chapter 2.

112. Wittgenstein, *Philosophical Investigations*, §§139–197.

113. Kripke, *Wittgenstein on Rules and Private Language*, p. 82

114. "It would be quite misleading...to call the words a 'description of a mental state'.—One might rather call them a 'signal'." (Wittgenstein, *Philosophical Investigations*, I.180, p. 73). As in our simulations of self-creation of meanings (see Chapter 2), these signals would have the property of triggering endogenous processes of creation and projection of meanings.

115. Elkana, "A Programmatic Attempt," p. 54. Elkana goes on to remark that this is precisely what we do in textbooks. "The tragedy...is...that, instead of using textbooks for the purpose of logical stock-taking, we use them for teaching."

116. See Chapter 6, p. 272.

117. Douglas, *Implicit Meanings*, p. 226.

118. Ibid.

119. For example, J. Weizenbaum's program Eliza, which carries on the psychiatrist's end of what appears to be a perfectly natural dialogue with a patient, or Kenneth Colby's Paranoia program, which had more luck in fooling a psychiatrist and simulating paranoiac speech than did a real patient! (See William Skyvington, *Machina Sapiens: Essai sur l'intelligence artificielle* [Paris: Le Seuil, 1976], pp. 179–185.

120. See Chapter 3, n. 61, and the teachings of Suzuki cited previously (Chapter 3, p. 103), those repeated by Fromm (Chapter 5, p. 220), as well as a celebrated aphorism from the *Ethics of the Fathers* (1,14): "If I am not for myself, who is for me? And if I am only for myself, what am I?" Even if these teachings always contain some measure—larger or smaller, depending on the tradition—of a dialectic of annihilation of the I (the "ego") by fusion with a cosmic Self or Subject, the subject's initial experience of his or her subjectivity serves as the irreducible point of departure for this fusion.

121. A particularly profound exposition of one aspect of this question can be found in the introduction by C. Mopsik to his French translation of a small kabbalistic tract—one of the few of that genre with an ethical purpose—by R. M. Cordovero, *Le Palmier de Débora* (Paris: Verdier, 1985).

122. Levinas, *De Dieu qui vient à l'idée*, pp. 54–55.

123. Emmanuel Levinas, *Otherwise than Being; or Beyond Essence* (The Hague: Martinus Nijhoff, 1974); *Totalité et Infini*.

124. Levinas, *De Dieu qui vient à l'idée*.

125. E. Levinas, *Transcendance et Intelligibilité* (Geneva: Labor et Fides, 1984)

126. Biological assimilation would be closer to such an opening than conscious cognitive assimilation of objective knowledge, because, for Levinas, one can uncover in it—unlike in cognitive awareness, which is always of the self-same—an "awakening" to mental processes, whereby the theology of the other can already come to the mind of an animal: "Aren't the mental processes of the animal already theological? That would be scandalous, wouldn't it?" he said to a Jewish-Christian audience (*Transcendance et Intelligibilité*, p. 40), concluding with a reference to the first of the benedictions recited by Jews upon waking up in the morning, in which

God is invoked as having granted the *rooster* the power to distinguish between day and night.

127. Levinas, *Transcendance et Intelligibilité*.

128. Levinas, *Nine Talmudic Readings*. [For Levinas, *sacré* (here rendered "hallowed") refers to pagan idolatry, as opposed to the *saint* ("holy") of authentic religion. ]

129. See BT *Shabbat* 30b (cf. Chapter 7, p. 289).

130. Ibid.

131. BT *Rosh Hashanah* 22a. Converting inconsequential games into serious activities, and perhaps even into a lucrative business, is the opposite of considering serious human affairs as constituting the "world-game." In the former case, what was formerly open is closed in, what was light is weighed down; in the latter, by contrast, the idolatry of business, closure within desire and the ego, are avoided. On the other hand, unlike games of chance, spectator sports and the theater seem to have an intermediate status, precisely because of the possibility of internalizing and "sanctifying" one's experience of them, by transposing it from the gladiators' arena to the stage of inner life and social life. In these "shows," combats of impulses and ideologies take place that the righteous experience as participating spectators, with just enough distance to be amused. Compare the spectacle, to which only the righteous will be admitted, of the great mythical hunts and the combats between marine and terrestrial monsters, Leviathan and Behemot (A. I. Kook, *Orot Haqodesh,* vol. 2, pp. 317–318, on BT *Baba Batra* 74ab, discussing Job 40).

132. Levinas, *Nine Talmudic Readings*, pp. 111f.

133. Fink, *Spiel als Weltzymbol*.

134. Wisdom says of itself (Proverbs 8:30–31): "I was with [the Creator before the Creation] like a child to be raised [or, reading with *Genesis Rabba* 1,1, like a teacher, a craftsman, or an instrument providing the plans for building the world], a source of delight every day, rejoicing [or playing] before Him at all times, rejoicing [or playing] in His inhabited world, finding delight with mankind" (see Chapter 3, p. 125). In the kabbalistic tradition (for example, *Sefer Habahir*, fragments 4 and 10, the *Zohar* on Genesis, *Tiqqunei Hazohar*, etc.), expanding on the Midrash (*Midrash Rabba* on Genesis 1 and Leviticus 19), wisdom and reason "precede" (logically, more than chronologically, "there is no beginning other than wisdom and Torah") creation, including that of divinity: the first verse of Genesis is read according to the strict sequence of its words, as "By means of 'beginning' [were] created god(s) with the heavens and the earth." The agent of this creation is left unstated, while the modality or tool is none other than the eternal Torah, the wisdom that the verse calls "beginning." But is this really a fundamental principle, in the sense of a sufficient cause, or is it rather an impetus in space, the impulse that triggered motion? It is noteworthy that "wisdom," in the context of the Book of

Proverbs on which the midrash is based, appears as both joy and play and as a source of ethics and law, which bear with them life for those who follow them and death for those who transgress them.

135. Deuteronomy 30:15–19. See Atlan, *Entre le cristal et la fumée*, Chapter 13, "La vie et la mort: biologie ou éthique."

*Chapter 9*

# Naked Truth

The common error about truth consists of seeing it as a metaphysical reality, or at least an epistemological entity, and to ask: "What is Truth?" For when we seek to pin it down we soon discover that we can only recognize and designate what it is not: falsehood, error, illusion, deception.[1] On the other hand, if we can fence it within a precise vision, then, very quickly, the enclosure shuts itself around death; the raw vision, unveiled, freezes what it wanted to animate, hides under nakedness what it wanted to unveil and what the veil of modesty had itself managed to suggest.

## The Garments of Modesty

The Talmud[2] recounts that a certain Rabbi Goodness (and some say his name was Goodness-of-Day) stated that he would not stray from speaking the truth even were he offered all the treasures of the world. One day his travels brought him to a town whose name was Truth. Its population spoke only the truth and no one died there prematurely. He settled down there, married, and had two children. One day, when his wife was getting dressed, a neighbor came and asked to see her. Out of modesty, he told her that his wife was not home. His two sons died immediately. The astonished townspeople came to investigate, and he told them what had happened. They asked him to leave immediately, lest he bring death on all of them.

According to another story,[3] when the Creator was about to create man, the ministering angels split into contending groups: some said, "Let

man be created"; others said, "Let him not be created"—as we read in the
Psalms (85:11): "Mercy and truth meet; justice and peace kiss." Namely,
Mercy said: "Let him be created, because he is full of compassion"; but
Truth said: "Let him not be created, because he is only lies." Justice said:
"Let him be created, because he will repair wrongs"; whereas Peace said:
"Let him not be created, because he is entirely violence." What did the Creator do? He took Truth and hurled it to the earth, as we read: "he hurled
truth to the ground" (Daniel 8:12). The ministering angels then said: "Master of the Universe, how can you thus despise your own sages? Let Truth
spring up from the earth"—as it is written: "Truth springs up from the
earth" (Psalms 85:12).

These legends and parables express the ambiguous value that their
authors accorded to truth: exalted from the ethical perspective, with regard
to both conduct and knowledge, where it is opposed to falsehood and error,
respectively; but certainly not so sublime from an ontological point of view,
where life and creative movement win out, and it is suspected of excessive
flirtation with death. Its models should be looked for not in some perfect
entity given to contemplation, but rather, for example, in judicial truth, as
opposed to falsehood, and scientific truth (or the truth of revelation, in traditional societies), as opposed to error; whereas its relationship with death
is perhaps best understood through what psychoanalysts call "the truth of
the subject." One form of truth always kills, and must therefore be itself
silenced; this is naked truth, stripped bare, in the name of the Good and
out of hatred for falsehood, to be sure, like a Greek statue in the light of
day, frozen, removed from its spatial context (the temple where it was
erected) and temporal context (the evolutionary process which led to its
existence). The veil of modesty that conceals this statue is language, with
the polysemic and creative richness that can explain or suggest what it
*means* behind what it says, who it is or could be behind what it appears to
be—in brief, that animates it and gives it life: at the risk of falsehood and
error, of course, if one believes that the garment is not a garment; but, in
any case, a source of movement. The garment, here, discloses more than
nakedness can, because the latter merely reveals, once and for all, a reality
that can only refer back to itself, whereas the former triggers the very
process of unveiling.[4] The truth of the subject is that which precedes language,[5] that which is silenced behind what language says and which slays
when it takes the place of this speaking. This is what the psychoanalyst
seeks to discover behind the multicolored garments of articulated language, which seems to be there only to cover it over, to disguise it, and to
stifle its voice for all those who do not pursue it (who themselves generally
hear only what the disguises of their own truth allow them to pick up).

If we admit that the unconscious speaks, it is certainly not in a formal, unambiguous computer language,[6] but rather in a natural language where what is said is more often what is not said, where several levels of organization and meaning make it possible to search continually for what the said "meant" to say in the silences of speech and the white spaces in the text, infinite sources of multiple meanings,[7] produced by the circumstances of the listeners at least as much as by the circumstances of the speaker. Thus the articulate language acquired in infancy and adolescence is the garment of deceit and illusion, opposed to the naked truth of the subject; but its nonacquisition leads to psychosis and death, in the blindness caused by the unfiltered light of that same truth. Reconciling the need for truth and the need for life is no simple matter.[8] It consists of hurling the truth down to the earth and afterwards doing everything so that it strikes root and grows there. What emerges then, perhaps, and with difficulty, is not truth just as it fell from heaven, but an approximative structure, an asymptotic process always to be taken up and reworked. What falls from heaven is inspiration, the flash of divination, the light of understanding, with all the attendant risks of error and illusion—if one believes that what it discloses is true.

## The Great Temptation of the Dogmatic

Thus judicial truth is built up step by step, in an inquiry that is never finished, where "facts" are triturated in all possible ways before being "established" by a consensus from which the arbitrary can never be totally excluded. It is this truth that springs from the earth, and not the immediately accepted evidence of someone who "knows" with certainty because he has "seen" and "heard."

As for scientific truth, many errors fatal to it derive from the fact that it is often considered to be fallen from heaven rather than planted, cultivated, and growing from the earth. Similarly, and to an even greater extent, the revealed truth of traditional wisdoms are in peril of freezing the revelation into dogma, of petrifying a truth that is vibrant and alive at the dazzling moment of its discovery into a dead idol, even if the latter is called God and monotheistic dogmas are supposed to fight against idols. Here the danger is inherent in the very process of discovery, in the illumination of the mystic and the revelation of the shaman and prophet, where everything is given at once and where criticism, as a matter of principle, seems to have no place. Scientific method, on the other hand, by virtue of its character of progressive construction, always open to criticism, seems to be forearmed against this danger. Nevertheless, the temptation—or the need—to contemplate in repose the naked truth is so great that every generation is witness to the flourishing of grand scientific cosmologies that finally disclose the Truth about the Ultimate Reality of things, the truth in which one must believe to be at long last rid of the illusions and errors of the false creeds of the past. Philosophers and epistemologists do indeed warn us that scientific theory has only an operational and provisional function, in a context limited by the techniques and languages employed; and that every generalization takes place only by means of analogies and shifts of meaning, sometimes fruitful but always disputable. This does not keep most cultured people, including scientists, from holding that the most recent physical and biological theories represent the Truth in which one cannot *not* believe, because it has been "scientifically established."

Certainly, for someone who is searching for a truth, it must appear unique, vis-à-vis the infinity of falsehoods that this truth makes possible. One can be mistaken, or deceived, in many ways; each of these lies or errors has a different face, which claims to replace *the one true* face that is to be discovered. But what the veils of modesty show better than the nakedness of the statue is that the search for truth is *nothing other than the hunt for potential errors to be eliminated.* This quest can be pursued only locally, according to the rules that establish the game in which error can exist. As Wittgenstein demonstrated in several ways, for a proposition to be false, it must not be absurd and it must respect the syntactical rules of the language in which it is enunciated, the rules of the game that any use of language constitutes. "When...no error is possible, it is because the move which we might be inclined to think of as an error, a 'bad move,' is no move of the game at all. (We distinguish in chess between good and bad moves, and we call it a mistake if we expose the queen to a bishop. But it is no mistake to promote a pawn to a king.)"[9] The habitual difficulty is that, because of the polysemy and ambiguities of natural language, it is much more difficult to show that propositions have no meaning than to prove that they are false. Meaningless propositions escape unnoticed from all the rules of the game and wander from one game to another while believing, and making us believe, that they are still playing. What is more, these meanderings may sometimes be fruitful and creative, in unexpected and unforeseeable ways, as sources of associations and analogies; but at this stage the question of their truth or falsehood cannot be posed in any manner.

## The Games of Scientific Legitimacy

In other words, the search for truth, in the form of a search for a true/false dichotomy, is inevitably circumscribed within a particular domain where the object and method are limited. There is always the question of the underpinnings of the rules that institute such a dichotomy; the legitimacy of these foundations depend on the domain of experience and discourse in which all searches—that is, their objects, what they concern—are necessarily circumscribed. The experience of truth is as it were located at the crossroads of two processes, two trials, that stem from two different sources. One, theoretical, descends from on high and permits discovery by understanding, reason, intelligence, and cleverness, or by witness and tradition, or by inspiration and illumination. The other, practical, which springs from below, legitimizes the grounds of the truth of this discovery with regard to some domain of reality and discourse that it is supposed to concern.

In other words, the rules of the game that are constituted by a particular logic and a particular language are supplemented by the metarules that legitimize applying these rules to a given domain. Popper's "rule" of falsifiability, as the criterion of scientificity, is only one specific case of the more general category of metarules. Constituents of theory and interpretations seeking to order data may come from any source and may be derived in any way, based on different conscious and unconscious, individual and collective efforts, in which elements drawn from all available memories are associated and distinguished. At this level, anything goes; any rules for theory formation can be only arbitrary. Or, rather, rules corresponding to all available logics are used simultaneously, with no metarule. This is Feyerabend's "anything goes."[10] As M. Neyraut has said:[11] "The matter would be quite simple if there were only a single logic, used at the same time by the determinism of dreams, the elaboration of myths, the articulation of Freudian concepts, the speech of madmen, speech about the speech of madmen, and the utterance of interpretations"; to which list should be added, of course, the determinism of the natural sciences. But there is no such unique logic. What is more, "every logic is captious and each of them tends to ensure the hegemony of its own process. But as soon as it is enunciated, that is to say as soon as it involves language, every word, every sign, every phoneme takes on power and indeterminacy, like a diapason played in a resonant cavity, and sets all the logical spaces it encounters to vibrating."[12]

Then, however—and only then—we can raise the question of truth vis-à-vis its contrary, error or falsehood. And judgment can be rendered only within a precisely circumscribed *domain*, that of the *legitimacy of the grounds* of this truth: the true/false character is grounded on procedures of decision that are themselves established or recognized within a particular domain of reality, which alone endows them with some legitimacy. As in games, it is possible that this domain of legitimacy is really delimited only by the conventions of its rules, to the exclusion of any other sort of consensus. But it is always a matter of consensus, and Neyraut quickly homes in on Pascal's rules of rhetoric as the art of *persuasion*[13] when he asks about the relationships of different logics among themselves and with a logic supposed to contain all of them, which, because it is "intelligible according to the laws of ordinary understanding," permits one to "speak of the irrational in rational terms."

It is also possible that the domain of legitimacy is segregated by some necessity, such as that of living in society, or by a desire for mastery over things or over other people; in that case, the rules of truth must be the object of a consensus that is more difficult to realize, because it bears precisely on the legitimacy of these very rules vis-à-vis the goal pursued, out of necessity or desire. This is how the rules of the scientific game are legitimated by technical success, that is, by effective control over recreated matter: in this game, the verdict of "untruth" is based especially on error, which itself seems to be a refutation adduced by "facts," themselves reconstructed in the framework of logico-mathematical rules of prediction for which the main objective is generalization in time and space.

On the other hand, in the domain of legitimacy of the rules of the judicial game, the verdict of "untruth" is based at least as much on mendacity. This too appears to be a refutation adduced by facts; but in this case the "facts" are reconstructed in quite a different framework, that of the rules of inquiry and evidence. In addition to these two domains of legitimacy—scientific method and the law—human communities recognize and accept many other domains of legitimacy, which make it possible to support judgments of truth that are clearly valid only within these domains: the truth or untruth of illumination, false prophets and true, the truth of the subject, or deception and illusion, the truth or falseness of esthetic feelings, themselves duplicated in the authenticity or falseness of works of art, and so forth.

## Speaking to Say Nothing

For the *Senchus Mor*, an introductory anthology to the law of Ireland, "truth is the common memory of several people."[14] In the scheme of different categories of being that is constituted by the framework of kabbalistic interpretations, it is remarkable that truth is found neither at the top of the tree nor at its base, but in the middle, where the categories of the knowing intellect link up with those of the senses, with those of sex (foundation and totality) and fecundity: "Let truth spring up from the earth." The multiplicity of worlds that this tradition describes can then be understood as the multiplicity of domains and rules of the game, which use reason and its "interests" in different ways.

The error about truth (it follows that there must be a truth about truth—perhaps this is no other than the experience of life; modesty would then uncover it by covering naked truth with its own veil; but is it possible to speak modestly about modesty?)—the error about truth would then consist of believing that explanations are true because they are coherent and operational in a certain domain, that they describe as an "ultimate reality" something about which there is a strange colloquy, conducted in total misunderstanding, of mystics looking for scientific justifications and spiritualist (and also materialist) physicists seeking mysticism. In fact, these explanations are merely ways of ordering the disparate elements of reality of which we are sensible and to which we give our attention in some circumstances and in the context of one research discipline or another.

Of course, there must be something in reality that makes it possible to order it. But one cannot truly speak of this something: neither by using scientific discourse, which it escapes by construction, nor by using "revealed" discourses, because the experience of revelation is always—as is stated, paradoxically, by those who speak of it—infinitely greater than the discourse that seeks to enclose it. To say that this something is God solves nothing; quite the contrary, considering the burden of the connotations that this word has in Western languages. Only Wittgenstein's "I" can be located at a perspective that encompasses and unifies all these worlds; more precisely, this "I" that can only manifest itself and that corresponds to only one of the two possible uses of this pronoun, the use that Wittgenstein calls "subjective" (as in the case of someone who says "I am suffering," without saying *who* he or she is, such that this expression is, strictly speaking, equivalent to a sigh).[15] But in what this "I" says, it cannot be mistaken; there is no room for error or truth; no room, in fact, for any discourse whatsoever. Of this "I" itself one can say nothing. It can only be manifested, and that in silence. Any discourse about this *subject* (about the subject of the subject) is merely speaking to say nothing: words that do not *mean* to say anything, that are there *in order* to say nothing, an isolated abracadabra without context. Just like someone outside a closed door who, to the question, "Who's there?", responds, "It's me"; but we do not recognize his voice, and before we can open up he vanishes without a trace.

## Notes

1. One can imagine the adepts of a sort of negative theology of Truth, in which the fact that truth can be defined only negatively would merely reinforce the habitual belief in the existence of Truth. It is this belief that generally makes it possible to load what is only a particular interpretive system, endowed with a certain power of persuasion, with the virtues of the revelation of the "hidden ultimate real-

ity of things"—whether the reference is to the natural sciences or to the "true hidden and unconscious motives of human actions" (including scientific knowledge), as propounded by the *sciences humaines*.

2. BT *Sanhedrin* 97a.

3. R. Judah Loew, the Maharal of Prague, *Netivot Olam* (Paths of the World [or Paths of eternity]), Chapter 3 (Prague, 1596), "The Path of Truth"; Midrash *Genesis Rabba* 8.

4. "One of Freud's lightning flashes of intuition concerning the order of the mental world is his grasp of the revelatory value of the peek-a-boo games that are the child's first games" (Lacan, *Ecrits*, p. 187).

5. "The language of man, this instrument of his lies, is traversed through and through by the problem of its truth" (ibid., p. 166). See also, for example, ibid., pp. 247–265, 551–552, 855–877.

6. "The speech of the unconscious, which is not language, is a polyphony, and its writing is a polygraphy staged on several registers dominating the frequency range that goes from the gravest to the most acute. The texture of language is too narrow to contain all of these registers by itself. Language is located between silence and a cry. The psychoanalytic experience scans this realm where transformations of substance carry us, moment by moment, from the cry of birth to the silence of the grave." (Green, *Le Discours vivant*, p. 140).

7. Atlan, "L'émergence du sens et du nouveau," in *L'Auto-organisation, de la physique au politique*.

8. Talmudic law seems to acknowledge this tension by instituting a zone in which modesty takes precedence over the dislodgement of falsehood, on condition that the individual involved is one whose status is a warrant for his vocation of searching for truth. This seems to emerge from an analysis of certain cases in which a scholar is believed on his word (whereas another would have to bring proof of his claim), because his status as a scholar is tantamount to a presumption of his sincerity and attachment to truth. Whether in fact the scholar really is worthy of this status of truth seeker is expressed in his adoption and application in his conduct of the precept that defines the sages' attitude toward falsehood: "The sages falsify their words with regard to these three things: how much they know, matters of the bedroom, and matters of hospitality" (BT *Baba Metzia* 23b–24a). In other words, by the (limiting) enumeration of the cases in which a sage is supposed to lie, all of which have something to do with modesty, his status as a truth seeker is defined and circumscribed. One who values truth makes it yield before modesty!

9. Wittgenstein, *Blue Book*, p. 67.

10. Feyerabend, *Against Method*.

11. Neyraut, *Les Logiques de l'inconscient*.

12. Ibid., p. 63.

13. Ibid., pp. 57–58.

14. Cited by M. Treguer, *Faces cachées* (Spezet, Finistère: Breizh Diffusion, 1984).

15. See Wittgenstein, *Blue Book*, pp. 66f., and *Tractatus Logico-Philosophicus* 5.6.

# Index